THE ECONOMIC SYSTEM

THE ECONOMIC SYSTEM

ELEANOR DOYLE

John Wiley & Sons, Ltd

Other Wiley Editorial Offices

John Wiley & Sons Inc., 111 River Street, Hoboken, NJ 07030, USA

Jossey-Bass, 989 Market Street, San Francisco, CA 94103-1741, USA

Wiley-VCH Verlag GmbH, Boschstr. 12, D-69469 Weinheim, Germany

John Wiley & Sons Australia Ltd, 33 Park Road, Milton, Queensland 4064, Australia

John Wiley & Sons (Asia) Pte Ltd, 2 Clementi Loop #02-01, Jin Xing Distripark, Singapore 129809

John Wiley & Sons Canada Ltd, 22 Worcester Road, Etobicoke, Ontario, Canada M9W 1L1

Wiley also publishes its books in a variety of electronic formats. Some content that appears in print may not be available in electronic books.

Library of Congress Cataloging-in-Publication Data

The economic system / Eleanor Doyle.
     p. cm.
Includes bibliographical references and index.
ISBN-13 978-0-470-85001-5 (pbk. : alk. paper)
ISBN-10 0-470-85001-9 (pbk. : alk. paper)
1.   Economics. I. Title.
HB171.5.D65 2005
330—dc22

2004027116

British Library Cataloguing in Publication Data

A catalogue record for this book is available from the British Library

ISBN-13 978-0-470-85001-5
ISBN-10 0-470-85001-9

Typeset in 11/15 New Baskerville by Laserwords Private Limited, Chennai, India
Printed and bound in Great Britain by Scotprint, Haddington, East Lothian
This book is printed on acid-free paper responsibly manufactured from sustainable forestry
in which at least two trees are planted for each one used for paper production.

C O N T E N T S

DETAILED CONTENTS

PREFACE

A good economics student manages to understand the workings of the components within the economic system. An excellent student manages to appreciate the broader picture of the system with all its complexity of networks, interrelationships and organization. This requires an ability to understand economic models and their role in supporting analysis of economic issues *plus* an appreciation of their usefulness when we attempt to understand economic phenomena at a particular point in time, within their specific, and often complicated, micro- and macroeconomic contexts. It was with this in mind that I wrote *The Economic System*. The aim of *The Economic System* is to provide an appropriate mix of topical and historical, practical and theoretical principles of economics that create a tool-box appropriate for understanding, analysing and addressing the economic issues that we face and attempt to understand.

Any writer or reader of economics textbooks, particularly those aimed at the principles of economics market, is aware of the variety of alternatives currently available. *The Economic System* is novel in that it does not follow a strict compartmentalization of chapters into microeconomics and macroeconomics distinctions but rather groups material appropriate to the central focus of the chapter to guide learning. The essentials of micro- and macroeconomic theory and analysis are provided within a context where their overlap within the 'economic system' is emphasized. A key focus of the book is on highlighting the *relationships* between microeconomic and macroeconomic analysis in a way that contributes to a better understanding of their intrinsic relationships and to a better appreciation of how the economic system works.

This approach addresses a limitation I have experienced where often even those students who appear to solidly grasp concepts and models display weaknesses in using them to better understand or analyse problems and to transfer their application to alternative settings or examples. Transferability of concepts is a real challenge especially for a subject that focuses on being a problem-solving discipline where students should learn skills useful to support decision-making, i.e. criteria for choosing between alternatives. An explicit aim in *The Economic System* is to clarify how models and concepts in economics are useful as tools that support rigorous, methodical analysis and not simply useful to solve mathematical 'puzzles'.

The use of a small number of chapters, nine in total, that focus on related material to highlight these system features of the economy achieves this end. There are some further topics that could also have been included in the text; however, I followed the view that learning should not be rushed and that understanding what is here is a solid foundation for further learning. The activity of information integration requires time and to learn and derive knowledge from that information is a complex cognitive process.

Another novel perspective is included with references to the 'Austrian approach' to economics and to entrepreneurship activity in particular, which is explained and referred to several times in the text. This presents students with an interesting focus on the *process* element of economic analysis as well as the *product* element provided in the appropriately comprehensive standard neoclassical analysis.

Real world examples and learning features

Also included within the text are many topical issues including globalization, outsourcing, EMU and the advantages and disadvantages of a single currency. Extensive end-of-chapter material is provided including mini case studies, further reading and review questions and problems. Students are required to develop their range of problem-solving, numerical, analytical and argumentative skills in generating their answers to these questions.

Online resource package

For students and lecturers, a comprehensive online support package is provided with the text. The website includes PowerPoint slides, multiple choice questions, weblinks, online glossary, and further review questions and exercises, plus model answers to all of the end-of-chapter questions provided.

ACKNOWLEDGEMENTS

The contribution of a network of individuals made work on the text substantially more enjoyable and challenging. Thanks must primarily go to the many students in the Principles of Economics BA course at University College Cork who have contributed to the development of this book and whose feedback has been gratefully received and much appreciated. The teaching assistants, including Krystle Healy, James Nolan and Rory O'Farrell, who have supplied their expertise to support the course delivery and test-driven the course materials, also deserve special appreciation.

I am extremely grateful to many colleagues in the Department of Economics, UCC who have generated a positive working environment where the role of teaching is highly valued. For providing many references and nuggets to be followed up or just reflected upon throughout this project sincere thanks to Connell Fanning. Edward Shinnick, the author of Chapter Six, whose timely and focused contribution was vital in achieving the end result, is deserving of many thanks. For valuable and timely feedback on various chapters that was much appreciated, I must thank Eoin O'Leary, Brendan McElroy and Niall O'Sullivan. Thanks to Kay Morrison and Emer Doyle for editorial and proofreading assistance. For support with content and development of online materials I am very grateful to Eileen O'Sullivan, Krystle Healy and particularly Gerard Doolan who did trojan work.

Staff at Wiley were supportive above and beyond the call of duty and Anna Rowe comes in for particular thanks here along with Deborah Egleton, Rachel Goodyear and Steve Hardman.

Without family support from Fred and Robert, who bore the brunt of 'book time', no text would have been possible. Thank you. Any remaining errors of omission or commission are, of course, mine alone.

THE ECONOMIC SYSTEM

LEARNING OUTCOMES

By the end of this chapter you should be able to:

✪ Define what is meant by an economic system.
✪ Describe the roles played by the main players in the system including individuals, firms and countries.
✪ Describe how and why:
  ● the principle of exchange;
  ● the existence of markets; and
  ● the role of prices
  are central to understanding how an economic system functions.
✪ Clarify the role played by concepts, theories and models in economic analysis.
✪ Explain how rules and laws facilitate and govern decisions within the economic system.
✪ Illustrate how each of the following concepts:
  ● scarcity;
  ● opportunity cost; and
  ● economic efficiency
  underpins economic analysis.

1.1 INTRODUCING THE ECONOMIC SYSTEM

This chapter provides an introduction to the economic system to illustrate the interconnectedness between the different participants in and features of an economy, which contribute to economic decisions and outcomes. An economy can aptly be described as a 'system' as it relates to the following definitions of what a system entails:

● a group of interacting interrelated or interdependent elements forming a complex whole;

- an organized set of interrelated ideas or principles;
- a functionally related group of elements;
- an organized and coordinated method; a procedure.

The main participants and features of an economy are outlined in the chapters that follow. The study of economics focuses on identifying and trying to understand the patterns and relationships between these elements.

To begin it is useful to define what a study of the economic system entails. It involves understanding how:

- the production of goods and services is organized and influenced by individuals, organizations (including companies – both publicly and privately owned, trades unions, employer groups, etc.) and governments;
- products and services are used to satisfy the requirements of these same individuals, households, organizations and government.

Analysis of production includes the consideration of decisions regarding what is produced and how production decisions are made, which inputs to use in production (factors of production) and the way in which they are organized together to produce output. How production meets the demands of buyers is a central factor in analysis of the economic system.

Factors of production: the resources necessary for production. They include:

- land – all natural resources (including minerals and other raw materials);
- labour – all human resources;
- capital – all man-made aids to production that have been produced (e.g. machines, factories, tools). It is used with labour to produce and/or market more goods and services;
- entrepreneurship in business organization and willingness to take business risks.

1.2 ECONOMIC RESOURCES AND MARKETS

A key focus of economists' attention is the relationship between an economy's resources, both in quantity and quality, and what it can produce again in quantity and quality. The concept of efficiency helps in the analysis of this relationship.

Economic efficiency: optimum production given the quantity and quality of available factors of production and their cost.

An economy is efficient if it is maximizing the output it can produce within the constraints of its available inputs or resources. These constraints may take the form of rules or laws governing how inputs may be used, such as limits to the hours people are permitted to work per week.

Economists' focus on output and production is driven by an inherent interest in trying to understand how society could be better off and this is evident as far back as 1776 in *An Inquiry into the Nature and Causes of the Wealth of Nations* by Adam Smith, the acknowledged 'father' of economics. What is produced in an economy has a direct bearing on the income – the flow of money earned – and wealth – the stock of money held – of people in that economy.

When an economy increases the quantity of goods and services it produces and can sell the output, economic growth occurs.

Economic growth: an expansion in the quantity of goods/services produced and sold.

Once economic growth is faster than population growth, material living standards can rise.

Living standards: the level of material well-being of a citizen. It is generally measured as the value of a country's production per person, e.g. UK national output divided by the population of the UK for a particular period of time.

Some data on international living standards are presented in Figure 1.1 for 20 countries with the highest living standards in 2002 (as reported by the OECD, the Organization for Economic Cooperation and Development). To ensure the data reported in Figure 1.1 can be compared, each country's output was initially converted to the same exchange rate – here all values are in dollars.

Because of the different international prices of goods, a further adjustment was made to the data to take account of these purchasing power differences. This is called the purchasing power parity adjustment as explained in the text box. Figure A.1 in Chapter 1 Appendix contains living standards data for 2000 over a broader selection of counties.

Purchasing power parity (PPP) is a measure of the relative purchasing power of different currencies. PPP is the exchange rate that equates the price of a basket

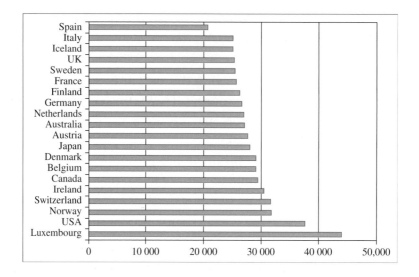

FIGURE 1.1 LIVING STANDARDS, TOP 20 COUNTRIES 2002, (US DOLLARS AND PPPs*)
Source: Main Economic Indicators, OECD, 2002
*See the nearby key term box for more on PPPs.

of identical traded goods and services in two countries. PPP is often very different from the current market exchange rate.

Since 1986 *The Economist* magazine has published a regular Big Mac Index. It indicates how many Big Macs dollars buy internationally when exchanged for local currencies. The Big Mac PPP is the exchange rate that would leave the Big Mac costing the same in the United States as elsewhere.

The logic underlying conversions using PPPs and not just standard exchange rates is that prices tend to be lower in poor economies, so a dollar of spending in a poor country buys more than a dollar in America. Using purchasing power parities takes account of these price differences. Comparing actual exchange rates with PPP often reveals differences. Some studies have found that the Big Mac Index is often a better predictor of currency movements than other more 'theoretically rigorous' currency models.

Since January 2004, *The Economist* also provides a Tall Latte Index where the focus is not on burgers but a cup of Starbucks coffee, another internationally available product.

Economists are interested in understanding the reasons behind economies' growth experiences and the reasons underlying the cross-country disparity of living standards. Several explanations as to why such disparities arise are offered and in our study of the economic system we will touch on some of these.

To fully appreciate how an economy functions also involves an understanding of the political context within which economies work as this too has an influence on the output produced and the available resources.

> **Political economy** is the term given to the study of how the rules, regulations, laws, institutions and practices of a country (or a state, region, province) have an influence on the economic system and its features.

Rules and laws on how resources and production can be organized and used influence the incentives for individuals and firms to conduct business and hence the output of an economy. One example would be rules on setting up new businesses and the time this takes.

> Research indicates time needed for setting up a new business varies considerably internationally, taking only two days in Canada and costing US$280, and 62 days in Italy, costing US$3946 (Djankov, *et al.*, 2001).

Rules and laws on how resources are shared or distributed among citizens also influence their income and wealth – if only a few receive most of the production (because of corruption or a caste system, for example) the income and wealth of the majority suffers.

How the value of output produced is distributed among an economy's stakeholders depends on the configuration of each economic system and the choices on distribution that are made. Stakeholders in the economic system are the individuals and groups that depend on the system to fulfil their own goals (be it to meet demands, generate income, create employment, provide wages or salaries, provide goods and services . . .) and on whom the economic system depends for its continued survival.

According to the above description of what an economy is, it is possible to interpret individual countries as economic systems, each with its individual economy, but it may also be useful, depending on some issues of interest to economists, to consider provinces, regions or cities as economies in their own right.

It is also often useful to examine an economy by focusing on sub-sections of organized resources within an economy, which are described as markets, e.g. the market for cars, apples, or labour. Knowledge of how the economic system functions based on analysis of markets, production and expenditure decisions and how economies grow will help to enhance understanding of why economies perform so differently.

> **Markets:** situations where *exchange* occurs between buyers and sellers or where a potential for exchange exists. Markets cover the full spectrum from physical locations where buyers and sellers meet to electronic markets (such as auction websites) facilitated by the Internet.

The familiar notion of a market where people come together in a particular location to buy and sell goods or services is the most straightforward definition of a market. The economist's definition is broader and does not limit a market to a specific time and place.

For example, we can refer to the market for apples, which covers the opportunities that exist for buying and selling apples between individuals and firms. Markets for products or services can usually be examined by considering the price at which producers or sellers are willing to supply and sell – the supply or production side of a market – and the price buyers are willing to pay – the demand or consumption side of a market. Depending on the price of a product (amongst other factors) sellers and buyers make their economic decisions about which products to produce/buy and the quantities to produce/buy. The model of demand and supply presented in Chapters 2, 3 and 4 and again in Chapter 6 develop these two elements of the economic system further.

The basic elements of the economic system therefore, involve, the organization of production and supply, consumption and demand, markets, exchange, prices, and the rules or laws that facilitate and govern decisions by individuals, households and firms relating to all of these elements.

1.3 THE ECONOMICS APPROACH: THEORY-BASED ANALYSIS

In recent years the scope of economics has expanded considerably due to the breadth of applications that are possible based on the concepts, theories and models that constitute the foundations of the discipline.

> **Concepts, theories and models** are simplified representations of phenomena, which are intended to serve as tools to aid thinking about complex entities or processes.

TABLE 1.1 ECONOMIC THEORY AND THE PROCESS OF ECONOMIC ANALYSIS

1. **Identify a question/issue** for analysis, e.g. the factors that explain why Luxembourg has relatively high living standards at a point/period in time.

2. **Identify theory** (and/or concepts and/or models) **relevant** to this issue, e.g. theory of economic growth that relates output and living standards to the quantity and quality of available factors of production.

3. From theory, **formulate hypotheses** about possible relationships between high living standards and high levels of education (affecting labour), investment (affecting capital) etc., e.g. one hypothesis would be that high living standards are caused by high levels of education.

4. **Test the hypotheses** against evidence (information/data) on high living standards in Luxembourg and competing potential explanations. From alternative explanations – e.g. education, investment, luck! – the economist must attempt to choose the most appropriate and convincing, given available evidence. To get to the root of the analysis it may also be necessary to focus on the causes of high levels of education or investment, which is not straightforward. If the cause of high levels of education (or investment) is high levels of income/living standards then the explanation is circular and is not very useful. Evidence used to test an hypothesis might be quantitative (numerical), or qualitative or a mixture of both, and might be published or might be collected by the economist themselves in interviews or surveys, for example.

5. **Draw *valid* conclusions**.

What constitutes what economists do is as much governed by the approach to analysis they use as by the issues they examine. Table 1.1 provides a framework illustrating how theory guides economic analysis.

An economic method of analysis involves using concepts, theories and models (that are transferable to a multitude of issues), which serve to structure thinking and clarify the fundamental features of interest in addressing an economic issue or answering an economic question. This method helps economists identify and organize the main features causing an economic phenomenon and perhaps rank the most important causes and effects and essentially to understand the most important features that explain how economies actually work. It is not sufficient to identify correlations between economic phenomena – high standards of living and education – because correlation is not causation! Overly focusing on data relationships without an underlying logical theory of causation is bad economics and does not give rise to valid conclusions. In relation to the example in Table 1.1

the essence of the issue is whether living standards in Luxembourg would be higher or lower at a particular time with different levels of education (or investment).

Models are sometimes criticized because of how they simplify reality but they are constructed in order to take into account the most important features of the economic system relevant to analysing a specific issue. For example, the standard economic model of supply and demand *abstracts* from all the various factors that feed into the determination of supply and demand to focus on the relationship between the price of a product and

- producers' decisions of how much to supply at different prices (supply);
- buyers' decisions of how much to purchase at different prices (demand).

Supply: the quantity of output sellers are willing to sell over a range of possible prices.

Demand: the quantity of output buyers are willing to buy over a range of possible prices.

The demand/supply model is the cornerstone of economic analysis (and is described in detail in Chapter 2) and is used throughout this book. We can acknowledge that a number of different factors feed into the decisions that suppliers (producers) make regarding what to produce, in what quantity and what price to charge. These decisions would take into account producers' available resources of money, machinery, production technology and know-how.

In their theories and models, economists abstract from all other factors to consider the essence of how economic units or phenomena are related. In focusing on the relationship between price and demand, for example, we consider how demand relates to price and price alone. The approach treats all the other potentially intervening factors *as if* they were unchanging, allowing one relationship to be considered in isolation. This method followed by economists is described as the *ceteris paribus* assumption.

The *ceteris paribus* assumption: from the Latin the direct meaning of this term is all things being equal or unchanged.

This could be rephrased as the '**economists are not stupid**' assumption! Economists know all things do not remain equal or unchanged. The power of the assumption allows them to construct models that highlight the fundamental nature of a relationship they are trying to describe and understand. Subsequently they use their models to incorporate other factors of most relevance to that relationship.

Economic analysis of demand can be extended to consider, for example, the effect that a general rise in income would have on a people's decision regarding Demand. In the case where consumers' incomes rise, *ceteris paribus*, we would expect rational consumers to buy more apples, or beans or CDs for example – more on this in Chapter 2! The objective of the model of demand is, therefore, not to simplify reality and assume that price is the only factor that feeds into consumers' decisions but to create a model whereby the analysis of any factor that is relevant can be considered in a clear and concise framework.

Many models are used in economics, which serve similar purposes of allowing the complexity of an economic issue to be understood and sometimes future behaviour (e.g. of suppliers or buyers, or economies) to be predicted. Clearly, despite their models and concepts, economists do not always predict future behaviour or outcomes correctly. Just like weather prediction, the models do not always allow for all relevant factors that affect the outcome to be considered or in some cases probabilities of occurrences are under/overestimated. This is due to the inherent uncertainty in trying to predict economic outcomes that arise due to individual behaviour and decision-making. It is precisely because the future is uncertain that economists try to argue logically which potential outcomes are most likely or not.

1.4   DESCRIBING AND INTERPRETING ECONOMIC RELATIONSHIPS

In attempting to draw sound conclusions, economists often use facts and figures to test their economic arguments. They compute percentages, they use index numbers, draw and manipulate diagrams and they analyse trends in data over time. If you are comfortable with such activities, you should skip this section.

To compute a percentage we are interested in the proportionate change in a quantity or value. Saying that employment increased by 10 000 jobs does not provide as much information as if you know what the initial level of employment was.

Consider an economy where 125 000 people are employed. Increasing jobs by 10 000 represents a percentage increase of 8% which is found by:

Percentage change = (Change/initial value)*100

In this example the relevant figures are (10 000/125 000)*100 = 8%

With data on changes in employment produced monthly and quarterly in many economies it would be possible to compute percentage changes over these periods and examine whether the general trend were up or down, or whether any patterns emerged such as seasonal increases – temporary summer workers are usually employed for a few months and then are laid off, students return to college, etc. – and this affects employment figures.

Alternatively, quantities or values can be expressed in index number form allowing them to be presented relative to one base point in time. Consider UK employment statistics. Table 1.2 shows employment between 1999 and 2003 based to 1999 = 100. By setting a base year value (1999 = 100) it is easy to read off the relative percentage changes in employment, which declined for both women and men across manufacturing industries. The total figure is the weighted average of men and women.

In 1999 men represented 72% of the workers while women accounted for the other 28%. Taking a weighted average of 72% of the 1999 value for men and 28% of the value for women gives 100 overall (0.72*100 + 0.28*100 = 100). The same weights apply for 2000 and 2001 and changed to 73% and 27% for the final two years.

Index numbers are commonly used in describing trends in prices and in weighted averages of prices, such as the retail price index, consumer price index, wholesale price index. Assessing changes in prices is important for all economic analyses of any variables measured in money terms over time – income, output, wages and so

TABLE 1.2 EMPLOYMENT STATISTICS MANUFACTURING INDUSTRIES: INDEX NUMBERS

Year	Total	Men	Women
1999	100	100	100
2000	98	98	97
2001	93	94	92
2002	88	89	86
2003	85	86	82

on. To see why this is so take the example of a car firm that produced £500m worth of output in 1990 and £800m in 2000. These amounts are in *nominal* or *current* terms which means they are the actual value of production not adjusted for price changes. Without further investigation you might consider that the economic activity of the firm increased over time since its output expanded by £300m or 60%. However, if you knew that over the same period average output prices increased too then without further information it is impossible to know what proportion of the extra 60% is due to rising prices or to any additional quantity of output. If prices rose by 60% then the firm's quantity of output would not have changed at all – only its monetary value.

It is possible to disentangle the two separate effects of price and quantity if we know the extent of the price rise over time. Assume it is 25% relative to prices in 1990. Essentially what is required is to quote output values in *real terms* so that the effect of price changes is removed and only quantity or real effects remain, as explained in the text box.

Nominal and real amounts: price and quantity effects

Changes in nominal amounts are made up of price and quantity effects. Economists are concerned with quantity effects.

e.g. Nominal change in value of output = change in price*change in quantity

In the above example the nominal change in the value of output is £300m. Using 1990 as a base year we can compute the following:

Nominal output index   1990 = 100   2000 = 160   [1990 = 500   2000 = 800]
Price index   1990 = 100   2000 = 125

A corresponding quantity index is found by *dividing* the nominal output index by the price index, i.e. (160/125)*100.

Quantity index   1990 = 100   2000 = 128   [1990 = 500   2000 = 640]

To double-check this is correct, the *product* of the volume and price indices should equal the total change in the nominal index (128*125)/100 = 160.

The real value of output in 2000 expressed in 1990 prices was £640m, representing a 28% increase in the quantity or volume of output.

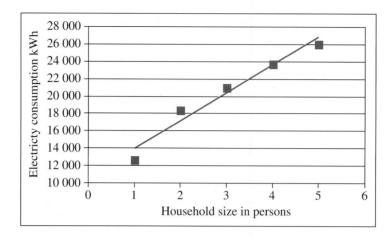

FIGURE 1.2 ELECTRICITY CONSUMPTION AND HOUSEHOLD SIZE
Source: *Statistics Norway*, 2004

Diagrams provide some indication of whether relationships exist between variables. For example, using data on average household size and electricity consumption indicates if and how both are related. Sample data are shown in Figure 1.2 and were taken from Statistics Norway. Such data are known as cross-section data as they provide information on different variables for one point in time (Figure 1.1 also shows cross-section data).

If data on electricity consumption were available over a number of time periods they would be called time-series data. For different household sizes (number of persons in the household) we see that smaller households had lower electricity consumption (measured in kilowatts per hour).

Linear relationships apply between many economic variables. In practice relationships are *approximately* linear as shown by the trend line added to the data points in Figure 1.2. The trend line approximately describes the relationship since only one data point actually sits on the line (a standard spreadsheet package was used to construct the line). For any *linear* relationship if the causal variable (X) changes it always brings about the same or constant effect on the variable it affects. Usually in mathematics, the causal or independent variable is put on the horizontal or X-axis while the dependent variable is on the Y-axis.

To draw a line we need:

1. The value of the dependent variable irrespective of the value of the causal or independent variable. This is called the intercept of the line.

2. A measure of how one variable reacts to changes in the causal variable. This is called the slope of the line.

A standard general expression for a line is presented and explained in the text box.

General expression for a line: $Y = c + mX$ where

- Y denotes one variable, e.g. electricity consumption;
- c denotes the intercept, i.e. the value of Y irrespective of the value of X;
- m denotes the extent to which Y changes as X changes, i.e. how electricity consumption varies with household size;
- X denotes the variable causing changes to Y, e.g. household size.

The specific line described in Figure 1.1 is $Y = 10759 + 3220.5X$
Electricity consumption is 10 759 kWh irrespective of household size and increases by 3220.5 with each additional one-person increase in household size.

From this relationship it is possible to predict what electricity consumption would be if household size were seven (*ceteris paribus!*).

$Y = 10759 + 3220.5 \times 7 = 10759 + 22543.5 = 33302.5$

Figure 1.2 is an example of a positive relationship because both variables move in the same direction and it is reflected in an upward sloping line. For negative relationships Y would fall if X rises, and rise if X falls, for example the relationship between the quantity of hours of sunshine per day and the quantity of umbrellas purchased.

Not all economic relationships are linear. For example, the price you pay for apples might be lower if buying in bulk from a grower. The more bought, the lower the unit price the grower quotes – why might a grower behave in this way? The reaction of quantity bought to changes in price may *not* be in constant proportion so that for each extra 10% decline in the price the quantity purchased increases at an increasing rate as shown in Figure 1.3.

Here, the 10% drop in price from 30p to 27p increases purchases by 10 apples while the 10% drop from 15.94p (to 14.35p) increases purchases by an extra 40 apples. Why might a buyer behave in this way?

Although mathematicians usually place the causal (independent) variable on the horizontal axis, economists by convention place quantity purchased on this axis. This goes back to Alfred Marshall's treatment of price as the dependent variable

Price	30.00	27.00	24.30	21.87	19.68	17.71	15.94	14.35	12.91
Quantity	10	20	35	55	85	120	160	210	275

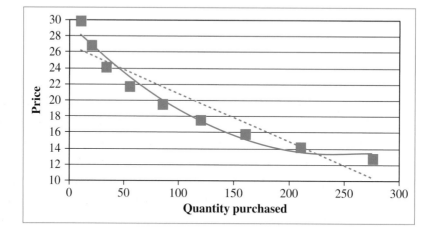

FIGURE 1.3   QUANTITY PURCHASED AND PRICE

and although most economists agree that price is the independent variable, and quantity purchased depends on price, they follow this convention. Alfred Marshall (1842–1924) was Professor of Political Economy at the University of Cambridge from 1885 to 1908. He founded the Cambridge School of Economics and taught renowned economists including Pigou and Keynes. Marshall's great work was *Principles of Economics* (1890), published in eight editions in his lifetime and considered the 'Bible' of British economics, introducing and explaining concepts still conventionally used.

A trend line has been added to Figure 1.3 to indicate how it would approximate the nonlinear relationship. The curved (nonlinear) trend is also included to show how it better describes the general pattern of the data.

Further nonlinear relationships are observed between economic variables and will be met and considered later on in the text.

1.5   MICROECONOMICS AND MACROECONOMICS

A distinction is made in most economics textbooks between the areas of microeconomics and macroeconomics.

Microeconomics: study of the causes and effects of the behaviour of individual economic units within the economic system (or groups with broadly similar interests and goals) such as consumers, producers, trades unions, firms and their impact on the markets in which they interact – e.g. the car, apple or labour markets.

Consumer theory assumes consumers wish to maximize their benefit or **utility**.

The theory of the firm assumes producers wish to maximize profits.

Many microeconomic decisions are based on prices, such as consumers' buying more apples if price falls, more people trying to work in the IT sector if wages (the price of labour) rises and so on. Hence microeconomics is also referred to as price theory. In considering economic units economists attempt to model and understand how the unit or related group of people behaves. Economic units are assumed to behave rationally, in the sense that they try to achieve the greatest amount of benefit, or utility, from their actions. With the assumption of rational behaviour the consideration of constraints on choices can be modelled in an attempt to estimate an optimal or most efficient outcome. For example, in attempting to increase utility by buying something I value, I am constrained by my income. I will try to maximize the utility I get from consumption, given my limited income. Many microeconomic issues are dealt with according to this 'optimal solution' method using the supply and demand model.

Once an analysis of individuals and units can be undertaken, it is possible to consider how all economic choices fit together and we can move to an analysis of economic aggregates such as aggregate production – not just of apples but of all goods and services. It is not always possible or feasible to consider the impact of an economic event across each of the individual units or markets that it may affect. Macroeconomic analysis is useful instead.

Macroeconomics is the study of:

- The relationships between aggregate or combined elements in the economic system such as national production and employment, for example.
- Causes of changes in aggregate economic performance including economic structure and economic institutions.

A model of the macroeconomy based on consumer, producer and government action is presented in Chapter 5.

National exchange rates reflect the price of one country's currency in terms of other currencies, and inflation rates indicate how average national prices change over time and these are also examined as macroeconomic issues that affect economies. Furthermore, from a government's perspective macroeconomic policies constitute a key element in their attempts to maximize the performance of their economies to achieve policy goals such as high employment and rising incomes and living standards for their citizens. Hence, macroeconomics also focuses on the impact of government policies on output, employment, inflation or exchange rates.

Although there has been a traditional division of economics into micro- and macroeconomics, an understanding of economics requires the appreciation that they are not independent of each other. Individuals' decisions feed into demand and supply in different markets. Aggregate or overall economic activity is clearly dependent on what happens in different markets, which is based on the choices and behaviour of individuals, firms and economic units regarding what buyers wish to buy and what producers wish to sell, for example.

A key focus of this text is on highlighting the *relationships* between microeconomic and macroeconomic analysis in a way that contributes to a better understanding of their intrinsic relationships and to a better appreciation of how the economic system works.

Hence, elements of both microeconomics and macroeconomics that provide useful frameworks for considering related issues are provided throughout the book.

1.5.1   THE ENVIRONMENT FOR ECONOMIC DECISIONS

Rules and laws also impinge on economic choices as rational people react to incentives with which they are faced. For example, interactions between consumers and firms are not independent of such rules because of the regulatory environment that exists, i.e. the rules and regulations, including laws, set down by governments in both national and international contexts which describe how citizens and businesses should operate.

Trade agreements are established by the international organization called the World Trade Organization (WTO) (see www.wto.org). Following prolonged discussions between government officials, the agreements are signed by governments. Firms in signatory countries must abide by the set rules and regulations or face penalties.

Various governments have appointed regulators of competition in attempts to promote greater competition in economies by tackling anti-competitive practices, and so contributing to an improvement in economic welfare. (Alternative market structures and their implications for competition, among other issues, are examined in Chapter 6.) Such practices might include firms:

- agreeing to 'fix' prices – not allowing prices to be determined freely in the economic system by demand and supply;
- limiting output to create *artificial* scarcity and keep prices high;
- dividing business between them or abusing their market position with no benefits to consumers.

Recently the issue of corporate governance has made the headlines because a number of big companies (e.g. Enron, WorldCom, Parmalat) have revealed poor and/or illegal methods of administration or accounting that resulted in a reduction of confidence in their financial reporting procedures, hence their reported earnings and most importantly their future performance. This impacts on people's willingness to invest in companies and may weaken their confidence in the ability of the economic system to operate efficiently or fairly.

Confidence and expectations can play an extremely important role in economic success – many surveys and 'barometers' of consumer confidence are reported and are considered to be key leading indicators of future economic performance. For one example, check out http://www.conference-board.org/economics/consumer-confidence/index.cfm. Why is consumer confidence so important? If consumers are not confident about the future, if they are fearful for their jobs they may prefer not to make purchases of goods and services in the immediate future, opting to save their money rather than spending it on consumer goods.

> **Consumer confidence:** the degree of optimism that consumers express (in surveys, for example) about the state of their economy through their saving and spending patterns.

A worker who thinks their job may be cut will probably put off upgrading their car until such time as they feel more secure about their prospects. If consumers are not in the 'mood' to buy, firms cannot sell as much of their output as they expected and so production might fall, leading to lay-offs and in worst-case scenarios slow economic growth (or even negative growth) for a period of time.

Appreciating the role played by each of the different components of the economic system and how interactions between the components all impact on the outcomes within the system itself is a key goal that guides this book. A good student manages to understand the workings of the components within the economic system. An excellent student manages to appreciate the broader picture of the system with all its complexity of networks, interrelationships and organization. This requires an ability to understand economic models and their role in supporting analysis of economic issues *plus* an appreciation of their usefulness when we attempt to understand economic phenomena at a particular point in time, within their specific, and often complicated, context.

1.6 RESOURCE SCARCITY AND PRICES IN THE ECONOMIC SYSTEM

A key issue that motivates the study of economics is how to resolve the discrepancy between scarce resources and the numerous potential uses for them (and how this is actually ordered and organized via the economic system). Resources are clearly scarce in the sense that we, the world's citizens, cannot fulfil all our economic desires, given our share of available resources. This arises to an extent because of difficult-to-defend policies on the distribution of income in some economies (which is discussed in Chapter 9). It arises also since some resources are finite – such as oil, gas, etc. – although new inventions and innovations allow new products to be developed constantly thus pushing out the boundaries we see for many resources (as Julian Simon explains in his article at http://www.cato.org/dailys/3-04-97.html). We make choices based on preferences regarding how and when we use our available resources to satisfy not simply our needs but our desires, and more generally throughout the economic system, choices are made based on subjective desires of individuals, companies and governments.

Choice inevitably involves precluding alternatives. Using resources in a particular way means those resources are unavailable for simultaneous use in another way since an opportunity cost is incurred. If I use all income on food I cannot buy clothes, or if I establish a manufacturing plant for tables it is not suitable for making chemicals.

> **Opportunity cost:** This is the cost of what is given up in following one course of action such that other choices are no longer possible. It is subjective and can be estimated in terms of the cost of the *next-best preferred alternative* but only when the choice made cannot be reversed.

It is via the economic system that decisions about how resources are used are made by the many buyers and sellers in markets. While we can view the economy as a system, the economic decisions made within that system are based on human behaviour and preferences. At the heart of economic decision-making is the necessity to select between alternatives. In making a choice, decision-makers should be aware of the costs of their actions in terms of what they cannot do once they make one particular choice, i.e. the opportunity cost of their decision to ensure the best – most efficient – use of scarce resources.

Consumers decide what to buy with their available income, and how much should be saved rather than spent, based on available information. For example, consumers' decisions about what to buy depend on the prices and availability of various products, their personal tastes, needs and available income (in no specific order). Employment choices depend on the jobs that are available, on individuals' qualifications and abilities and the wage rate. Firms also make economic decisions as they attempt to produce and sell their products or services (at prices that consumers are willing to pay) basing their decisions on perceptions of what is happening in their market, which is affected by consumers' demands, the available production technologies, the firm's know-how, and how competing firms behave. A firm's choices are, therefore, bound up in the network of decisions that result in what potential buyers want and what other firms are doing to compete.

Decision-making by individuals and firms is facilitated by the prices they observe in most markets. This means that prices play a central role by signalling information to consumers regarding how best they should use their available resources (including monetary, entrepreneurial, land and labour resources). Prices also act as a signal to producers of the price they can expect to earn for their products which will lead them to make particular decisions about what inputs to use (employees, machines, computers, etc.) how much they can afford to pay for inputs and so on. Hence, the price mechanism provides a means for coordinating the goals and choices of the various decision-makers in a market-based economic system.

Interestingly, from an objective point of view, not all economic outcomes might be considered to enhance the overall well-being of society. Take for instance the fashions that lead to rising expenditure on mobile phones and their accessories that might, arguably, be better spent on improving education or health. Instead of allowing the market system to organize the use of resources and what is produced based on the price mechanism and individuals' and companies' responses to prices, it would be possible to consider handing over total control for such choices to an ultimate decision-maker who 'knows best'. But this would not necessarily lead to a better overall outcome. Economists consider that it is through the dispersed decision-making by individuals and organizations in the economic system that the best use of dispersed economic knowledge regarding demands, supplies and markets is facilitated which allows prices to act as signals to all participants in the system. This highlights one issue at the heart of economic debate – the costs and benefits of centralized versus dispersed decision-making.

Economists argue that centralized decision-making about how resources should be used and what products should be produced leads to inefficient resource use where surpluses of some goods and shortages of others would be created (as in many former centrally planned economies). Furthermore, such systems take away individuals' freedom of choice. In fact, the dependence of a substantial proportion of our market-based economic system on the price mechanism actually means that individuals' choices are affected by the choices and decisions of other members of the system. This happens because the sum total of all individual choices (by producers on the supply side of the economy and buyers on the demand side) feed into the economic system to generate the market prices we observe (analysed in detail in Chapter 2). Hence, subsequent decisions by buyers and sellers are disciplined and organized by the price mechanism. This is what Adam Smith alluded to in his discussion of the invisible hand that guides the economy – a guiding mechanism that is no one individual's responsibility, desire or goal, but is the outcome of myriad decisions taken by buyers and sellers.

In the decisions made by governments, opportunity costs also apply to choices taken regarding how to use resources, e.g. how to divide up spending between building hospitals or schools or to build roads; choice between competing alternatives must be made. Clearly, however, political decisions relate not only to how best to use available resources but also to preferences made by governments and ministers with the knowledge that decisions may impact on their future election prospects. Thus, political economy concerns introduce additional complexity into the economic system.

1.6.1   USING RESOURCES AND CENTRALIZED DECISION-MAKING

In the case of centrally planned (or command) economies, it is possible to examine how resources were centrally controlled and allocated, guided by a 'visible hand' of the central planner that focused mostly on the supply side of the economy and the organization of production.

The prevailing economic system in such economies was not based on markets driven by prices to guide decision-making. The price mechanism was not influenced by consumers' competing demands for various goods as prices were set by central government. Neither were prices used as signals to where profitable opportunities lay for entrepreneurs and where they should best direct their resources. In most cases private property was not prevalent. Hence, free markets did not underpin how the economy was organized.

A further implication of command economies is in terms of innovation incentives. Innovation plays an important role in improving the processes used and the types and quality of goods produced within firms and industries that feed into improving national labour productivity and living standards.

> **Labour productivity:** the average output of a citizen. It is generally measured as the value of a country's production per worker, e.g. UK national output divided by the employed workforce of the UK for a particular period of time.

Yet in economies where goods are provided based on central planning, and resources are largely centrally owned, individuals do not enjoy rights to own private property and hence lack the incentives of their counterparts in 'market economies' to be as innovative or enterprising. The *self-interested* (not selfish!) desire to improve individual well-being that translates into broader benefits for the larger community (via creating employment or better technology) is more difficult to operationalize in a society where property and resources are owned centrally because individuals see fewer of the direct benefits.

It is true, however, that the world's economic system does not rely solely on the market system and price mechanism to provide all goods and services. A considerable portion of economic activity involves public provision of some goods and services where government ministers (and civil servants) are responsible for allocating resources to meet targets for street lighting, flood controls or defence, which are known as public goods. A public good is not provided by a private citizen or private company but by the government.

> **Public goods:** goods that would not be provided in a free-market system. They are goods that
>
> - if consumed by one person can still be consumed by others; non-rival in consumption. Private goods once consumed are not available to others.
> - if provided, cannot be excluded from the consumption of anyone who desires the good, even if they do not wish to pay for it. Public goods are non-excludable in consumption.

The benefits of a public good are available to all citizens who consume it and those benefits cannot be withheld from any individual in the economy. Governments supply public goods because of the free-rider problem.

> **The free-rider problem** exists due to the non-rival and non-excludable nature of public goods. There is no incentive to supply or pay privately for goods with public-good characteristics. Such goods, if desired, are provided by governments and paid for collectively through taxes.
>
> The free-rider problem is one example of **market failure**, a reason why the market requires government intervention to change what would otherwise be produced.

Some economies, such as the French and Swedish, display greater public provision based on national preferences than other economies such as the US or Japanese.

Some goods have some public characteristics such as rail and road networks. Both networks are not fully non-rival since a completely full train does not permit further consumption. Toll costs and ticket prices are methods of excluding some potential consumers so the condition of non-excludability is not necessarily met either. However, it would be difficult to envisage either network being fully privately supplied, and collective preference and choice means they are publicly provided, for the most part.

The price mechanism has traditionally played a less important role in governments' decisions about how government-controlled resources should be allocated between competing uses.

> Governments internationally are increasingly examining both the provision of public (and other) goods and services and the processes by which they are provided in order to adopt more efficient provision. Indeed, the issue of the extent to which governments should provide goods is debated in many countries – consider the complexity of the UK government's U-turn on owning and running the rail system, where they initially organized and ran the rail transportation system then privatized it only to take over its running once again.

1.7 RESOURCE USE, OPPORTUNITY COSTS AND EFFICIENCY

The concept of opportunity cost is a powerful and useful concept for considering how scarce resources are used in an economy and it can be considered

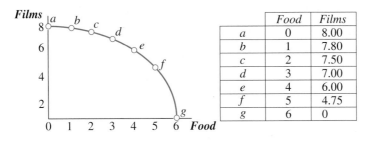

	Food	Films
a	0	8.00
b	1	7.80
c	2	7.50
d	3	7.00
e	4	6.00
f	5	4.75
g	6	0

FIGURE 1.4 PRODUCTION POSSIBILITY FRONTIER: EFFICIENCY, SCARCITY AND OPPORTUNITY COST

using a production possibility frontier (PPF) shown in Figure 1.4. The main productive resources or factors of production in an economy are land, labour, entrepreneurship and capital. Land and labour resources contribute to production and their quantities and qualities vary across economies. Entrepreneurship refers to the organization, management and assumption of risks of a business or enterprise and often implies an element of change or challenge and a new opportunity to exploit in a market. Sometimes entrepreneurship is successful, sometimes not. While it is possible to measure and compare the land and labour resources to some extent across economies, entrepreneurship is more difficult to measure. It may be reflected in estimates of the number of new companies established, new products launched, or the development or adoption of new technologies in an economy but is a complex concept which serves to explain some of the reasons why some economies perform better than others.

Capital goods are not used for consumption. Capital includes the factories that produce saleable output, apple trees grown to produce apples sold in the apple market, the machinery in factories or the computers in offices used to produce further products and services (but not those home computers used for leisure rather than productive purposes!). Inventories held by shops and factories are also classified as capital goods and only become consumption goods when households buy the goods for consumption purposes – the function served by the goods implies whether they can be classified as capital or consumption. Furthermore, when people engage in education, training or any activity that increases their personal productivity (how much they can produce with the factors of production at their disposal), they increase their human capital that can also contribute to producing further goods and services.

Human capital includes all the skills, knowledge and expertise that people accumulate over time that allow them to increase their productive capacity as individuals, members of firms and within society more broadly.

The production possibility frontier is a model useful for considering the maximum feasible combinations of goods an economy can produce. The differences between efficient and inefficient production can be considered via the PPF. The PPF is not an attempt to describe the complexity of decisions that feed into national production, instead just two products are considered, but the points illustrated by the model reveal its appropriateness for its purpose.

Figure 1.4 presents a PPF showing all possible outputs of food and films that could be produced by an economy. Production at points lying on the PPF indicate efficient production.

Efficient production: all available resources are used to produce a maximum combination of goods/services with no resources unemployed. Resources are used in their most productive way, in Figure 1.4 in either food or film production.

An example of inefficient production would be if 4 films and 4 food were produced since this point lies inside the PPF and would leave some resources unemployed in the economy. Any points outside (north-east) of the PPF cannot be produced given the economy's scarce resources.

Of all the possible output combinations that *could* be produced, the actual output choice will depend not only on production possibilities of the economy (what the economy can supply) but also on the demand that exists for films and food. If the economy's citizens prefer more films than food output might occur at a point such as *b*. Where production takes place matters from the citizens' perspective because they will be better off if resources are not left unemployed but are fully used to meet their needs and demands.

The concept of opportunity cost can also be illustrated using the PPF. Specifically, the opportunity costs associated with changing the output combination in the economy can be analysed. At Figure 1.4 point *a* output of 8 films and 0 food is a feasible output combination: a unit of food can be thought of as a basket of various food items. At point *b* 7.8 films are produced as well as 1 unit of food and at *c* 7.5 films and 2 food are produced. The opportunity cost of food in terms of films can be calculated based on the example. In changing output of the economy from *a* to *b*, less films but more food can be produced as some resources are switched from films to food production. Film production drops by 0.2 film (from 8 to 7.8) while food production increases by 1 (from 0 at point *a*). Therefore, the opportunity cost of switching from point *a* to *b* is the amount of films that can no longer be made, hence the opportunity cost of films in terms of food is 0.2 films 'lost' for 1 unit of food 'gained'.

If production changed from *b* to *c*, film production would decline further from 7.8 to 7.5 films while food production would increase from 1 to 2 units. Here, the opportunity cost is the decline of 0.3 of a film for a 1 unit increase in food.

The reduction in film production releases sufficient resources to allow food production to increase by 1 unit. A further decline in film production by 1 unit would move output from point *c* to *d*, allowing an additional unit of food to be produced. Hence, the opportunity cost changes over the range of the PPF: when no food is initially produced (Figure 1.4 point *a*) switching some resources best suited to food production out of film production allows more food to be produced than if the economy was already using a lot of its resources to produce food and wanted to produce more (points *b* or *c* or *d*). As more food is produced, the amount of films that must be 'sacrificed' to produce each additional unit of food increases. Therefore, the opportunity cost of films in terms of food increases as more food is produced (moving from *a* towards *d*). The same analysis can be conducted for the opportunity cost of food in terms of films beginning at point *e* where only food is produced and moving back to points *d*, *c*, *b* and *a*. Again, the opportunity cost of food in terms of films increases as more films are produced in the economy.

> **Increasing opportunity costs of production** that underlie the curved shape of the PPF occur since not all of an economy's resources are equally suited to the production of different goods. Rational producers use the resources most suitable to their output, where possible.

Another way of thinking about this change in opportunity cost is to consider the marginal cost of producing goods.

> **Marginal cost** is the opportunity cost of producing one additional unit of a good.

The marginal cost is different depending on how much of a good is already produced. Initially, resources least suited to producing films would be transferred to produce food, but as more and more food is produced, the resources transferred from films to food will be less and less productive in producing food. Hence, as

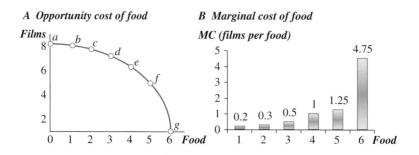

A Opportunity cost of food *B Marginal cost of food*

FIGURE 1.5 MARGINAL COST AND OPPORTUNITY COST

additional units of food are produced, the marginal cost of producing each extra unit (measured in terms of films) increases, because more films must be 'sacrificed' to release sufficient resources to make additional food. Rising marginal cost is shown in Figure 1.5.

If all resources are devoted to film production (*a* panel A), no food and 8 films are produced. If 1 unit of food is produced – moving from point *a* to point *b* – the output of films falls by 0.2. This provides a measure of the opportunity cost of this first unit of food (shown in panel B). Moving production from *b* to *c* involves a further increase in food production of 1 unit and a decline in film production of 0.3; producing the second unit of food requires a greater reduction in film production than the first unit. The marginal cost of each additional unit of food production is computed as 0.5, 1, 1.25 and 4.75 units of films.

Two further economic concepts are illustrated using the PPF. Points on the PPF represent *static efficiency* where each point reflects one state of efficiency for the economy – moving from any point on the frontier to any other point means that the economy uses its resources at their maximum efficiency albeit to produce a different combination of goods. Over a short time period it is possible that an economy faces limits to its productive capacity because resources do not usually increase significantly over short periods (unless there's an oil strike or gas is found, for example). However, over longer time periods it is possible that an economy's productive capacity increases.

Dynamic efficiency (economic growth): the outward expansion of the PPF.

Economic growth or dynamic efficiency would be possible with:

- *Increased quantity of labour*: if more people were available for work and could find employment so more output could be produced.

- *Improved quality of labour*: if people's skills and education improved sufficiently for them to be more productive – i.e. get more out of the resources they use.
- *Improved technology*: due to domestic or imported innovations technical progress occurs where more output could be produced from available resources.
- *Ease of start-ups*: if new businesses can easily be set up by entrepreneurs new products can be introduced to markets (or old products provided in new ways).
- *Increased capital resources*: if firms' investment in new capital grows, workers have more capital to work with and could produce more output.

Importantly, however, growth would only occur if demand for the additional output also existed so firms could sell their extra production (the issue of economic growth is addressed explicitly in Chapter 9).

Substantial challenges exist for economies regarding how to move closer to static efficiency and encourage dynamic efficiency. Economies do not necessarily produce to the maximum of their productive capacity – some labour may be unemployed, machines and factories may be idle, entrepreneurs may not wish to engage in risky ventures – so actual output might lie inside an economy's potential production possibilities. The trick is to strike the right balance to maximize potential possibilities and actual output, while also taking account of environmental and any other social costs.

It is worth noting that the PPF is not an attempt to describe reality but a model to help think about issues of interest to economists. Economists consider that most economic activity should be left to a market-based economic system for an economy to achieve an efficient state rather than via central planning. However, economists differ regarding the role they consider governments should play in the economic system and the quantity of public goods that should be provided.

1.8 ALLIANCE OF ECONOMIC PERSPECTIVES

There is a tradition in economics that emphasizes the need for government or government agencies to oversee the activities of the business community in order to protect consumers from being deceived or exploited by firms – to protect what is referred to as the 'public interest'. Using economic theories and concepts to make such arguments could be called a public policy perspective and holders of this view often consider that governments should enact policies that 'police' the business sector and regulate the economy to ensure consumers are shielded from any negative or undesirable effects of business activities. Government regulation might take the form of competition policy and it may try to ensure that the rights of consumers are protected.

This perspective acknowledges the role that governments can play in economic life. The actions of government can influence an economy in many ways, not only through the regulation function, and have an impact on the general performance of the economy and its competitiveness over time.

> **Competitiveness:** a range of factors from measures of income and prosperity to economic creativity and innovative ability that describe the performance of one economy relative to others.

The purpose of examining economic competitiveness is to get closer to understanding the process by which countries and economies (local or regional) can enjoy rising living standards. Policies relating to taxation, government spending, labour, education, business creation, technology, environmental protection and many other areas have direct and indirect effects on the ability of an economy to generate income to support its citizens over time and allow them to enjoy rising living standards.

Viewing the business sector with mistrust or suspicion, however, ignores the critical role played by companies in generating wealth and employment and in leading and facilitating economic development. Businesses clearly play an active and contributory role in competition and the market process in economies; hence, the need to understand the economic system from a 'business' perspective also. Applying economic theories and concepts to the business environment increases understanding of the role played by business firms in improving competitiveness and generating rising living standards in economies on a sustainable basis.

In fact, an appreciation of *both* perspectives by economists is essential in order to understand the complex interplay that goes on between businesses and government sectors and how they both affect the outcomes in any economy. For example, economic efficiency as presented in the production possibility frontier model clearly depends on what decisions are made by firms (e.g. what to produce) *and* the environment in which firms operate which, in turn, is affected by the policies followed by government.

Participants in an economy need to be aware that both business and government sectors have a contributory role to play in developing the factors that allow economies to achieve their potential and raise the living standards for their citizens. This means that all participants need to work towards developing processes within the economic system so that citizens/clients receive high standards of goods and services from private businesses, public organizations and bodies and public representatives. This could mean that ethics and standards should be set and followed by both policy-makers and business people and that the actions of individuals, organizations and public representatives are transparent and open to scrutiny and that accountability for actions is enshrined. This would mean that citizens could have trust in their economic and political systems. These are admirable goals but they are certainly not always met in practice.

1.9 POSITIVE/NORMATIVE ECONOMICS

Economic analysis based on objective facts is called positive economics.

> Various reasons behind strong growth in the Irish economy have been proposed including a young well-educated English-speaking workforce, sound management of the government finances, moderate wage increases, and attracting investment by multinational companies. Although it is difficult to distinguish which factor is most important, economists generally agree that each of these reasons provides part of the explanation, offering analysis based on positive economics that attempts to get at how the economic system works.

When economists make judgements about what *should* occur – making statements such as education spending should increase, government spending should be reduced – they move from objective analysis of facts to a more subjective analysis based on personal beliefs, values, norms or political persuasion. Such analysis is known as normative economics.

The distinction between positive and normative economics matters because economists often differ regarding opinions on what should be done because of their personal opinions, which are based on factors including their education, background, culture, etc. Decision-makers in companies, government organizations and elsewhere, who rely on economists for advice, need to know the basis and reasoning underlying the advocation of a particular opinion or policy and sound objective analysis is a more reliable basis for selecting a policy than one based solely on personal beliefs.

This does not mean that normative issues are ignored by the economics discipline. Such topics are studied in welfare economics. The focus of this stream of study is on assessing:

- how efficiently resources are used;
- the fairness of how the economic system functions from the perspective of various stakeholders.

Efficiency can be examined adopting a positive economics approach based on objective analysis. The fairness issue, however, is rather more problematic and one on which people hold alternative normative positions.

1.10 SUMMARY

- **The economic system is a web of interactions between individuals, economic units and institutions that determine how resources are best used to satisfy competing demands.**
- **Choices about how resources are used, which goods are produced and in what quantities, are made via the economic system.**
- **Choices are made dependent on what is demanded and the factors of production and technology available, supported by the operation of markets where prices provide information on how best resources may be used. Political considerations also feed into the economic decisions as laws and regulations govern the activities and behaviour of the stakeholders within economies.**
- **Studying economics is useful for understanding and improving how the best economic choices possible are made based on individual and/or organizational preferences and the available usually limited resources.**
- **An economics approach follows a logical method of analysis based on assessing, and sometimes estimating, causal relationships.**
- **The participants and features of the economic system are further discussed in the chapters that follow. Both macroeconomic and microeconomic concepts, principles and models are used to explain how the features interrelate within the economic system.**

CHAPTER 1 APPENDIX

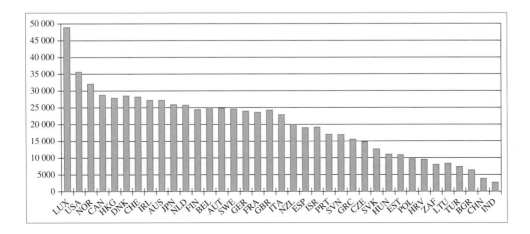

FIGURE A.1 LIVING STANDARDS, $, 2002

Source: Excerpted from the Penn World Table 6.1 (Heston *et al.*, 2002).

Note: The Penn World Table is a great source of comparable data on 168 countries going back to 1950 in many cases. To see the range of information presented in the tables visit http://pwt.econ.upenn.edu/

REVIEW PROBLEMS AND QUESTIONS

1. How would you define the economic system? Describe the role played by each of the following in the economic system: individuals, firms, countries.

2. What role is played by theory in economics? Does this mean we already as good as know the answer to a question before we begin analysis?

3. What differentiates microeconomics from macroeconomics?

4. What are the main differences between market-based and centrally planned economies? Refer to the principle of exchange, the existence of markets and the role of prices in your answer.

5. What is the relationship between resource scarcity and prices in economics? Refer to the signalling function of prices in your answer.

6. Draw a production possibility frontier for two goods, housing and entertainment. The maximum amount of entertainment and shelter that could be produced is 100 and 80 units respectively.

    a. Based on your drawing, what is the opportunity cost of producing 20 units of entertainment? 40 units? 80 units?

b. Why does the opportunity cost change for different outputs of entertainment and shelter?

7. Which individuals in the economic system are most likely to have a public policy approach to economics? Which individuals in the economic system are most likely to have a business economics approach to economics? Why? Is it of any importance which perspective people hold?

8. Leaf through some good newspapers. Provide *three* examples of normative economic statements and *three* examples of positive statements they contain.

FURTHER READING AND RESEARCH

- To put some context behind the data provided in Figures 1.1 and A.1 the OECD's Economic Survey publications provide comprehensive economic assessments of nations and recommendations for their future development. These contain information on some topics that will be new to you as you start out in economics, but by the end of the course should become substantially more comprehensible. The OECD also provides a range of specific articles from its research departments as well as free access to much of its data.

- For daily economics-related features and articles, the *Financial Times* provides timely national and international information and can be used to answer some of the review questions in this chapter.

- The weekly *Economist* magazine also presents accessible descriptions and analyses of current and topical national and international issues. Search through past editions and see how long it takes you to find 10 articles that touch on issues discussed in this chapter!

- For those with an interest in finding out more about the European Union and its economy, see El-Agraa, 2001.

REFERENCES

Djankov, S., R. La Porta, F. Lopez de Silanes and Shleifer, A. (2001) *The Regulation of Entry*, CEPR Discussion Paper No. 2593.

El-Agraa, A. (ed.) (2001) *The European Union, Economics and Policies*. 6th edn, Pearson.

Heston, A., R. Summers and B. Aten (2002) *Penn World Table Version 6.1*. Centre for International Comparisons at the University of Pennsylvania (CICUP), October.

OECD, *Economic Outlook* (2002) Annex Table 24, December (www.oecd.org).

Smith, A. (1970) *An Inquiry into the Nature and Causes of the Wealth of Nations.* Penguin, Harmondsworth [original publication 1776].

Statistics Norway (2004) 'Energy statistics: energy consumption per household', Table 1: Average energy consumption by house type, household size and net income, kWh supply of energy per household, 2001.

CHAPTER 2

MARKET ANALYSIS: DEMAND AND SUPPLY

2.1 INTRODUCTION

Knowing how markets function is fundamental to understanding the interactions between the various elements in the economic system. Through our desires not to be self-sufficient, we reveal how we need a system that can facilitate organized transactions. The market mechanism of buyers and sellers coming together allows the coordination of economic activities, although no one person or group have control over the free-market outcome; it is the result of all of the decisions made by individual buyers and sellers. Through this mechanism prices emerge and goods are bought and sold. Understanding how this process proceeds is crucial for economic analysis. In this chapter the market model of demand and supply is presented in sections 2.3 and 2.4 after the logical reasons as to why buyers and sellers exchange have been discussed in section 2.2. Attempts to 'organize' prices in markets rather than allowing them to emerge from markets have interesting implications that are examined in section 2.5.

The roles of information and knowledge in the economic system are also considered in this chapter in section 2.6. When we are involved in economic transactions to buy or sell goods we are engaged, to some extent, in the buying or selling of knowledge that we value but do not possess. We buy a computer because most of us do not have the required knowledge to make it ourselves. The logic applied in Chapter 1 to argue that resources should be used most efficiently also applies to how information resources are used. Factors that increase the probability of using knowledge most efficiently are considered.

In section 2.7 the purpose and role of equilibrium in the demand and supply model is examined as alternative views exist, both of which provide arguments as to why the model helps in understanding the operation of economies. Finally, in section 2.8, the main features of the labour market are presented as one example of how the demand and supply framework can be used to consider the behaviour of sellers and buyers in this complex market. This example indicates the appropriateness of the demand and supply framework for understanding the complexity of how markets work.

2.2   EXCHANGE – A CENTRAL FEATURE OF MARKETS

Markets are an intrinsic feature of economies, especially developed industrialized economies, and represent an important mechanism for coordinating economic activity. Facilitated by markets, buyers communicate explicitly or implicitly with sellers, and decisions about what transactions to make and when to make them are made. A key principle underlying the existence of markets is that people wish to engage in exchange, each party placing a lower value on what they give up in the exchange compared to what they receive from it. When I buy a can of beans I place greater value on the product than on holding onto the money it costs; the expected benefit derived from the product is balanced against its cost.

The concept of value is widely debated. Although value is entirely subjective the amount consumers are willing to pay for products provides some information regarding the value placed on purchases. The expected benefit derived from a purchase is the incentive to buy in the first place and it can be estimated using the principle of opportunity cost, i.e. what is the value of the next best alternative the consumer gives up in order to make their purchase? Consumers cannot be asked this question by economists for each and every purchase they make but the amount of goods or services they are willing to forego in order to make a purchase is reflected in the money they are willing to give up in the transaction. (This is still problematic though because if I pay 55p for a tin of beans, this reflects the market value of the product and I might have been willing to pay more than this based on my perception of my expected benefit.) The benefits or gains from exchange are related to differences in preferences and in the values sellers and buyers place on goods and services.

Each consumer's individual preferences feed into their purchasing decisions, their willingness to pay and ultimately their demand for goods and services. The economic concept of demand refers not just to a desire to make purchases, but to those desires that are supported by an ability to pay – I would love to buy a Ferrari Enzo but I do not feature in the economic 'demand' for it because I could not effectively purchase the product at its retail price (around £430 000 and 349 models only were manufactured!).

Gains from exchange may also arise due to differences in productivity. An example can be used to illustrate this point. Consider the production possibilities of two regions – North and South – which produce both food and clothing and which have different quantities of available resources. If all North's resources were devoted to food production then each worker could produce 2 baskets per day and if resources were devoted solely to clothing, 10 outfits could be produced on average. The corresponding productivity figures for South are 10 baskets of food and 2 outfits, shown Table 2.1. These figures for output indicate the opportunity cost (see Chapter 1) of producing one good in terms of another for each region. (For simplicity this example deals with two regions only but additional regions or countries could be added to the analysis and would not change the main conclusions made.)

Table 2.1 indicates that for clothing Northerners are five times as productive as Southerners (10 compared to 2) while Southerners are five times as productive as Northerners in food. If each region specialized and exchanged any surplus production to buy the good in which they are less productive, both regions could be better off than if they tried to be self-sufficient in both goods.

When a product is produced more efficiently (using less resources) in one country, that country has an **absolute advantage** in that product. It is measured

> ## TABLE 2.1
> ## DAILY PRODUCTIVITY OF FOOD AND CLOTHING IN NORTH AND SOUTH
>
> | | Food (baskets) | Clothing (outfits) |
> |---|---|---|
> | **North** | 2 | 10 |
> | **South** | 10 | 2 |

by comparing relative output across countries, e.g. in Table 2.1 South is more productive in food than North.

Economies that are self-sufficient and which produce efficiently can be considered to produce and consume an output combination on their production possibility frontier, but by engaging in trade with another economy, it may be possible to consume more than what is produced in the economy itself. Imagine that North spends half a day producing clothing and the other half producing food so its total output is 1 basket of food and 5 outfits. South could produce 5 baskets of food in half a day and 1 outfit in the other half-day. Their combined output would be 6 baskets of food and 6 outfits.

This combined output is less than what could be produced across the 2 regions with specialization by each region in the good of its absolute advantage. With specialization, combined output increases as North can produce 10 outfits and South 10 baskets of food. Assuming demand for both goods exists in both regions, trade would be required to allow both goods to be consumed in each region.

International trade makes sense when countries have different opportunity costs of production and specialize in the good in which they have a productivity advantage – a lower opportunity cost of production.

Trade and specialization make sense even when one region (South) has no absolute advantage as illustrated in Table 2.2. Here North remains more productive in clothing but the regions are equally productive in food. When each region spends half a day producing both goods, total output is 10 baskets of food and 6 outfits: 5 baskets of food and 5 outfits in the North and 5 baskets of food and 1 outfit in the South. With specialization, North could produce 10 outfits and South 10 baskets of food so specialization still allows greater combined production than self-sufficiency.

TABLE 2.2
ALTERNATIVE DAILY
PRODUCTIVITY IN NORTH AND
SOUTH

	Food (baskets)	Clothing (outfits)
North	10	10
South	10	2

The opportunity costs of production indicate where each region should specialize. The opportunity foregone in the North if only food is produced is 10 outfits per day, i.e. the opportunity cost of each basket is 1 outfit. In the South, the opportunity cost of each basket is one fifth of an outfit (and the opportunity cost of each outfit is 5 baskets of food). The opportunity cost of producing each basket of food is lower in South than North – one fifth of an outfit compared to 1 outfit. Hence, it makes economic sense for South to specialize in producing food, the good in which its opportunity cost of production is lower. Since South's opportunity cost of clothing is 5 baskets of food, compared to only 1 basket in the North, North should specialize in producing the good in which it has a lower opportunity cost of production – a comparative advantage.

> When output is produced at a lower opportunity cost in one country, that country has a **comparative advantage** in production. It is measured by comparing relative opportunity costs between countries, e.g. in Table 2.2, the opportunity cost of food in South is 0.2 outfits which is lower than the opportunity cost of food in North (1 outfit).

If South's productivity dropped to 6 food baskets instead of 10, an incentive to trade would still exist. The opportunity cost of production would be unchanged in the North but the opportunity cost of producing each basket of food would still be lower in South – one third of an outfit compared to 1 outfit in the North.

> The incentive to trade is present even when one economy is less productive in all goods *once* opportunity costs of production differ.

Each region benefits if it specializes based on its comparative advantage and trade occurs in surplus production. Once the regions can agree on a price for trading the goods, trade can occur. If price reflects the opportunity cost of production, then trade between North and South makes economic sense.

In exchange there are essentially two parties – a buyer and a seller. Demand exists that might be met by supply – once quantity demanded and quantity supplied coincide at a price which the buyer is willing to pay and which the seller is willing to accept. The next section explains the process through which prices are set.

2.3   DEMAND

The economic concept of demand is quite specific.

> **Demand** describes the desire to purchase, supported by an ability to pay together with an *intention* of making the purchase over a specific time period, e.g. the demand for cars in 2003 describes the quantity of cars that buyers intend to buy and can pay for in that period. Across all possible buyers demand (usually) exists over a range of prices.

Demand can relate to a particular group of people, e.g. the demand for cars by fleet buyers (company cars), or demand might be related to a specific geographical area as in the demand for fish in the UK, Germany, France, London, etc. Demand is the relationship between the quantity of a good (or service) buyers intend to buy and their willingness and ability to pay.

Economists refer to a law of demand according to which at higher prices the quantity demanded of a good is expected to be lower than at lower prices. The price of a product is considered to be a central factor affecting the intention to make a purchase. Figure 2.1 presents demand for cars in Europe, i.e. the relationship between the price of cars and the quantity demanded in Europe. (See www.autoindustry.co.uk where quantities of cars sold across Europe are provided.)

Graphs of demand conventionally present quantity on the horizontal axis and price on the vertical axis. This convention is followed despite the fact that quantity is the dependent (Y) variable while price is the causal (X) or independent variable. We saw in Chapter 1, that mathematicians place the independent variable (Y) on the horizontal axis.

A negative relationship exists between price and quantity demanded, reflected in the downward slope of the demand curve since, at relatively high prices, we expect quantity demanded to be low or, if price is relatively low, we expect quantity demanded be high.

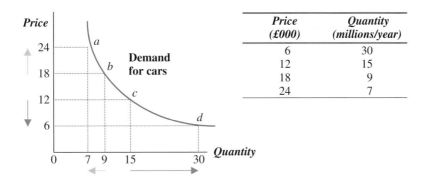

Price (£000)	Quantity (millions/year)
6	30
12	15
18	9
24	7

FIGURE 2.1 THE DEMAND CURVE AND DEMAND SCHEDULE

The table presented in Figure 2.1 is a demand schedule of the quantity of cars demanded by those individuals with plans to buy cars over a range of prices. At a price of £6000, 30 million cars would be demanded. At a higher price of £12 000, the quantity demanded would be lower at 15 million. At higher prices, quantity demanded would decline further to 9 million at a price of £18 000 and to 7 million at £24 000.

For a given demand curve and demand schedule, a change in price gives rise to a change in quantity demanded.

Two reasons explain the negative relationship between price and quantity demanded. Most goods have potential substitutes – goods that might serve a similar purpose from the buyers' perspective. For cars, possible substitutes include public transport, bicycles or motorcycles. If the price of cars increases relative to the price of substitutes, it may change people's behaviour in terms of their intended purchases of cars.

As the price of one good increases, people buy less of it preferring its relatively cheaper substitutes. This is known as the **substitution effect**.

If the price of one good changes, this affects buyers' purchasing power which is their ability to buy quantities of goods and services. Purchasing power depends on income and prices; given their income, if car prices rise, car buyers' purchasing power is adversely affected as their income allows them to buy fewer cars (or put another way, if they buy a car they have less to spend on other goods and services). At the level of individual car buyers, effects of higher car prices will include some buyers opting for cheaper brand cars, some opting for smaller cars than they would otherwise choose, some buyers postponing their decisions to buy, and some moving to substitute products.

Alternatively if car prices dropped, the purchasing power of car buyers would increase and economists would expect that due to the income effect more cars would be bought.

> Economists expect that in the face of higher car prices and a fixed income, buyers would plan to buy fewer cars. This is known as the **income effect**.

2.3.1   NON-PRICE DETERMINANTS OF DEMAND

Car buyers' intentions are related to the price of cars but price is by no means the only factor that enters into the buyers' decisions. Other relevant factors include:

- prices of related goods/services;
- buyers' income;
- preferences;
- Population;
- Expected future prices;
- consumer confidence.

The effect of each of these factors on demand, *ceteris paribus*, is considered in turn. In practice, any number of these factors might have an influence on demand at any point in time.

Prices of related goods/services: complements and substitutes

Many products are consumed in conjunction with others as with cars and car insurance, or cars and petrol/diesel. Car insurance and petrol are described as complements to car consumption. Changes in the prices of complement goods like petrol and insurance can have a knock-on impact on the demand for cars.

> The price of oil has an effect on petrol prices. Oil prices hit a 25-year low of $11 per barrel in February 1999 but rose to a peak of almost $35 per barrel in the first week of September 2000. In many European countries, soaring fuel prices brought protesters onto the streets and road blockades were common.
>
> Similar rises in oil prices in 1973/4 (when oil prices tripled) and 1979/80 (when prices doubled) are known as the oil-price shocks and these unexpected economic events had significant consequences on most economies dependent on oil imports because resources that would have been spent on buying other goods and services had instead to be spent on oil imports.

Increases in the price of complement products (petrol/diesel) can alter the demand for a good (cars). The effect may not be immediate as in the case of cars where owners require fuel for their transportation needs and the fuel costs may be small relative to the cost of the purchase itself; however, rising fuel costs might tempt some individuals to alternative modes of transport, where it is available. Cars come under the category of durable consumption goods (bought by households for non-business use with a lifespan of at least three years – cars, washing machines, PCs) that are not purchased regularly (by most people) and are therefore considered a 'lumpy' or irregular type of purchase as opposed to other non-durable purchases made on a more regular basis (food, clothing, cigarettes). For both durable and non-durable goods, the usual expected effect of an increase in the price of a complementary good (e.g. petrol) is a decline in demand for the good for which it is a complement (cars). Further effects could include an increase in demand for low-fuel consumption or smaller and lighter vehicles or increased research into vehicles that can run on alternative fuels.

Insurance costs are another complement good of cars and large increases in insurance premiums could cause some consumers to change their plans to buy a car, leading to a drop in quantity demanded at each price. Again, it is reasonable to consider that a substantial insurance price increase would be required to change demand behaviour as the decision to spend £12 000, for example, on a car will not be greatly affected by a minor change in the price of a complementary good.

As explained above, changes in prices of substitute goods can also affect demand. If public transport becomes cheaper, relative to transport by car, demand for cars could conceivably decline.

Congestion charges (£5) were introduced for motorists driving in inner-city London from February 2003. Six months after its implementation 50 000 fewer cars were entering the congestion zone daily, a drop of 16%, meeting one objective of reducing congestion (estimated at 30%) and saving time (car journeys were reduced by 14%). If as is anticipated, this makes public transport a relatively more attractive option for some drivers, demand for cars in London will fall. Hence, council or government regulations impact Demand also (this point is further developed later).

Buyers' income

Planned expenditure on any goods or services depends on disposable income (after-tax or net income; pre-tax income is known also as gross income). As a general rule of thumb, if disposable incomes rise, demands for most goods rise also. This is true for goods called normal goods. For inferior goods, demand falls as income rises. Examples of such goods might be cheap cuts of meat or lowest-priced products.

If incomes rise, economists expect that the demand for cars would also rise, especially where the rise was believed to be permanent. Planned purchases might not change significantly for a temporary or one-off increase in income (a tax rebate) but would be more likely to change following a salary increase. Consumers' expectations about their future income also play a role in their buying decisions and although they cannot know with certainty what income will be earned in the future, they make plans based on available information.

Preferences

Consumer demand also depends on tastes and preferences, which are subjective and vary across consumers. Tastes are shaped by factors as diverse as culture, background, education, past experience and advertising. An environmentally conscious consumer with access to public transport has less demand for cars than other consumers.

Population

Generally speaking, in regions with large populations, the demand for all goods and services is greater relative to regions with lower populations. Demand for cars is greater in the USA than in the UK, in cities rather than rural areas and is greater in the UK than in Ireland. The *ceteris paribus* assumption is relevant here, though differences in living standards are also relevant. For example, in India or China, with low relative living standards, demand for some goods will be lower than in more developed countries, irrespective of population differences.

Expected future prices

Demand for some goods is affected by expectations of future price changes. If car prices are expected to fall in the future, many consumers will postpone car buying until prices fall as the opportunity cost of the car is lower in the future. Buyers choose to purchase at different points in time depending on their expectation of prices.

Consumer confidence

Surveys of consumer confidence are conducted based on questions posed to a representative sample of consumers to gauge their opinions about their future buying plans.

Consumer confidence reflects consumers' opinions on their future purchasing plans.

It relates to the psychology underlying decisions about spending or saving and if consumers are pessimistic about the future, they may prefer to save rather than spend, reducing demand for some goods and services. In times of weak consumer confidence, purchases of durable goods such as cars usually fall. Often demand for non-durable 'comfort products' like alcohol, books or chocolate increase simultaneously.

The cause of weak consumer confidence is uncertainty about the future. Fear of future income due to job insecurity could be one cause. Expectations of higher prices could be another and there is some evidence that higher energy prices in 2001 in the USA explained some of the decline in consumer confidence. A decline in consumer confidence may be explained in terms of a negative wealth effect, according to which some consumers who feel richer as stock markets climb perceive themselves to be poorer when the markets decline, not because their earnings or savings lose value but for psychological rather than wholly rational reasons.

Businesses are concerned by consumer confidence because around two thirds of economic activity consists of consumer purchases. If consumers are not buying, businesses are not selling, stocks of unsold goods (inventories) build up and it may only be a matter of time before employees are made redundant.

Implications of changes in the influences on demand

When all other factors that could affect demand are unchanging, the effects of a price change alone on the quantity demanded can be considered. Staying with the car example, if the price of cars changes there is a movement from one point on the demand curve to another point along the curve; *quantity demanded changes*. If price increases from £12 000 to £18 000 quantity demanded moves from point *c* to *b* in Figure 2.1, i.e. a decline in quantity demanded from 15 to 9 million cars.

If any of the other factors influencing demand change, however, it causes a movement/shift in the demand curve; *demand for the product changes*. If customer preferences for sports utility vehicles (SUVs) increase, and they are substitute products for standard cars, the demand for cars is affected as illustrated with a movement of the demand curve shown in Figure 2.2.

At each price on the original demand curve (D_1), the change in preferences causes a decline in quantity demanded resulting in a new demand curve (D_2) that lies to the left of the original curve. The new demand schedule shows this decline

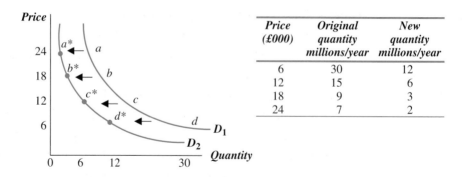

FIGURE 2.2   A MOVEMENT OF THE DEMAND CURVE (AND NEW DEMAND SCHEDULE)

in demand for cars at each possible price caused by consumers' plans to substitute away from cars towards SUVs.

Alternatively, if D_2 were the original demand function, a fall in preferences for SUVs would lead to a rise in demand for cars over the entire price range, to D_1 for example.

2.4   SUPPLY

Consumers' buying plans can only be satisfied if there are goods and services supplied to them.

> The economic concept of **supply** relates to the activities of firms that organize the factors of production to produce output and make it available to buyers.

Producers have an incentive to engage in supplying output to markets if they see that a profit can be made, where profit is the difference between the costs of production and the revenue received from buyers. From an accounting perspective the nature of profit is evident from a company's accounts but the economic concept of profit is not equivalent.

> An **economic profit** is made if a producer earns enough from supplying their product (or service) to the market to cover all their costs *and* pay themselves for the cost of the time and effort put into the business.

This economic definition of profit takes the opportunity cost of the suppliers' efforts in their business into account and from an economic perspective a supplier should only stay in business if all the costs of supply *including the opportunity cost* of the owner of the business's efforts are covered. Each business person has their own subjective view of how much they need to earn to cover their opportunity costs; it is impossible to say objectively what amount of income must be earned for a business person to remain in business rather than sell up and do something else.

Factors apart from a desire to make an economic profit also affect supply. Suppliers must be able to supply output, which implies having the required resources, factors of production and technology to produce. Over a specific time period, suppliers will take all information available to them regarding their available resources, the type and costs of the factors of production needed for production and assess if it is worthwhile to produce.

Similarly to their use of the law of demand, economists use the law of supply, which states that at higher prices the quantity supplied of a good is expected to be higher than at lower prices. Figure 2.3 presents the relationship between the price of cars in Europe and the quantity supplied for the year 2000. The logic of the law of supply is that firms are willing to supply greater quantities only if they receive higher prices because of the increasing marginal costs encountered in increasing output (see Figure 1.5).

In terms of the supply curve, a firm is only willing to supply more output if it receives a higher price for a higher output since its marginal cost increases with production. This implies that the marginal cost of producing the 1000th car is higher than for the 999th car so suppliers require a higher price to cover their higher marginal costs. The logic of this assumption relates to the need to attract more resources into car production from other uses if suppliers want to increase output. There is an opportunity cost of using resources in car production rather

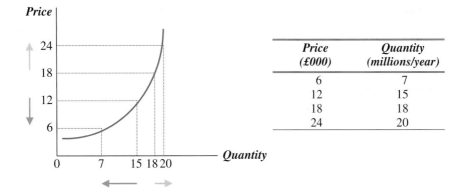

Price (£000)	Quantity (millions/year)
6	7
12	15
18	18
24	20

FIGURE 2.3 **THE SUPPLY CURVE AND SUPPLY SCHEDULE**

than other alternatives, and hence the increasing marginal cost of production in a specific market is conceptually similar to the argument used earlier that there are increasing opportunity costs of production underlying a production possibility frontier. (When we consider differences in the supply decision in the short run and long run later, we will see that there are additional reasons why short-run supply curves are upward sloping.) Hence, we observe a positive relationship between price and quantity supplied and this is reflected in the upward slope of the supply curve.

The supply curve indicates the amounts all car firms plan to sell at different prices (not how much they actually sell). The table presented in Figure 2.3 is a supply schedule showing the quantity of cars supplied for a range of prices: at a price of £6000, 7 million cars would be supplied; at a higher price of £12 000, quantity supplied would be 15 million and, at higher prices, quantity supplied increases to 18 million at a price of £18 000 and to 20 million at £24 000.

For a change in price, suppliers react by changing the quantity of goods supplied to a market. A supply curve is drawn *ceteris paribus*, as if factors apart from price affecting supply are unchanging. These other factors include:

- prices of the factors of production (and technology);
- expected future prices;
- government regulations.

- prices of related goods;
- the number of suppliers;

If any one of these factors changes, it causes a movement/shift of the supply curve.

Prices of the factors of production (and technology)

The price that a firm earns for its output provides the firm's revenue. This can be calculated as the price of output times the quantity of output (e.g. if the price of a car was £12 000 and a firm supplied 20 000 cars its revenue would be £240 million). Using its revenues the firm hopes to cover its costs and make at least a normal (economic) profit.

> **Normal (economic) profit:** the minimum profit a firm is willing to make rather than go out of business. Any level of profit beyond this is called **supernormal profit**.

In producing its output the firm uses factors of production and if the costs of the factors increase, this reduces the firm's profits. Possible sources of increased costs would be higher wages, raw materials prices, rent, or interest rates on loans.

Costs might also be changed considerably by the introduction of new technology. When economists refer to technology we mean not just machinery, equipment or robots but also the level of knowledge or know-how that exists about production at a specific point in time.

The car industry's extensive use of robotics (for the welding of seats onto chassis, for example) represented a significant investment by the firms in the industry but allowed considerable cost savings once the robots were functional on assembly lines since they could perform a number of tasks (placing and fitting of components) more efficiently, removing the necessity for thousands of manual workers. Many of the activities performed by robots were those in the harshest of working conditions, which were uncomfortable and even risky for workers and since a robot has an advantage of being able to perform repetitive tasks without feeling the boredom often associated with such activities, the accuracy and speed of output also improved.

Restructuring of organizations also allows for cost savings. The concepts of downsizing and rationalizations (used extensively in the 1990s) refer to the process of laying off considerable numbers of employees by firms that substantially reorganized their production. Quite often this occurred in conjunction with outsourcing which involved firms contracting out work to others that was previously performed by the firms themselves. The logic for such restructuring allows a firm to focus on its most important activities, what it does best, and buy in any other non-essential activities that could be more efficiently supplied by other firms. There is a substantial debate on the downsizing that occurred over the 1990s and whether it made sense economically and socially. (Refer to www.geocities.com/WallStreet/Exchange/4280/ for an interesting discussion on the phenomenon.)

Costs for firms can also be affected by government policies. If subsidies are provided, firms' costs fall, such as happened in the UK in 1999 when the government provided more than £150 million to BMW to maintain production of Rover models at the Longbridge plant in Birmingham. BMW had threatened to move production to Hungary, where a free site was available and production costs were considerably lower.

Since BMW was making substantial losses on the cars, the subsidies received served to cut their losses rather than increase profits. A further example of the effects of government policy on costs is the EU directive on *End of Life Vehicles* which attempts to make car makers responsible for dealing with the waste caused by cars that end their useful lives (approximately 12 million in the EU annually). If car manufacturers have to bear such costs (estimated at £50bn) then this will affect car supply.

The effect of higher costs on the supply curve for any product can be considered at any price on the supply curve. A supply curve is drawn for a given set of costs (*ceteris paribus* strikes again!). If costs change, this causes a movement of the supply curve. For example, any supplier willing to supply at a price of £12 000 incurs higher costs if labour costs rise. Given higher costs and the total cost outlay suppliers are willing to incur to earn revenues of £12 000 per car, suppliers are willing to supply a lower quantity of output at point x^* in Figure 2.4 than at point x (with lower costs).

More generally, depending on their line of business, it is possible that some suppliers might wish to switch production to other products for which costs have not increased. With sufficient advance information of cost changes, suppliers will take any new information into account and may change their supply decisions. In Figure 2.4 there is a reduction of supply from 15 million cars to 8 million cars caused by an increase in production costs. At every price on the original supply curve, once production costs increase, producers cut back their production and this leads to a leftward shift in the supply curve from S_1 to S_2.

Beginning with S_2 a cost reduction would have the opposite effect; some producers are enticed to supply greater quantities resulting in a shift of the supply curve to S_1 for example.

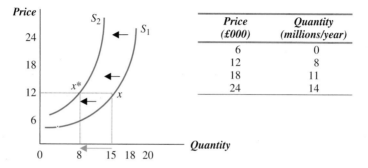

Price (£000)	Quantity (millions/year)
6	0
12	8
18	11
24	14

FIGURE 2.4   A MOVEMENT OF THE SUPPLY CURVE (AND NEW SUPPLY SCHEDULE)

Prices of related goods

Supply is influenced by the prices of related goods, substitutes and complements. In car production, different types of vehicles can be produced from a given factory – saloons or sports utility vehicles (SUVs) – with minor alterations to the production line, which means they are substitutes in production. The quantity of saloons supplied is affected by the price of SUVs because if the price that can be earned from supplying SUVs increases, suppliers of saloons have the incentive to switch towards producing SUVs (so the supply curve for saloons moves leftwards).

Complements in production also exist where at least two goods are produced jointly from the same resources, e.g. beef and leather. If the price of leather increases, leather suppliers have the incentive to supply more, which would lead to the joint additional supply of beef (the supply curve for beef would move rightwards).

Expected future prices

Suppliers who can store their output over time would have the incentive to do so if prices in the future were expected to be higher than the current price they could earn on their supply, hence a lower current supply would be offered on the market than if no change in the future price was expected. The alternative is also true. In the car market when new editions appear, previous models become more difficult to sell – in buying a new car, many customers prefer to buy the most up-to-date model rather than earlier editions. If suppliers have stocks of the older models available and know that future models are about to be launched they often offer good deals on the old models to try to sell them before new models reduce the demand for the old. Expectations about the future prices that can be earned on the old models create incentives for suppliers to sell in the present rather than stock up their supply for the future.

The number of suppliers

The supply of cars or any product is the sum total of each car firm's supply in that market. The entry of a new firm into the market adds extra supply moving the supply curve rightwards.

This effect could be short term if the new firm supplies more attractive cars or better value cars than other firms. Reaction by competing firms may follow. Some firms might be forced out of the market if they can no longer compete with the new firm and the end result might be a replacement of a supplier with no significant impact on the overall supply.

Government regulations

The regulation function of governments permeates many different activities in an economy. It can affect supply through various channels, such as through the policy regarding *End of Life Vehicles* explained above, and various other environmental and safety regulations that limit the activities of suppliers across a range of industries. Various policies apply to the chemicals industry, for example, from food labelling requirements and the classification of dangerous substances to general health safety and environmental regulations. To the extent that new regulations force firms to deal with additional costs (e.g. to pay for anti-pollution systems, to employ people with regulatory expertise) the supply curve may move leftwards.

This may not necessarily be all bad news for a firm, though. Some buyers might be attracted to products when they know the suppliers apply stringent standards. Some firms go beyond government regulations to make their products even safer or more environmentally friendly because the additional cost is more than covered by the extra demand generated by the product.

Although costly to manufacture, cars that are capable of withstanding a 64 kmph (40 mph) head-on smash and a 48 kmph (30 mph) side-on collision are currently being engineered and developed to deal with European New Car Assessment Programme tests reported regularly on new cars – for more on this see www.euroncap.com. Manufacturers realize that safety is an important selling feature for cars and invest substantial funds into safety improvements that increase their performance.

2.5 MARKET INTERACTION: DEMAND AND SUPPLY

Each market consists of buyers and sellers, demand and supply. Bringing both together allows for analysis of how market prices are arrived at, showing how both sides of the market combine to give rise to the outcome in terms of the price and quantity of goods bought and sold. Using the example of the car market, the market demand and supply curves can be shown together as in Figure 2.5.

There is only one price at which the quantity buyers are willing to buy coincides with the quantity sellers are willing to sell. This price is £12 000 and is called the market clearing price because if all good supplied at this price are sold, all buyers

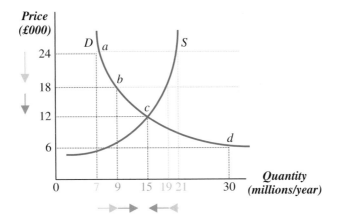

FIGURE 2.5 DEMAND AND SUPPLY: THE CAR MARKET

wishing to buy at this price can do so. At this price firms do not build up stocks of unsold cars and no consumer demand is left unsatisfied. A market does not clear if demand cannot be met (shortage) or if suppliers provide more than is demanded in the market (surplus).

This price is also called the equilibrium price. The term equilibrium is used widely in economics and it refers to a situation from which there is no tendency to change – unless something to cause a change occurs. An equilibrium quantity corresponds to the equilibrium price. In Figure 2.5 this quantity is 15 million cars, the amount of goods that are bought and sold when the market is in equilibrium.

The market for cars will tend towards the market-clearing equilibrium price and quantity. This happens if you consider the forces at work at any other price. If the price were £24 000, demand would be 7 million cars while corresponding supply would be 21 million. Such a high price means few buyers are willing and able to buy cars while quite a number of suppliers are willing to supply at such a high price.

At a price of £24 000 the market does not clear because the quantity demanded does not correspond to the quantity supplied:

$$Q_D < Q_S$$

Quantity demanded is less than quantity supplied. The discrepancy between these quantities is 14 million cars which suppliers are willing to supply, for which no demand exists; hence, a surplus exists in the market. The expected reaction to this non-equilibrium situation is for firms to try to do something to sell their unsold stocks. One rational response might be to cut their price. If price declines to £18 000, quantity demanded increases to 9 million while quantity supplied falls to 21 million. This reduces the surplus or excess production to 12 million cars but does not eliminate it. Reducing the price further will further reduce the surplus. Only if the price falls to £12 000 will the surplus production be eradicated. If firms wish to sell all their output, the price needs to fall to this level, otherwise they are left with unsold stocks of cars.

If the price were below the equilibrium level, that too would create problems and represent a disequilibrium situation in the market. Take the case where the price of cars was £6000. The quantity demanded at this price would be 30 million cars (high demand at such a relatively low price) but suppliers are willing to supply only 7 million cars. A shortage would exist in the market; 23 million more cars would be in excess demand compared to the available supply.

$$Q_D > Q_S.$$

Customers lucky enough to get their hands on cars at £6000 are surely very satisfied but a large number of potential customers willing and able to pay this amount just cannot buy cars as supply does not meet demand at this price.

The method by which cars are allocated to customers could be extremely problematic – first come first served might be a possibility but someone who really wanted the product might not be happy to settle for a straightforward queuing system. Attempts at bribery might occur, preferential treatment might be given to some customers, and corruption is a real possibility. Any supplier happy to supply at this price can sell their output but because the price is relatively low, the supply of cars is also low. If this situation existed in a market, suppliers would be aware of the excess demand and might try to react to it. Sellers might decide to increase the price a little which would have the effect of encouraging greater production of cars while reducing the quantity demanded. At any price greater than £6000 but less than £12 000 suppliers will have the incentive to charge a higher price which means that the quantity supplied will rise. As price rises, quantity demanded is reduced but since supply does not match demand, a portion of it is unsatisfied at prices below £12 000.

Hence, in a free market – where price and quantity are set by market demand and supply – a tendency for the price and quantity to change exists if the market is not in equilibrium. In equilibrium, the market price is the equilibrium price and neither excess demand nor supply is observed as the market clears.

2.5.1 CHANGES IN EQUILIBRIUM

Market analysis based on demand and supply can be used to consider the effects of changing circumstances on equilibrium.

Staying with the car market, city councils in both London and Paris were considering banning SUVs due to their environmental impacts; they are big, relatively more dangerous to pedestrians and other motorists in crashes, and they generally have higher emissions than cars.

Figure 2.6A shows a possible scenario for the international car market, should a ban be imposed. *D1* indicates initial demand for cars before the outlawing of SUVs, when *P1* was the equilibrium price and *Q1* represents equilibrium quantity. *D2* shows the increase in demand for cars indicating that changes in regulation affecting the use of goods change demand. With no change to supply, the effect of the rightward shift of the demand curve is a new equilibrium at *P2* and *Q2*. Increased demand leads to both a higher price and quantity in equilibrium.

If such bans become commonplace internationally, many SUV producers might switch their production to more standard cars as their equipment and factories could be adapted without too much difficulty. Should this lead to substantial new entrants into the market, Figure 2.6B indicates a possible outcome. Supply expands from *S1* to *S2* giving rise to another new equilibrium position. Focusing on *D2* and *S2* as the relevant demand and supply curves, *P3* and *Q3* represent the equilibrium position where price falls relative to *P2* and where quantity expands to *Q3*.

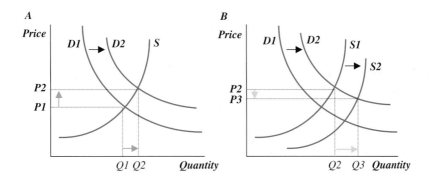

FIGURE 2.6 POSSIBLE SCENARIOS FOR THE CAR MARKET

2.6 GOVERNMENT AFFECTING PRICES

Attempts are sometimes made by government to influence the price in a particular market. Examples are price ceilings and price floors, which are cases when the actual market price is not the same as the equilibrium price.

2.6.1 PRICE CEILING

A **price ceiling** or *price cap* is a price that puts an upper limit on the price that suppliers can charge.

The purpose of a price ceiling is to allow consumers to buy products at relatively low prices.

> In January 2002 the Filipino government implemented a price ceiling on utility vehicles in an attempt to reform taxes in that industry. The price ceiling applied to basic models only and meant they were tax exempt.

The general effects of a price ceiling are shown in Figure 2.7 for the case of a price ceiling on cars of £6000. The result is excess demand of 23 million cars (30 – 7), but prices cannot adjust upwards to clear the market since it is illegal to charge more.

Economists generally do not favour price ceilings because of the costs they generate. There is a cost to consumers who wish to buy the product at £6000 but who cannot because of the limited supply. Suppliers have an incentive to maintain supply at a relatively low level because of the low price and so industry

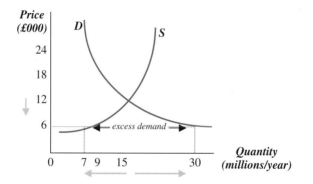

FIGURE 2.7 PRICE CEILING IN THE CAR MARKET

output, employment and taxes paid to government may all be lower as a result. Furthermore, potential problems exist regarding how the 7 million cars will be allocated among the people demanding 30 million cars.

2.6.2   PRICE FLOOR

A **price floor** is a price that suppliers can be sure to receive for their output.

A price floor is a minimum price with the purpose of helping the producer/supplier attain a price higher than the equilibrium price. It is common in the agriculture sector, as with Europe's Common Agricultural Policy. The general effects of a price floor are shown in Figure 2.8.

The price floor is set at £24 000. Suppliers are willing to supply 19 million cars, 4 million more than if the equilibrium price could be earned. The result is excess supply in this market since quantity demanded is 12 million cars less than quantity supplied of 19 million. The surplus output may be taken up by a government agency or perhaps exported. Prices cannot adjust freely downwards to clear the market and bring demand and supply to equilibrium.

2.6.3   PROBLEMS OF PRICE CEILINGS AND FLOORS

Economists generally do not support the use of price ceilings and floors as they interfere with the free working of the market system and mean that markets do not clear. Problems are created which are worse than those the policies are aimed at solving. Instead of allowing the accumulated choices taken by people on both demand and supply sides of markets to feed into the market price and quantity of goods bought and sold, individuals with decision-making power judge what the

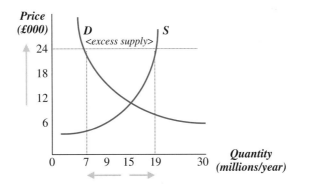

FIGURE 2.8   PRICE FLOOR IN THE CAR MARKET

'correct' market price should be. This removes the contributions of some individuals to the market process meaning less collective information feeds into the market outcome. This means that some information of relevance to the market is not used, or is purposefully ignored, and hence, the economic outcome is not as efficient as it could otherwise be.

2.7   INFORMATION AND KNOWLEDGE IN THE MARKET SYSTEM

You will appreciate already that demand and supply curves are not simple features of an economy but relate to a complex range of factors that together reflect the behaviour of individual buyers and sellers in markets. The behaviour results from all of the information used by buyers and sellers when making their economic decisions and is, therefore, the result of numerous independent decisions made by unrelated and non-directly communicating individuals seeking to satisfy their personal economic goals – maximizing their utility. Information available to each individual informs their decision-making so all relevant information distributed across a range of individuals is reflected in supply and demand.

The market system is built on individuals' use of information and their incentives about how best it should be used. Some of this information is generally available. Take the case of a firm trying to decide if it should hire an additional worker. It will know how much the employee will cost, based on the going or market wage rate, and it will have to make a guess about how much additional revenue the worker will be able to generate for the firm, maybe using information they already have about other workers. Using this information, the economic decision to hire or not is taken.

General information or knowledge that we all possess provides no economic advantage to us relative to others in the economic system although it is useful for some decision-making. Specific knowledge is also used in the economic system. Specific knowledge differs from general knowledge because it is not generally known or available and can be difficult and/or costly to share with others. It includes:

- *Scientific knowledge* – e.g. the laws of quantum physics or astrophysics that are not easily shared with non-specialists.
- *Assembled knowledge* – e.g. an administrator who has worked dealing with students in a university department has assembled knowledge about courses offered, timetables, the marks and standards of the courses, details of assignments,

deadlines and so forth; e.g. the knowledge of how a machine works and how it can be fixed if it breaks down. Such assembled information would take time to be learned by new staff.

- *Idiosyncratic knowledge* of particular circumstances which if not acted upon swiftly leads to missed opportunities and, hence, wasted resources – e.g. if more output is required in a factory then information on whether a specific machine is operating to capacity will be known to individuals working closely with that machine; if more products must be distributed, information about which containers/lorries are not fully loaded is known to employees on the spot.

Some knowledge may be easily redistributed if it can be expressed in facts, phrases or drawings. Depending on the time it takes to distribute the knowledge, however, it may still be costly to transfer to other people. Other types of knowledge are of a tacit nature, made up of perceptions, beliefs, experience and other types of specific knowledge and can be impossible to explicitly transfer.

The role of knowledge within firms and its central role within the economic system is discussed by Stewart (1997).

Knowledge is more valuable and more powerful than natural resources, big factories, or fat bankrolls. In industry after industry, success comes to the companies that have the best information or wield it most effectively – not necessarily the companies with the most muscle. WalMart, Microsoft, and Toyota didn't become great companies because they were richer than Sears, IBM, and General Motors – on the contrary. But they had something far more valuable than physical or financial assets. They had intellectual capital . . .

Intellectual capital is the sum of everything everybody in a company knows that gives it a competitive edge. Unlike the assets with which business people and accountants are familiar – land, factories, equipment, cash – intellectual capital is intangible. It is the knowledge of a workforce: the training and intuition of a team of chemists who discover a billion-dollar new drug or the know-how of workmen who come up with a thousand different ways to improve the efficiency of a factory. It is the electronic network that transports information at warp speed through a company, so that it can react to the market faster than its rivals. It is the collaboration – the shared learning – between a company and its customers, which forges a bond between them that brings the customer back again and again.

In a sentence: intellectual capital is intellectual material – knowledge, information, intellectual property, experience – that can be put to use to create wealth. It is collective brainpower. It's hard to identify and harder still to deploy effectively. But once you find it and exploit it, you win. (Stewart, 1997. Reproduced by permission of Currency Publishers.)

From the perspective of encouraging an economy to be efficient it is a challenge to ensure that all resources, including knowledge, are used in the best way possible. As outlined in Chapter 1, economists generally believe that the free-market system provides the most appropriate form of economic organization to encourage efficient resource use. Each person or organization has the incentive to use their knowledge to maximize their utility.

Adam Smith discussed the concept of the 'invisible hand' when he referred to how the economic system performed as though it were guided towards getting the most out of its resources in spite of the fact that individuals in the economic system do not make their economic decisions with such a goal in mind. Within the free-market system any 'guiding' activity is the result of how people and firms react to the prices and the market opportunities they observe. Prices are the signals that feed into economic decisions about what to buy and what to sell, how to use resources, or whether to supply labour or not.

Hayek (1945) described how the price system operates in by allowing all relevant information and knowledge to be incorporated into the functioning of markets without the participants necessarily being fully aware of why changes occur, but by reacting to them and taking any new information into account in their decision making.

It is worth contemplating for a moment a very simple and commonplace instance of the action of the price system to see what precisely it accomplishes ... [S]omewhere in the world a new opportunity for the use of some raw material, say, tin has arisen ... All that the users of tin need to know is that some of the tin they used to consume is now more profitably employed elsewhere and that, in consequence, they must economize tin ... If only some of them know directly of the new demand and switch resources over to it, and if the people who are aware of the new gap thus created in turn fill it from still other sources, the effect will rapidly spread throughout the entire economic system. This influences not only all of the uses of tin but also those of its substitutes and the substitutes of these substitutes, the supply of all things made of tin, and their substitutes and so on. All this takes place without the great majority of those instrumental in bringing about these substitutions knowing anything at all about the original cause of these changes. The whole acts as one market, not because any of its members surveys the whole field, but because their limited individual fields of vision sufficiently overlap so that through many intermediaries the relevant information is communicated to all. The mere fact that there is one price for any commodity – or rather that local prices are connected in a manner determined by the cost of transport, etc. – brings about the solution which (if conceptually possible) might have been arrived at by one single mind possessing all the information which is in fact dispersed among all the people involved in the process. (Hayek, 1945. Reproduced by permission of the American Economic Association.)

Economic decision-making in free markets is decentralized across all the individuals dispersed in each market and is synchronized or coordinated by the price system.

Decisions in command economies are not made on the basis of price signals because the central planners decide what should be produced and in what quantities, without reference to supply and demand. Central planners attempt to assemble as much information as possible in making their decisions but given the dispersion of knowledge throughout an economy; it would be impossible for central planners to gather all relevant information for each economic decision that must be made. In the case of specific knowledge, even when it is possible to transfer knowledge it is often costly. Centralized decision-making creates problems for the effective use of information and knowledge within an economy and so leads to a less efficient use of resources than a free-market system.

Another principle that differentiates free markets from centrally planned economic systems is the right to own private property. Private property rights are often taken for granted by those of us in free markets. Since we have the rights to personally own and use property – as opposed to a system of centrally owned and operated property within a centrally planned economy – both individuals and firms have the incentive to use their specific knowledge to maximize their utility. Economists argue that, in general, when decision-makers do not own resources that they may have control over, their incentive to make optimal use of the resources is reduced. Bring this close to home by focusing on the incentive to take care of a TV (or room) you rent rather than one you own!

2.7.1   DECENTRALIZED DECISION-MAKING – THE OPTIMAL FORM OF ORGANIZATION?

Allowing economic decisions to be the outcome of market decisions rather than central planning appears to be Hayek's conclusion. Even the expressions 'free-market system' or 'market economy' indicate the central role of markets in how many economies are organized. However, it would be incorrect to argue that decentralized decision-making is *always* the most efficient form of economic organization. Look at how firms function by making many of their decisions centrally – by the chief executive officer (CEO) or board of directors – with staff 'lower down' in the hierarchy making few, if any, decisions.

Economic activity within the market system relies largely on firms for the markets to function. In principle, it would be possible for economic decisions to be made without the existence of firms – if I want a new wooden table I could contact a timber supplier and organize a carpenter to assemble it. In practice, however, most tables are manufactured by firms and sold on to consumers because some transactions are more efficiently conducted by firms rather than in markets. Consumers save time, effort and, therefore, money in buying from a firm rather than having to deal with what may be a multitude of different suppliers of individual parts and assemblers.

Searching out suppliers is more time-consuming the more complex the product and such search costs represent just one element of what are called transactions costs.

> **Transactions costs** are the complete price plus non-price costs of a transaction, including search, information, bargaining and policing costs.

Consumers incur information costs when they must find out about suppliers or about the quality of different parts; they incur bargaining and decision costs when they must haggle to negotiate the final price with the supplier and decide between alternatives; policing and enforcement costs when the consumer must ensure that the other party to the transaction is honouring the agreed terms of the transaction.

The most efficient way of organizing a transaction minimizes transactions costs. Firms will make and supply goods and services and consumers will buy from them when the transactions cost to the consumer is lower than using markets. Firms too incur transactions costs in organizing their economic activities but exist when these costs are lower than the costs of organizing in markets. Usually transactions costs in firms increase as the firms grow and it becomes more difficult for the management to keep track of all relevant knowledge for their decision-making. Hence, there is a limit to the size of firms that is related to the cost of their transactions and this is one explanation as to why firms do not grow indefinitely.

2.8 MORE ON EQUILIBRIUM IN THE DEMAND AND SUPPLY MODEL

The demand and supply model and the role of equilibrium within it outlined in this chapter is the foundation of the economics discipline, allowing analyses of different markets and assessment of the implications of changes across a range of factors on market outcomes. The demand and supply model, however, does not provide any answers. Rather, it provides a framework for economists who use the model as best they can for making sense of what they observe. Despite its place at the centre of the economist's toolbox there is disagreement among economists as to the purpose of equilibrium analysis, which is viewed alternatively by some as a description of reality or by others as a theoretical construct.

- *Equilibrium as a description of reality*: According to this view, real markets come sufficiently close to being approximated by the supply and demand model – tending towards equilibrium – and in cases where an individual market does not, the supply and demand model allows us to make better explanations and predictions of that market than any alternative model available.
- *Equilibrium as a theoretical construct*: Holders of this view consider that the supply and demand model can help us to understand things that might occur in reality but it is through our observations of the economy that we figure out what is going on in any particular market and why. Allowance is made for a market that is in disequilibrium and this helps us to understand how markets change over time as individuals (on demand or supply sides of the economy) learn from available information and incorporate it into their economic decisions.

The definition of equilibrium as a state from which there is no tendency to change does not describe markets all of the time as the quantities of goods bought and sold change over time as does their price. Hence we need to understand what equilibrium means, how it comes about, its implications for sellers and buyers and causes and consequences of changes in factors that feed into economic decision-making. Irrespective of your preference for one description or other, the supply and demand model allows us to address these issues.

2.9   A MARKET AT WORK: THE LABOUR MARKET

The labour market can be analysed using the supply and demand framework but in many respects it is a unique market and a number of different elements require analysis in considering how it functions. As labour is one of the factors of production, the labour market is also described as a factor market. Since labour is an input into production, labour demand is a derived demand since it depends on the demand for goods and services.

Firms demand labour taking into account, among other factors, the cost of the labour, which in turn depends on the wage rate that must be paid. At higher wage rates we expect firms to hire fewer workers than at lower rates. Labour supply refers to people's willingness to make some of their time available for paid work and also depends on the wage rate. We expect more people to wish to supply their labour if wage rates are high rather than relatively low. When we discuss price in relation to the labour market we refer to the price of labour, which is the wage rate. The wage rate in a labour market is determined similarly to any equilibrium price, i.e. via supply and demand for labour, which are discussed in more detail below.

2.9.1   LABOUR DEMAND

Labour demand is graphed like other demand curves with quantity (of labour) on the horizontal axis and the price (wages) on the vertical axis, as in the example in Figure 2.9. Firms in the industry shown wish to employ 60 000 workers if wages are £10 per hour; at higher wage rates, firms would demand fewer workers because costs rise as wages rise.

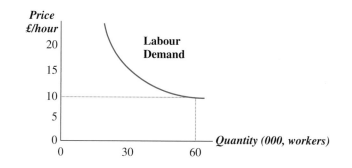

FIGURE 2.9   INDUSTRY LABOUR DEMAND CURVE

The wage rate enters into the labour demand decision of firms but the firm must also take into account the output that the workers they employ can produce for the firm, and the revenue the firm can earn from that output. The firm must try to work out how many workers it can profitably employ. This process involves consideration of the output of each worker.

> The following example is considered to figure out the number of workers demanded by Safelock, a hypothetical company manufacturing steering locks (anti-theft devices for steering wheels).

Given the available machinery and equipment in the steering lock factory, the firm considers that output could be produced as shown in Table 2.3. In the second column Table 2.3 shows the output that could be produced if the firm employed between one and 10 workers. One worker could produce 25 locks per day, rising to 55 if two workers were employed and so on. In the third column the marginal physical product of Labour is computed.

> The **marginal physical product of labour** is the change in the quantity of output (ΔQ) produced by each additional worker (ΔL).

TABLE 2.3   LABOUR OUTPUT

No. of workers	Output (per day)*	MPP_L
1	25	25
2	55	30
3	82	27
4	102	20
5	116	14
6	124	8
7	130	6
8	132	2
9	130	−2
10	125	−5

*A working day is assumed to consist of 8 hours.

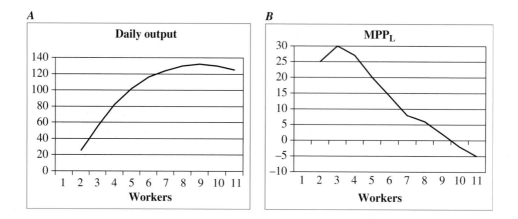

FIGURE 2.10 **TOTAL OUTPUT AND MARGINAL PHYSICAL PRODUCT OF LABOUR**

For example, the change in output generated by hiring the first worker is 25 ($\Delta Q/\Delta L = 25/1$) since when no workers are hired output is zero. In hiring the second worker output increases from 25 to 55, a change of 30. The second worker adds 30 steering locks extra to total output, the third adds 27 locks and so on.

When a second worker is hired the two can cooperate to divide up the work between them and there are advantages of this division of labour that allows them to produce more than double the output of the first worker (55 compared to 25). Hiring the third worker changes the division of labour too but in this case the additional output is 27 locks extra. This happens because of how the materials and equipment are shared and used among the workers. The total output increases with each worker up until worker 8 but when the next worker is hired, they do not add any additional output. In fact output falls by half a unit – this is because given the available equipment, there is nothing for this worker to do. Hiring the ninth worker leads to a fall in output (from 132 to 130 locks) because the worker actually gets in the way of others trying to do their job. The total output of the factory and the marginal physical product of labour are shown in Figure 2.10.

Once any more than two workers are employed, the additions to total output decline (from 30 to 27 to 20 to 14, etc.) by diminishing amounts. This is reflected in the flattening slope of the total output curve in panel A of Figure 2.10 and in the downward (negative) slope of the MPP_L in panel B. This reveals the law of diminishing marginal returns.

The law of diminishing marginal returns states that when a firm adds workers to a given amount of capital – machinery, equipment, etc. – it *eventually* leads to a less efficient match between labour and capital to the extent that if all capital is used by workers, hiring an additional worker will only lead to workers getting in each other's way and the marginal product of labour declines.

The law of diminishing returns helps us to understand why when capital input is fixed supply curves slope up and the marginal costs of production rise. This is relevant over short periods of time when firms use their available capital rather than changing it by building new factories, buying new machinery, etc.

Safelock uses the above information in considering how many workers it should profitably hire. It also takes into account the price it can earn for its output. There are a large number of competing products and Safelock is aware that if it wants to be successful in selling its product it cannot charge above a price of £30. Using this price information, the firm can move from an analysis of output to the revenue it can expect to earn from its product. Each worker's MPP_L can be considered in terms of MRP_L.

> MRP_L – **marginal revenue product of labour**. This is the change in total revenue (price of output × number of units sold) generated by each additional worker. It is computed by multiplying the product price by the MPP_L.

In Table 2.4 these additional estimations are shown for the Safelock example, with some blanks left for you to fill in. Table 2.4 shows how the first worker adds £750 to Safelock's total revenue which is computed as the worker's $MPP_L \times P = 25 \times 30$. With the second worker, the total revenue (output × P) earned by the firm increases to £1650 which represents an MRP_L of £900 (since £1650 − £750 = £900).

A final element in the firm's decision on how many workers to employ is the cost to the firm of the workers (the cost to the firm is assumed here to be the wage rate only). If the firm knows it will only attract workers by paying £10 per hour, it can calculate its labour costs for varying numbers of workers as shown in Table 2.5 and Figure 2.11. When the working day is 8 hours and the wage rate is £10, it costs the firm £80 to employ each worker each day.

Hence, total labour costs per day rise steadily by £80 for each worker employed and the extra costs to the firm of employing each additional worker is computed as the daily wage. This is the marginal cost of labour for the firm.

All of the previous information on the output of workers, the revenue they generate for the firm and the costs of employing them enter into the firm's decision about its demand for labour. In particular, the information regarding marginal revenue and marginal cost are central to the demand for labour.

TABLE 2.4   LABOUR OUTPUT: EXTENDED ANALYSIS

No. of workers	Output (per day)*	MPP_L	TR (P = £30)	MRP_L
1	25	25	750	750
2	55	30	1650	900
3	82	27		810
4	102	20	3060	600
5	116	14	3480	
6	124	8	3720	240
7	130	6		180
8	132	2	3960	60
9	130	−2	3900	−60
10	125	−5	3750	−150

*A working day is assumed to consist of 8 hours.

TABLE 2.5   LABOUR COSTS: WAGES OF £80 PER WORKER DAY

Workers	1	2	3	4	5	6	7	8	9	10
Labour cost: total (£)	80	160	240	320	400	480	560	640	720	800
Labour cost: marginal (£)	80	80	80	80	80	80	80	80	80	80

It is possible to consider how many workers it makes economic sense for Safelock to hire at the (daily) wage rate of £80. Simply put, if the benefits to the firm outweigh the costs they should continue to hire additional workers:

- First worker: benefit = MRP_L of £750   cost = £80   £750 > £80
- Second worker: benefit = MRP_L of £900   cost = £80   £900 > £80
- ...   .
- Eighth worker: benefit = MRP_L of £60   cost = £80   £60 < £80

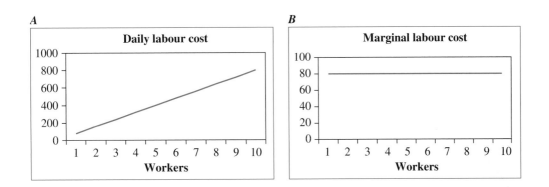

FIGURE 2.11 LABOUR COSTS: TOTAL AND MARGINAL

When the decision of whether to hire the eighth worker is taken, the cost outweighs the benefit so the most efficient workforce for Safelock is seven workers. This solution could also be found graphically by drawing marginal cost and MRP_L on the same graph and examining where they intersect.

The hiring decision would differ under different economic circumstances (another case of *ceteris paribus*). For example, at a wage rate of £25 per hour (£200 per day) it would make sense to keep hiring workers up to the sixth worker since the seventh worker would add more to the costs of Safelock (£200) than to the revenue (£180). The sixth worker will be hired as long as their MRP_L is sufficient to cover their wage costs which means that once the wage rate does not rise above £30 per hour (£240 per day) it makes economic sense to hire the worker. This process shows that Safelock continues to hire workers once their MRP_L (marginal revenue product of labour) is greater than or equal to the MLC (marginal labour cost), i.e. the wage rate. We can also see from Table 2.4 that it will never make economic sense to hire any more than eight workers (if price remains at £30) because after this level, MRP_L is negative – given the available equipment and factory space more than eight workers leads to losses.

The above information allows us to conclude that Safelock's demand for labour differs for different wage rates:

- at a wage rate of £10 demand is seven workers;
- at a wage rate of £25 demand would be six workers and at £30, five workers would be employed.

The demand for labour follows the general law of demand – the higher the price, the lower the quantity demanded, *ceteris paribus*. To find the demand for labour in an industry (or a country) requires the summing up of the demand for labour across each firm in the industry (or the country).

2.9.2   LABOUR SUPPLY: INDIVIDUAL SUPPLY DECISION

Whether to supply labour to firms is a subjective decision made by individuals who vary with regard to their incentives to supply their labour and the amount of time they are willing to supply. One factor that individuals usually take into account in this decision is the price that they expect to receive for their labour, the wage rate. Generally speaking, the higher the wage rate, the more attractive it is to work because the reward is higher. This can be restated in terms of opportunity costs.

> People wish to work or not, and those that do seek employment. There is an opportunity cost of working, which is the leisure time given up. Or, there is an opportunity cost of not working, which is the income foregone.

In choosing between alternative employment possibilities, people also take the wage rate into account and will usually try to secure the highest wage possible, *ceteris paribus*.

In the case of labour supply for individuals, supply does not keep rising indefinitely as wages increase, simply because there is a limit to the hours any individual can and is willing to work. Someone who works 35 hours a week for £10 per hour might be enticed to work additional hours at a higher wage rate – this would happen if the person placed a higher value on the extra income they could earn rather than the extra leisure time given up. Someone else working 55 hours a week might actually cut down on their labour supply if they could earn a higher wage because they consider 55 hours to be the limit of the time they are willing to devote to work. A higher wage rate would cause the person to cut back on their labour supply if they place a higher value on their leisure time compared to the income they forego. Hence, the labour supply decision is different for different individuals and opportunity cost of work (or leisure) is a subjective and personal value. The supply of labour for one worker is shown in Figure 2.12.

> A **reservation wage** indicates the lowest wage a worker will accept to take a job.

No labour is supplied if wages are below £4 per hour, the reservation wage, as the worker does not consider it worthwhile to work for less than this wage. If the wage rate rises to £16, the worker is willing to work 55 hours (income = £880). At any

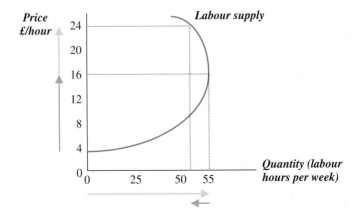

FIGURE 2.12 INDIVIDUAL LABOUR SUPPLY CURVE: BACKWARD BENDING

higher wage than £16, the worker prefers to cut back on hours worked and labour supply declines to 50 hours if the wage rises to £24 (income = £1200).

Moving from the individual to industry labour supply, we can think of labour supply as consisting of a mix of different skills. High skills command higher wages, *ceteris paribus*. So too do more 'dangerous' jobs, and some unpleasant jobs also attract a premium wage unrelated to skill levels but as recompense for the perceived unpleasantness. The supply curve for an occupation is likely to display a positive slope implying that to increase the quantity of labour supplied to one occupation the wage rate must rise.

2.9.3 EQUILIBRIUM IN THE LABOUR MARKET

By considering labour demand and supply together, as shown in Figure 2.13, we can see how equilibrium wages and hours worked are determined. The demand and supply curves shown are those for the European Steering Lock industry, for manufacturing workers. The equilibrium wage in the industry is £10 per hour in equilibrium, and 10 000 workers are employed in the industry. Safelock is one average firm in this industry, and it pays the equilibrium wage rate.

As long as there are no changes in the factors determining either demand or supply, the equilibrium situation will prevail. Since information on the output of workers, the revenue they generate for the firm and the costs of employing them enter into the labour demand decision, a change in any one of these factors will impact on the demand curve. Going back to Tables 2.4 and 2.5, for instance any

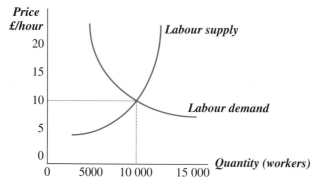

FIGURE 2.13   EQUILIBRIUM IN THE LABOUR MARKET

factor that changes element in these tables will give rise to a new demand curve. Any factors that change supply (such as a change in the rate of income tax) would generate a new supply curve, with implications for equilibrium workers and wages. Government policies too might have an impact if, for example, a minimum wage was imposed. The effects of all such changes can be analysed using the demand and supply model outlined in this chapter.

2.10   SUMMARY

- The demand and supply model is the framework that allows us to examine how markets function. We can consider the most relevant features that need to be taken into account for any market we wish to consider.
- Both buyers and sellers benefit from exchange.
- The equilibrium situation in a market is an outcome that is the intention of no single buyer or seller. It is the result of all buyers' and sellers' decisions in that market, and includes all available information used when making those decisions.
- Prices act as a signal that create incentives for exchange and help to explain the behaviour of both buyers and sellers in markets.
- If a market is in disequilibrium, that information creates incentives for the behaviour of buyers and sellers to change and move the market towards equilibrium.
- Where governments are unhappy with the prices determined in markets, they may intervene to change the market-determined outcome.

- **One of the most interesting markets to analyse is that for labour because of the need to understand the underlying principles governing firms' decisions to hire or demand labour and people's decisions to supply labour. Once these principles are understood, however, equilibrium in the market is found just as in any other and it is possible to consider the effects of changes on demand, or supply on equilibrium.**

REVIEW PROBLEMS AND QUESTIONS

1. Explain how differences in (1) preferences and (2) opportunity costs of production can give rise to gains from exchange.

2. Using examples, illustrate that you understand the concepts of absolute and comparative advantage.

3. Arguments are sometimes put forward that countries should reduce their imports from other countries – reducing the amount of exchange that takes place. Does this argument make sense, given what you know about absolute and comparative advantage?

4. Use a diagram to explain what would happen to the quantity demanded of personal stereos if their price doubled, *ceteris paribus*. Add in supply curves to your diagram to indicate how the doubling of equilibrium price would be caused by a movement in supply. What possible effects on supply might be responsible for a doubling of the price?

5. Use a diagram to explain what would happen to demand for personal stereos if MP3s become a preferred substitute by a substantial portion of the population. Add in a supply curve for personal stereos and explain what happens to equilibrium price and quantity.

6. Explain how the principle of opportunity cost underlies the supply curve.

7. Use Table 2.4 to examine the equilibrium implications of a fall in workers' output on the demand for labour. Update the table if output per worker falls by 5 units for each worker. What are the implications for MPP_L, and MRP_L (if price is £30)? What are the effects on the demand for labour? Would you expect any changes in the supply of labour? Can you think of any factors that might cause the average worker's output to fall?

8. Read the following case study on the ELV initiative and answer the questions that follow.

The end of life vehicle case

Each year across the EU somewhere between 8 and 10 million cars are scrapped (out of a car 'population' of around 170 million). Before the 1990s the imperative to recycle had not been taken on board by car manufacturers and the issue was only beginning to be considered by consumers and governments. In May 2002, an EU directive came into force which means that from 2006 onwards end-of-life-vehicles (ELVs) will be categorized as hazardous waste requiring careful disposal. The directive will force the final owner of a vehicle to return their ELV to an authorized collection point to deregister the vehicle. Furthermore, the directive indicates that delivery of the vehicle to this point should not involve any cost for the vehicle owner. Essentially this means that car manufacturers must have networks in place to support the collection and treatment cost.

Treatment of vehicles that reach their end of life between 2006 and 2014 must ensure that 85% of materials (based on the weight) must be reused/recovered. From 2015, this percentage rises to 95%. Currently, about 75% of materials are recovered.

Support from car manufacturers for the directive has been generally positive except in relation to the decision to force them, from 2007, to bear recollection cost for all cars they produced (not just those produced from 2002).

a. What do you see as the potential implications of the ELV initiative for each of the following: car manufacturers, dismantlers and recyclers?
b. What arguments do you see for/against the initiative?
c. Can you think of any obstacles to reaching high recycling targets?
d. Do you expect any effects on either demand or supply of cars by the imposition of this law?
e. Look up the websites of car companies or car associations (such as the ACEA) across Europe to consider their views on this directive and how they are currently dealing with meeting this directive.

FURTHER READING AND RESEARCH

- An interesting example of market analysis can be found in Lindsey, 2003. Using this and other publicly available information, such as
  - Coffee Research Institute: www.coffeeresearch.org
  - International Coffee Organization: www.ico.org/ed/edmark.htm
  you could apply the demand and supply framework to explain:
  a. what has been happening to equilibrium price in this market;

   b.   what has been happening to equilibrium quantity in this market;

   c.   why equilibrium has changed.

   You should be able to identify demand-related issues of relevance, supply-related issues of relevance and any other relevant issues to a, b and c.

- Writings by Friedrich August von Hayek (1899–1992) are insightful and thought provoking for market analysis. Hayek was awarded the Nobel Prize in Economic Sciences in 1974 (jointly with Gunnar Myrdal). See Hayek, 1948, 1984.

- For statistical and other information on labour markets in terms of the proportion of the employed population, unemployment rates, check out the World Bank's annual *World Development Report*, Eurostat's *Basic Statistics of the EU* and *Statistical Review* and various OECD labour and employment-related publications.

REFERENCES

Hayek, F. (1945) 'The use of knowledge in society', *American Economic Review*, **35**, 1–18.

Hayek, F. (1948) 'The meaning of competition', in *Individualism and Economic Order*. University of Chicago Press, Chicago, 92–106.

Hayek, F. (1984) 'Competition as a discovery procedure', in Nishiyama, C. and Leube, K. (eds) *The Essence of Hayek*. Hoover Institution Press, Stanford, 254–265.

Lindsey, B. (2003) *Grounds for Complaint? Understanding the 'Coffee Crisis'*, Trade Briefing Paper No. 16, CATO Institute, May.

Smith, A. (1970) *An Inquiry into the Nature and Causes of the Wealth of Nations*. Penguin, Harmondsworth [original publication 1776].

Stewart, A. (1997) *Intellectual Capital: The New Wealth of Organizations*. Currency.

CHAPTER 3

BEYOND DEMAND: CONSUMERS IN THE ECONOMIC SYSTEM

LEARNING OUTCOMES

By the end of this chapter you should be able to:

- ✪ Identify how demand is related to consumers' choices at a microeconomic level and to macroeconomic consumption behaviour.
- ✪ Highlight the importance of consumers' spending across international economies.
- ✪ Explain consumers' choices in terms of consumer satisfaction.
- ✪ Relate the law of demand to consumer satisfaction.
- ✪ Consider how price changes impact on consumer choices and demand.
- ✪ Illustrate how consumers' welfare can be estimated using the demand curve.
- ✪ Show how consumers' responsiveness to price changes can be measured and explain why it is useful for economic decision-making.
- ✪ Analyse how consumers choose between different varieties of similar products.
- ✪ Describe macroeconomic consumption behaviour using the consumption function.
- ✪ Discuss how governments try to influence consumers at macro- and micro-economic levels.

3.1 INTRODUCTION

Understanding the 'demand side' of the economy is important in appreciating how an economy works and this chapter delves into an important component of demand – the consumer. Much of the economic system is organized to meet the demands of consumers. Consumers' demands and moreover their willingness to pay for products and services provide incentives for entrepreneurs that attempt to meet their requirements and produce what consumers wish to buy. Purchases of 'consumption' goods represent a substantial component of economic activity, as shown in section 3.2. The choices that consumers make are based on their expected benefit or utility, which is discussed in section 3.3.

As rational people, consumers take all available information into account in making their consumption decisions. As explained in section 3.4, information about prices is relevant to consumers' decisions and, taken with consumers' subjective views of their expected utility, serves to help us understand why consumers make the choices they do. Using demand analysis it is possible to examine the benefit or utility that consumers earn when they consume and this is shown in section 3.5. How consumers' decisions about what to buy are affected when prices change is examined, again using demand analysis, in section 3.6. Many consumer decisions are between different brands of quite similar products and section 3.7 focuses on how such choices are made. The focus of the chapter moves to macroeconomics when the behaviour of all consumers together is considered in section 3.7 through analysis of the consumption function. This allows for consideration of how consumption spending relates to a country's national income. The final section in this chapter considers some examples of how and why governments try to affect consumption decisions.

3.2 DEMAND AND THE IMPORTANCE OF CONSUMERS

Governments buy goods and services both for current (everyday) use and to make capital expenditures that are expected to meet more long-term requirements (e.g. road building or providing funds for future pensions). Firms also make purchases for current and longer-term purposes. But consumers buy the vast majority of goods and services produced.

The value of all economic activity is the sum of the output or income of that economy over a specific period of time – this is discussed in more detail in Chapter 5. For now, note that national output or national income is conventionally denoted as Y.

National output or income, denoted Y, is calculated as the *value* of

- all the goods bought for consumption purposes; C **plus**
- all the investment expenditures by firms; I **plus**
- all government expenditures; G **plus**
- the net value of all goods traded by the economy, exports minus imports: $X - M$.

Economic Activity $(Y) = C + I + G + (X - M)$

When classifying the purchases and expenditure that occur in an economy (as C, I or G, X or M), economists classify them according to their *purpose* or *function*. A pair of shoes bought by a consumer for the purpose of wearing them would be part of consumption expenditure (C). The same pair of shoes in the manufacturer's factory before being distributed for sale is a component of investment – *inventory investment* (I). If the pair of shoes were bought by the government for a member of the army the expenditure would be part of G – government expenditure. Shoes produced abroad and imported appear under imports while if the shoes are produced for an external market they appear as exports. To ensure that output is not counted twice, imported shoes would not also be included in consumption or government expenditure.

Each component of economic activity can be studied separately and in this chapter we deal with consumption, the most substantial component. Table 3.1 shows the percentage share of consumption expenditures out of the value of total economic activity for a number of economies.

Table 3.1 illustrates the sizeable share of consumption in economic activity for those countries considered. Almost 70% of the income in the USA was spent on consumption goods and the value of US consumption is estimated at 20% of world output. It is important for economists to understand what impacts on this component of economic activity.

TABLE 3.1 CONSUMPTION SHARE (%) OF ECONOMIC ACTIVITY, 2000

	USA	UK	France	Ireland	Germany	Japan
Consumption Share	68	75	66	60	69	62

Source: Excerpted from the Penn World Table 6.1 (Heston *et al.*, 2002).

3.2.1 CONSUMPTION GOODS

Consumers derive benefit, satisfaction or utility from the goods they consume. Consumption goods are made up of three broad categories of goods that consumers demand – durable and non-durable goods, and services.

If consumer confidence is low or declining, it indicates that consumers consider economic activity to be slowing down or that the economy is in a *recession* so they prefer to put off durable purchases because they expect the economy to improve in the future. An economy is in recession if economic activity declines for a substantial period. Recessions are characterized by periods when consumers buy fewer goods and services than previously and when many people who are willing and able to work lose their jobs as demand for their output declines. A recession that lasts for a long period is called a depression – as in the Great Depression that followed the Wall Street Crash of 1929.

THE GREAT DEPRESSION

Economically speaking, the roaring twenties were a good time in the USA for business growth, jobs, share prices and profits. Stock market speculation, riotous spending and real estate booms sent prices skyrocketing. On 24 October 1929, many shareholders began to lose confidence and, believing that the prices of the shares they owned could not rise forever, decided to sell.

Within the first few hours of the stock market opening that day, prices fell so much that all the gains that had been made in the previous year were wiped out. Public confidence was shattered because the stock market had been viewed as a chief indicator of the state of the American economy.

The cause of the crash has been much debated. Some blame an interest rate increase a couple of months before, others the fact that naïve investors had bought stock with credit which was too freely available, believing that stock prices only moved in an upward direction. Some observers believed that stock market prices in the first six months of 1929 were overpriced, but not all agreed. The most likely scenario is that a combination of factors united together to bring about such dramatic outcomes.

Clearly, no one knew what the outcome of the crash would be. Given the economic uncertainty, many firms cut back their plans to purchase producer durables, until a clearer picture emerged. But this caused a further decrease in the demand for producer durables, and led to a fall in production. As production fell, firms needed fewer workers. Unemployed consumers and those who feared they might soon be out of work cut back on their consumer durable purchases. Therefore, firms producing consumer durables faced falling demand as well.

The vicious circle continued as America sank steadily into the worst depression in its history. Millions of people lost every cent they owned. Half of all US banks failed, factories shut down, shops closed and almost every business seemed paralysed. By the end of 1930 more than 6 million Americans were out of work; by 1931 that had doubled to 12 million. Between 1929 and 1939 real output fell by 30% and living standards in 1939 were lower than in 1929. Over 5000 banks failed and over 32 000 businesses went bankrupt. The slide into the Depression, with increasing unemployment, falling production, and falling prices, continued until the effort for World War Two started.

The USA was far from the only country affected by the Depression. Unemployment rates of over 30% in Germany into the 1930s provided an environment for the policies of the National Socialist German Workers Party, and the career of its leader Adolf Hitler, to flourish with the devastating consequences that ensued internationally.

Non-durable goods include food, clothes, petrol, drugs, and top-up cards for mobile phones and these are usually consumed in less than one year. Services include things like telephone calls, health services (a visit to the doctor, or an operation), or a trip to the cinema.

> **Services** are non-material or intangible items of consumption that are consumed as they are created.

In proportionate terms, consumption spending in developed economies is made up of mostly services (60% plus of total consumption spending), with non-durable goods of approximately 30% and the remainder made up by durable goods. Services are the least volatile component of consumption tending not to vary too much over time, with non-durables next and durable goods the most volatile of the three.

3.3 CONSUMER SATISFACTION – UTILITY

Using the concept of utility, it is possible to consider consumer behaviour and how it underlies demand. Utility increases with the consumption of goods up to a point. For example, the utility or satisfaction from consuming a fifth chocolate bar in a day will surely not be as great as that derived from the first, and this is

TABLE 3.2   TOTAL AND MARGINAL UTILITY: CONSUMING CHOCOLATE BARS

Number of bars (Q)	Total utility (TU)	Marginal utility ($\Delta TU/\Delta Q$)
0	0	–
1	33	33
2	53	20
3	65	12
4	71	6
5	71	0
6	65	−5

the same for the majority of goods. Table 3.2 shows the total utility and marginal utility from consuming chocolate bars for one consumer who was asked to try to quantify and rank the satisfaction they derive from consuming chocolate bars over one day.

Total utility (TU) is the total benefit perceived by the consumer from consumption of a good/service.
Marginal utility is the change in total utility for each additional good/service consumed. It is estimated as $\Delta TU/\Delta Q$.

Considering the total utility column in Table 3.2, we see that the satisfaction derived from consuming four bars is 71 and has risen with each bar consumed. Above four bars, the consumer's utility rises no more and with six bars, total utility actually declines because the consumer has chocolate overload!

Looking at the marginal utility column in Table 3.2, we consider the additional benefit derived from each extra bar consumed. This shows a decline from 33 units of satisfaction from the first bar, to 20 units from the second and so on. By the time the consumer consumes the fifth bar, they derive no additional satisfaction as their appetite for chocolate has been adequately satisfied.

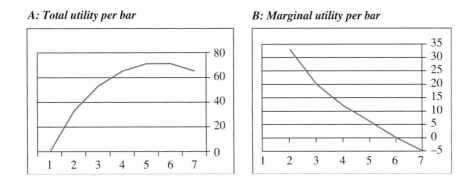

FIGURE 3.1 TOTAL AND MARGINAL UTILITY: CHOCOLATE

Consuming a sixth bar makes little sense because it leads to a decline in overall satisfaction, reflected in negative marginal utility. This information is also presented in Figure 3.1, with total utility in panel *A* and marginal utility in panel *B*.

When using the concept of utility, economists analyse consumption *as if* people can rank and quantify their preferences and can establish how much satisfaction they acquire from consuming different quantities of goods or services. In practice if you were asked to explain your satisfaction from consuming various quantities of chocolate, you might find it difficult and even more so if a number of different goods and cross-rankings were involved.

Economists do not assume that people engage in this process every time they consume something. However, economists do consider that *rational* people reveal their preferences by what they purchase and that they know what they like, what provides them with consumer satisfaction and that the utility generated from total and marginal consumption follow the *general* patterns as shown above; initially increasing and eventually falling total utility and declining marginal utility.

3.3.1   THE ASSUMPTION OF RATIONALITY IN ECONOMICS

When economists use the term 'rational' in relation to consumers, the implications are that consumers are capable of estimating the satisfaction they derive from consuming goods or services, they can rank their preferences (e.g. if they prefer chocolate to cheese and cheese to sausages, they prefer chocolate to sausages) and that they act generally to maximize their own utility. Rationality assumes that consumers use all available information in making their decisions. It must be acknowledged that consumers do not have full information at all times to support their decisions, hence they are bounded by their knowledge and the available information, or, people possess, as Herbert Simon put it, *bounded rationality*. This means that people do not always make the choices that would objectively maximize their utility – if they had more complete information their choice might be different. It is relevant in complex decisions where receiving, storing, retrieving, transmitting (i.e. processing) relevant information can be complicated and time-consuming. In many economic models people are assumed to display approximately rational behaviour.

If a choice arose between consuming a chocolate bar or a packet of crisps, the rational consumer would compare the utility they would derive from each product and make their preferred and subjective choice. They would also take an additional piece of information into account in this decision – the prices of the goods. Why? Because consumption preferences are limited by individuals' income and they rationally make decisions about what to buy with this in mind, taking prices into consideration.

3.4 MARGINAL UTILITY, PRICES AND THE LAW OF DEMAND

Consider a person trying to decide how to spend money she has received and who knows her top preferences are either nights out (including taxi fare, entrance to a night club and food/drinks) which cost on average £50 or call credit for her mobile phone, at the same price. Analysis of marginal utility for both goods is provided in Table 3.3.

Her prime choice is a night out because the extra utility generated from one night out is greater than the extra utility generated by £50 call credit. After spending one night out, the next best choice for consumption would be a second night out because 19 units of utility is greater than 16 units generated from the first unit of call credit consumed. The next preferred option is call credit and so on. If she has received £200, it is possible to list what her preferred purchases will be because she will be rational and consume the goods that provide her with the greatest utility.

The preferences can be estimated simply as the marginal utility per pound generated by the goods. The marginal utility per pound for both goods is shown in Table 3.4 with the ranked preferences for consumption shown in parentheses.

With £200 to spend, the top four choices are a night out, followed by a second night out, followed by £50 call credit, followed by a third night out. With more money to spend, the remaining choices would come into play. After making six

TABLE 3.3 MARGINAL UTILITY: CALL CREDIT AND NIGHTS OUT

Quantity	Marginal utility call credit (£50)	Marginal utility nights out (£50)
1	16	21
2	14	19
3	12	15
4	10	13
5	9	12
6	7	11

TABLE 3.4 MARGINAL UTILITY AND PRICE RATIOS

Quantity	MU call credit	MU/P (P = £50)	MU nights out	MU/P (P = £50)
1	16	0.32 (3)	21	0.42 (1)
2	14	0.28 (5)	19	0.38 (2)
3	12	0.24 (7)	15	0.30 (4)
4	10	0.20 (10)	13	0.26 (6)
5	9	0.18 (11)	12	0.24 (7)
6	7	0.14 (12)	11	0.22 (9)

choices, the consumer is indifferent between either a night out or call credit because they yield the same marginal utility/price ratio.

Such analysis indicates what the individual's demand for nights out and call credit are, given prices, income and preferences. All consumers' demand decisions summed together give rise to the demand curve. From the information here, when the price of call credit or a night out is £50, and this individual has £200 to spend, one unit of call credit and three nights out are demanded.

Since demand decisions result from the marginal utility/price ratio, demand decisions would be different if prices changed. Consider what happens if the cost of a night out increased to £60. This changes the ranking of preferences since the marginal utility per pound changes, as shown in Table 3.5. The result is that with £200 to spend, two nights out and two units of call credit would be demanded. Consumers change their mind about what to consume in response to the changes in the marginal utility/price ratio. In other words the quantity demanded changes in response to price changes.

Although the price of call credit is unchanged in Table 3.5, the *relative price* of call credit decreased as the price of a night out increased and so the quantity demanded of call credit increased. It is in terms of relative prices that economists conduct their analysis. Another way of stating the same idea in terms of the concepts already introduced is to say that following the price rise, the *opportunity cost* of a night out has increased. More call credit must to be foregone to release the money for a night out. When prices change the consumer rearranges their consumption choices, always preferring goods with the highest possible ratio of marginal utility to price.

We can go further than this to say that the rational consumer will make their consumption choices so that the marginal utility/price is equal for all goods consumed. This is logical since consumers would always prefer to allocate their money to goods that yield the highest marginal utility per pound but each time they consume one more of any good, the marginal utility from that good declines while the marginal utility of another good which they buy one unit less of increases. In equilibrium, consumers make their consumption choices so that they end up

TABLE 3.5   MARGINAL UTILITY AND PRICE RATIOS – NEW PRICES

Q	MU call credit	MU/P (P = £50)	MU nights out	MU/P (P = £60)
1	16	0.32 (2)	21	0.35 (1)
2	14	0.28 (4)	19	0.32 (2)
3	12	0.24 (6)	15	0.25 (5)
4	10	0.20 (8)	13	0.22 (7)
5	9	0.18 (10)	12	0.20 (8)
6	7	0.14 (12)	11	0.18 (10)

consuming quantities of goods where the last pound spent on each good yields the same marginal utility per pound as the last pound spent on every other good. If this were not the case total utility could be further maximized of consuming less of one good and more of another.

3.4.1 THE LAW OF DEMAND – INCOME AND SUBSTITUTION EFFECTS

The foregoing analysis can be further examined making reference to Income and Substitution effects, as mentioned in Chapter 2. The income limits facing consumers can be presented using a graphical tool called the budget constraint, which shows the different combinations of goods that can be purchased with a set income, given prevailing prices.

A consumer's preferences can be illustrated using another graphical tool, the indifference curve, which illustrates various consumption combinations of two goods, which generate the *same utility* for a consumer. These tools are presented in Figure 3.2 using the information from Tables 3.3 and 3.4. Since the consumer has an income of £200 and the prices of credit or a night out are £50, the maximum amount of either good that could be purchased is 4 units, reflected in the budget line/constraint.

The indifference curve has a curved shape because of the diminishing marginal utility from consuming additional units of each good. The more of one good being consumed, say nights out, the lower the marginal utility from additional consumption of that good. If a consumer consumes many nights out, they would be willing to forego a night out for some call credit, and when little call credit is

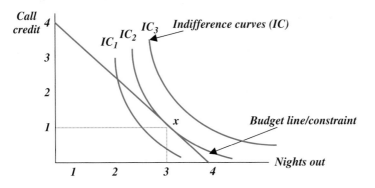

FIGURE 3.2 BUDGET LINE AND INDIFFERENCE CURVE ANALYSIS

consumed, its marginal utility is high. This is why different combinations of credit and nights out on the indifference curve give rise to the same level of utility.

At different points on the indifference curve, the consumer is willing to trade different amounts of call credit for nights out reflecting the **marginal rate of substitution** of the goods. This is also reflected in the slope of the indifference curve at any point.

Consumers have a set or map of indifference curves, each with the same shape, that reflect their preferences. Each indifference curve refers to one specific level of utility. On indifference curve IC_3, the consumer has a higher utility level than on IC_2 or IC_1. Rational consumers attempt to maximize their utility which is equivalent to a desire to consume on the highest possible indifference curve. The actual consumption decision results from preferences indicated by the set of indifference curves and limited income represented by the budget line.

In line with our earlier observation, the consumer in Figure 3.2 chooses to consume 3 nights out and 1 unit of call credit with income of £200, prices of £50 for both goods and given their preferences. Consumption is at point x on IC_2.

The indifference curves drawn for this consumer lie closer to the nights out axis than the call credit axis, which indicates this consumer's tastes. Another consumer may prefer fewer nights out relative to call credit (if they are new to an area, have not yet made too many friends and prefer to chat to friends back home).

The consumer's demand decision changes with a price change. If the price of a night out rises to £60, then the maximum number that could be purchased with £200 is 3.3 (£200/60 = 3.33). The budget line changes as shown in Figure 3.3 and consumption moves from x to y. The steeper slope of the line indicates that following the price rise, more call credit must be sacrificed, in opportunity cost terms, to afford one night out. The consumer's decision to change their quantity demanded of both goods can be broken down into a substitution effect and an income effect.

A price change induces consumers to change their demand decisions. The **substitution effect** indicates the adjustment in quantity demanded by a consumer due to the change in relative prices alone.

The **income effect** reflects the adjustment in quantity demanded due to the change in real income alone.

The substitution effect can be examined by considering the price effect alone on the consumer's choice. To see this we draw a line with the same slope as the new

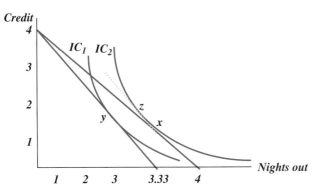

FIGURE 3.3 CONSUMPTION WITH NEW BUDGET LINE

budget line and examine where it intersects the original indifference curve IC_2. In Figure 3.3, this occurs at point z.

The substitution effect is measured from x to z. The change in relative prices alone leads to a reduction in quantity demanded of nights out but an increase in the quantity demanded of call credit. The rational consumer substitutes away from the relatively more expensive good towards the relatively cheaper good.

The income effect involves examining the effect on quantity demanded of the reduction in real income caused by the price rise in one good holding relative prices constant. It is shown by the comparison of point z with point y where the same relative prices are used, reflected in the same slope of the two lines. Less of both goods are consumed at point y on IC_1 compared to point z on IC_2. The increased price reduces the consumer's purchasing power and is reflected in reduced demand for all goods, not simply for the good which has become more expensive. This is the pure income effect of the price rise for one good, a normal good.

> **Normal good**: one for which demand falls if real income falls or for which demand rises if income rises.
> **Inferior good**: one for which demand rises if real income falls or for which demand falls if real income rises.

Inferior goods are bought when consumers do not have the required purchasing power to buy other preferred goods. Examples would be many of the goods bought by low-income households – cheaper cuts of meat, non-brand items, etc. The pure income effect of a price fall leads to increased purchasing power and an increase in demand for all normal goods, which are most goods.

CONSUMER PREFERENCES

Where do our preferences come from? Parents, school, friends, experience, advertising? Interesting new research has revealed that neuromarketing – brain scanning via electroencephalogram mapping and functional magnetic-resonance imaging – can be used to analyse consumers' purchasing decisions and reveal how preferences feed into purchasing decisions.

Neuromarketing is particularly useful for explaining the value of branding. Blind taste tests repeatedly put Pepsi ahead of Coke, which shows up in brain scans that identify greater response of 'reward centres' in the brain to Pepsi. Yet Pepsi is not the brand leader. In non-blind taste tests, where subjects were told which cola they were tasting, Coke won out.

Such consumer behaviour was explained in terms of the strength of its brand in the minds of the subjects, which was evident in activity in another area of the brain associated with thinking and judging.

If such thinking and judging activity can be stimulated and influenced by advertising, for example, companies will be able to shape our preferences more clearly! Such research is in its infancy but holds interest for anyone interested in processes that create and change our preferences.

Before we get too carried away with such tests, it has also been pointed out that there is a clear difference between a taste test using a small quantity of product and consuming a larger quantity. Specifically in the cola example, the immediate sugar 'reward' from drinking Pepsi is apparently much higher and is preferred in taste tests for this reason. Drinking more than a taste changes the consumer's perception and the product is found 'too sweet' by a majority of the population – no neuromarketing explanation required.

3.5 DEMAND, CONSUMERS AND CONSUMER SURPLUS

Since consumer satisfaction is examined by means of utility, it should be possible to consider the satisfaction of more than one person in isolation. A problem arises though because utility is subjective and while it is possible to consider one person's preferences, by asking them to rank them and try to quantify the satisfaction derived from consumption, it is impossible to sum up the satisfaction of more

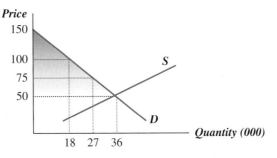

FIGURE 3.4 DEMAND FOR CALL CREDIT AND CONSUMER SURPLUS

than one consumer or try to rank their different preferences. Economists try to get around this problem by means of moving analysis from utility to demand, in the knowledge that the sum of individuals' consumption choices (based on their marginal utilities) are revealed in the demand for any good. (Economists also use community indifference curves as approximations for the preferences that may be gauged for a group of individuals, despite the difficulties involved.)

Consider the demand for call credit shown in Figure 3.4, with supply included also. Given demand and supply as shown, the equilibrium in the call credit market is for 36 000 units at £50 per unit (the single consumer considered in earlier analysis is just one buyer in the market). The demand at this price is the result of the decisions of many different individuals based on their derived utility from consuming call credit, and their marginal utility/price ratios.

The overall satisfaction generated by the equilibrium consumption can be estimated using the concept of consumer surplus.

> **Consumer surplus** – the benefit to consumers due to the difference between what consumers actually pay to consume a good and what they would have been willing to pay.

In Figure 3.4, although the equilibrium price is £50, many people are willing to pay a higher price. At a price of £75, 27 000 units are demanded while at a price of £100, 18 000 units are in demand. In fact the area under the demand function and above the price provides an estimate of the value of satisfaction generated from consumption of this product (shown as the shaded triangle). The area of this triangle is computed as £1.8 million (the area of a triangle is half the base × perpendicular height which here is $18\,000 \times 100 = 1\,800\,000$). This indicates the estimated value of the satisfaction generated from the consumption of equilibrium call credit.

3.5.1   CONSUMER SURPLUS AND CONSUMER WELFARE

Welfare economics focuses on assessing the effects of economic policies on both consumers and producers. Such assessments depend to a large extent on the values (or normative judgements) of the assessors because issues of fairness come into play. Issues considered include the conditions under which an economy is most efficient and how goods and income are distributed within economies, and how different economic policies impact on stakeholders. The effect of an economic policy on consumers can be investigated by looking at changes to consumer surplus.

For example, if a government ensures that there is additional competition in the taxi market (by allowing extra taxis to be registered), this could lead to an increased supply of taxis. This is shown in Figure 3.5 as the increase in supply in panel B compared to panel A.

The result of expanded supply (from *S1* to *S2*) with the same demand, is a lower price for taxi fares with a greater quantity supplied: compare *P** to *P*** and *Q** to *Q***. The welfare effects can be considered by examining consumer surplus (CS) in both cases, which is the area above the price and below the demand curve. At lower taxi fares, in panel B, consumers' welfare is improved since some consumers unwilling to pay higher taxi fares become willing to demand taxis and those who were willing to pay higher prices still benefit given the gap between the price paid and willingness to pay. Consumer welfare can be said to have increased since a comparison shows that *CS1* in panel A is smaller than *CS2* in panel B.

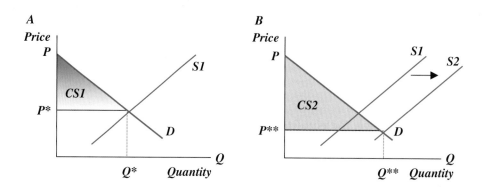

FIGURE 3.5   CONSUMER WELFARE AND THE TAXI MARKET

3.6 CONSUMERS' RESPONSE TO PRICE CHANGES

The quantity of goods demanded changes in response to price changes, resulting from new marginal utility/price ratios. If the price of all goods fell by 10% consumers would demand more of most if not all goods, but the rise in demand in response to the price fall would not be the same across all goods. This is because consumers are more or less price-sensitive for some goods relative to others. No matter what price cow's tongue is I will never choose to increase my demand for it from zero! While individual preferences play a key role in demand decisions and in reactions to price changes we know they are not the only explanatory factor for consumers' responses to price changes.

A 10% fall in the price of standard pens will not substantially change the quantity demanded for most people since pens are inexpensive and only a small portion of consumers' income is spent on them. In the case of goods that are not bought very often, and for which the income share is very small, demand is usually not very price-sensitive. This information is useful in drawing a demand curve because it helps us to decide whether the demand curve is relatively steep or flat. For pens the demand curve will be relatively steep indicating that a change in price has little impact on quantity demanded (see panel A in Figure 3.6).

Demand for theatre tickets is somewhat more responsive to changes in price as they can be relatively expensive and are quite a discretionary purchase. Hence, the demand curve is relatively flat such as in panel B in Figure 3.6.

The extent to which substitutes are available for a good also impacts on its price-sensitivity. If the price of one brand of pen were to fall by 10%, rational consumers

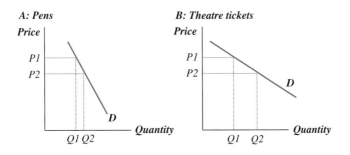

FIGURE 3.6 PRICE SENSITIVITY AND DEMAND

would substitute away from more expensive pens to the cheaper available brand. For a specific brand, price sensitivity is higher than for a broad category of goods.

In general it is also the case that the higher consumers' income, the less price-sensitive they are because there are fewer limitations on what can be purchased than for people on lower incomes. This means that the demand curves of higher-income households would be steeper than for lower-income households and their quantities demanded would change relatively little in response to price changes.

The issue of time is also relevant for analysis of price sensitivity since consumers can adjust their purchasing behaviour more easily over longer periods. If one supermarket chain cuts its prices overnight, many people will continue to shop at their usual shops until they become aware of the price cuts elsewhere and until they are willing and able to change their shopping patterns to take advantage of the cheaper prices (clearly convenience, location and other factors matter for the consumer). This may take time but over longer time periods economists expect consumers to be more price-sensitive than over shorter time periods.

FACTORS EXPLAINING SENSITIVITY OF QUANTITY DEMANDED TO PRICE CHANGE

Ceteris paribus, sensitivity of quantity demanded to price change is *low*

- for inexpensive goods;
- for goods with a low income share (e.g. clothes pegs);
- for goods in general rather than a specific good, e.g. all pens vs. Papermate pens;
- for consumers on high incomes;
- over short relative to longer periods.

3.6.1 PRICE ELASTICITY OF DEMAND

In the taxi example, when supply expanded the result in equilibrium was a lower price. As predicted by the law of demand, at a lower equilibrium price consumers demanded more taxis. The reaction of quantity demanded can be quantified if information is available on the quantities demanded over a range of prices.

The responsiveness of quantity demanded to a change in price is called the **price elasticity of demand (PED)**.

$$PED = \%\Delta Qd / \%\Delta P$$

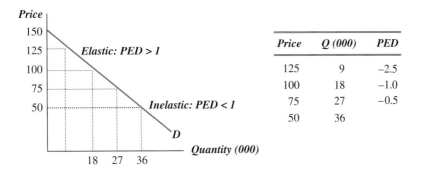

Price	Q (000)	PED
125	9	–2.5
100	18	–1.0
75	27	–0.5
50	36	

FIGURE 3.7 ELASTICITY AND THE DEMAND FOR CALL CREDIT

If the quantity of taxi rides rose by 10% following a price fall of 5%, price elasticity of demand is −2 (%ΔQd is 10 and %ΔP is −5 so PED is −2). Demand elasticities are always negative numbers but many economists report demand elasticities without the negative sign, assuming that other economists correctly interpret the number.

As the following example shows, information on elasticity is of particular interest to firms in terms of the effects of price changes on their revenues. Returning to the call credit example, price elasticity can be computed, based on the formula above and the information in Figure 3.7.

- Price rise from £50 to £75: PED = 25%/50% = **−0.50**
  decline in quantity from 36 to 27 is 9, expressed as a percentage of 36 = 25%
  price rise of £25, expressed as a percentage of £50 = 50%.
- Price rise from £75 to £100: PED = 33%/33% = **−1.00**
  decline in quantity from 27 to 18 is 9, expressed as a percentage of 27 = 33%
  price rise of £25, expressed as a percentage of £75 = 33%. Here, the percentage changes in price and quantity exactly cancel each other out. This is called **unit elasticity**.
- Price rises from £100 to £125: PED = 50%/20% = **−2.50**
  the decline in quantity from 18 to 9 is 9, expressed as a percentage of 18 = 50%
  price rise of £25, expressed as a percentage of £125 = 20%.

PED differs at different points on the demand curve.

In absolute terms (ignoring the minus sign) **PED** is greater than one when the percentage change in quantity demanded is greater than the percentage change in price. This is **elastic PED.**

PED is less than one when the percentage change in quantity demanded is less than the percentage change in price. This is **inelastic PED**.

An alternative estimation method may be used. Instead of computing elasticity relative to one point on the demand function, it can be estimated as an average over a section of the demand function:

Arc price elasticity of demand:

$$\frac{\Delta Qd}{\Delta P} \times \frac{1/2[P1 + P2]}{1/2[Qd1 + Qd2]}$$

Arc price elasticity differs to the earlier method by estimating average price and average quantity demanded. It is most appropriately used for large price changes.

Re-calculating elasticities from the data above according the arc elasticity method reveals:

- Price rise from £50 to £75: Arc PED $= -\dfrac{9}{25} \times \dfrac{1/2[50 + 75]}{1/2[36 + 27]} = \mathbf{-0.72}$

- Price rise from £75 to £100; Arc PED $= -\dfrac{9}{25} \times \dfrac{1/2[75 + 100]}{1/2[27 + 18]} = \mathbf{-1.40}$

- Price rise from £100 to £120; Arc PED $= -\dfrac{9}{25} \times \dfrac{1/2[100 + 125]}{1/2[18 + 9]} = \mathbf{-3.00}$

Price elasticity of demand and total revenue

If a firm wishes to change the price of a good, it can estimate the impact on the quantity demanded of its product by using PED. Staying with Figure 3.7, if the firm is considering an increase in price it can consider the impact on its revenues. From consumers' perspectives firm revenue is the same as consumers' expenditure.

A firm's **total revenue** is price times the quantity of goods sold: *TR = P × Q*

Example: following Figure 3.7

$P = £0$	$Q = 0$	$TR = £0$		
$P = £50$	$Q = 36\,000$	$TR = £1\,800\,000$	**Price ↑ 0–50**	**TR ↑**
$P = £75$	$Q = 27\,000$	$TR = £2\,025\,000$	**Price ↑ 50–75**	**TR ↑**
$P = £100$	$Q = 18\,000$	$TR = £1\,800\,000$	**Price ↑ 75–100**	**TR ↓**
$P = £125$	$Q = 9\,000$	$TR = £1\,125\,000$	**Price ↑ 100–125**	**TR ↓**

Conclusion: increasing price can lead to rises in *TR* **OR** to falls in *TR*.

The relationship between quantity demanded, price, elasticity and total revenue is also evident from Figure 3.8. In the elastic part of the demand curve, where quantity demanded is very responsive to changes in price, a fall in price leads to an increase in total revenue.

In the **elastic** portion of the demand curve, **TR changes in the opposite direction to a price change**: in the case of a price increase *TR* falls and in the case of a price fall *TR* rises.

In the **inelastic** portion of the demand curve, **TR changes in the same direction as a price change** implying that if price increases *TR* rises also.

Changes in the price of a good *almost* always result in changes in total revenue. The exception is at the point on the demand curve where PED $= -1$ at point c in panel

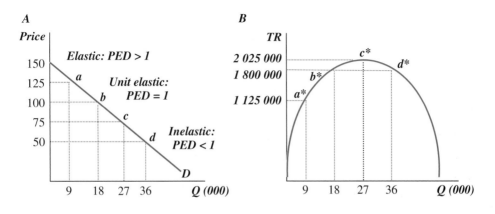

FIGURE 3.8 DEMAND, ELASTICITY AND TOTAL REVENUE

A when the PED is neither elastic nor inelastic but unit elastic. We saw earlier that unit elasticity arises when the percentage change in quantity demanded is the exact same as the percentage change in price so that there is no change in total revenue.

Price elasticity of demand: some special cases

It is possible to envisage situations where irrespective of what price is charged for a product, the quantity demanded would remain constant. Some necessities would fall into such categories where irrespective of price consumers have to bear any price change. Demand functions for goods to which consumers are addicted might also display such characteristics. Such a demand function would be a vertical line, shown in Figure 3.9. Since quantity demanded does not react *at all* to any change in price, it is described as a demand function with perfectly inelastic demand. At a relatively high price of *P1* in panel A, the same quantity is demanded as at the lower price of *P2*. At the higher price, the firms' revenue and consumers expenditure is higher.

At the opposite end of the spectrum it is also possible that demand exists for a product at only one price, also shown in Figure 3.9. This is possible if we consider the output of a single firm with many competitors which can only charge the market price for their product, i.e. the price determined by *market* demand and supply (this case is considered in more detail later in Chapter 6). Quantity demanded reacts perfectly to any change in price by completely disappearing! The firm can sell as much as it wishes to produce at *P3* in Panel B of Figure 3.9. If the firm produces *Q2* it will earn higher revenues than if it chooses to produce *Q1*.

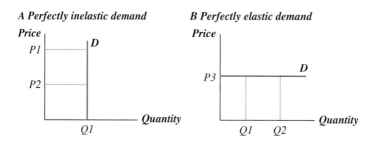

FIGURE 3.9   PRICE SENSITIVITY AND DEMAND

3.6.2   APPLICATIONS OF ELASTICITY ANALYSIS

If a firm seeks to increase its revenue and wishes to change the price it charges for a product, it needs to know to what extent quantity demanded is responsive to the price change. The above analysis shows that there would be little point in a firm raising its price with the intention of boosting its revenues if quantity demanded was in the elastic part of the demand curve. In terms of a firm's pricing strategy, therefore, it makes sense for the firm to have information on the price elasticity of demand for its product(s).

Information on elasticity is not just of interest to business but can be useful for policy-makers also.

> If a government is thinking about increasing taxes on cigarettes with the intention of reducing the quantity demanded, it needs to have an estimate of the PED for cigarettes.
>
> If the function of the tax is to reduce aggregate expenditure on cigarettes, a price increase (via the tax) would have to result in the price rising to the elastic portion of the demand curve. The result of the tax would be that the percentage increase in price would bring about a larger proportionally percentage fall in quantity demanded – consumers would buy fewer cigarettes, and the total revenue to cigarette firms would decline. Hence, the responsiveness of consumers to price provides useful information for decision-making.

3.6.3   OTHER ELASTICITY EXAMPLES

Income elasticity of demand

In general if a consumer's income increases, it is expected that their demand for goods and services would increase too, but not necessarily by the same proportion. The relationship between the quantity demanded of any goods and income is described by the income elasticity of demand.

> **Income elasticity of demand** measures the responsiveness of the quantity demanded of a good to changes in consumers' income (I).
> It is computed as $\%\Delta Qd / \%\Delta Y$

Goods are described as normal goods, if their income elasticities are greater than zero implying the quantity demanded changes in the same direction as a change in income. Most goods fall into this category – we buy more of them if our income rises. In the case of inferior goods their quantity demanded declines if income increases. Income elasticities for inferior goods are negative because a percentage increase (fall) in income leads to a decline (rise) in quantity demanded of the good.

Goods for which the percentage change in quantity demanded is greater than the percentage change in income are described as income elastic (with income elasticity greater than one). This would be the case if income rose by 15% and the quantity demanded of package holidays, for example, increased by 20%. Other goods are called price inelastic when a change in income results in a less than proportionate change in quantity demanded: an example would be a 3% increase in quantity demanded of electricity following a 15% increase in income. Income elastic goods are also known as luxury goods whereas income inelastic goods are necessities.

Cross-price elasticity

The relationship between the quantity demanded of one good and the price of another good is described by the Cross-price elasticity.

> **Cross-price elasticity** indicates the responsiveness of the quantity demanded of one good (good A) when the price of another good (good B) changes.
> It is computed as $\%\Delta Qd_A/\%\Delta P_B$

Cross-price elasticity is of interest for goods that display some economic relationship, such as complement or substitute goods.

If car insurance rises by 20%, this may have an impact on the quantity of new cars demanded, a complement good for car insurance, which might be expected to fall and so the cross-price elasticity would be negative. Since new cars are substantially more expensive than insurance, the effect on demand should not be close to 20% and so the cross-price elasticity would be less than one. Among young drivers and focusing on the first-time drivers' second-hand car market, the cross-price elasticity might be considerably higher, when annual insurance costs may even be greater than the price many pay for their first car.

If Indian and Chinese takeaway food are substitute products, it would be expected that if the price of Chinese takeaways rises, the demand for Indian food would rise as consumers substitute away from the more expensive to the cheaper good, presuming the consumer is indifferent between the goods. This means that the cross-price elasticity would be positive since the price change (rise or fall) in one good leads to a change in quantity demanded of the substitute good in the same direction (rise or fall) as the price change.

3.7 CONSUMER CHOICE AND PRODUCT ATTRIBUTES

Many purchasing decisions are made not between very different products such as call credit and nights out, but between different brands or types of similar products. Such decisions can be analysed using the attribute model of consumer demand. This model explains that consumer utility, and therefore demand, is the result of product characteristics, performance features or attributes, other than price. In selecting one brand of a good over another, consumers compare and subjectively rank their preferred attributes, which are those that generate highest utility for them.

> The features or attributes that explain consumers' decisions to buy one variety or brand instead of another are the basis for **product differentiation**.

3.7.1 THE ATTRIBUTE MODEL: BREAKFAST CEREALS

An individual considering buying one of the variety of competing cereals has decided on the two most important non-price attributes for their subjective purchasing decision as wholegrain cereal and low sugar content. Having evaluated four possible products, the product information is as shown in Table 3.6.

This information is also presented in Figure 3.10 where each of the four products is drawn as a line against the two attributes and where the slope of each product line reflects the computed ratio of the attributes. The difference in the slopes of the product lines reflects the different trade-offs of the two attributes in the

TABLE 3.6 PRICE AND ATTRIBUTE INFORMATION FOR BREAKFAST CEREALS

Brand	Price	Attribute rating (on scale of 1–10 where 1 is lowest) Wholegrain	Sugar content	Ratio of attributes
A	£2.35	9	4	2.25
B	£2.59	7	5	1.40
C	£2.85	5	7	0.71
D	£2.99	3	9	0.33

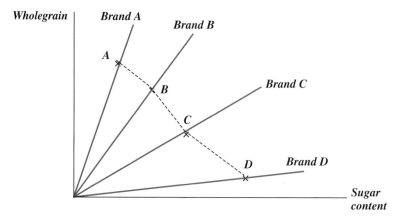

FIGURE 3.10 THE ATTRIBUTE MODEL

eyes of the consumer (similar to the concept of marginal rate of substitution discussed earlier).

Points *A, B, C* and *D* in Figure 3.10 indicate the cost of acquiring each product (which can alternatively be called an attribute combination) as measured from 0 and the distance reflects the budget the consumer wishes to allot to buying cereal and the price of each brand. We can simplify having to guess the budget the consumer wants to spend on cereals by assuming our consumer here has sufficient income to buy any of the four products but their purchasing decision is about buying one pack only (for their weekly shopping). This assumption corresponds more closely to how purchases actually occur – in terms of one cereal brand versus others. Hence, points *A, B, C* and *D* are each one unit out from 0. Points *A, B, C* and *D* represent the buyer's maximum satisfaction/utility frontier and, for example, reflect that at point *A* the attribute combination corresponding to one unit of Cereal *A* is 9 for wholegrain and 4 for sugar content.

In making the purchasing decision the consumer must evaluate their marginal rate of substitution between the attributes and these are shown by the addition of indifference curves as in Figure 3.11. The decision of which cereal to purchase is seen from selecting the brand that corresponds to the highest indifference curve, which is Brand *B* on *IC4*. The 'next best' option is Brand *C* on *IC3*, next Brand *A* on *IC2* and finally Brand *D* on *IC1*.

The attribute model can also be used to consider the effect of price changes as this will impact how far on each product line the consumer can purchase and hence a change in price of one brand changes the utility frontier and the highest indifference curve that could be reached. If the price of Brand *B* increases, for

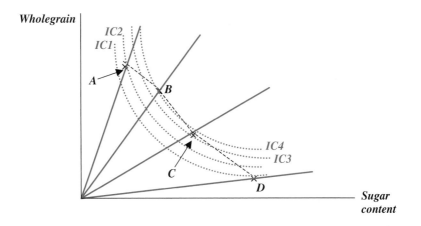

FIGURE 3.11 THE ATTRIBUTE MODEL WITH PREFERENCES

example, then with the same amount of money fewer attributes can be bought (or more must be paid for a given set of attributes). This would have the effect of moving the satisfaction frontier reflecting brand *B* from point *B* to a point on the same line but *closer to* 0. Following the price change, Brand *B* might no longer be the consumer's preferred choice.

3.8 AGGREGATE CONSUMER BEHAVIOUR

Moving from individual microeconomic consumer behaviour to macroeconomic behaviour we now turn our focus to the general trend that emerges from analysing macroeconomic consumption behaviour. The higher people's disposable income – gross income less direct taxes – the more they plan to spend on consumption goods. If Y denotes income and t denotes the income tax rate, then disposable income Yd can be defined as $Y - tY = Yd$. If Y is £30 000 and t is 25% then Yd is £30 000 less £7 500, which is £22 500. The relationship between planned consumption expenditure and disposable income for an economy is represented by the consumption function, as shown in Figure 3.12.

Total expenditure on consumption is made up of two components, autonomous consumption (a) and a fraction of disposable income (b), in other words:

$$C = a + bYd$$

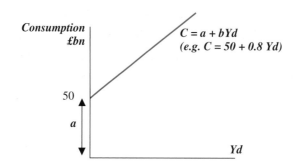

FIGURE 3.12   THE CONSUMPTION FUNCTION

From the consumption function in Figure 3.12, we see that even if disposable income is zero, some consumption still occurs. In the figure, this value of autonomous consumption is £50bn. This is the intercept value of the consumption function.

> Consumption expenditure that is independent of the level of income is called **autonomous consumption.** It occurs if people borrow to buy consumption goods or if they spend their savings (or borrow) when they have no income to pay for consumption goods.

People also spend some of their disposable income. This portion of income is represented by b in Figure 3.12 and is the slope of the consumption function. The value of b is different in different countries, and varies over time in countries also. It is a fraction lying between 0 and 1. This means that if disposable income increases by £1, for example, planned consumption expenditure will rise but by less than £1. Any disposable income not spent on consumption is saved. The term b in Figure 3.12 is known as the marginal propensity to consume – MPC.

> The **MPC** describes the relationship between a change in disposable income and the resulting change in aggregate consumption expenditure.

As with demand, the *ceteris paribus* assumption applies to the consumption function. Many factors help to explain the shape of a consumption function for a group of consumers. Changes in the factors lead to changes in the consumption function, in either the autonomous component or in the marginal propensity to consume or sometimes in both.

Disposable income is not the only factor that determines consumption behaviour. Other relevant factors include consumers' wealth, and their expectations about future prices and income levels. The higher their wealth, whether measured as savings, inherited wealth, property or shares, the higher people tend to consume out of their current disposable income. The rationale is that those with higher wealth have less need to save than other less wealthy consumers. Expectations of higher future prices would induce rational consumers to purchase sooner rather than later as would the expectation of a higher future level of income.

Income distribution across a population also affects consumption behaviour since poorer consumers tend to have a higher MPC and tend not to have the luxury of being able to save out of their low incomes. Tastes and preferences regarding borrowing and buying on credit also affect consumption and this is true both for individuals and groups or nationalities.

A consumption function shifts with changes in:

- *Wealth*: greater wealth → increased consumption (reflected in either higher autonomous consumption or a higher MPC).
- *Expectations of future prices and future income*: expectations of higher prices or higher income → increased current relative to future consumption (reflected in either higher autonomous consumption or a higher MPC). The specific effects depend on consumers' opinions as to how long higher prices will prevail and the expected increase and size of the increase in income.
- *Income distribution*: the higher the share of rich people in the population the lower the marginal propensity to consume as rich consumers have more discretion in how to spend income. A rise in the proportion of rich people in the population would reduce the MPC and may change autonomous consumption also.
- *Preferences regarding buying on credit*: an increase in preferences to borrow for consumption purposes increases the MPC and may increase autonomous consumption also.

If the MPC is 0.8 this means that 80p out of every additional £1 is spent on consumption goods. Furthermore, it implies that the marginal propensity to save is equal to 0.2 and that 20p will be saved out of each £1. A savings function can be drawn to correspond to the consumption function above as shown in Figure 3.13.

The savings function describes the relationship between income and the desired level of savings. If consumers in Figure 3.13 consume £50bn with an income of 0, they must be borrowing or dis-saving. This is why the savings function in Figure 3.13 begins at −£50bn on the savings axis. Since whatever income is not used for consumption is saved, the slope of the savings function is $(1 - b)$ which is 0.2 in this case.

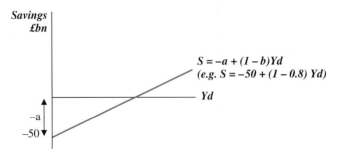

FIGURE 3.13 THE SAVINGS FUNCTION

The extent of borrowing or dis-saving in an economy is of interest since some economists have argued any growth in consumer credit can be beneficial or detrimental for an economy. The value of economic activity increases when consumers borrow whether it is to buy cars, pay for holidays or whatever the consumption goods purchased. However, if consumers take on too much debt relative to their income, it is argued that there may come a time when consumers can no longer spend on new goods and services and focus instead on paying off old debts. Potentially, that could slow down economic activity.

Consumers' demand for credit also has a direct bearing on interest rates. Interest rates are the price of money determined in money markets by demand for money and the supply of money (both of which are considered in more detail in Chapter 7). As in any market, if the demand (for borrowed money) exceeds the supply (provided by lenders), prices (interest rates) rise. If demand for credit falls and lenders are trying to fight for customers, they may offer lower interest rates to attract business.

The **paradox of thrift** is an example of the **fallacy of composition** which holds that although a certain action might make sense for an individual it does not follow that the same activity makes sense for an economy overall. Increased saving by an individual consumer provides the consumer with increased opportunities for consumption in the future. It does not follow that an economy benefits from increased savings. Why?

An unexpected increase in savings implies decreased consumption expenditure. Firms will sell less than they planned and require fewer employees to produce output. Unemployment may rise with the result of lower incomes being earned at the level of the economy overall. Falling income has a knock-on effect of reducing consumption expenditure. If such a scenario unfolds, the paradox of thrift is observed. Further implications may follow with firms reducing their planned investments in line with lower expectations of consumer expenditure so the process continues on and on until the cycle is ended by changes in behaviour once again.

3.9 GOVERNMENT POLICIES – CONSUMER FOCUS

Many government policies are microeconomic in focus and attempt to influence the demand for specific products – such as in the case of cigarettes. Annual government budgets often include increased taxes on alcohol and petrol as governments try to increase their tax revenues. Following the law of demand, with an increase in the price of a good, whether caused by an increase in taxes on the goods or any other factor, the expectation is that quantity demanded will fall. We saw earlier that the extent to which quantity demanded changes in response to a price change depends on the price elasticity of demand for the product, which is related to the initial price and quantity demanded of the good – it may be price elastic, unit elastic or inelastic.

Macroeconomic policies are also used to affect consumer spending at a broader level. Since consumption expenditure is such a substantial share of economic activity, governments sometimes try to focus policies on increasing consumer demand. This is particularly relevant before and during recessions when consumer demand slows down as people put off purchases that are not entirely necessary. During recessions consumer confidence is low and unemployment can be high as firms lay off workers when their output is not in demand.

One policy that governments use to affect macroeconomic consumption behaviour is through the tax system. During recessions governments often cut income taxes so that consumers have more disposable income that they can spend on consumer goods. This is one example of how government attempts to affect the consumption function. By cutting taxes, consumers have more disposable income, and hence their consumption expenditures would probably rise. Any change in the tax rate alters consumption behaviour via the consumption function, as explained in this worked example.

THE TAX RATE AND CONSUMPTION

Consider the following consumption function: $C = 50 + 0.8Yd$

If the net tax rate is 20%, this means disposable income is 80% of national income or

$$Yd = 1 - 0.2Y = 0.8Y$$

A change in the net tax rate to 30% would affect consumption behaviour by changing the amount of disposable income to

$$Yd = 1 - 0.3Y = 0.7Y$$

This indicates that *when the net tax rate changes consumption is affected.*
If the change in disposable income had no effect on autonomous consumption or the marginal propensity to consume then the function itself would remain at

$$C = 50 + 0.8Yd$$

However, the impact of having lower disposable income would imply lower planned consumption by consumers. If consumers reacted to higher taxes by saving less, the MPC could increase. The change in tax rate would probably have no impact on autonomous consumption.

Alternatively, governments trying to slow down activity in a booming economy might attempt to make savings a more attractive option.

Special savings accounts might be introduced such as in the case of the Irish Special Savings Investment Accounts (announced in the Finance Act 2001). In this case the Irish Government provided an additional 25% on each €1 saved in these special accounts (minimum monthly savings were €12.70: maximum were €254), which would be valid for a five-year period. To qualify for such attractive returns, savings could not be withdrawn before the five-year period or taxes equivalent to the government's contribution would have to be paid. Approximately 40% of the adult population opened such accounts, which should mature for withdrawals around the time of the next General Election, should the government serve its full office.

Another government policy that focuses on trying to influence aggregate consumption is the expansion of public sector employment, which includes teachers, police, civil servants, nurses, doctors, etc. By increasing employment in this way fewer people are unemployed and the wages and salaries of the public sector workers can be spent on consumer goods, boosting demand. Unfortunately there are some examples of cases where governments created additional public sector jobs, which although resulting in generating extra consumer demand in the short term also created long-term problems of inefficiency in certain parts of the public sector and increased government expenditure via wages and salaries (see Johnson and Scholes, 2001).

Other less direct policies are also used by governments to stimulate consumer demand – as in the car industry example in the Philippines (outlined in Chapter 2). Because a price ceiling was set, consumer demand for a certain type of utility vehicle was boosted; however, since demand outstripped supply, many consumers willing and able to make their purchase were unable to do so due to the limited supply. This is interesting since it shows how government policies do not always have the desired effects.

Governments also try to affect consumer behaviour by policies such as banning smoking in the workplace, as in Norway, New York and Ireland. This means such governments have decided that the social costs of smoking outweigh the benefits to consumers who wish to smoke. Many debates rage regarding the right of government to affect consumption behaviour so drastically and point to the tension between protecting the public on the one hand and impinging on individual freedom from a 'nanny' state, on the other.

3.10   SUMMARY

- **Expenditure on consumption goods is a substantial component of economic activity.**
- **Consumption activity can be analysed from a number of perspectives – how individual rational consumers make their consumption decisions, how this is reflected in the demand for a product in a specific market and how this relates to aggregate consumption.**
- **Concepts that allow us to understand the choices consumers make include total utility, marginal utility and consumer preferences. Price changes impact on planned consumption expenditure, i.e. on quantity demanded, which can be analysed using the marginal utility/price ratio or using budget line and indifference curve analysis.**
- **Consumer welfare can be analysed using the concept of consumer surplus.**
- **Economic decision-making regarding consumer behaviour can be supported by analysis of price elasticity.**

- The attribute model allows for analysis of demand for differentiated consumer products.
- Aggregate consumption behaviour is described by the consumption function.
- Government can influence aggregate consumption and/or demand for individual products.

REVIEW PROBLEMS AND QUESTIONS

1. Using the information provided, fill in column 3 by computing the marginal utility of car and motorbike consumption.

No. of cars (Q)	Total utility (TU)	Marginal utility ($\Delta TU/\Delta Q$)	No. of bikes (Q)	Total utility (TU)	Marginal utility ($\Delta TU/\Delta Q$)
0	0	–	0	0	–
1	50		1		20
2	88		2		15
3	115		3		11
4	135		4		7
5	150		5		3
6	162		6		0

2. If the consumer in question 1 had £60 000 to spend and a car or bike cost £15 000:
   a. Compute the marginal utility per pound for car and bike consumption.
   b. Rank the consumer's preferred consumption choices.
   c. What difference does it make to your answers to (a) and (b) if the price of the bike is £10 000?

3. Given the following information on demand for roses in a small town:

Equilibrium price	£10.00
Quantity demanded when price is zero	480
Quantity demanded when price is £20.00	0

   a. Estimate the consumer surplus.
   b. If there is a change in the supply of roses that leads to an increase in the equilibrium price to £12.00, estimate the change in consumer surplus. Answer this question by drawing supply and demand curves. Can you think of any reasons that might cause supply to change?

4. List five products that you consume and *explain* why you are/are not price-sensitive in the case of each one. Which products do you think have the steepest and flattest demand curves? Why?

5. Using the given information, consider if Fair Furniture Ltd should or should not increase its price of tables (*hint: compute the total revenue*).

Current price	£275
Quantity sold	500
Proposed price	£325
Expected sales at price = £325	480

In increasing price from £275 to £325, does this correspond to the elastic or inelastic portion of the demand for tables? Explain your answer.

6. For an economy with a consumption function of $C = 50 + 0.8Y$ and a tax rate of 0.2 (or 20%)

   a. Rewrite the consumption function in terms of disposable income rather than national income.

   b. Sketch both consumption functions to consider the effect of taking account of taxation.

   c. If the tax rate rises to 0.4, what effect does this have on the consumption function?

7. What other products, apart from breakfast cereal, could be analysed using the attribute model? For one of the products you selected, ask two friends to indicate the most important attributes they consider in purchasing the product. Ask each of them to rank their preferences for each attribute (on a scale of 1–10) for four alternative products. Construct a table like Table 3.6 and draw a figure like Figure 3.10 showing the relative performance of the products in terms of their attribute ratings.

8. Read the following brief case study and answer the questions that follow.

The European car industry: consumers being taken for a ride?

The price of cars across the EU varies considerably for some makes and models. Many consumer groups have voiced concern over this issue and campaign for reform in this market that will result in greater standardization of prices. Despite the introduction of the euro, price divergences were still widespread in 2002, although recent information points to some convergence of prices within the euro zone.

An examination of manufacturers' recommended retail (pre-tax) prices showed considerable diversity between the cheapest and most expensive countries in the euro zone with the average difference being approximately 10%

in November 2002, down slightly on the previous estimate of May 2002. The euro zone countries where cars are cheapest are Denmark, Greece and the Netherlands while the most expensive are Germany and Austria. The most expensive EU country is still the UK.

For individual cases, some very wide price differences have been recorded, the greatest being for the Fiat Seicento, which costs 59.5% more in the UK than in its cheapest source, Spain.

In theory, at least, it should be possible for a European consumer to source a car from a cheaper location. However, in practice the process is not straightforward. For reports on car price differentials across the EU visit:

http://europa.eu.int/comm/competition/car_sector/price_diffs/

a. Would you expect that manufacturers' recommended retail (pre-tax) prices would differ for consumers in different countries? Why or why not?

b. Why might the introduction of the euro have been expected to reduce any price discrepancies across the euro zone?

c. What obstacles might stand in the way of a consumer wishing to purchase a car from another country?

FURTHER READING AND RESEARCH

- For more on Simon's concept of bounded rationality see Simon, 1957.
- Interesting recent research on the implications for economics of research into human behaviour was published in Kopcke, Sneddon Little and Tootell, 2004.
- For related reading see Jensen and Meckling, 1994.

REFERENCES

Heston, A., R. Summers and B. Aten (2002) *Penn World Table Version 6.1*. Centre for International Comparisons at the University of Pennsylvania (CICUP), October.

Jensen, M. and W. Meckling (1994) 'The nature of man', *Journal of Applied Corporate Finance*, Summer, 4–19.

Johnson, G. and K. Scholes (2001) *Exploring Public Sector Strategy*. Prentice Hall.

Kopcke, R., J. Sneddon Little and G. Tootell (2004) 'How humans behave: implications for economics and economic policy', *New England Economic Review*, First Quarter, 1–35.

Simon, H. (1957) 'A behavioral model of rational choice', in *Models of Man*. John Wiley & Sons, Inc., New York.

CHAPTER 4

BEYOND SUPPLY: FIRMS IN THE ECONOMIC SYSTEM

LEARNING OUTCOMES

By the end of this chapter you should be able to:

✪ Describe the main activities of firms in the economic system.

✪ Clarify why firms are necessary within the economic system.

✪ Compare and contrast accounting and economic definitions of profit.

✪ Use marginal analysis to consider efficient production for a firm taking its costs and revenues into account.

✪ Explain how producer surplus is a measure of producer welfare.

✪ Apply the concept of price elasticity of supply and explain how it is useful for economic decision-making.

✪ Outline the reasons why firms invest and how investment contributes to economic growth.

✪ Apply the demand/supply model to discuss how government tries to influence producers with specific reference to:
  ● production subsidies;
  ● environmental taxes.

4.1 INTRODUCTION

Just as the economic system relies on consumers for its existence, suppliers play an equally important role in the organization and functioning of an economy. Suppliers facilitate the exchange of goods and services, which is a cornerstone of the economic process. But to see their function as simple intermediaries between people and goods and services would miss the variety of contributions made by firms to the continuation, growth and expansion of the economic system. In section 4.2, these contributions are discussed. The reasons why firms exist at all are presented in section 4.3 and the basic building blocks for microeconomic analysis of firms are presented in detail throughout this section, i.e. output, revenue and costs. This analysis is developed further to examine the concept of efficient production from a single firm's perspective in section 4.4 in the context of a profit-maximizing firm. Efficient production in the face of a lower cost competitor is also considered here and the extent to which the production decision differs for firms in the short run or long run is examined.

Producers' welfare is analysed in section 4.5 by estimating producer surplus and this is followed by consideration of how producers react to changes in prices in section 4.6. The discussion turns to focus on aggregate macroeconomic investment behaviour by firms in section 4.7, since the investment function fulfilled by businesses is a vital contribution by firms to the economic system. The role played by government in attempting to influence production is dealt with in section 4.8 where the examples of using subsidies and environmental taxes are analysed.

4.2   FIRMS IN ECONOMIC ACTION

Producers make and supply products and/or services to consumers. Most firms operate in the private sector which means those companies are owned and operated by private individuals. Firms owned and/or operated by governments make up the public sector. Firms contribute to economic life in many ways through:

- the goods and/or services they provide;
- the employment they offer;
- the wages and salaries they pay employees;
- the money they spend on buying goods and services from other firms;
- the money they spend on improvements to their businesses (to buy new premises or new machinery and equipment, for example);
- the taxes they pay for their employees and on their profits;
- their expenditure on innovation to advance and increase the quantity or quality of products/services they provide.

As we saw in Chapter 3 the consumption behaviour of consumers provides firms with revenue so in terms of attempting to approximate the contribution of firms to economic life, this provides some information. If we consider the overall amount of economic activity conducted in an economy (whether measured as income or output) we note that firms also contribute to each of the other components of activity by:

- providing some of the goods and services that are provided to government and which appear under *government expenditure*;
- supplying goods and services for exports and by importing such goods also, appearing under *net exports*;
- their attempts to maintain and improve the level of capital stock of their companies, and thereby the economy, classified as *investment*.

The monetary value of firms' involvement in economic activity in no way exhausts all the ways in which firms contribute to economic life. Indeed it would be difficult, if not impossible, to put a value on the utility that individual entrepreneurs derive from setting up and running their own businesses rather than working for other employers.

4.3   WHY ORGANIZE AN ECONOMIC SYSTEM AROUND FIRMS?

As outlined in Chapter 2, hypothetically speaking, economic life does not need to include firms. However, it does make better sense for firms to organize some economic activities because it is a more efficient way to use economic resources than if individuals instead engaged in those same activities. Hence, one reason why firms are needed is to save on unnecessary transactions costs that would arise if economic activity were conducted by individuals, instead of by firms.

If you were to ask those people actually running firms, the chief executive officers or managing directors, why their firms exist, they probably would not explain that it is to help society save on transactions costs. Similarly, although society benefits from firms' advances to create new and innovative products, most firms would probably not rate society's benefit as their reason for existing. Firms exist rather to generate income for their owners or shareholders and such income is generated as long as the firm's total costs (in the economic sense) are less than its total revenues. This excess of revenue over costs amounts to a firm's economic profits. Economists generally assume that firms exist to generate the maximum possible economic profit they can. This is the principle of profit maximization. This means firms make their decisions about how much to produce and what price they should charge with the aim of making the largest economic profit possible.

4.3.1   DECISIONS OF FIRMS AND THE ROLE OF TIME

Economists constantly use the terms short run and long run and the distinction is particularly relevant when considering the decisions taken by firms. The short run and long run are not just set periods of time and are firm- and industry-specific.

> **The short run** describes the period of time it takes for a firm to change its scale of production and this depends on its fixed factor of production – usually capital.

In the short run a firm has one or more fixed factors of production, which constrains its possible output.

> An ice-cream seller who travels around in his van selling ice-cream cones cannot sell more than his machine, van and supplies can produce unless he decides to put another van on the road. This would take some time depending on his finances and the ease of finding a suitable van, equipment and driver but could possibly be done quite quickly so the short run would be quite short, i.e. the time to get another van up and running.

> On the other hand for a ship-building company the short run would be much longer. A significant amount of equipment and machinery is required to build ships and it could take a long time to build new hangars, buy the necessary equipment and find the skilled labour if a ship-builder decided to expand its scale of production. The short run in that case could run into several years.

Usually we consider capital to be the fixed factor in the short run. When economists conduct analysis in the short run it is also assumed that there are a fixed number of firms in an industry, there is no entry of new firms or exit of existing firms.

The expressions short-term, medium-term and long-term are also commonly used in economic forecasting and refer to time-periods of up to three years, three to five years and five years plus respectively.

> **The long run** – when a firm's output is not limited by fixed factors of production – the amount of any factor of production can be changed and firms can enter or leave an industry.

Essentially the distinction between short run and long run is useful for dealing with day-to-day decisions a firm takes, i.e. short-run decisions – and more long-term or strategic issues the firm has to deal with, i.e. long-run decisions. The distinction is useful in the context of how theory is applied in economics because it provides a framework for focusing on a more constrained set of decisions in short-run analysis which can be extended as required to focus on long-run issues.

In considering how firms try to maximize their profits the sections that follow highlight relevant issues for firms separately for the short and long run. This requires consideration of the revenue and costs of a firm. Decision-making based on economics – such as the decision to produce the quantity of output that allows a firm to maximize its profits – uses marginal analysis and this is why not only total revenues and costs but also marginal revenues and costs are examined in the sections that follow.

Marginal analysis is the process of considering the effect of small changes in one factor relevant to an economic decision (e.g. on output levels or pricing) and identifying whether an economic objective will be met. The objective may relate to profit maximization, benefit maximization, cost minimization or revenue maximization as examples.

The logic of marginal analysis is that a small incremental change should be made once an economic objective is met – there is economic rationale to increasing price only if profits rise, if that is the economic objective. If no change enhances the economic objective (if it is already maximized/minimized) the decision variable should be changed no further.

Marginal analysis a method for optimizing decision-making within a reasonably well-defined setting.

4.3.2 FIRM REVENUE

The general pattern followed by the total revenue of a firm with a 'standard' linear downward sloping demand function was presented in Chapter 3 and is repeated here in Figure 4.1. Total revenue received by a firm is calculated as price × quantity (in equilibrium) so if price is £20 and quantity sold is 50, total revenue is £1,000. Depending on the amount of output the firm sells its total revenue varies. Since quantity demanded varies with price (higher price corresponding to lower quantity demanded and vice versa), then the price the firm charges has a bearing on its revenues. A firm's demand curve provides the information needed to sketch its total revenue curve.

Consider the total revenue curve in panel A of Figure 4.1. We refer to the call credit example used in earlier chapters except here we deal with one firm supplying some of this market. If the firm charges a price of £150, consumers are not willing to

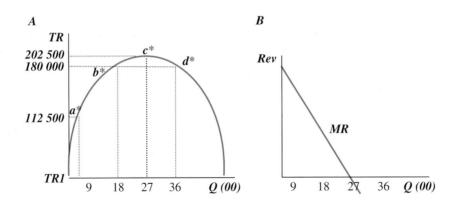

FIGURE 4.1 TOTAL REVENUE AND MARGINAL REVENUE

buy its product and no revenue is earned (shown as *TR1* in the bottom left corner of Figure 4.1) At a price of £125 the firm would sell 900 units and earn revenue of £112 500 (see a*). If price is relatively lower at £100, more consumers buy the product and 1800 units are sold. Hence, total revenue rises to £180 000 (see b*). If price is cut further to £75, more consumers are enticed to buy the product, 2700 units are sold and total revenue rises further to £202 500 (see c*). Two effects are associated with the quantity increase from 1800 to 2700 for example. On the one hand there is a negative impact on firm revenue since the price has dropped from £100 to £75. However, the effect of increasing quantity demanded *more than* offsets the price effect and so total revenue rises.

Any further cuts in price still increase the quantity sold (e.g. 3600, etc.) *but* the extra sales at the lower price required to entice more consumers to make their purchase result in lower total revenue for the firm; the effect of the price reduction offsets the rise in sales. The firm maximizes its total revenue if it sells the quantity 2700 but this amount of output can only be sold if the firm chooses the 'correct' price.

If revenue maximization is the firm's objective it needs to consider what demand for its product is in order to set the required price to sell the optimal amount of output. In panel B of Figure 4.1 marginal revenue (MR) is graphed.

Marginal revenue is defined as the change in total revenue associated with a change in quantity demanded.

The **marginal revenue** function shows the amount of additional revenue generated for a firm at different levels of quantity demanded. It is computed as the change in total revenue divided by the change in quantity demanded: $\Delta TR/\Delta Q$.

To understand the linear MR curve, take the example of a firm that sets a high price for its product (say £800 for a wooden table) so that quantity demanded is just one unit. The firm earns total revenue of the price of the table × 1 unit = £800.

If the firm drops its price to £725, it could sell two tables. If it did so it would earn total revenue of £725 × 2 = £1450. Since total revenue changes when different prices are charged, so too does marginal revenue.

The change in total revenue when two tables are sold compared to when one was sold is £1450 – £800 = £650.

Therefore, the marginal revenue for the first table sold is £800 while the marginal revenue for the second table is £650. To sell additional tables the firm would have to cut its price further so that the marginal revenue declines further as quantity demanded and sold rises.

Focusing on Figure 4.1 marginal revenue can be computed as:

Price	Quantity	Total revenue	Δ TR	ΔQ	MR Δ TR/ΔQ
£150	0	0	0	0	0
£125	900	£112 500	£112 500	900	£125
£100	1800	£180 000	£67 500	900	£77.20
£75	2700	£202 500	£22 500	900	£25
£50	3600	£180 000	−£22 500	900	−£25

Conclusion: marginal revenue declines as quantity demanded rises. Firms must lower price to increase quantity demanded and this impacts on total revenue and on marginal revenue.

In Figure 4.1 panel A, total revenue rises up until its maximum at 2700, after which it drops. This means that a small, marginal increase in output from 2699 to 2700 corresponds to the change in output where the effects on total revenue of the drop in the price and increase in quantity of output exactly cancel each other out. Beyond quantity demanded of 2700 any change in total revenue is a decline and this is reflected in the MR function, which dips below 0 beyond this level of output.

The effect of the price reduction beyond £75 has a greater negative effect on total revenue than the effect of increasing quantity demanded.

Firm revenue is just one component in the profit-maximizing decision of the firm. The next relevant component is output.

4.3.3 FIRM OUTPUT (PRODUCT): MARGINAL AND AVERAGE OUTPUT

What a firm can produce depends on the inputs available to it, both in terms of the quantity and quality of those inputs. At its simplest, what comes out of a firm depends on what goes in. The exact relationship between inputs and output will be different for each firm since different firms are in different lines of business and will have very different input requirements, different resources, both capital and human. Even for firms within the same industry or line of business, the relationship between inputs and outputs will vary as firms will have different inputs available to them and different strengths and weaknesses in successfully converting their inputs into output. A general relationship between inputs and output, however, can be graphed, as shown in Figure 4.2.

Putting one input (labour) on one axis, total output, also referred to as total product, can be drawn. If we consider the output of a firm in the short run, we assume that its capital input is fixed while its labour input can be varied. This is the simplest case that we can use to display the relationship between output and factors of production.

The S-shape of the total product curve represents the general relationship between variable input(s) and output for any firm, where *L1*, *L2* and *L3* represent different numbers of workers. In the short run, the more workers a firm employs, the higher its total output up to a point. Beyond that point (C), additional workers just get in each other's way and total output begins to fall.

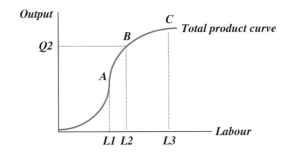

FIGURE 4.2 **TOTAL OUTPUT (PRODUCT)**

The relationship between output and labour input is not a simple linear relationship, as the S-shape indicates. Up to a certain number of workers – *L1* – total output rises more and more with each additional worker. This is reflected in an increase in the slope of the total output curve up to point *A* in Figure 4.2. This is the portion of the total product curve that reflects *increasing* marginal physical product of labour (the *MPPL* was discussed in Chapter 2).

Marginal physical product of labour: the change in the quantity of output produced by each additional worker: $\Delta Q/\Delta L$.

When *L1* workers are employed, *MPPL* is at its maximum, as seen in Figure 4.3. After point *A*, the *MPPL* declines implying that although total output still increases as the quantity of workers increases, its rate of increase slows down. This is reflected in a decrease or flattening of the slope of the total output curve beyond point *A* in Figure 4.2.

The pattern in the average product of labour can also be considered with reference to Figures 4.2 and 4.3.

Average product of labour: total output divided by the number of workers: Q/L.

For example, with *L2* workers, the firm shown in Figure 4.2 produces *Q2* output – at point *B* on the total product curve. If this output corresponds to 200 tables, produced by 160 workers, each worker produces 1.25 tables on average. For all values of total output below *Q2* (and the corresponding number of workers below *L2*) the average product of labour is less than at point *B*. For example, at *L1* 120 workers produce 140 tables, a lower average of 1.2 tables each. For all values of total output above *Q2*, and the corresponding number of workers above *L2*, average

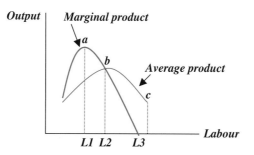

FIGURE 4.3 MARGINAL AND AVERAGE OUTPUT (PRODUCT) OF LABOUR

product of labour is lower than at point B. (At any point apart from B on the total product/output curve, the slope of a line drawn between zero and that point on the total product curve is lower than at point B. The slope expresses the vertical distance between zero and the output quantity relative to the horizontal distance between zero and the quantity of labour, i.e. the measure of average output per worker: Q/L.) At $L3$ with 260 workers, output is 240 tables, or 0.92 of a table.

This explains why in Figure 4.3, point b is the highest point on the average product of labour curve. From this figure we see that:

- When the marginal physical product of labour lies above the average product of labour, hiring one extra worker leads to an increase in the average product of labour.
- When the marginal physical product of labour lies below the average product of labour, hiring one extra worker leads to a fall in the average product of labour.
- The marginal physical product of labour curve intersects the average product of labour curve from above at the highest point on the average product of labour curve.

The shape of the marginal product curve can be understood from the analysis of the labour market and the discussion of the law of diminishing marginal returns discussed in Chapter 2.

MARGINAL AND AVERAGE RELATIONSHIPS

Linda is taking a course with five continuous assessment exercises, each counting for 20% of the overall course mark. Linda would like to do well in all exams but her key objective is to score 50% overall so she can pass the course and move on to the next year of her studies.

Linda scores as follows in the exams:

Exams	#1: 60%	#2: 65%	#3: 52%	#4: 60%	#5: 64%
Total marks:	60	125	177	237	301

Linda's *average mark* after the first exam was 60%.
Her average mark over the first two exams is $[60 + 65]/2 = 62.5\%$.
Her average mark over the first three exams is $[60 + 65 + 52]/3 = 59.0\%$.
Her average mark over the first four exams is $[60 + 65 + 52 + 60]/4 = 59.25\%$.
Her average mark over the five exams is $[60 + 65 + 52 + 60 + 64]/5 = 60.2\%$.

The marks received in each exam correspond to the definition of marginal marks – the change in total marks for each extra exam completed: the change in marks after the second exam is the total marks 125 minus the marks for the first exam or $125 - 60 = 65$.

You can see that:

- When the marginal mark rose (eg. 60% to 65%), the average also rose (from 60% to 62.5%).
- When the marginal mark fell (eg. 65% to 52%), the average also fell (from 62.5% to 59%).
- When the marginal mark was greater than the average, the average increased (look at exams #1 and #2).
- When the marginal mark was less than the average, the average declined (consider exams #2 and #3).

4.3.4 FIRM COSTS

Firms must pay a range of different costs, depending on their circumstances and line of business – costs for rent, rates, insurance, taxes, wages, salaries, production inputs, machinery, computers, refuse collection, accountants' fees, etc. A firm's total costs are the sum of variable and fixed costs.

Total costs (TC) are the sum of variable costs and fixed costs.
Variable costs (VC) or **total variable costs (TVC)** depend directly on the amount of output the firm produces, such as the costs for production inputs and workers. The higher the quantity produced the higher the variable costs.

Other costs such as rent and rates must be paid even if the firm produces no output and these costs are called **fixed costs (FC)** or **total fixed costs (TFC)**.

$$TC = TVC + TFC$$

Total fixed costs can be graphed easily, as shown in Figure 4.4, since they do not change as output changes. If when adding up all a firm's fixed costs, total fixed costs are £2750 per week, then these costs must be paid by the firm if output is zero or not.

In panel *B* of the figure, average fixed costs are shown. The average fixed cost of the first unit of output is £2750/1 = £2750; for the second unit it is £2750/2 = £1375;

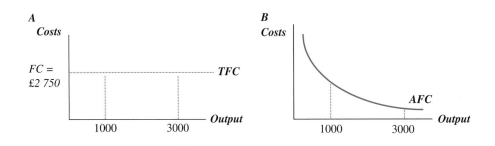

FIGURE 4.4 TOTAL FIXED COSTS (TFC) AND AVERAGE FIXED COSTS (AFC)

for the third unit it is £917 and so on, so the more the firm produces the lower its average fixed cost as the fixed costs can be spread across a greater amount of output. The average fixed costs of 1000 units of output would be £27.5 while the average fixed cost for 3000 units would be £0.92.

Variable costs change with output, which was shown above as total output. The total variable costs curve for any firm follows an *inverted S-shape* since it is related to the total output curve. It is drawn based on available information on the price of inputs and knowledge about the best available techniques (technology) for converting inputs into output. In short-run analysis, technology is assumed to be fixed so the cost curves are drawn assuming a certain level of technology.

The best technique for transforming inputs into output can depend on the amount of output produced. It may make sense for a large car producer to invest in robotic technology because of the quantity produced but this technology would be too expensive and make no economic sense for a small-scale car producer. Large dairy companies use large container vats for cheese-making; such investment in equipment would be unsuitable and too expensive for smaller homemade cheese producers.

The general shape of any firm's total variable cost curve (*TVC*) is shown in Figure 4.5. The first units of output generate high initial costs for a firm – the first worker is hired, initial inputs must be bought (often in bulk) and the most efficient ways to produce output are yet to be learned by the workforce – often it is only from working on-the-job (learning by doing) that the best ways to produce efficiently are understood and put into practice. Hence, in the initial stages of production, until point *a* on the *TVC* curve, total costs rise proportionately faster than output. Once efficiencies are realized, production costs still increase but not as quickly as output. Beyond point *b*, there is no point in producing extra output as costs rise significantly faster than output.

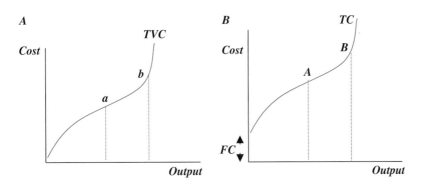

FIGURE 4.5 TOTAL VARIABLE COST (TVC) AND TOTAL COST (TC)

A firm's total costs are found by adding up its total fixed and total variable costs. Graphically this gives rise to a figure similar to Figure 4.5 panel A, the only difference being it does not start at zero cost when output is zero since fixed costs (*FC*) must be paid. This is shown in Figure 4.5 panel B, which differs from panel A only with respect to fixed costs that have been added on at each point on the total cost curve.

4.3.5 MARGINAL AND AVERAGE COSTS

The marginal and average cost curves that correspond to the total cost curve is shown in Figure 4.6.

> **Average cost (AC)** is total cost per unit of output. AC is computed as total costs divided by output (*TC*/*Q*).
>
> Average total cost (ATC) is made up of average variable cost (AVC) plus average fixed cost (AFC): ATC = AVC + AFC.
>
> **Marginal cost (MC):** the change in total costs as output changes (*ΔTC*/*ΔQ*).

Firms' average cost (AC) curves tend to follow a general U-shaped pattern. The AC curve for a firm with relatively low costs would lie below the AC curve for a higher-cost firm.

The minimum point on a firm's AC curve corresponds to the level of output the firm should produce in order to produce at its minimum average cost. However, an individual firm cannot always sell this amount of output – there may not be a market for it. Producing at minimum average cost would be a welcome outcome from the perspective of making efficient use of economic resources but firms do

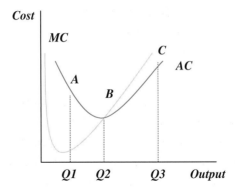

FIGURE 4.6 MARGINAL COST (MC) AND AVERAGE COST (AC)

Notes: If TVC = €2500 when 250 units are sold, AVC = €2500/250 = €10.

If TVC rise to €3000 when 275 units are sold, the MVC of the additional 25 units of output is €500 in total or €12 per unit.

not always produce this amount of output as it does not always coincide either with demand for their products or with the output level that allows firms to maximize their profits. This is explored further below.

From Figure 4.6 we see that:

- When the marginal cost curve lies below the average cost curve, producing one extra unit of output leads to a fall in the average cost.
- When the marginal cost curve lies above the average cost curve, producing one extra unit of output leads to an increase in the average cost.
- The marginal cost curve intersects the average cost curve from below at the lowest point on the average cost curve.

Explaining U-shaped cost curves

The reasons for U-shaped cost curves differ in the short run and long run. In the short run the firm has some fixed (usually capital) and some variable (usually labour) factors of production.

A short-run cost curve is drawn for *one* specific size or scale of plant.

Because capital is fixed in the short run and the scale of the plant is limited, a firm finds that beyond a certain amount of production the fixed factor leads to diminishing returns to other factors of production meaning that average costs rise – as we see in Figure 4.6 beyond point *B* when output is greater than *Q2*. This also helps to explain the shape of the short-run supply curve.

When selling ice cream, when one van operates and with both the driver and another employee selling cones, beyond a certain amount of sales trying to expand output by employing an extra worker would only lead to the workers getting in each other's way, given space and machine constraints, and would not necessarily expand output at all although the worker would have to be paid and so costs would rise.

In the long run, all factors are variable and each firm can decide on what scale of production it wants, such as how many ice-cream vans to operate and what technology to use. The implications of these decisions will be evident in a firm's costs and will depend on its size or scale of production. The U-shape of the average cost curve arises because of the ways efficiencies may initially be generated within firms over a certain range of output and how inefficiencies may eventually result beyond a certain scale of output.

Efficiencies and inefficiencies arise that are associated with a firm's scale of output which can vary over the long run. They are known as **economies and diseconomies of scale**.

Economies of scale are enjoyed when average costs of output decline as output increases.

Diseconomies of scale are experienced when average costs of output rise as output increases.

For a given set of input prices, if all a firm's inputs were increased by 20% and

a) its output increased by more than 20% it enjoys *economies of scale* and its average unit costs would fall as output rises. See Figure 4.6 up to point *B*.
   OR

b) its output increased by less than 20% it experiences *diseconomies of scale* and its average unit costs would rise as output rises. See Figure 4.6 from point *B* on.
   OR

c) its output increased by 20%, it would experience constant costs (more on this below).

There are a number of potential reasons as to why falling average costs might be observed in the long run:

1. specialization;
2. indivisibilities in production;
3. returns to large-scale production.

Specialization: It was Adam Smith who first explained with his example of a pin factory that splitting up a manufacturing process into separate tasks (18 for pins) made for greater productivity from a given set of inputs. The focus of some workers on specific limited tasks allowed them to specialize and develop the skills most suited to those tasks as opposed to trying to carry out all of the various tasks in the production process. This logic underlies assembly lines that still characterize many manufacturing processes including those for vehicles.

Indivisibilities in production: Fixed costs by their nature are a source of economies because the greater the output, the more units over which fixed costs can be apportioned. Such costs are also known as indivisibilities in production because they are independent of output.

Returns to large-scale production: There are physical or engineering reasons that explain why, in some circumstances, large-scale firms can achieve lower average costs than smaller firms. The engineer's rule of two thirds explains how the volume of cylinders expand by 100% if the surface area rises by only 66% (based on the mathematical formula for the area of a cylinder). Similarly for *some* machines and factories, where their cost represents only two thirds of the value of the additional output they can produce. Large-scale firms might also be able to benefit by being in a position to buy machinery and equipment appropriate for large-scale production only. A large furniture manufacturer might be able to buy sophisticated technology that is both appropriate and cost-effective for its high output level allowing it to have relatively low average costs compared to a smaller-scale operation producing lower output and for which the same equipment would not be cost effective because its associated fixed costs would be simply too high and inappropriate for the scale of output.

Any output greater than *Q2* in Figure 4.6 leads to a rise in average costs or diseconomies of scale. This is usually due to the fact that, as the scale of the firm's

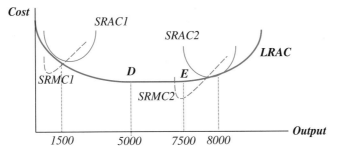

FIGURE 4.7 LONG-RUN AVERAGE COST (LRAC) AND CONSTANT RETURNS TO SCALE

operations becomes so complex and bureaucratic, management finds it increasingly difficult to coordinate the operations and average costs rise with scale.

At point *B* on the average cost curve, average costs are neither rising nor falling but constant. This corresponds to a size of plant where there are constant returns to scale. For some firms constant returns to scale are possible not just at one point on their average cost curve but over an entire portion of it – as shown in Figure 4.7 between points *D* and *E* when output is between 5000 and 7500 units.

The firm that might have such a cost curve needs to produce a lot of output before its costs decline to their minimum level but once a large scale of output is produced (5000 units in this case), minimum average costs apply until output expands beyond 7500 units. This cost curve could describe the situation for a large-scale car producer. Once at least 5000 cars can be produced, it makes sense for the firm to buy sophisticated and expensive robotic equipment that can be used to produce such a large quantity of output efficiently, so technology can give rise to economies of scale. Point *D* is referred to as the minimum efficient scale (MES) of production.

> The **minimum efficient scale (MES)** of production is the size/scale of plant required if a firm wishes to produce sufficient output to allow it to produce at its lowest long-run average cost.

If the car firm in Figure 4.7 has markets for its output it would continue expanding its production to achieve economies of scale implying it could efficiently produce up to 7500 cars.

CHALLENGES FOR CAR PRODUCERS

The car industry in developed countries is often described as 'mature' because growth in the market is relatively modest compared to the growth observed in markets for newer products – such as for MP3s. In the mature car market, firms face a challenge since most people who wish to have a car have already purchased. Demand still exists because consumers replace their vehicles over time but no substantial jump in sales is expected as the penetration of cars is considered to have levelled off.

Large-scale producers in the market have adopted similar technologies of production and have similar average cost curves. Large-scale production is required to minimize costs and diseconomies of scale set in beyond a certain scale of organization.

One approach to competing in such saturated markets is to attempt to take market share from other competitors by offering more valued attributes. Alternatively, companies can acquire or buy out competitors and increase scale, which may be profitable once increased coordination costs do not outweigh scale benefits. For some companies it might be possible to develop new technology that effectively creates a new market for them – such as Ryanair and easyJet in the air travel market.

For car manufacturers the tendency over recent years has been towards consolidation across companies via mergers and acquisitions: Daimler acquired Chrysler while Nissan and Renault have merged. Analysts of the industry predict that over the next decade three main international players will dominate the market.

It is possible to link long-run and short-run average cost curves since each short-run average cost curve (*SRAC*) corresponds to one scale or size of plant; in other words, one fixed level of capital. In the short run, with a fixed level of capital, a range of output can be produced depending on how many workers are employed, and each quantity of output within that range has an associated cost. In Figure 4.7, two examples are shown for outputs of 1500 and 8000. These *SRAC* curves indicate the costs associated with producing output when plant size is limited to either a small or a large scale. Neither of these plant sizes allows the firm to produce at its minimum average cost because in the first case economies of scale cannot be fully exploited because of the small size of the plant while in the second case, the plant size is too big to be optimally efficient and diseconomies of scale have kicked in.

Finally, you will see that the *LRAC* in Figure 4.7 does *not* pass through the minimum points on *SRAC1* or *SRAC2*.

The long-run average cost curve is *not* a map of minimum SRACs

- The LRAC displays all the minimum average cost methods of producing output when all factors of production can be varied.
- The SRAC displays the average cost of production of a range of output for one plant.

4.4 MAXIMIZING PROFITS IN THE LONG RUN

If firms are to make the most efficient use of their resources, they should produce as much output as possible from the factors of production they use. To decide how much output each firm should produce firms need to consider their profits. Initially here, the case of the long-run output decision is considered. Using analysis as in previous sections, we can examine the marginal revenue and marginal cost position of a sample firm to work out what the best or optimal output should be to maximize its profits. These are shown in Figure 4.8.

The firm faces the downward sloping demand curve shown in Figure 4.8. The corresponding *MR* curve for this demand curve is also shown. The costs facing the

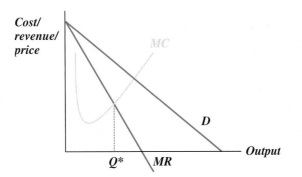

FIGURE 4.8 PROFIT-MAXIMIZING OUTPUT: REVENUE, COST AND DEMAND

firm are graphed by the marginal cost curve (the corresponding average cost curve is not included to keep the diagram clear initially).

To maximize its profits the firm wants to produce output up to the point where the additional revenue earned on its last unit of output covers the costs of that unit. This occurs at output of Q^* and is found by examining the point where the MR and MC curves intersect and checking the level of output that corresponds to this point. It makes sense to produce output up to Q^* because up to this output level the marginal revenue curve lies above the marginal cost curve – increasing output adds more to revenues than to costs. Beyond Q^*, this is no longer the case as the marginal cost curve lies above the marginal revenue curve and the marginal costs of further units of output are greater than the marginal revenue earned by the firm.

> The profit-maximizing output level is found by identifying the quantity that coincides with $MC = MR$.

Once the decision regarding output has been made, this also suggests the profit-maximizing price that the firm should charge, as shown in Figure 4.9. If the firm wishes to produce Q^*, this quantity corresponds to one price only on the demand curve and that price is shown as P^*. If price were other than P^*, a quantity other than Q^* would be demanded.

To maximize profits in the long run a firm should:

- Establish the quantity that coincides with the point where its marginal costs and its marginal revenues intersect.
- Based on this quantity, set the price of its product from its demand curve.
- Ensure that the price it charges customers is sufficient to cover its average production costs.

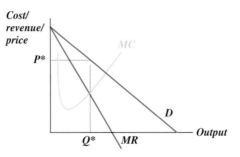

FIGURE 4.9 PROFIT-MAXIMIZING PRICE: REVENUE, COST AND DEMAND

This final point is of huge importance. Consider Figure 4.10, which now also includes the average cost curve. In Figure 4.10 it is possible to compare the price the firm receives if it sells Q^* to the average cost it incurs for this output. The price and average cost of Q^* units of output are P^* and AC^* respectively. The difference between P^* and AC^* indicates that at Q^*, the price earned is more than sufficient to cover the firm's average costs, meaning economic profits are earned. The size of the profits is given by the shaded rectangle.

> If $P^* = £100$, $AC^* = 50$ and output at $Q^* = 1800$ total revenue $(P \times Q) = £180\,000$, total costs $= £90\,000$ and profits $= £90\,000$.

4.4.1 PROFIT MAXIMIZATION, NORMAL PROFIT AND EFFICIENCY

For the example shown in Figure 4.10 we can comment on the efficiency of the production of the firm in question. The firm is producing the quantity of output for which its average costs are minimized. The quantity Q^* corresponds to the lowest point on its average cost curve so the firm is operating at the minimum efficient scale of production. The price charged of P^* is greater than the costs of AC^* so this firm earns supernormal profits (explained in Chapter 2) because its revenue more than covers the average costs. Remember that the firm's costs include payment to the owner of the business that is sufficient to keep them in business, i.e. enough to cover the opportunity costs of the time and efforts of the owner.

Quite often it is considered that industries where firms make supernormal profits are not as efficient as they could be because profits are being made beyond normal

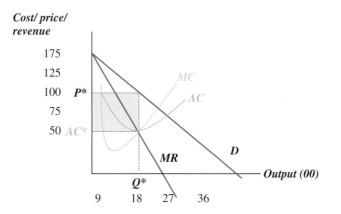

FIGURE 4.10 PROFIT MAXIMIZATION AND AVERAGE COST

levels. Rather than having a portion of society's resources used as profits, the argument is sometimes made that excess profits (excess relative to what business owners would be satisfied to receive to keep them in business) would be better be used for some other purpose.

One way of trying to reduce such supernormal profits would be to encourage greater competition in industries where supernormal profits exist and are considered high. This is the function of national competition authorities and national competition policies which is discussed in more detail in Chapter 6. Competition between firms *could* lead to a new lower-cost firm coming into the industry (if it has access to a more cost-effective technology for example) but as we will see in Chapter 6 whether this is possible depends on the overall structure of the market and how firms compete with others.

Also, we already know that firms compete more than just on price (other attributes also matter from consumers' perspectives) so charging a lower price might in itself be insufficient to create a real alternative product in the eyes of consumers.

Finally, having noted that the firm in Figure 4.10 is operating efficiently in production terms, this is not the only possible outcome, as Figure 4.11 indicates. Another firm with different cost structures could have the cost curves as shown.

Here the firm's profit-maximizing level of output is found where its *MR* intersects its *MC* which occurs at the output level *Q1*. This firm also makes supernormal profits since the price of its output *P1* is greater than the average cost of production of *Q1*. The extent of the supernormal profit is indicated by the grey rectangle.

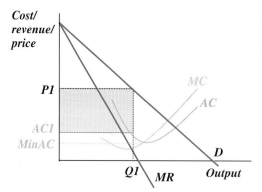

FIGURE 4.11   PROFIT MAXIMIZATION: OUTPUT *NOT* AT MINIMUM AC

If we knew that $P1 = £75$, that $Q1 = 2700$ and $AC1 = £35$, the firm's total revenue (P × Q) = £202 500, total costs = £94 500 and profits = £108 000. This firm, facing the same demand conditions as the firm in Figure 4.10, would produce a higher level of output (900 units extra) at a lower cost (£25 lower) but manages to make greater profit given its cost conditions.

Comparing Figures 4.10 and 4.11, the firm in Figure 4.11 (despite its higher super-normal profits) could be argued to operate less efficiently than the firm in Figure 4.10 since its output level does not coincide with the quantity at which it could minimize its average costs. However, $Q1$ makes economic sense for the firm because this is the quantity that generates maximum profits.

> Because of cost conditions and demand conditions, profit-maximizing firms do not necessarily produce the level of output that minimizes costs.

If substantial supernormal profits are being made in an industry, it is usual to expect that some other firms would be anxious to enter the industry to try to compete and earn some supernormal profits for themselves. A competitor firm might be tempted to enter the industry and charge a price slightly less than the price that would maximize its profits so it would 'grab' the market for itself. Such behaviour, however, could lead to a price war in the industry with different firms cutting price in a 'tit-for-tat' strategy that might end up with all competing firms cutting prices down to their average costs.

The only way that firms can earn supernormal profits over the long run is if there are some obstacles or barriers to entry in the way of other firms entering and competing in the industry.

> **Barriers to entry** exist when new firms *cannot* freely enter and compete in a new market. With no barriers all firms competing in the same market would have access to similar technology allowing them to have similar cost structures.

Many examples of such barriers to entry exist including:

- product differentiation, where firms attempt to offer attributes that differentiate their products from available substitutes;
- absolute cost advantages, where one firm's costs may be so low that no others can compete efficiently (if the firm has a patented technology which others may not legally use, for example);

- scale economies, where established firms producing on a large scale have such low costs that a new firm producing a smaller share of the market output would not expect to compete.

Government-granted licences might confer rights to some firms but not to others. Patent restrictions operate somewhat similarly in terms of their impact on potential competitors. For example, newly developed drugs that are patented cannot be manufactured by competitors so pharmaceutical companies enjoy supernormal profits and benefit from barriers to entry for whatever period of time the patent is applicable. Such firms enjoy a 'first-mover advantage' because they are the first to come up with the drug even though others may have been trying to do so also. Any innovative firm that successfully launches a new product (or invents a new process) will wish to protect its investment in innovation to maximize its return and will benefit as long as imitators lack the required expertise or legal permission to imitate and if they operate in an environment where their patent is respected.

Society, however, also benefits from the dissemination of new inventions and innovations as resources can be used in more efficient ways and to produce previously unavailable products or services. The benefit from imitation can be perceived where increased supply of a product leads to a lower equilibrium price for consumers. However as prices fall, the return on the initial investment by the innovating firm declines. Hence, there can be a social effect of the private invention in the sense that society gets the benefit of lower prices and/or new previously unavailable products but the original developer loses out. The economist Joseph Schumpeter pointed out that without the incentive of making supernormal profits, some business would never be created and so some inventions and innovations might never occur.

> Supernormal profits should not be considered always to reflect inefficiency in the economic system but rather may be the stimulus for creativity that leads to benefits both for users of invention or innovations and more broadly if economic resources are used more efficiently.

This explains why patents, which slow down the dissemination of inventions and innovations, are used as a policy to create incentives for producers to engage in some research activities. It also provides reasons for public – i.e. government – funding of basic research in universities, in government-owned laboratories and in private industry.

4.4.2   MAXIMIZING PROFITS OVER THE SHORT RUN

We know that the short run is distinguished by the existence of a fixed factor, or factors, of production. In the short run, a firm has fixed and variable costs whereas in the long run all factors of production are variable, and hence long-run total costs are variable also. Figure 4.12 includes the cost information for examining the short-run profit-maximizing decisions for a firm.

> Short-run average total costs are equal to short-run average variable costs plus short-run average fixed cost.
> $SATC = SAVC + SAFC$

The marginal cost curve *SMC* drawn is relative to the average total cost curve *SATC*. The decision about what output level to produce in the short run is based on the same logic as for the long-run decision i.e. where

$$SMC = MR.$$

One important distinction, however, between short- and long-run output must be noted. The firm in Figure 4.12 chooses its profit-maximizing output in the short run, Q^*, from the $SMC = MR$ decision rule. The firm also sets its price from the corresponding point on the demand curve, P^*. If you compare P^* to the average cost of producing this level of output, you see that AC^* lies above the price while AVC^* lies below. This means that the price is sufficient to cover average variable costs but not to cover total costs. Should this firm remain in business? What is in the firm's best economic interest?

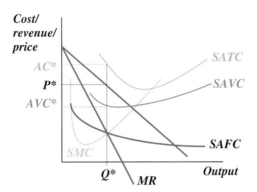

FIGURE 4.12   PROFIT MAXIMIZATION IN THE SHORT RUN

If the firm decides to produce and sell its output at the price P^*, it makes an economic loss because its average costs are not covered. However, all average variable costs can be paid and *some* of its average fixed costs. If the firm did not produce in the short run, its fixed costs would still have to be paid. The firm has to choose between:

- producing zero output and paying for its fixed costs;
  or
- producing Q^* at a short-run loss.

  As long as a firm can generate at least enough revenue to cover its short-run average variable costs of production, it should stay in business *in the short run*.

The firm needs to cut its costs somehow (or earn a higher price) to ensure the price covers average total costs in the long run or else the firm faces closure. The firm might be able to negotiate new prices with its suppliers, or lower rent from its landlord, or use its equipment more efficiently, for example, so that it can reduce its costs and its short-run cost curves would move down over time.

A firm that cannot cover its average variable costs in the short run should stop production. Its losses are lower at no output than if its variable costs cannot be covered by the price it earns on output.

Economic analysis

To follow the economic analysis of profit maximization conducted above, economists use demand, cost and revenue curves. The general patterns of the demand, cost and revenue curves have emerged from economists' analysis of how firms operate and are *analytical tools* that help the economist to think about and examine the decisions facing firms. Many firms would probably not be able to draw exact or even inexact diagrams of these curves, however, in their knowledge of how their businesses operate day-to-day and over the longer term, they learn and understand how much they should produce to make profits, when they should cut back on production as their costs rise faster than revenue, and how their customers react to changes in prices. Such information allows firms to change their output in order to improve their profit position. Hence, the analytical tools of the economist are grounded in the reality facing firms and contribute to our understanding of how firms behave.

4.5 SUPPLY, PRODUCERS AND PRODUCER SURPLUS

The supply curve shows us the amount of output suppliers wish to supply at different prices and the upward slope of the curve indicates that the higher the price, the more suppliers are willing to supply, which is related to the increasing marginal costs of production. The benefit or utility that producers generate can be analysed using the concept of producer surplus.

> **Producer surplus** – the benefit to producers due to the difference between the price suppliers are willing to receive for their output and what they actually receive.

To calculate producer surplus we need to examine the supply curve in equilibrium, as shown in Figure 4.13.

In equilibrium, the quantity of output bought and sold and the price charged are shown as Q^* and P^*. If price were $P0$ producers would supply no output in this market because there is no economic incentive – supply costs would not be covered.

At a price above $P0$, for example, $P1$, $Q1$ would be produced as only those producers who have sufficiently low costs would be willing to supply to the market. In equilibrium, however, the price is higher at P^* so more suppliers produce for this market. While price is P^*, this means that all the suppliers who would have willingly supplied at a lower price can earn P^* for their output, thus they benefit from receiving a higher price than they require as an incentive to supply the market. The shaded area in the figure above the supply curve and below P^* represents the sum total of the benefit to all such suppliers a measure of producer welfare.

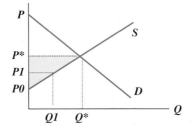

FIGURE 4.13 SUPPLY AND PRODUCER SURPLUS

4.6 PRODUCERS' RESPONSE TO PRICE CHANGES

From the shape of the supply curve we know that at different prices producers wish to supply different quantities of output. The extent to which they wish to supply more or less of their output if price changes is measured by the price elasticity of supply.

> **Price elasticity of supply** (PES) is the responsiveness of quantity supplied to changes in price. It may be elastic, inelastic or unit elastic.
>
> It is computed as the proportional change in quantity supplied divided by the proportional change in price: **%∆QS/%∆P**
>
> Arc PES is computed as $\dfrac{\Delta QS}{\Delta P} \times \dfrac{1/2[P1 + P2]}{1/2[QS1 + QS2]}$

If price increases we would expect producers to supply more and for a price fall, we would expect producers to cut back on their output. Thus, price elasticity of supply is usually a positive number. For a PES of 1.5, for every 10% rise in price, quantity supplied would rise by 15%. For values of PES greater than 1, quantity supplied is elastic or relatively responsive to changes in prices. Where PES is less than 1 PES is inelastic – a price change of 10% would lead to a quantity change of less than 10%. Where PES is 1, a small change in price has the same proportional effect on quantity supplied.

The extent to which suppliers are able to change their output in response to a price change depends on the business and time frame being considered.

> A ship-builder cannot expand its capacity as quickly as a car manufacturer and the same is true for a car manufacturer relative to an ice-cream van.

In the case of all businesses, however, price elasticity of supply will be lower in the short run than in the long run because in the short run firms will be unable to respond as completely to the change in price as in the long run.

> The supply curve is flatter in the long run than in the short run. In the long run, firms can fully adjust to the price change.

The long-run/short-run consideration also has implications in terms of the availability of factors of production. The elasticity of supply of factors of production is relevant in determining the elasticity of supply of the products for which they are inputs. If suppliers cannot source inputs required to expand their production when the price of their product rises, they simply cannot expand output. A factory producing cars that cannot source extra steel required to produce additional cars (or that can only source extra steel at relatively high prices) will have little ability or incentive to respond to expected price increases in cars.

> The quantity firms are willing to supply to a market may not always respond to changes in the price. If the price of potatoes doubled overnight, growers would be unable to adjust their supplies quickly to the new price. Over a short time period, supply would be *perfectly inelastic* (vertical) where quantity is 'stuck' at the output growers selected before the price change. Rational producers would react over time and where possible expand their output. Some new entrants would switch from growing other crops and still others might establish new businesses in the industry.
>
> If the price of cinema tickets doubles, the short-run capacity of a cinema is fixed and supply cannot respond immediately.
>
> In other markets supply may be *perfectly elastic* (horizontal) implying that quantity supplied is unlimited at one price only.

Information on price elasticity of supply can be useful for those interested in the future supply of products.

> Within the EU estimates of supply elasticities are useful in the context of agricultural prices. The EU has an overproduction of many agricultural products – milk, butter, beef, mutton, etc. – due to its practices of supporting the prices of the products via *floor prices*. Since the EU wants to reduce the output of these products it has decided to cut the prices gradually over time.

To examine the effect of cutting prices, it would be useful to carry out research on the price elasticities of supply of the products to provide information on the expected supply effects of price changes.

PRICE CEILINGS, US OIL, INCENTIVES AND PRICE ELASTICITY OF SUPPLY

In the United States prior to 1978/9 a price ceiling was in place on domestically produced oil. The country was heavily dependent on imported oil, the price of which was determined by demand and supply. Limits on supplies by the Organization of Petroleum Exporting Countries (OPEC) kept the price high.

Although the objective of the US oil-price policy was to keep oil prices low for consumers and businesses, the low price was reducing incentives for firms in the industry to engage in more exploration and drilling. A debate followed that focused on the effect of removing the price ceiling in terms of domestic producers' responses. How much extra would suppliers supply at higher prices? Estimates of the price elasticity of oil put it at just under 1, meaning that to increase quantity supplied by 10%, the price would need to rise by just over 10%.

When the price ceiling was removed the price increased and quantity supplied rose also. Rational consumers and businesses reacted by using oil somewhat more conservatively. Rational suppliers reacted to the higher prices by engaging in further exploration.

4.7   FIRMS' INVESTMENT BEHAVIOUR

A key function of firms in the economic system is to maintain and upgrade the productive capacity of their companies; firms engage in investment.

Investment leads to the creation of capital assets.

Firms invest in fixed capital – which is plant, machinery and equipment – and in working capital, which is stocks of finished goods (inventories) waiting to be sold. In the national accounts, investment also includes the construction of business premises and residential construction. Investment by firms is also called private investment. If a firm wishes to produce a set level of output into the future it must invest sufficiently to cover the depreciation of its fixed capital.

Depreciation is the decline in value of an asset over time attributable to deterioration due to use and obsolescence.

If a firm wishes to increase its output in the future it needs to invest sufficiently in its capital to cover more than just depreciation. An increase in investment by most firms increases an economy's productive capacity pushing out its production possibility frontier and leading to economic growth, assuming of course that consumers buy the additional output produced with the new capital (this is expanded on in Chapter 9).

> **Net investment** is the term used to describe only that investment which creates new capital assets, whereas **gross investment** includes the value of capital depreciation plus new capital investment.

Expectations about the future play a central role in a firm's investment decisions and firms make their best guesses today on what future demand for their products will be and attempt to make the most appropriate investment decisions on that basis. Firms' expectations about the future vary over time and the investment component of aggregate demand is actually the most changeable or volatile portion of aggregate demand in the national accounts. Much of the volatility derives from firms' behaviour regarding their inventories. Firms' inventory levels fluctuate widely depending on their expectations about business conditions. While holding a lot of inventories might not make sense due to storage costs or perishability, it makes sense for firms to have some stocks as their predictions about demand are not perfect and having inventories allows them a buffer to deal with unexpected demand so shortages are minimized.

In analysing the investment behaviour of firms using the definition of economic activity as planned consumption plus planned investment, planned government expenditures plus net exports, economists usually begin with the assumption that planned investment demand (denoted I) is autonomous, i.e. independent of the level of national income. This assumption is not far removed from reality because the level of national income today is not a crucial decision variable for a firm thinking about investing; rather the focus for firms is on their expectations of the future and demand for their output in the future. Graphically, this can be represented by the investment function as in Figure 4.14.

> The **investment function** describes the macroeconomic or aggregate investment behaviour in an economy.

In Figure 4.14, the level of autonomous investment I^* is constant, whatever the level of national income, Y. Since much of firms' investments are financed by loans, investment decisions are sensitive to changing interest rates, and hence investment

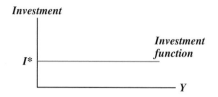

FIGURE 4.14 THE INVESTMENT FUNCTION

can be influenced by policies and activity in the financial sector of an economy that cause rates to change (these are discussed further in Chapter 7).

4.8 GOVERNMENT INFLUENCE ON SUPPLY AND PRODUCTION

As the EU agriculture and US oil examples indicate, governments sometimes wish to influence production. In the case of oil the objective was to increase domestic supply whereas the EU agricultural policies focus on reducing production. For governments trying to increase the output of certain industries, targeted industrial policies may be used. Subsidies are one instrument used by governments to try to support domestic industries.

> **Subsidy**: a payment or a tax concession from the government that reduces producers' average production costs.

A government might wish to use subsidies for an industry that is not competitive and facing a declining market share. Or a strong lobby group with its own particular interests might be successful in negotiating subsidies to stave off competition in the future.

In the car industry in the 1970s and 1980s both European and US producers faced stiff competition from Japanese car manufacturers that were using new ways of organizing their factories – 'lean production' – which facilitated the Japanese firms' reduction of their average production costs. In attempts to support domestic car producers, policies were used to try to support domestic output and producers at the expense of foreign output and producers. This meant reducing imports of cars allowing domestic (and higher-cost) producers to serve their home market.

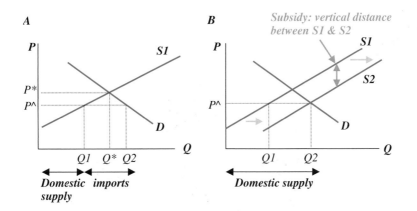

FIGURE 4.15 SUPPLY AND SUBSIDIES

4.8.1 USING SUBSIDIES – AN EXAMPLE WITH INTERNATIONAL TRADE

By using subsidies, the government transfers some of its revenue (paid to it by various taxpayers) to businesses. This affects the supply curve of the industry receiving the subsidy as shown in the example described in Figure 4.15. In panel A, $S1$ represents the supply curve of the European bicycle industry, D represents the European demand for bicycles so that P^* and Q^* are the equilibrium price and quantity of bicycles bought and sold in Europe.

Foreign bicycle manufacturers decide to sell on the European market but they can produce bicycles profitably for $P^\wedge$ and consumers are happy to buy at this price. At the lower price, some European producers cannot profitably produce because their costs are too high so they go out of business and European suppliers supply $Q1$ (which is less than Q^*). At the lower price consumers increase their demand from Q^* to $Q2$ which means the difference between $Q2$ and $Q1$ is made up of bicycles produced by foreign suppliers – imported bicycles.

The European bicycle industry, unhappy at losing some of its market to producers from outside the EU, lobbies the EU for subsidies to protect the EU market from foreign supplies (imports). The EU agrees and offers a subsidy of 40% of the international price $P^\wedge$. If $P^\wedge$ is £180, the subsidy received by each European bicycle manufacturer is £72 per bicycle.

Subsidizing an industry results in a rightward shift of the supply function.

The size or amount of the subsidy per unit of output is the vertical distance between the original and new supply functions. (See $S1$ and $S2$ in Figure 4.15B).

This affects the European supply curve because all producers who were previously willing to supply to the market can now supply more bicycles at each possible price, at no additional cost. Looking at Figure 4.15 panel *B*, compared to the original supply curve, *S1*, suppliers who receive the subsidy will supply extra bicycles at each price, which means the post-subsidy supply curve is *S2*.

With the new supply curve and no change in the demand curve a new equilibrium position arises with equilibrium price of $P^\wedge$ and equilibrium quantity of *Q2*. Since the new European supply curve intersects the demand curve at a price of $P^\wedge$ there is no longer any incentive to purchase from abroad, hence imports fall to zero.

Economists generally consider subsidies to be an inefficient use of society's resources. To see why this is so, look again at Figure 4.15 panel *B*. At a price of $P^\wedge$ on *S1* European suppliers wished to supply *Q1* bicycles. Once the subsidy is offered, however, this increases to *Q2*. From the cost-curve perspective this means because of the subsidy, firms' average cost curves have shifted downwards.

Suppliers who were unable to produce competitively at $P^\wedge$ prior to the subsidy have been attracted by the subsidy to bring some of their resources into the market. Without the subsidy the resources would be used in some other way and economists consider the best use of resources occurs when people freely react to the prices of products that emerge from markets where demand and supply are set by the market without government intervention.

The use of subsidies as shown here has become increasingly less prevalent for a number of reasons. Take the case where the foreign producers, unhappy at being 'shut out' of the European market, would probably complain to their own government who would retaliate by subsidizing some of their industries to keep some European products out of their markets. Such policies are not efficient because the situation where subsidies are paid to different industries in different countries creates artificial prices that provide poor signals within the economic system as to how best resources should be allocated to different uses.

There is also the argument that it is unfair to use subsidies to protect domestic markets and keep foreign products out, especially in the case of poorer countries that are attempting to develop economically via their agricultural and basic manufactured exports. Such countries may be unable to retaliate against subsidies, thus affecting their economic development (this argument is followed up in Chapter 9).

For these reasons industrial subsidies attract a lot of attention internationally and under the agreements signed by countries party to the World Trade Organization (WTO) agreements about the use of subsidies have been reached. WTO rules indicate that any subsidies on exports that distort trade are forbidden and while industry-specific subsidies that harm trade are not allowed either, it is sometimes difficult to differentiate between illegal subsidies and permitted practices like providing research assistance and support for taking new environmental technologies on board.

4.8.2 ENVIRONMENTAL TAXES – EFFECTS ON PRODUCTION

In the case of some industries that create pollution there is pressure, through the Kyoto Protocol for example, to regulate the amount of pollution created and reduce it where possible. (Named after the city in Japan where the agreement was signed, the Kyoto Protocol set national targets for greenhouse gas emissions.) Governments can influence pollution production by the process of limiting the quantities of pollutants allowed in products or by imposing taxes. The costs of pollution that are not borne by the firms that generate pollution and are external to the transactions that give rise to the pollution in the first instance are an example of what are known as externalities.

> **Externalities** – either positive or negative effects of a transaction by one set of parties on others who did not have a choice and whose interests were not taken into account.
>
>   Pollution is an example of a negative externality when producers have no incentive to take account of the pollution that is a by-product of production.
>
>   Expenditure on successful research and development may have positive externalities if firms learn the technological advances achieved and can put them into practice.

By imposing taxes on polluting firms, governments force them to take account of the pollution they create. Imposing taxes on producers of pollution increases their costs and pushes their cost curves upwards. The imposition of taxes would have consequences as shown in Figure 4.16.

Figure 4.16 panel *A* shows the equilibrium position for an industry that produces aerosol deodorants – which use CFC gases (chlorofluorocarbons) that are harmful to the environment due to damage they cause to the ozone layer – which is not legally bound to take the cost of the pollution it creates into account. Figure 4.16 panel *B* presents the situation for the same industry where the government has decided to tax the producers in an attempt to reduce pollution. The amount of the tax is measured as the vertical distance between *S1* and *S2*.

Because suppliers have to pay tax on every unit they produce, there is a wedge or difference between the price they receive and the revenue they can keep. When

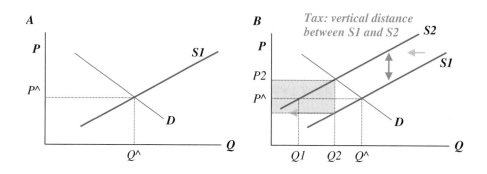

FIGURE 4.16   SUPPLY AND ENVIRONMENTAL TAXES

no tax must be paid (Figure 4.16 panel A), at a price of $P^\wedge$ suppliers were happy to supply $Q^\wedge$ in equilibrium. When the tax must be paid and if the market price of the product were $P^\wedge$, the producers would receive $P^\wedge$ less the tax. The reduced revenue received by the suppliers means they no longer have the incentive to supply the same quantity to the market. At the price of $P^\wedge$ on $S2$ in Figure 4.16 panel B, suppliers wish to supply $Q1$. Once a tax must be paid, suppliers wish to supply less output at every price, hence the new supply curve $S2$.

With the new supply curve and no change to the demand curve, a new equilibrium is the outcome with $P2$ a higher equilibrium price and $Q2$ a lower equilibrium quantity. We can see that although the tax is the vertical distance between $S1$ and $S2$, the price has not increased by the full value of the tax which means suppliers have not passed on the whole tax to the consumers. The amount of tax paid, or the tax revenue received by the government, is shown by the shaded rectangle in Figure 4.16 panel B, which is equal to the amount of the tax (vertical distance between $S1$ and $S2$) multiplied by the amount of goods bought and sold ($Q2$).

> If $Q2 = 27\,000$ units, $P2 = £50$ and the vertical distance between $S1$ and $S2$ is £20, the amount of tax paid is £540 000. If $Q^\wedge$ were 36 000, the decline in output resulting from the tax is 9000 units or 33%. If the amount of pollution is directly related to output, pollution will decline by 33% also.

Taxing a polluting industry results in a leftward shift of the supply curve. A new equilibrium ensures with a lower quantity of output and a higher tax-inclusive price.

4.8.3 TAX INCIDENCE

Tax incidence focuses on who ends up paying taxes. In the case of Figure 4.16 we see that when a tax is imposed the effects in equilibrium lead to a reduced level of output but at an increased price. The post-tax price of $P2$ is higher than the pre-tax price of $P^\wedge$; however, the price has not increased by the entire amount of the tax. A portion of the tax is paid by consumers via higher prices, but some of the tax is also absorbed by the producers. The incidence of tax falls approximately 66% on consumers (prices are 66% higher) and 34% on producers. Consumers pay £13.20 of the tax on each unit with producers absorbing the remaining £6.80.

The tax incidence or the degree to which taxes are paid by producers or consumers depends on demand and supply conditions reflected in demand and supply curves. Consider the case shown in Figure 4.17. In Figure 4.17 panel A, a tax has been imposed (the same amount as in Figure 4.16); however, the demand curve in this case is quite flat, indicating relatively higher consumer responsiveness to price changes.

The outcome after the tax is imposed is similar to the previous case. The supply curve moves left or upwards and a lower equilibrium quantity, $Q3$, is produced at a higher price, $P3$. The tax revenue generated for the government is shown as the shaded rectangle. With similar supply conditions, and the imposition of the same tax (£20 per unit), but a flatter, more price elastic demand curve the increase in equilibrium price is less than in Figure 4.16. The quantity decline is greater and the tax incidence is not the same. Here the tax incidence falls more on producers than consumers as the price consumers pay has risen from $P^\wedge$ to $P3$ which is approximately 40% of the tax (£8 per unit); hence producers absorb the difference of 60% (£12 per unit). If $Q3$ is 20 000 units, the tax revenue collected is £400 000.

If suppliers did not absorb a large proportion of the tax, the fall in equilibrium quantity would be much larger, as shown in Figure 4.17 panel B. Here the demand

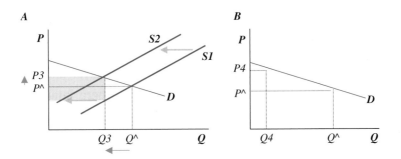

FIGURE 4.17 TAX INCIDENCE

curve is presented and the pre-tax price $P^\wedge$ is shown along with *P4* where *P4* represents the tax-inclusive price that would prevail if suppliers passed on the full cost of the tax to their customers. The quantity on the demand curve corresponding to the full tax-inclusive price is *Q4*. The quantity *Q4* is substantially less than $Q^\wedge$ or *Q3*. Thus, suppliers react by absorbing some of the tax because they know their market and appreciate how price-sensitive their consumers are.

The more price-sensitive consumers are, *ceteris paribus*, the greater the proportion of a tax that suppliers are willing to absorb. High price-sensitivity is reflected in a relatively flat demand function.

4.9 SUMMARY

- The contribution of the business sector (the supply component of the demand and supply model) within the economic system is substantial.
- We assume firms operate in order to maximize their *economic* profits.
- Firms decide on the amount to produce and what price to charge for their output to maximize their profit. A useful distinction for examining some of the most important decisions firms must make is between short- and long-run decisions.
- To decide on the profit-maximizing level of output requires some analyses of the general patterns exhibited by firms' costs and revenues, i.e. total, average and marginal.
- A supply-side welfare perspective is possible by examining the concept of producer surplus.
- Economic decision-making by suppliers in response to price changes can be analysed using the price elasticity of supply.
- Firms' investment behaviour has a direct bearing on both the state and growth of a country's capital stock. Several factors feed into firms' investment decisions.
- Governments affect firms' supply decisions in many ways. Examples presented here refer to subsidies, shown here for an industry where international trade is conducted, and environmental taxes. Both are analysed using the Demand and Supply framework.
- The effect of government intervention when taxes are imposed can be analysed using the tax incidence approach.

REVIEW PROBLEMS AND QUESTIONS

1. Identify which of the following are short-run decisions and which are long-run decisions for a business. Explain your rationale in each case.

   a. hiring one extra worker,   c. building an extension to a factory,
   b. buying a new computer,   d. producing 20% more output.

2. Grandon's Nursery sells roses and their demand curve is presented below.
   a. Compute total and marginal revenue that correspond to the demand information in the table below.
   b. Sketch the company's demand, total revenue and marginal revenue curves.

Price	Demand	Total Revenue	Marginal Revenue
20	0		
15	25		
12.5	37.5		
10	50		
7.5	62.5		
5	75		
0	100		

3. Information on Grandon's costs are presented below.
   a. Using the table below and data from question 2, decide on the profitable level of output for the firm. Hint: you need to compute marginal costs.
   b. Sketch marginal revenue and marginal cost on one graph.

Output	Total costs	Average cost	Marginal cost
0	100		
25	325		
37.5	337.5		
50	425		
62.5	525		
75	750		

4. a. If Grandon's fixed costs are £80, compute Grandon's Average Fixed Costs and Average Variable Costs.
   b. Graph Total Average Costs, Average Fixed Costs and Average Variable Costs on one graph. Comment on how the three sets of costs are related.

5. Given the profitable level of output for Grandon's you chose in question 3, what price should the firm charge for its roses?
   a. Does the firm earn profits at this price?
   b. Are supernormal profits earned?
   c. Explain if the firm should charge either a higher or lower price.

6. Consider that Grandon's can produce their profit-maximizing level of output.
   a. How would you expect Grandon's to react in terms of their supply if they could increase the price they receive by 12.5% in one month's time?
   b. How would you expect Grandon's to react in terms of their supply if they could increase the price they receive by 12.5% in six month's time?

7. As part of a government policy to boost the horticultural industry, a subsidy is to be paid to all nurseries growing organic products. Grandon's nursery receives a subsidy of 12.5%.
   a. Show, using a diagram, the effect of the subsidy on Grandon's supply of roses.
   b. What is the impact of the subsidy on Grandon's equilibrium price and quantity of roses?
   c. Do you think this policy makes good use of the resources available to the Government?

8. Read the following brief case study and answer the questions that follow.

The grey market for cars

Based on the principal of comparative advantage, economists agree that free trade improves welfare. An example of trade is the substantial number of cars, both used and new, imported into the EU each year, which are known as grey or parallel imports. Such grey imports are a feature across many different product markets. Parallel imports/grey imports occur where the goods of a particular producer are imported into a particular territory by a third party in competition with the licensed distributor in that territory. They are called grey imports in allusion to the 'black' market as grey products are sometimes considered to be legally questionable. Producers are usually not in favour of grey imports citing that goods that are distributed through 'normal' distribution channels are targeted and correspond to the needs of buyers in the markets for which they are designed.

Consumers are sometimes happy to buy grey products because they cost less than 'the real thing' but problems can occur later when they realize that grey products may not meet the standards of the same product that was designed for their market. This is certainly the argument put forward by car manufacturers and there are countless examples of issues relating to grey car imports: lack of warranty – because the specification of the car is different for different markets, failure to meet national emission standards, fewer features, failure to meet crash-test standards of domestic cars, etc. Consumers argue that because suppliers try to charge different prices for the same product in different countries (see the case study at the end of Chapter 3), the consumer is right to attempt to source the product legally from another market.

Governments appear to be unable to agree on a consistent approach to the resolution of whether parallel imports are justified or not. Therefore, it is left to intellectual property rights to determine the position (intellectual property refers to intangible property that includes patents, trademarks, copyright and any registered or unregistered design rights).

a. Use demand and supply analysis to consider how trade has an impact on welfare – consider the affects of trade on both consumer and producer surplus.

b. Show, using demand and supply analysis, the impact of grey imports on the market for standard (non grey-import) cars.

c. Why do you think suppliers (car manufacturers) are unhappy with grey imports – are they not still managing to sell their cars?

FURTHER READING AND RESEARCH

There is a rich variety of accessible academic research on supply, firms and firm behaviour. A *brief* selection is cited below, all of which are worth reading, but which focus on different aspects of firms' purpose or functions in the economic system.

Coase, 1937; Williamson, 1991; Jensen and Meckling, 1976; Foss, 1997; Penrose, 1955.

REFERENCES

Coase, R. (1937) 'The nature of the firm', *Economica*, **4**, 386–485.

Foss, N. (1997) 'Austrian insights and the theory of the firm', *Advances in Austrian Economics*, **4**, 175–198.

Jensen, M. and W. Meckling (1976) 'Theory of the firm: managerial behavior, agency costs, and ownership structure', *Journal of Financial Economics*, **3**(4), 305–360.

Penrose, E. (1955) 'Limits to the growth and size of firms', *American Economic Review*, **15**(2), 531–543.

Williamson, O. (1991) 'The logic of economic organization', in Williamson, O. and Winter, S. G. (eds), *The Nature of the Firm – Origins, evolution, and development*. Oxford University Press.

CHAPTER 5

ECONOMIC ACTIVITY: THE MACROECONOMY

LEARNING OUTCOMES

By the end of the chapter you should be able to:

○ Explain how income and resources circulate in an economy between consumers, firms, government, financial and international sectors using the circular flow of income model.
○ Describe and sketch the business cycle of short-run output trends.
○ Discuss causes of business cycles and their implications for government and business.
○ List the components of real output.
○ Compare alternative approaches to measuring 'real' economic activity: relating personal income and national output/product.
○ Apply the aggregate demand (AD) and aggregate supply (AS) model to:
  ● determine equilibrium economic activity and aggregate prices;
  ● analyse how changes in aggregate demand and supply affect equilibrium.
○ Apply the concept of the multiplier to assess the effect on equilibrium economic activity of changes in planned expenditure.
○ Examine government's effect on economic activity via government expenditure, budget, deficit and debt.
○ Apply a production function approach to analysing economic activity.

5.1 INTRODUCTION

Economic activity for an economy is the outcome of the various decisions taken by consumers (households), firms at home and abroad, and government; in other words the sum of $C + I + G + (X - M)$. When the value of economic activity is analysed over time, it follows a cyclical pattern in the sense that short periods of growth in economic activity have been followed by periods of contraction and the pattern is observed across all developed economies over the last century.

One approach to examining economic activity is to consider the flow of income generated within an economy over a specific period such as a year, a quarter, a month, etc. using the circular flow model as presented in section 5.2. This allows for analysis of the various sources and destinations of flows of income and resources around an economy. From analysis of such income flows over time, short-term fluctuations in economic activity are evident and are referred to as the business cycle, which is examined in section 5.3 (economic growth over the longer term is considered separately in Chapter 9). Economic debate on the possible causes of the cyclical pattern in output is also addressed.

The components of economic activity defined according to expenditure categories $(C + I + G + [X - M])$ are considered in section 5.4 and alternative measures of economic activity based on value-added and income methods are also presented. In section 5.5 a model is introduced that helps to understand how macroeconomic equilibrium economic activity is reached. Using this model of aggregate demand and aggregate supply the equilibrium effects of changes of either aggregate demand or supply can be considered. In section 5.6 the multiplier – an important feature of this model – is examined in some detail. This analysis provides information as to how changes in expenditure have repercussions in an economy that can give rise to changes in equilibrium output and prices. The contribution of international trade in economic activity is examined in section 5.7. In section 5.8 an alternative and equally valid model for considering aggregate economic activity is presented and its main features are discussed.

5.2 ECONOMIC ACTIVITY AND THE CIRCULAR FLOW

Economic activity over any period is the result of all the decisions of the many different economic units in an economy over that period – consumers (households), firms at home and abroad, and government. Production and consumption are the results of the various transactions between these groups, as they buy and sell their goods and services, labour and financial assets. These transactions are shown in Figure 5.1.

> **The circular flow** denotes all transactions in the economic system describing how products, services, resources and money flow around the economic system.

Beginning with the market for products and services, we see that goods and services flow from firms to households (consumers). In payment for the goods and services money flows from consumers back to firms. The government also buys some goods

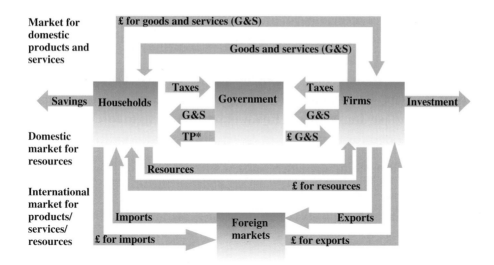

FIGURE 5.1 THE CIRCULAR FLOW OF INCOME, RESOURCES AND OUTPUT

*TP denotes transfer payments, explained further below.

and services from firms and pays for them while the government also provides some goods and services to households, which are partly paid for in the form of taxes paid to it by households and firms. Many of the goods provided to households by government are called public goods, as outlined in Chapter 1. When government provides goods or services that the private sector is unwilling to provide, this is known as market failure since the market incentives do not exist that entice private firms to supply (this issue is further discussed in Chapter 6).

An additional transaction involves the government making transfer payments to households. These are payments made to individuals who are not part of the production process, i.e. they do not supply either capital or labour to the economic system. These payments include unemployment benefit, pensions, disability payments, income supplement programmes and subsidies. They are called transfer payments since the government transfers some of the money paid to it by firms and consumers (via taxes) to those who qualify for the payments due to their age, level of income, or economic status. Incidentally, to avoid counting transfer payments twice in national income, the receipts of the government count in national income, since they are derived from the income of individuals and firms, but not the transfer payments themselves.

Moving to the market for resources, this refers to the various factors of production used by firms to produce their output. For example, households supply their labour resource to firms and receive payments in return. Out of households' savings in banks and other financial institutions, firms can also borrow and thus some firms' capital is also derived from households' resources.

The final set of transactions conducted in the circular flow involves foreign markets. Imports are purchased from foreign markets and payments are sent to the foreign markets to pay for them and finally exports are sent to foreign markets and payments are received for them.

In the circular flow of income, **injections** of income into the flow include:

- investment expenditure by firms;
- government expenditure;
- income earned as payment for exports.

Leakages of income out of the circular flow include:

- savings;
- taxes;
- income paid for imported goods.

Although not mentioned explicitly in Figure 5.1, the financial sector, which consists of banks and various national and international financial institutions, plays a role in facilitating transactions within the economic system. The role of this sector in the economic system is considered in more detail in Chapter 7.

Underlying the two-dimensional representation of the circular flow in Figure 5.1 are all the varied and complex institutions that support and underlie its activities. These include (in no specific order) the local, domestic and international financial systems, systems of corporate governance, legal and political environments, social and cultural background, technological capability and the myriad standards, business and personal ethics, and codes of conduct that are embedded in the economic system. Keeping these in mind helps us to better understand the functioning of the various resource, factor and money markets that are outlined in the circular flow diagram.

5.3   REAL OUTPUT AND THE BUSINESS CYCLE

Economies across the world appear to follow cycles in their production.

Graphing countries' output over time reveals **business cycles** – a tendency for *real output* to rise and fall over time in a reasonably regular pattern.

As explained in Chapter 1, economists focus on real output because it provides a more accurate picture of how much an economy produces in quantity terms over time than the actual or current value of output. Quoting values in *real terms* effectively means that the effect of price changes is removed and only quantity or real effects remain.

Examining real output trends in Figure 5.2, we see that periods of growth in real output are followed by declines in growth. There are periods when real output

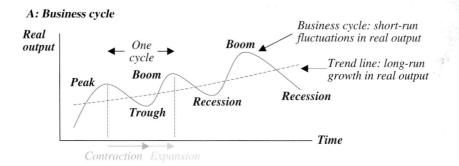

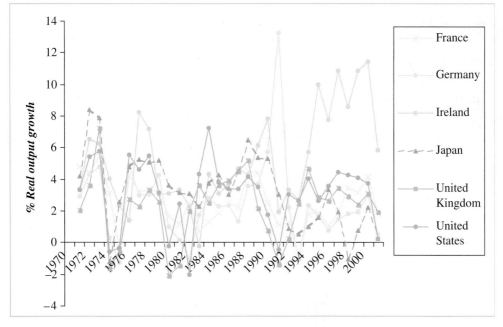

FIGURE 5.2 PATTERNS IN REAL OUTPUT – THE BUSINESS CYCLE

Source: (Panel *B*) International Financial Statistics of the International Monetary Fund

grows quickly and when this growth slows down in a cyclical fashion. The length of a business cycle is measured from peak to peak (also described as boom to boom) where peaks imply the summit of growth of real output. Following a peak/boom although growth remains above its long-run trend for a period, it eventually begins to slow down or contracts. Over time the growth rate falls below the long-run trend and the contraction becomes a recession (trough). The next phase corresponds to the growth rate expanding and ultimately the expansion brings the economy into another boom. Over the course of a business cycle, firms are not always operating at full capacity as there is not always sufficient demand to meet their planned supply. The business cycle is a short- to medium-term phenomenon and usually, although not always, *booms* (periods of high or fast growth) or *recessions* (periods of slow or sometimes negative growth) last months rather than years.

In comparing Figure 5.2 panels *A* and *B* it is clear that observed business cycles are not as regular as the stylized or model case. However, we see that booms are invariably followed by recessions although the regularity varies from cycle to cycle. From examining the average periods for economic expansions and contractions, economists have concluded that economies spend more time in the expansion phase (lasting three to five years) rather than the contractionary phase (lasting around one year) of business cycles.

While business cycles are observed in the short to medium term, long-run growth follows an upward trend. A graph of real output over the last century, for example, shows that internationally real output grew on average by over 3% per annum. This means that the *quantity of output* produced internationally increased each year by approximately 3%. Since 3% is an average figure, growth was lower in some periods and higher in others depending on the prevailing business cycle. Sometimes output is above the long-run trend (if an economy is booming, workers may be working a lot of overtime and capital equipment may be used at more than recommended full capacity) and at other times it lies below trend. If output is below trend an output gap is said to exist.

> **The output gap** is the difference between **potential output** (also known as full employment output) and actual output.

To figure out whether long-run economic growth was of benefit in welfare terms we would need to figure out whether the international population grew faster or slower than 3%. If population growth were also 3%, then the growth in output just kept pace with the population and average living standards would be unchanged. In other words people, on average, were no better or worse off (*ceteris paribus*). If population growth were 1%, then output growth exceeded population growth and people experienced a welfare improvement. This issue is considered again in Chapter 9. (See exercise 5 at the end of this chapter to draw a conclusion regarding the welfare effects of growth.)

5.3.1 EXPLANATIONS/CAUSES OF BUSINESS CYCLES

The question of what causes business cycles is of interest to economists since one of their challenges is to advise on how to increase real output. Because of the interdependent nature of the economic system, an economic shock could have adverse consequences on elements in the system that lead to the cyclical pattern observed in real output.

> An **economic shock** is an *unexpected* event that affects the economy.
>
> Some economic shocks affect *one economy or a part of one economy more* than other economies or other parts of an economy. Such shocks would be described as asymmetric shocks. For example, oil price shocks affect countries dependent on imported oil more than others and affect manufacturing firms more than services firms.

Central to the pattern of business cycles are people's perceptions of what is happening in their local, domestic and international environments and their expectations of what will happen in the future. In terms of trying to identify specific causes of business cycles economists have put forward a number of possibilities but no single source can be identified. In fact some economists view business cycles as the efficient reaction of markets to new information or events somewhere in the economic system while others view them as a signal that markets are not operating efficiently.

Contractions and recessions may be caused by consumers, who fear a future downturn where unemployment will become a problem and who prefer to hold on to more of their income rather than to spend. In such circumstances a recession could arguably be caused by a change in demand or consumer expenditure. However, the ultimate cause would be the information that led to the initial change in demand. This could be because firms' output becomes difficult to sell as it is too expensive and not competitive either at home or abroad (for export goods) and so firms cut back on production. Or maybe firms cut back on their investment expenditure because they are pessimistic about the demand for goods and services in the future (and hence their future profits) or because the loans they need to take out for investment are too expensive. Booms could be explained by opposite economic effects.

Particular features of the nature of investment might serve to exacerbate business cycles. There is much evidence to indicate that much of the investment undertaken by individual firms is 'lumpy', meaning it is discrete and takes place occasionally rather than steadily. If different firms make their investments at the same time as others, investment activity will be decidedly cyclical. Rising productivity levels in firms may also drive investment since increases in current output will put upward pressure on the amount of capital equipment required to produce the output and on capital requiring replacement or renewal. As mentioned in Chapter 4, investment is the most volatile component of national income.

The explanation of cycles may also have some relationship to cycles in governments, which change regularly – every five years or so if no early elections are called – and often patterns of political business cycles are observed. Before elections there is a lot of evidence to indicate that incumbent governments try to present themselves in the best possible light with their electorate by announcing extra government spending, or tax cuts, or both which would boost economic activity. The new government must then deal with any pre-election spending, which might require cutbacks later, contributing to a cycle of economic activity.

Variation in the money supply in an economy represents another potential cause of business cycles. While the money market is discussed in detail in Chapter 7, what we can say here is that central banks' decisions about how much money to supply to an economy has an effect on an economy's interest rate (which is the price of money); and the interest rate, in turn, is assumed to feed into firms' decisions about production and employment. An alternative view (of proponents of real business cycle theory) is that changes in money supply and interest rates are reactions to changes in output and/or employment. Real business cycle (RBC) theory is quite a recent approach to explaining business cycles.

Real business cycle theory is based on the view that changes in technology, long considered to provide an explanation for long-run economic growth (and expansion of the PPF), also explain business cycles.

The deterioration in technology that followed the oil price shocks of the 1970s meant that the standard production technology became substantially and unexpectedly more expensive over a short period of time due to increased energy costs.

Such unexpected and adverse technology shocks change the decisions of

- firms that wish to cut back on costly production and attempt to pass on the price increases to customers;
- consumers who demand higher wages to compensate them for price increases and who plan to spend less when faced with such price increases;
- investors who reduce planned investment since they are pessimistic about a future of high energy prices.

Under such circumstances the market signals lead to reductions in employment, low wage increases (if any), and reduced investment. A positive technological change would have quite the opposite effects. Because of its technology-based approach, RBC theory offers a supply-side explanation for business cycles.

There are many similarities between the relatively new RBC theories and the creative destruction explanation of the economic system put forward by the Austrian economist Joseph Schumpeter (e.g. in 1911 and 1939). Schumpeter's view of economic development centred on the role of the entrepreneur whose function in the economic system involved spontaneous and persistent (but irregular) introductions of innovations. Schumpeter linked the business cycle to the process of innovation in an economy. When inventors or entrepreneurs try to launch new products they often meet resistance but if a profitable opportunity is exploited imitation is likely with new variants of successful products being launched in imitation of successful first-movers. Production rises until the market becomes saturated and an economic downturn is experienced until the next wave of innovation and new products come along and the process repeats itself again. To fund such innovation requires the supply of credit to entrepreneurs, which highlights the role of the financial system in innovation and economic development. Entrepreneurs relying on bank loans are found in clusters within the economic system and as successful innovations emerge economies experience booms, while recession phases occur as the economy deals with creative destruction as described by Schumpeter (1975).

> As we have seen in the preceding chapter, the contents of the labourer's budget, say from 1760 to 1940, did not simply grow on unchanging lines but they underwent a process of qualitative change. Similarly, the history of the productive apparatus of a typical farm, from the beginnings of the rationalization of crop rotation, plowing and fattening to the mechanized thing of today – linking up with elevators and railroads – is a history of revolutions. So is the history of the productive apparatus of the iron and steel industry from the charcoal furnace to our own type of furnace, or the history of

the apparatus of power production from the overshot water wheel to the modern power plant, or the history of transportation from the mailcoach to the airplane. The opening up of new markets, foreign or domestic, and the organizational development from the craft shop and factory to such concerns as U.S. Steel illustrate the same process of industrial mutation – if I may use that biological term – that incessantly revolutionizes the economic structure *from within*, incessantly destroying the old one, incessantly creating a new one. This process of Creative Destruction is the essential fact about capitalism. It is what capitalism consists in and what every capitalist concern has got to live in. (Schumpeter, 1975, pp. 82–85)

An alternative view – that business cycles are indicative of markets failing to work – is attributed to John Maynard Keynes who wrote *The General Theory of Employment Interest and Money* (1936). Writing in the aftermath of the Great Depression of 1929–1932, the focus of Keynes's work was on explaining how economies might in some circumstances be unable to prevent themselves from addressing the joint problems of low output and high unemployment and might need some intervention by governments to help them proceed and grow. Economists argue regarding which, if any, markets should be aided by government – goods markets where there may be insufficient competition, examined later in Chapter 6, or labour markets if wages are too high, examined in Chapter 8. There are also arguments that the financial sector through providing insufficient credit represents another example of market failure and any one or all three markets failing to operate as they should could provide an explanation for business cycles.

Economists have come a long way from the sunspot theory expounded in the nineteenth century by Jevons, who believed that storms on the sun, observed through telescopes as sunspots, caused crop failures. Since the nineteenth century economy was heavily organized around agricultural production, sunspots were considered an explanation for low production and recessions. Better harvests were associated with booms. This sunspot theory of business cycles had no basis in fact but since it was the initial focus on the question of what causes business cycles, it still receives economists' attention. As Benjamin Franklin said, 'A question is halfway to wisdom.'

To date, economists have come up with many theories, some of them competing, that provide explanations for business cycles. Despite the lack of agreement on any single cause, what economists appear to agree on is that people's expectations of what will happen in the future (firms, consumers, government) underlie the pattern displayed in real output.

5.3.2 IMPLICATIONS FOR BUSINESS AND GOVERNMENT

The fact that business cycles appear as regular short/medium-run features of economies means that business and government are regularly faced with them. Businesses must take account of them in their planning cycles and in the development and execution of their business strategies. Declines or increases in sales should not be interpreted as major strategic problems if they are just part of a business cycle, but a business must somehow be able to analyse whether such a feature is simply a reflection of a business cycle or a symptom of a more serious problem that must be identified for their firm to retain and improve its competitive position.

Firms need to manage their production and inventories in the knowledge that there will be cycles in demand, sales and profits, over which they have little if any control. In managing their factors of production, management of labour is vitally important. Firms may need to reduce output, which will sometimes require making people redundant. In doing so they must try to ensure minimal adverse impact to their reputation as they may well require additional staff once the economy experiences its next boom period. Given that many countries' labour laws are quite strict regarding redundancies and labour regulations generally, letting workers go is not easy in many situations, which sets constraints on firms' flexibility in dealing with the business cycle.

As well as the argument that governments may play a role in causing business cycles, governments are also faced with the challenge of dealing with them. Governments attempt to manage expenditures and tax revenues in their economies, where the business cycle creates some problems. For example, in recessions, when unemployment rises, governments will pay out substantial amounts in benefits and at the same time receive fewer tax receipts as economic activity slows down, and may find that it must borrow to meet its requirements. The hope would be that, when the recession ends and economic growth recommences, enough resources are raised through taxes and reduced benefits to cover the costs of any borrowing. How governments try to deal with business cycles is discussed further below and again later in Chapter 8.

5.4 REAL OUTPUT AND ITS COMPONENTS

Any estimate of economic activity, whether over the short or long run, involves measuring the total value of the flow of income/output generated by an economy over a specific period. The definition of economic activity presented in Chapter 3 corresponds to real output if all components are in real terms, i.e. real output (Y_r) consists of real consumption (C_r) plus real investment (I_r) plus real government expenditure (G_r) plus real net exports $(X_r - M_r)$ as follows;

$$\text{Real economic activity: } Y_r = C_r + I_r + G_r + (X_r - M_r)$$

This approach to measuring economic activity is called the *expenditure approach* as it consists of summing up the various parts of economic expenditures by consumers, firms and government. This measure of economic activity is called *gross domestic product* (GDP).

> **Gross domestic product (GDP)** is a location-based measure of economic activity. It measures the value of real output produced in an economy

Not all real output remains in the economy where it is produced creating a wedge between the values of real output produced and earned by the citizens of a country. Profit repatriation may occur where foreign companies send some of their profits back to their headquarters in their home country. Property income from abroad may be earned by citizens earning returns on assets they own in other countries. When real output takes all the flows of real output to and from an economy into account, *gross national product (GNP)* is measured.

> **Gross national product (GNP)** is the value of real output that is retained by the citizens in a country after all inflows and outflows are allowed for.
>   The difference between GDP and GNP is called **net property income from abroad**.

If a country's net income flows from abroad are positive, then inflows exceed outflows and GNP is greater than GDP. If net income flows are negative, GDP is greater than GNP. For most countries the difference between GDP and GNP is minor, although countries that have many multinational companies that repatriate substantial profits usually experience a large wedge between GDP and GNP (GDP is larger than GNP). Since both GDP and GNP are used to measure economic activity nationally and internationally it is worth remembering the distinction between them.

> GNP is also called **gross national income (GNI)**, since national economic activity is the same whether measured in terms of output (the *product* in GNP) or income that is generated by citizens providing their factor resources to markets for payment.

5.4.1 OTHER MEASURES OF ECONOMIC ACTIVITY

The income method and the value-added method are alternative approaches to measuring economic activity. The income method involves summing up all income received by an economy's citizens in payment for supplying resources to the economy. Payments of wages or salaries are received by owners of labour, interest by owners of capital, rent by owners of land, and profit by those who apply their entrepreneurial ability successfully. In each country's national accounts (published annually or in many cases also quarterly) the corresponding income categories are called employee compensation, interest, corporate profit, rental income and proprietors' income. Summing up these payments gives us an estimate of national income.

The value-added method involves summing up the value added by different economic units (usually firms) as products or services are provided for the market. In the example in Table 5.1 four firms are involved in the transactions that produce wooden tables. Initially the tree grower sells trees to a sawmill for processing. The tree grower receives £125 from the mill for each tree it produces. Once the mill transforms the tree into planks of wood, the value of the wooden planks bought by a carpenter is £200. The value added by the sawmill is £75 (£200 − £125). Once the carpenter transforms the planks to tables, their value has risen to £550. The carpenter has added value of £350 to the planks he bought (£550 − £200). The carpenter supplies the tables to a furniture shop which sells the tables for £1000 adding value of another £450.

If the market values of each transaction are added up the total is £1875 while totting up value added gives rise to £1000. In assessing the value of economic activity, value added is the relevant amount to be considered because summing up the value of each transaction gives rise to double counting. For example, payment

TABLE 5.1 VALUE ADDED

Firm	Product	Market value	Value added by firm
Tree grower	Trees	£125	£125
Sawmill	Wood planks	£200	£75
Carpentry firm	Tables	£550	£350
Furniture shop	Tables	£1000	£450
Total		*£1875*	*£1000*

for the planks sold by the sawmill for £200 includes the payment to the tree grower of £125. To avoid double counting, the value of intermediate goods is ignored in computing the value of economic activity.

> **Intermediate goods** are sold by firms to other firms and are used in making final goods (goods that are not resold to other firms).
> **Final goods** are not purchased for further processing or resale but for final use.

In measuring national economic activity it is the total value of all final goods and services produced in an economy over a specified period that is of interest. In theory, whether economic activity is measured using the expenditure, income or value-added method, the same amount of activity is measured. In practice, some statistical discrepancies are common due to how data are collected.

5.4.2 ECONOMIC ACTIVITY: GNP, GDP AND INCOME

The relationship between measures of economic activity is illustrated in Figure 5.3 where it is possible to see at a glance the components of the different measures and their relationship to each other.

Beginning on the left of Figure 5.3 in column 1, GNP and GNI are presented. The relationship between GNP (GNI) and GDP is clear from the first two columns,

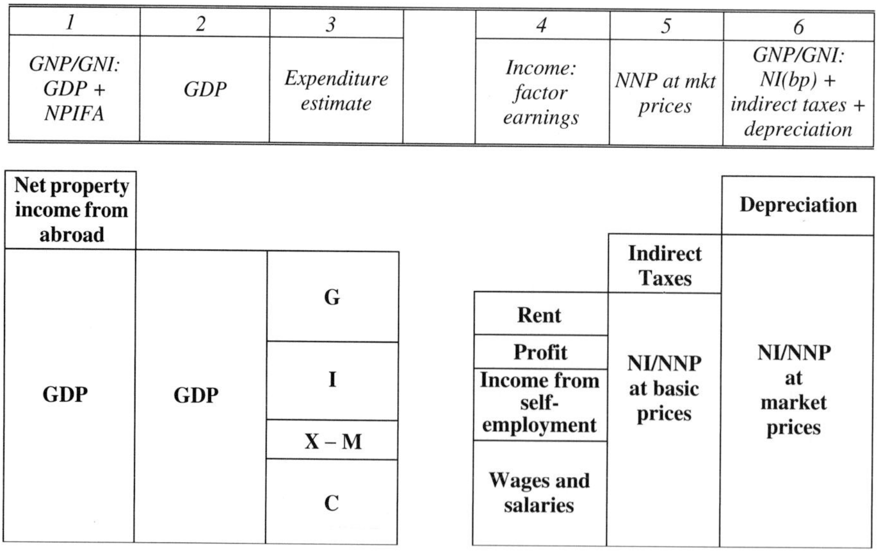

1	2	3		4	5	6
GNP/GNI: GDP + NPIFA	GDP	Expenditure estimate		Income: factor earnings	NNP at mkt prices	GNP/GNI: NI(bp) + indirect taxes + depreciation
Net property income from abroad						**Depreciation**
		G			**Indirect Taxes**	
				Rent		
		I		**Profit**	**NI/NNP at basic prices**	**NI/NNP at market prices**
GDP	**GDP**			**Income from self-employment**		
		X – M				
		C		**Wages and salaries**		

FIGURE 5.3 COMPARATIVE MEASURES OF ECONOMIC ACTIVITY

which show that GNP is made up of GDP plus net property income from abroad (assuming NPIFA is a net inflow into the economy). If NPIFA is a net outflow then GDP would be greater than GNP. Figure 5.3 column 3 shows the expenditure components of GDP. Next we see that the sum of income (factor earnings) plus indirect taxes add up to national income at market prices, which include indirect taxes. Basic prices exclude indirect taxes.

Indirect taxes are paid on expenditure whereas **direct taxes** are paid on income.

Adding on the value of *depreciation* to NI (national income) at market prices provides a measure of GNP or GNI. Depreciation is included because it is the rate at which the capital stock is reduced each year (for annual accounts) due to wear and tear.

If economic activity of £100bn is generated in a year, the economy 'loses' some of its capital stock since it deteriorates over the year and *net* measures of economic activity subtract the value of depreciation from measured economic activity.

To summarize, there are several measures of economic activity and sometimes it is necessary to decide which is most suited to a particular purpose. GDP is generally accepted as a sound measure but for countries where a significant amount of net property income flows to or from abroad, GNP might be a more appropriate measure. There are several ways to compute GNP (adding indirect taxes and depreciation to national income at basic prices or adding net factor inflows from abroad to the components of GDP) but irrespective of which method is used the same measure is being estimated.

WHAT GNP OR GDP DO NOT MEASURE

Not all economic activity is measured and reported in national statistics. A **black economy** is said to exist where people do not declare income for tax purposes and hence the activity is not accounted for in national statistics. The extent of hidden economic activity varies across countries and some countries are culturally more comfortable with not reporting income than others.

Some economic activity goes unmeasured if not unnoticed because it is unpaid. Stay-at-home women/men who take over childcare or household duties for no pay do not have their contribution to economic activity measured although the value of their activity could be measured by using estimates of market costs for childcare and housekeeping.

Arguably the production of pollution, noise, and congestion should be deducted from measured economic activity since they are also part of economic activity but represent negative outcomes. However, this would be difficult to put into practice since there is wide debate about how to decide on the value of their output or to place a cost on it. Hence, measures of economic activity are not perfect but do provide us with some information about economic activity and allow us to make comparisons across countries and for countries and regions over time.

5.5 EQUILIBRIUM ECONOMIC ACTIVITY

Different methods can be used to estimate the value of economic activity. An interesting question arises as to what determines whether a country's economic activity is relatively high or low. Many economists enter the discipline with a desire to understand better how to encourage higher rather than lower economic activity. Another way of thinking about the same question is to try to imagine what factors generate high expenditure on each of the components of economic activity, i.e. C, I, G, $X - M$.

Having considered short-term business cycle fluctuations in economic activity it is also possible to think about modelling equilibrium economic activity, the long-run trend. This involves assessing those factors we think are the most important determinants of economic activity. A number of different approaches have been used to examine the determinants of economic activity. It is necessary to identify whether the issue of interest is:

- the determination of the level of economic activity; or
- the determination of growth in economic activity;

as the determinants are related but not exactly the same in both cases. In this chapter we focus on the first issue and return in Chapter 9 to the second.

At the level of an economy, analysis of both the demand and supply is required to consider equilibrium economic activity. However, different concepts are used to examine demand and supply in relation to national economic activity compared to those we have met so far.

National economic activity is the sum of activity by all of the economic decision-makers including households, producers and government. For this reason it is also called **aggregate economic activity.**

Aggregate economic activity is examined by using the concepts of aggregate demand and aggregate supply and an examination of equilibrium economic activity requires both.

5.5.1   THE PRICE LEVEL

Aggregate supply (AS) is the amount of output firms are willing to supply at different price levels.

The price level of interest for aggregate economic activity is, not surprisingly, aggregate prices. National statistics providers collect information about prices on a regular basis using survey techniques and estimate the average price level, which is a weighted average of the prices of all goods and services. Taking a simple example, if citizens' main expenditure is 30% on food, 25% on clothing and 45% on entertainment and if in 2002 and 2003 average prices of food, clothing and entertainment are as shown in Table 5.2, the change in price level can be estimated.

If the average price level rises, **inflation** is observed while if average prices fall, **deflation** occurs. (Inflation is discussed further in Chapter 8.)

TABLE 5.2   AVERAGE PRICE LEVELS AND INFLATION – AN EXAMPLE

	Food	Clothing	Entertainment	Total
Value of expenditure 2002 (2002 prices)	5150	2850	3250	11 250
Value of expenditure 2003 (2003 prices)	5325	2915	3450	11 690
A: Weights* × 2002 prices	1545	712.5	1462.5	3720
B: Weights × 2003 prices	1597.5	728.75	1552.5	3878.75
Inflation rate ((**B** − **A**)/**A**)*100	3.40%	2.28%	6.15%	4.27%

Note: *Weights used are those given in the text: 30% on food, 25% on clothing and 45% and are assumed to be the same for 2002 and 2003.

While we know there is no such aggregate good as 'food', we can consider that it is made up of rice, pasta, cheese, fruit, etc. – a representative basket of goods bought by the 'average' person. We can further assume that an 'average' price for all the various components of 'food' can be computed with information on expenditure shares. Similarly for an aggregate good such as 'clothing' or 'entertainment'.

In Table 5.2 the prices of the same amounts of the same goods are measured in both years so a like-with-like comparison can be made. In practice, this is almost impossible to implement since many goods are not exactly the same from month to month or year to year. The quality of food goods might increase or decline or different materials might be used in clothing, for example. In trying to measure price levels over time, however, we assume that quality is reasonably similar to allow reasonable comparisons to be made.

The level of average prices is shown for each year in rows 4 and 5 of Table 5.2. The *same quantities* of goods that cost £3720 in 2002 cost £3878.75 in 2003. This indicates that the average level of prices went up. The extent of the increase is found by measuring the increase in the average price levels between 2002 and 2003 and expressing it as a percentage of the average price level in 2002.

Thus, the annual inflation rate for the economy is computed as 4.27%, with components for each of food, clothing and entertainment as shown. Inflation was highest in entertainment and lowest in clothing. Inflation is often measured using the *consumer price index*, which is essentially a weighted average of a comprehensive list of the prices of goods and services taking into account their shares in expenditure. It is a more complex but essentially similar process to the example in Table 5.2.

5.5.2 AGGREGATE DEMAND

Aggregate demand is the demand for output (of all goods and services) at different price levels.

Demand for output can be thought of in terms of the demand for consumption, investment, government and traded goods (remember $C, I, G, X - M$). *As a result the aggregate demand curve is a far more complex concept than the demand curves considered so far.* This becomes evident when considering its shape and how it is derived. Before examining aggregate demand, it is necessary first to understand the link between aggregate expenditure and aggregate demand, shown in Figure 5.4.

Figure 5.4 panel *A* shows two *aggregate expenditure* functions which graph planned expenditure against national income (Y): planned expenditure consists of $C, I, G, X - M$.

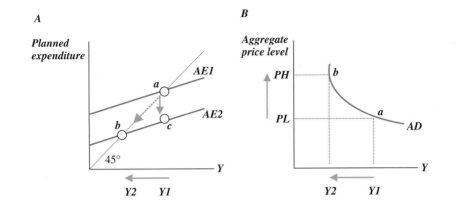

FIGURE 5.4 AGGREGATE EXPENDITURE AND AGGREGATE DEMAND

An **aggregate expenditure function** indicates total planned expenditure in an economy for different levels of income or output (denoted Y).

The aggregate expenditure functions slope upwards indicating that the higher national income (Y), the higher planned expenditure. This makes sense since plans to spend depend on income and the higher (lower) income is, the higher (lower) planned spending will be.

Each aggregate expenditure function is drawn for a specific price level so we can see citizens', firms' and government's expenditure plans at different levels of income for one specific price level. If the price level changes, people's planned expenditures change too. In the case of an increase in the price level, planned aggregate expenditure falls.

We see this in a comparison of $AE1$ with $AE2$ where $AE2$ is the aggregate expenditure curve after an increase in the price level. Beginning at point a on $AE1$ when income is $Y1$, this corresponds to the lower price level. If the price level rises, then with the same amount of income, $Y1$, people will cut back on planned expenditure to point c on $AE2$ because they cannot buy the same amount of goods with the same amount of income.

At the higher price level, planned aggregate expenditure falls (from $AE1$ to $AE2$).

The dashed line in Figure 5.4 panel A needs some explanation. At all points on this line, planned expenditure coincides with national income (output):

$$AE = Y.$$

An economy in equilibrium generates sufficient income (output) to match planned expenditure; hence this occurs at only one point on each *AE* function, such as *a* on *AE1* and *b* on *AE2*.

In Figure 5.4 panel *B* the aggregate demand function is shown. Each point on an aggregate demand function is taken from the point on a corresponding expenditure function where the economy is in equilibrium where planned expenditures = national income. When the price level is relatively low at *PL*, the corresponding level of income shown in Figure 5.4 panel *B* is at *a* (and this corresponds to the point of equilibrium at *a* on *AE1*). When the price level rises to a higher level at *PH*, this corresponds to a lower amount of national income at point *b* (which corresponds to the equilibrium point *b* from *AE2*). Each point on an aggregate demand curve corresponds to an equilibrium point on an *AE* function.

There are three reasons **why the aggregate demand curve slopes down**:

- the real wealth effect;
- the interest rate effect;
- the international trade effect.

The real wealth effect: When there is a change in the price level, this has an impact on consumers' utility because with the same amount of income they can buy more consumption goods if the price level falls (or less if the price level increases). In 'real terms' a change in the price level affects consumers because of the effect on their purchasing power. A 10% increase in the price level means for a given amount of income, 10% less goods can be bought. Because consumption is such a significant portion of aggregate expenditure, the change in planned consumption brought about by a change in the price level is clearly reflected in a negative relationship between the price level and income observed in the aggregate demand function.

The interest rate effect: If the price level increases, people need and demand more money for their purchases (some purchases can be put off until the future but others cannot). In the short run the amount of money in an economy is fixed (by the relevant central bank, to be explained later in Chapter 7). Any increase in the demand for money puts upward pressure on the price of money, the interest rate. Higher interest rates have implications for many components of aggregate expenditure. If the interest rate rises, this has implications for business investment, since much of it is financed by bank loans. Buying consumption goods on credit is also adversely affected by increased interest rates and some government expenditure may also be reduced due to a higher interest rate. An increase in the price level that leads to a higher interest rate leads to lower aggregate demand – hence the AD curve slopes down.

The international trade effect: Any change in a country's price level relative to the price level of its trading partners has an impact on the attractiveness of international trade. A country's exports become less attractive if the exports become relatively more expensive. If an exporting country's prices rise faster than its importing partner countries, rational buyers will prefer the products for which prices are not rising so rapidly (this will be the case where similar products – substitutes – are available and where the prices were quite similar before the exporter's prices rose). Changes in price levels affect both export and importing activities and since both exports and imports are components of aggregate demand the effect of an increasing price level that reduces net exports $(X - M)$ is reflected in the downward slope of the aggregate demand curve.

5.5.3 AGGREGATE SUPPLY

To consider aggregate supply, it is useful to return to the concept of efficient production discussed (in Chapter 1) when we dealt with the production possibility frontier. There is a constraint on the maximum amount of output firms in an economy could produce irrespective of the price level because an economy's resources are limited. An economy that produces the maximum feasible output with all resources fully employed operates at potential output and this is shown as $Y^\wedge$ in Figure 5.5. The relationship between the average level of prices and aggregate supply is shown here.

Potential output is a country's output level if all resources were fully employed.

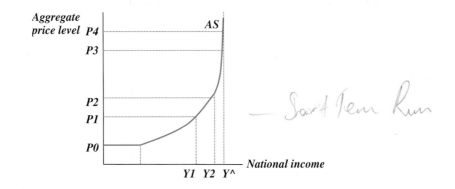

FIGURE 5.5 AGGREGATE SUPPLY

The shape of the aggregate supply curve indicates that the relationship between output and the price level varies, depending on the economy's output level. Initially aggregate supply is flat, then slopes gently upwards only to become steep as it coincides with potential output. This relationship describes how firms react to the price level. There is a minimum price level required for firms to consider it worth their while to supply a market with goods. In Figure 5.5 this level is *P0*. This corresponds to a situation where an economy has low income (recession phase of the business cycle), firms have a lot of spare capacity and many resources are unemployed. Firms are willing to sell at the going market price and would like to sell more output at the going price.

If an economy is producing output *Y1* at a price level *P1*, any change in the price level will cause firms to change their output. A decline in the price level would lead to lower output because firms would perceive that they would have to cut their prices to sell their output and lower prices would make some firms uncompetitive; they would stop producing and output would fall (in Chapter 8 we will look at the factors that might bring about such a fall in the price level). An increase in the price level from *P1* to *P2* would have the opposite effect and output would expand from *Y1* to *Y2* indicating firms' willingness to expand supply as the higher price level allows them to remain competitive and charge higher prices.

A proportional increase in the price level from *P3* to *P4*, however, does not have the same impact on output. If the economy begins from a position where the aggregate price level is *P3* then the economy is producing very near its potential output. Any rise in the price level, such as to *P4*, has no significant impact on output because firms' have little extra capacity.

Analysis of aggregate supply depends on whether the short run or long run is of interest. In the long run, it is assumed that an economy will operate at full employment and hence the long-run aggregate supply curve is that shown in Figure 5.6.

The **long-run aggregate supply (LRAS) curve** is a vertical line drawn at potential output.

The quantity and quality of the available factors of production and the available technology (for converting inputs into output) determine the amount of **potential output** an economy can supply.

Hence, *LRAS* is not influenced by the price level – the same amount is produced irrespective of the price level. (The aggregate supply curve illustrated earlier in Figure 5.5 may be considered to correspond to the short-run aggregate supply,

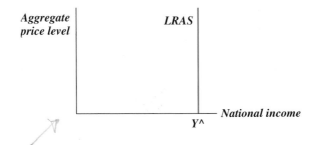

FIGURE 5.6 LONG-RUN AGGREGATE SUPPLY

or it can be treated as a 'combination' *AS* curve that combines elements of both short-run and long-run behaviour.)

The determinants of $Y^\wedge$ are influences on the quality and quantity of factors of production including the local, domestic and international financial systems, systems of corporate governance, legal and political environments, social and cultural background, technological capability and the myriad standards, business and personal ethics, codes of conduct that are embedded in an economic system, as referred to earlier in the discussion of the circular flow.

5.5.4 BRINGING AD AND AS TOGETHER: THE SHORT RUN

A country's equilibrium output and price level are determined jointly by its aggregate demand and aggregate supply functions, as shown in Figure 5.7 for the short run. Here, equilibrium output is SRY^* (where *SR* denotes the short run) and the equilibrium price level is P^* corresponding to the intersection of aggregate demand and aggregate supply. The economy shown is not producing its potential output, so some resources are not being employed and the government might want to try to boost output.

There are different avenues to encouraging the use of more resources – boosting either aggregate demand or aggregate supply. (You may wish to sketch this situation using Figure 5.7 as your starting point: this analysis is further considered in Chapter 8.)

Any increase in aggregate demand moves the *AD* curve upwards (to the right) bringing about a new equilibrium position involving increased output and an increased aggregate price level.

Any expansion in aggregate supply moves the *AS* rightwards leading to a new equilibrium position involving higher output but a lower aggregate price level than P^*.

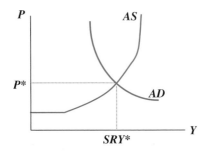

FIGURE 5.7 SHORT RUN: AGGREGATE SUPPLY AND AGGREGATE DEMAND

The challenge in intervening in the economy is to implement policies that have the desired outcome. While this may appear straightforward using the theory of AS-AD presented here, in practice it represents a problem for governments and businesses alike for a number of reasons considered in more detail in Chapter 8.

5.6 EQUILIBRIUM ECONOMIC ACTIVITY AND THE MULTIPLIER

When there is a change in aggregate demand, whether caused by a change in C, I, G or $(X - M)$, equilibrium output changes. In sketching a movement in the AD curve, however, we lose sight of the process according to which this change occurs in the economy. Take the example of a change in consumption expenditure. Autonomous consumption drops by £25bn from £50bn, for example. This leads to a new consumption function (this can be sketched using Figure 3.12 as the starting point) and also a new AD curve. The immediate effect of a drop in autonomous consumption is that equilibrium income drops by the same amount (as the AD shifts down or to the left).

The initial drop in autonomous consumption, however, has knock-on or domino effects. The drop in income caused by the drop in consumption also causes a further drop in consumption because consumption also depends on the level of disposable income (refresh your memory by returning to section 3.8 if required). This further drop in consumption causes a further drop in income, causes a further drop in consumption ... and so on. The total effect of the drop in autonomous consumption is greater than the initial change that caused it, with a multiplicative effect. This implies that if autonomous consumption falls by £25bn, the effect on equilibrium output will be *an even greater* fall. Each economy has its own national income multiplier.

The multiplier indicates how much income/output changes after a change in autonomous expenditure.

The size of the multiplier for an economy that does not engage in international trade (and therefore has no exports or imports) can be found according to the following formula:

$$\text{Multiplier} = \frac{1}{(1 - MPC^*)}$$

The value of the multiplier depends on the value of an economy's marginal propensity to consume out of national income (MPC^*). In Chapter 3, the marginal propensity to consume out of disposable income was discussed (MPC). The relationship between the marginal propensities is:

$$MPC^* = MPC \times (1 - t)$$

where t is the tax rate.

If the tax rate is 0.2 (equivalent to 20%) and people's marginal propensity to consume out of disposable income is 0.95, then the marginal propensity to consume out of national income, according to the above equation, is $0.95 \times (1.0 - 0.20) = 0.76$.

The ratios of disposable income to GDP for 2001 were 71.3% for the euro area, 73.3% for the USA, and for Japan, 60.3%. These data are from the international statistics of the European Central Bank, http://www.ecb.int/stats.

To compute the multiplier if the MPC^* is 0.76, then $1 - MPC^*$ is 0.24 and the multiplier is $1/0.24 = 4.16$.

This implies that any change in autonomous expenditure (e.g. autonomous consumption, I or G where each is independent of the level of national income) leads to a new equilibrium income/output of 4.16 times the initial change.

For a higher tax rate, this would change the MPC* and the value of the multiplier, as shown in Table 5.3. As the tax rate rises, a greater proportion of aggregate income is paid in taxation, representing a leakage out of the circular flow. As the leakage increases (with t), the impact of any change in autonomous expenditure declines, as shown by the fall in value of the multiplier.

The size of the multiplier for an economy that is involved in international trade is different to that presented above and is found as:

$$\text{Multiplier} = \frac{1}{[1 - (MPC^* - MPM)]}$$

where MPM denotes the marginal propensity to import.

TABLE 5.3 VALUE OF THE MULTIPLIER AS TAX RATE RISES

MPC	t	$(1 - t)$	$MPC^*: MPC \times (1 - t)$	$1 - MPC^*$	Multiplier: $\frac{1}{(1-MPC^*)}$
0.95	0.20	0.80	0.76	0.24	4.16
0.95	0.30	0.70	0.665	0.335	2.99
0.95	0.40	0.60	0.57	0.43	2.33

Conclusion: for a given MPC, an increase in the tax rate leads to a reduction in the multiplier.

TABLE 5.4 VALUE OF THE MULTIPLIER INCLUDING MPM

MPC	t	$(1 - t)$	MPC^*	$MPC^* - MPM$	$[1 - (MPC^* - MPM)]$	Multiplier: $\frac{1}{[1 - (MPC^* - MPM)]}$
0.95	0.20	0.80	0.76	0.51	0.49	2.04
0.95	0.30	0.70	0.665	0.415	0.585	1.71
0.95	0.40	0.60	0.57	0.32	0.68	1.47

Conclusion: inclusion of the MPM reduces the value of the multiplier because it represents an additional leakage of income from the circular flow.

TABLE 5.5 TRADE SHARES OF ECONOMIC ACTIVITY (% GDP) 2002

	USA	UK	Ireland	Germany	Japan
X: exports	6.5	18	72	30	10
M: imports	−11	−21	−43	−24	−7.5
X − M: net exports	−4.5	−3	29	6	2.5

Source: Economist Intelligence Unit, Country Data except for Ireland: Trade Statistics of Ireland, Irish Central Statistics Office.

Payments for imports represent a further leakage of income from a country's circular flow, hence the multiplier is different. For a country with an *MPM* of 0.25, the impact on the multiplier is shown in Table 5.4, which extends Table 5.3.

The extent to which imports and net trade is important for different countries is shown in Table 5.5 which presents the share of exports (X) and imports (M) as values of each country's GDP, for a sample of countries.

Both the USA and UK experienced trade deficits in 2002 because the value of their imports exceeded their exports. Japan, Germany and Ireland displayed trade surpluses. Countries' comparative advantages (see Chapter 2) help us to understand a considerable portion of the international trade that takes place between them.

5.7 INTERNATIONAL INTEGRATION

A key characteristic of the current international economic system is the extent to which individuals, firms and countries are exposed to influences from foreign goods, services, firms, capital and labour. Individuals and economies are increasingly faced with contributions by far distant people and places to their lives. Evidence for this is found, for example, in the growth in international trade.

World growth in exports outstripped world GDP growth between 1995 and 2000 by a factor of more than two (7% per annum compared to 3%). Over the longer period spanning 1948–2002, the figures are 6% for exports and 3.7% for GDP (see www.WTO.org for more national and international trade information and statistics).

Trade provides outlets for countries' output when domestic demand is insufficient to allow firms to sell all produce. The trade option also provides firms in some industries with the possibility of reaping scale economies, allowing them to reduce their average costs of production as their output expands. Hence, not only can trade lead to greater quantities of output produced in an economy in response to access to more markets, but it can also generate greater efficiency in terms of how resources are used within economies.

5.7.1 EXPLAINING GROWING INTERNATIONAL TRADE

A number of factors explain the growth in world trade. Declines in trade barriers such as tariffs and quotas certainly play a role.

> **Trade barriers** are policies or practices that reduce the amount of imports into a country. Examples include tariffs and quotas.
>
> Import tariffs operate like a tax on goods originating in a different customs area.
>
> **Tariffs** raise the price paid by consumers for imported goods making them less attractive to buy. Tariff rates are decided by governments but are increasingly outlawed under the WTO. Sufficiently high tariffs on goods for which domestically produced substitutes exist can eliminate any incentive to buy the imports. Governments receive the revenue generated by tariffs.
>
> **Quotas** raise the price paid by consumers for imported goods making them less attractive to buy. Quotas are quantitative restrictions set by governments on the amount of imports permitted from another customs area. Because quotas limit the supply of a good, they drive the price of the goods up.

Declining trade barriers reduces the costs of buying foreign goods for consumers and provides them with greater product choice. Another important explanation lies in the form of falling transportation costs allied to the types of goods currently being traded.

Historically when the majority of goods traded were agricultural products, raw materials and processed commodities like steel and meat, their cost of transportation was high given their weight and bulk. In such a world it made most sense to trade with countries in close proximity.

> **A commodity** is an undifferentiated product such as wheat or oil or computer memory chips. Commodities are usually of uniform quality, often produced by

many different producers where each producer's output is considered equivalent or interchangeable. Futures markets exist for many commodity products.

The majority of traded goods today are finished manufactured products. Due to technological developments these products often consist of low-weight components (relative to steel) and micro technologies (microprocessors replacing heavy control panels) that mean their value relative to their transport cost is high. For many firms, low and relatively stable transport costs make shipping such goods beyond the nearest countries an increasingly viable option.

Shipping technology itself was reorganized from the 1950s with the advent of 'containerization', which involved substantially less unloading and reloading of cargo and hence, lower related labour costs. Ships were redesigned to transport such containers more efficiently. In the 1970s road and rail transportation began to be reorganized and deregulated in the USA – until then the government was involved in decisions on transport costs and often licensed lorries to ship goods only on one leg of a return journey. (The Japanese waited until the 1990s before beginning such transport deregulation.) Currently, air transportation is being deregulated. Transport deregulation to date has allowed costs to fall, encouraged greater trade and generated productivity gains for firms in time and resource savings.

Transformation of the transport sector has not just impacted shipping final goods to customers but also firms' coordination of transport and production of components and intermediate goods produced internationally. Computer and car manufacturers are prime examples of industries where global coordination of the manufacturing process has been facilitated by reductions in international transport (and communications) costs. It often makes economic sense to source some components in East Asia, others in the USA and others in Europe and to conduct some sub-component assembly and final assembly in different locations. The complex set of activities that go into sourcing raw materials and components and organizing them to create the product sold to customers is all associated with a firm's supply chain.

A **supply chain** describes the resources and processes that are involved in acquiring components and raw materials and includes delivery of end products to final consumers. It includes the activities of sellers, distributors, manufacturers, wholesalers and any other service providers and contributors to the buyer's decision to buy.

To help firms coordinate such activities, supply chain management companies have emerged. By outsourcing successfully, firms are able to reduce costs substantially.

An outsourcing firm can hold inventories to save on storage costs for its clients, for example. It is also often possible to shorten the time to bring a product to market because the logistical maze of procuring components is left to the 'expert' outsourcing firm which can do so at lower cost by exploiting scale economies. More cost-effective and efficient distribution can also result. The benefits of greater efficiencies and improvements in time to market can allow businesses that outsource to reorient their focus towards their most important business activities.

Offshore outsourcing (known as offshoring in the United States) involves relocation of elements of the supply chain to a foreign location for more efficient production. Both production and services may be outsourced. Because of its low cost base, China has become an important player in production offshoring while India has emerged as a competitive provider of services. (The website of the National Association of Software and Service Companies www.NASSCOM.org provides information on offshoring activity in India.)

5.7.2 BENEFITS AND COSTS OF INTERNATIONAL TRADE

Heated debates ensue about international trade in general and offshoring in particular. Trade and international integration are viewed, by some, as threats to economic stability and growth. On the one hand this is strange since, as we saw in Chapter 2, specialization and comparative advantage generate a better international outcome for *all* countries that trade.

As Adam Smith pointed out in 1776, it is possible for Scotland to produce grapes suitable for wine-making using glasshouse-technology but it would cost approximately 30 times more than available imported wine; it would be difficult to argue in favour of tariffs to encourage Scottish wine production.

Smith highlighted the opportunity cost of limiting trade and encouraging production in goods for which a country may have no inherent comparative advantage. It may make economic sense for Scottish grape growers to respond to import tariffs by producing wine yet the resource cost (products not produced by those resources devoted to wine production) means more efficient and productive use of the resources is not possible. Trade without barriers would leave the Scottish economy free to produce and specialize based on its comparative advantage. If this is true for Scotland and wine then why not for the USA or France or Japan and why not for components or services as well as products?

Smith's Scottish wine example is interesting because the Scots were not producing wine in sufficient quantities for producers to have a strong voice to complain about cheaper imports. Nor were sufficient Scottish workers employed in the industry to lobby for the protection of their jobs. These are crucial issues in the context of today's trade debates.

Industry, trade associations and trades unions are often unhappy about the effects of cheaper imports on their companies' profitability and members' jobs and wages, respectively. And so they should be – they are correctly looking out for their own and their members' interests. Certainly we can all come up with examples of jobs which have been moved abroad due to 'the current international trading environment' or similar explanations which essentially boil down to lower opportunity costs of production elsewhere. At various points in time, it seems that some jobs are inevitably displaced to other locations by imports.

We know that offshoring and imports help domestic companies maintain their competitiveness and, hence, support rather than displace domestic jobs. US imports of steel make the Caterpillar tractor company more competitive, allowing it to sell more, allowing it to provide more jobs. Distributors of tractors could sell more vehicles and farmers get more tractor for their money, allowing them to be more competitive. But fewer jobs in the US steel industry result from steel imports. Unemployed steel workers suffer. Others gain.

Price changes and the economic adjustment they bring about always create 'winners' and 'losers' and real income is redistributed as a result.

Deciding to restrict imports protects some industries and domestic jobs but it is not without costs.

In the 1980s US restrictions on textile and apparel imports kept prices of such goods relatively high. This meant fewer jobs in the clothing retail sector and higher consumer prices. Estimates of the cost of protecting textile jobs where annual wages were approximately $15 000 to $20 000 was put at about $50 000 *per job* (Hufbauer and Elliott, 1994).

As a group of disparate consumers and taxpayers funding protectionism, we do not feel the direct link between our tax payments, higher prices and trade policy but it is definitely there. Logically, workers whose jobs are threatened or lost to trade feel the pain and voice their dissatisfaction.

Some jobs are displaced by technological change or product innovations but we rarely hear protests in favour of limiting technological improvements or innovation. Arguing for limits on trade seems to be an easy target, implicitly placing more value on jobs under threat from lower-cost foreign production rather than jobs that may be created elsewhere in the economy based on its comparative advantages. From a political perspective this makes sense. Workers who lose their jobs often reflect this in their voting patterns. Workers who 'gain' jobs often do not attribute it to free trade or the policy of the government of the day. Nor do increased product variety and lower costs for consumers often appear as underlying people's voting preferences.

At the microeconomic level for individuals and for firms, arguing against imports can sometimes seem logical but if it occurred across all areas of an economy, the macroeconomy would suffer and lower aggregate output and per capita incomes would result.

> The fallacy of composition arises here. Although the net effect of trade is positive, this does not necessarily translate into positive effects for every individual in trading countries. The results of trade – availability of a broader variety of goods and services at lower prices – is easily forgotten by an unemployed worker whose job has been lost to imports.

From the perspective of developing countries, it is also worth noting that both the United States and the European Union maintain trade restrictions that harm such countries by limiting their ability to export goods. Through the WTO (and its predecessor, the General Agreement on Tariffs and Trade) improvements have been attempted but reform has been promised for many years without substantial results. It is still the case that average tariff levels in agriculture (predominantly exported by developing countries) are about *nine* times those in manufacturing. Industrial countries subsidize agriculture, effectively cutting world prices because of the supply incentive subsidies create for farmers in industrialized countries. Not only does the EU spend around £2.7bn *per year* to make sugar profitable for European farmers but it also shuts out low-cost imports of tropical sugar through trade barriers.

Minimizing or overlooking the negative microeconomic effects of trade is a problem with many free-trade advocates. It may well make the free-trade argument more palatable and popular if these issues were dealt with explicitly.

There is a link between the arguments for free trade and for greater focus on national income distribution, addressed in Chapter 9. Both require examination of the economic repercussions on the least well off of economic measures that may well favour an economy overall and perhaps even the majority of its citizens. Yet, economic models or explanations indicative of welfare improvements for 'average' or 'representative' citizens should not ignore costs borne by minority groups, which are insufficiently compensated for their losses.

5.8   GOVERNMENT ACTIVITY

Government exerts its economic influence in a number of ways through its interactions with consumers and firms both domestic and foreign. A government's actions are important for an economy in terms of its role in setting the tone for how business is conducted generally. While the extent of government activity within the economic system varies from country to country, governments' activities are generally focused on a number of goals such as:

- *Stabilization policy*: Stabilizing the economy by minimizing the short-run fluctuations of GDP (output) and unemployment associated with the business cycle.
- *Dealing with AS and AD shocks*: these are any unpredicted events that cause changes in equilibrium national output and the price level.
- Making *transfer payments.*
- *Public good provision.*
- *Taxation*: to enable government to make transfer payments, to pay for national administration and the provision of public goods. Countries that have larger public sectors need relatively high taxes to pay for them.
- *Allocating (or reallocating) resources*: by making transfer payments and imposing taxes, the government reallocates/redistributes the economy's resources.
- *Regulation*: some markets are regulated by imposing tariffs, quotas, etc. Other markets are regulated depending on what competition laws are enacted and enforced (more on this in Chapter 6). Governments also assume responsibility for ensuring law and order.
- Creating an *environment to support expansion of AS*: implementing appropriate policies – education, research and development, business support, etc.

Despite a considerable amount of research (e.g. Slemrod, 1995), no clear link can be established between the size of the public sector and the state of countries' economies. What does seem to be important for economies is the effectiveness of the public sector rather than its size.

When a government manages its economy well, its spending plan or budget can be met by the revenue generated by the economy. If spending is greater than revenues, the government generates a budget deficit while, if revenues are greater than expenditure, a government surplus results. Whether the revenue is sufficient to cover the budget depends on the amount of government spending (G), the tax rates (t) levied, and the level of economic activity.

> Governments use **fiscal policy** whenever they affect G or t (which affect aggregate demand).
>
> An **expansionary fiscal policy** is followed if the government manages to increase activity by injecting extra income into the circular flow.
>
> A fiscal policy that results in lower activity is described as **contractionary** and results in a reduction in the circular flow of income.

If a government tries to stabilize economic activity, this means attempting to maintain a regular growth rate in real output, with no significant fluctuations up or down. To implement a stabilization policy, governments should follow contractionary fiscal policy in booms and expansionary policies in recessions to mitigate the affects of the business cycle; such polices would be countercyclical.

> **Countercyclical fiscal policies** have the *opposite* effect on economic activity to that caused by the business cycle, reducing income flows during booms, increasing income flows in recessions.

To figure out whether governments follow contractionary or expansionary policies, what is at issue is whether the government tries to affect equilibrium output over and above the effects of automatic stabilizers. Examples of automatic stabilizers include income tax rates, VAT rates and unemployment benefit.

> **Automatic stabilizers** result in reducing the response of national income to changes in autonomous spending. They are measures that automatically counter the business cycle without government action. For example, in a boom, government net tax receipts rise, taking income from the circular flow.

In the case of a demand shock, such as an unexpected fall in investment demand, aggregate demand falls, leading to a new equilibrium situation in the short run with lower output and a lower price level (sketch this situation using Figure 5.7 as your starting point). Depending on the size of the fall in output, this might also lead to a rise in unemployment. Firms might keep on all their workers if the drop in output is small, but would be more likely to make workers redundant if there was a big drop in output. We know that due to the multiplier effect the total effect on output would be larger than the initial cause of the drop in income/output. However, automatic stabilizers act to stabilize the economy because the drop in income/output would automatically result in a fall in the government's tax take (due to lower income, the government takes in less revenue in taxes) and, if workers are unemployed, a rise in payments for unemployment benefit. The drop in tax receipts and rise in payments to the unemployed helps people to deal with the decline in income/output. These changes occur automatically in the economy.

Depending on the stage of the business cycle, a government might be receiving high or low tax revenues or be paying out high or low amounts in benefits. To correctly assess the discretionary fiscal policy stance of the government requires removing the business-cycle impact on government revenues and expenditure. When this is carried out the result is a cyclically adjusted budget, which may show a deficit or surplus.

A **cyclically adjusted budget** provides information about the discretionary fiscal policies a government has followed to deliberately achieve specific macro-economic goals. These might include trying to achieve a particular level of inflation, or employment or government deficit, for example.

Quite often, as is evident from Table 5.6, governments end up with budget deficits. Borrowing must be repaid and the extent of past borrowing is revealed in countries' national debts. Most countries in Table 5.6 ran deficits in 2003. Sweden alone ran a surplus. Japan is an outlier in terms of its debt situation – it owed the value of over 154% of its 2003 GDP in debts.

TABLE 5.6   BUDGET AND DEBT SITUATION, 2003 (AS % OF GDP)

	USA	UK	Ireland	Japan	France	Sweden	Germany
Budget balance*	−3.5	−3.1	−0.2	−7.4	−4.1	0.1	−4.0
Public debt**	62.4	51.4	32.4	154.6	69.1	52.8	63.9

Notes: *Negative data imply budget deficits were run.
**This corresponds to the definition used under the Maastricht criteria relevant for European Monetary Union (more on this in Chapter 7).
Source: Country Data, Economist Intelligence Unit.

When public debt increases, economists tend to open the issue to debate. Debts generated for sound economic reasons are not considered problematic but the issue of whether debts are sustainable – i.e. if they can be repaid – is often raised. Debts need to be repaid in the future so the cost will be borne by tomorrow's taxpayers if the government borrows today. While voters may desire high levels of government spending, high debts may require future high tax rates, and hence will not be popular with voters. The effects of high tax rates on incentives to work, employment and running a business may very well create headaches for a government trying to repay future debts and could very well deepen the problem.

Some economists consider that since much of national debt is owed to domestic citizens, it may not be a problem; the most important consideration regarding debt is how it is used. Debts generated to invest in infrastructure or education that will increase future economic activity should help pay for the debt. Debts generated to pay for day-to-day costs like public sector pay or the running of government departments is more difficult to defend because such expenditures should really be met by day-to-day revenues where at all possible, since in many cases they are unlikely to generate their own revenue streams to be self-financing in the future. Economists should be concerned with the purpose of expenditures and the efficiency of expenditure when analysing the sustainability of public debt.

5.8.1 ANOTHER PERSPECTIVE ON ECONOMIC ACTIVITY: THE ECONOMY AS A PRODUCTION FUNCTION

Depending on the issue of interest, different models of economic activity are useful. Earlier the model of aggregate demand and supply was presented. For some purposes, however, it is useful to view an economy as a production function.

> The **production function** is a relationship describing how economic activity, specifically output, depends on the factors of production and technology. It describes a technically efficient use of the factors of production and technology necessary to produce output, i.e. no resources are unemployed.

Examples of 'standard' production functions are:

$$Y = F(K, L, T) \qquad PF1$$
$$Y/L = F(K/L, T) \qquad PF2$$
$$Y/L = F(K/L, E) \qquad PF3$$

For each production function output, Y, is related to the factors of production, which are capital (denoted K), Labour (denoted L) and technology (denoted T). The term F indicates that there is some functional relationship between output and inputs but because these are general equations, the precise relationship or functional form is not specified. The above relationships hold for firms, industries and economies. If you look back to Figure 4.2, you will see a sample production function for a firm for the short run when capital is fixed. For the focus and purpose of this chapter we refer here to economies.

While the three production functions are quite similar, *PF2* and *PF3* are expressed in per worker terms. In *PF1*, output depends on inputs and technology. In *PF2* output per capita depends on capital per worker (K/L) and technology. (Remember these factors of production were highlighted earlier as contributing to aggregate supply.) The capital/labour ratio (K/L) of an economy provides information on the capital intensity of the economy.

> **Capital intensity** is the amount of capital each worker in the economy (on average) has at their disposal.

Usually in economies that generate a high level of economic activity, the K/L ratio is relatively high. In terms of policy options for government, trying to increase this ratio ranks quite high. An economy's capital intensity rises if investment expenditures on capital machinery and equipment grow faster than what is required just to replace depreciation of an economy's capital stock.

In *PF3* output per worker depends again on capital per worker and on the efficiency of labour (E). The efficiency of labour itself depends on both technology and the efficiency of business and general market organization. Explicit inclusion of the efficiency of labour allows for the consideration of learning in the process generating economic activity. For example, the efficiency of labour can improve if nothing else in the economy changes except workers' ability to 'work smarter' from using their specific knowledge of their job more efficiently. It is often only by on-the-job experience that workers figure out the best ways to achieve their work goals via learning by doing.

Output (or output per worker) can grow if factors of production increase and are used for production. If the amount of capital in an economy rises due to increased capital investment, for example, that economy can grow. This can happen only if the capital can be put to productive use to produce something in demand, i.e. for which people are willing to pay. If labour increases output can grow, once (as discussed in Chapter 2):

1. there are jobs for the additional labour; and
2. those jobs generate sufficient return to cover workers' wages/salaries, other business costs and the opportunity cost to the owner of the business.

If technology improves more output (or output per worker) can be produced from a given set of inputs which implies improved production methods either through innovations, invention or better management and organization. These improvements will lead to lower production costs once the technology is not too costly.

This production function approach to describing economic activity allows for analysis of many interesting questions regarding economic activity, although unlike the aggregate demand/aggregate supply approach, the aggregate price level is *not* an explicit feature of the approach. Hence, inflation is not directly part of the model, nor indeed is unemployment. However, the relationship between output and inputs, technology, the efficiency of labour and the role of learning can be considered using the production function approach. Hence, the most appropriate model to use when considering economic activity must be chosen based on the issue of interest and the model most suited to that issue. In Chapter 9 we return to the production function approach in discussing economic growth and its sources.

5.9   SUMMARY

- **Macroeconomic or aggregate economic activity is represented by the circular flow diagram encompassing all income flows between the various markets in the economic system. These include markets for products and services, labour and other factors of production.**

- **Standard measures of economic activity are GDP and GNP. Methods for measuring GDP or GNP include the expenditure, income or value-added methods. All methods should lead to an equivalent measure.**

- **The distinction between short and long run is relevant for aggregate economic activity. In the short run, economic activity displays business cycles. In the long run, a trend growth rate can be estimated.**

- **The aggregate demand and aggregate supply model can be used to analyse economic activity at macroeconomic level and helps us to understand how aggregate national output (or income) and the average aggregate price level are determined.**

- The concept of the multiplier is *crucial* to understanding how changes in autonomous spending ultimately impact on economic activity.
- Given the various functions of government, governments affect equilibrium economic activity through a number of channels.
- For open trading economies, trade creates aggregate benefits, but costs of trade also arise for some economic units.
- A production function approach is one appropriate model for aggregate economic activity. This method can be appropriate in analysis of economic activity, depending on the issue of interest.

REVIEW PROBLEMS AND QUESTIONS

1. Separately in the case of firms, households and government, explain all of the transactions that they are involved in within the circular flow. Make sure to discuss their role regarding products, services, resources and money.

2. Separately in the case of resource, factor and money markets, explain how you think local, domestic and international financial systems, systems of corporate governance, legal and political environments, social and cultural background, technological capability and the myriad standards, business and personal ethics, and codes of conduct that are embedded in the economic system all play a role in understanding the circular flow.

3. a. Using data for five countries of your choice, graph their long-term growth path from 1950 to the last year of available data (use data from the Groningen Growth and Development Centre website http://www.eco.rug.nl/ggdc/index-dseries.html). Compute the average rate of growth for the period overall and for each decade. Try to identify boom periods and recessions from your graph.

   b. For the same five countries as in 3a, compare the growth rate of population with real output growth and comment on whether welfare can be argued to have improved for each country. The data are also available from the same source.

4. Go to the website of your national statistics provider. Find the section on prices and plot the trends in average consumer prices for the last five years. Has the trend been rising or falling? Compare this trend with the Harmonized Index of Consumer Prices for all EU Member States (which is available from http://www.cso.ie/principalstats/princstats.html under the Prices heading).

5. Use an aggregate expenditure curve and an aggregate demand curve (similar to Figure 5.4) to explain what you would expect to happen to equilibrium output and the price level if the average price level fell by 5%. Explain the individual effects you would expect for aggregate demand in terms of the real wealth effect, the interest rate effect and the international trade effect.

6. a. Use the following table to compute the multiplier when the MPC is 0.90 and the tax rate is 20%.

MPC	t	(1 − t)	MPC* : MPC × (1 − t)	1 − MPC*	Multiplier: $\dfrac{1}{(1 - MPC^*)}$
0.90	0.20				

b. Indicate in the following table what happens to the multiplier if the MPC falls to 0.85. Explain why this is so.

MPC	t	(1 − t)	MPC* : MPC × (1 − t)	1 − MPC*	Multiplier: $\dfrac{1}{(1 - MPC^*)}$
0.85	0.20				

c. Indicate in the following table what happens to the multiplier if the tax rate falls to 15%. Explain why this is so.

MPC	t	(1 − t)	MPC* : MPC × (1 − t)	1 − MPC*	Multiplier: $\dfrac{1}{(1 - MPC^*)}$
0.85	0.15				

d. If an MPM of 0.20 is included in the tables above, compute the new multiplier in *each* case.

7. For your domestic economy look up appropriate sources to find out and explain what your government has done in relation to each of the following over the last three to five years.

- Stabilization policy, reaction to economic shocks, transfer payments, provision of public goods, taxation, resource reallocation, regulation, policies likely to encourage expansion of aggregate supply.

8. Use the latest available data from your national statistics provider or the WTO (www.wto.org) to identify the main sectors and goods that your country exports and imports. Do the same exercise for 10 years previously. What does your information reveal about your country's comparative advantages?

FURTHER READING AND RESEARCH

- Two of the greatest minds in economics – Hayek and Keynes – provided theories of business cycles. See Hayek, 1975 and Keynes, 1936.
- For research on economic performance and the size of government see Slemrod, 1995.
- For analysis of trade related issues, *Foreign Affairs* contains topical articles. Regarding the offshoring/outsourcing debates see Drezner, 2004.
- Some good books on international integration have been published recently, including Wolf, 2004 and Bhagwati, 2004.

REFERENCES

Bhagwati, J. (2004) *In Defence of Globalization*. Oxford University Press, New York.

Drezner, D. (2004) 'The outsourcing bogeyman', *Foreign Affairs*, May/June, 22–34.

Hayek, F. (1975) *Monetary Theory and the Trade Cycle* [original publication 1933]. Augustus M. Kelley, New York.

Hufbauer, G. and K. Elliott (1994) *Measuring the Costs of Protectionism in the United States*. Washington: Institute for International Economics, 5, 13.

Keynes, J. (1936) *The General Theory of Employment, Interest and Money*. Macmillan, London.

Schumpeter, J. (1975) *Capitalism, Socialism and Democracy* [original publication 1942]. Harper & Row, New York.

Slemrod, J. (1995) 'What do cross-country studies teach about government involvement, prosperity and economic growth?', *Brookings Papers on Economic Activity*, **2**, 373–431.

Smith, A. (1776) *An Inquiry into the Nature and Causes of the Wealth of Nations*.

Wolf, M. (2004) *Why Globalization Works*. Yale University Press, New Haven.

CHAPTER 6

COMPETITION IN THE ECONOMIC SYSTEM

By EDWARD SHINNICK

LEARNING OUTCOMES

By the end of this chapter you should be able to:

- Explain why competition is a complex process in the economic system.
- Explain the Austrian perspective on competition as an ongoing process within an economy which includes an explicit function for entrepreneurs.
- Describe the traditional models of competition (non-Austrian) using figures including demand, costs and supply.
- Compare and contrast the assumptions and outcomes for consumers, producers and society as a whole, of alternative models of competition.
- Compare and contrast the traditional and Austrian approaches to competition.
- Use the five forces framework to highlight the factors that explain why some industries are more attractive – more profitable – than others.
- Discuss what is meant by market failure, how it may arise and its implications.
- Explain what is meant by the structure, conduct, performance paradigm and how it provided a foundation for competition policy. Explain the implications of changes in the formulation of the SCP paradigm for competition policy.
- Provide some examples of why competition may give rise to problems for an economy.
- Analyse how competition policy can be used to address competition problems.

6.1 INTRODUCTION

Previous chapters have outlined the demand and the supply sides of the economy and how these two elements interact within the economic system. This chapter explores this interaction further by analysing how and why firms compete in the marketplace. Pick up any business magazine or newspaper and undoubtedly you will find a reference to 'competition' in a report on the economy. The term is widely used yet we may not fully understand what it means and its importance. The role of this chapter is to explore the meaning of competition and the beneficial consequences of competition for the economy and society as a whole.

The Austrian influence is present again in this chapter with the Austrian perspective on how competition can be viewed as an ongoing process in the economic system outlined in section 6.2. This incorporates the concept of discovery and provides an explicit role for entrepreneurship as a factor of production.

This is followed in section 6.3 by presentation of the main economic models of competition that characterize different industries. These complementary perspectives on competition in sections 6.2 and 6.3 are compared and contrasted in section 6.4.

In section 6.5 the focus shifts to why markets may not always work to the satisfaction of governments and what can be done to correct such outcomes. This re-introduces the role of government in the economic system and what it can do in the form of a national competition policy to address market problems. Analysis of competition policy, its aims and how it is implemented completes the chapter.

6.2 COMPETITION IN THE ECONOMIC SYSTEM

When economists use the term 'competition' or advocate greater competition they generally have in mind some mechanism that brings about an increase in supply leading to a reduction in equilibrium price and an increase in equilibrium quantity (*ceteris paribus*). However, the term 'competition' involves much more than just an increase in supply.

The extent of competition in an economy has implications for a whole set of interacting issues such as innovation, efficiency, availability of a variety of goods and services, and prices that together influence and enhance the welfare of individual consumers. When individual consumer benefits are aggregated, the economy too is better off as a result of competition.

Within the economic system we have a series of interacting agents that act independently of each other and yet are part of a complex interrelated web. In the context of competition, the marketplace is a crucial element in this web where the interaction of different economic units, each motivated to maximize their utility, results in an outcome that benefits both these individuals and the entire economy.

Despite the potential benefits from economic interactions, markets do not always operate to generate positive outcomes. Instead markets can become distorted and can end up serving one group of people at the expense of others. For example, some market conditions result in producers gaining the most from market exchange, while consumers end up with fewer benefits (from a consumer surplus/producer surplus analysis). In such cases, the government may deem it necessary to intervene in the market to achieve a more balanced outcome, from a public-policy perspective. Such intervention can take the form of removing restrictions on, for example, quantity restrictions on supply, on prices or on foreign trade. Arguments for interventions also come from lobby groups or vested interests whose focus is on maximizing their own benefits and depending on the lobby group will adopt either a public-policy or business perspective.

When governments intervene in markets truly open, competitive free markets do not exist. There are many examples of how competition is limited by the entry of new firms being blocked or in some way made more difficult. Government intervention is by no means the only way in which entry can be restricted but it is one example of restricting competition by setting a limit on the number of competitors in an industry – a case in point is the pub industry where competition is limited as pubs require licences from the government to operate in that market. Naturally occurring restrictions also occur where a firm has access to the sole supply or knowledge required to produce a good, and examples include oil, and coke, for different reasons. Barriers to entry can arise due to the type of product (standardized or differentiated), the existence of economies of scale, initial or ongoing capital requirements or cost disadvantages independent of size, such as access to distribution channels.

> **Standardized products:** products for which many substitutes are available and which use readily available technology in their production.
> **Differentiated products:** products for which several different varieties are provided (e.g. cars). Differentiation between varieties depends on producers' choices of the product attributes for which consumers are willing to pay.

Competition, therefore, is a complex concept that is often not fully understood in terms of what it actually means and its implications in the marketplace, for prices and supply, and therefore for economic growth and employment.

6.2.1 COMPETITION AS A PROCESS

One view of competition is that it is a process whereby through learning over time, economic units on the demand and supply sides of the economy reach a state where their plans become mutually consistent. Hayek, in particular, and the Austrian School of Economics in general, would subscribe to such a view where competition is a discovery procedure, where people discover knowledge on an ongoing basis. Competition is perceived as being similar to a game of gathering knowledge and exploiting that knowledge for economic gain. The concept of competition as a game has several useful implications. For example, in any game, we do not know the results beforehand, skill is required to influence the outcome and the outcome is unpredictable. The following quote from Hayek (1978) illustrates this point: 'Competition is valuable only because, and so far as, its results are unpredictable and on the whole different from those which anyone has, or could have, deliberately aimed at.' (p. 180)

Unlike in standard games where there are winners and losers (also called zero-sum games), competition often generates greater gains than losses or costs. For example, the result of a new more efficient competitor entering a market and charging lower prices might be to put some other firms out of business, but consumers gain from the lower prices charged and more efficient use of society's resources is made.

An important implication of Hayek's description is that we cannot set out to create an outcome that is in itself unpredictable. If competition is a discovery procedure, then we cannot know beforehand what is to be discovered. In addition, the outcomes of a game can only be temporary because as new knowledge is discovered and used, new outcomes are likely to emerge. Therefore, rather than analysing whether competition has achieved a particular outcome, we should instead focus our attention on making comparisons across similar markets, across industries and/or across countries and consider which outcomes are economically superior.

This concept of competition is appealing because the knowledge that exists and that is developed over time within a marketplace is unlikely to be generated as efficiently through any other mechanism. Therefore the miracle of the marketplace is that it allows the market system to achieve results that are not only unpredictable but are also the 'best' outcome possible.

In a similar vein to Hayek, Schumpeter offered us the notion of competition as creative destruction (discussed in the treatment of business cycles in Chapter 5). Schumpeter viewed competition as a dynamic process that is based on innovation and change, arguing that in the process of economic growth and in the development and expansion of new products, technological change results in the displacement of old products and old technologies by new products, jobs and technologies. Old jobs and factories become obsolete and defunct and are no longer productive within the economic system.

Knowledge and the use of this knowledge are central to this process-view of competition. As outlined in Chapter 2, such knowledge is dispersed throughout the economic system and its application is central to the functioning of this system. Prices become signals of this knowledge. Again Hayek (1978) illustrates this point:

> Utilisation of knowledge widely dispersed in a society with extensive division of labour cannot rest on individuals knowing all the particular uses to which well known things in their individual environment might be put. Prices direct their attention to what is worth finding out about what a market offers for various things and services. This means that the, in some respects always unique, combinations of individual knowledge and skills, which the market enables them to use, will not merely, or even in the first instance, be such knowledge of facts as they could list and communicate if some authority asked them to do. The knowledge of which I speak consists rather of a capacity to find out particular circumstances, which become effective only if possessors of this knowledge are informed by the market which kinds of things or services are wanted, and how urgently they are wanted. (p. 257)

Hayek highlights several useful ideas worth noting. Knowledge plays a central role in the view of competition as a process, where each individual knows something but nobody knows everything. The existence of tacit knowledge is also recognized, as is the role of the entrepreneur in discovering and using knowledge in a profitable way.

> **Tacit knowledge:** is highly personal, not easily visible or expressible and cannot easily be copied. It usually requires joint, shared activities in order to transmit it. Examples of tacit knowledge include subjective insights, intuitions and hunches.

Finally, the concept of demand is referred to in terms of things or services wanted and 'how urgently they are wanted'.

6.2.2 ENTREPRENEURSHIP, DISCOVERY AND THE MARKET PROCESS

At the heart of the use of knowledge in market economies lies the entrepreneur.

> **Entrepreneurs** exploit knowledge by converting knowledge discovered into profitable gain.

Crucial to entrepreneurs' ability is the freedom to enter existing markets or develop new markets so discovery is fundamental to the notion of an entrepreneur. The entrepreneur's skill lies in discovering knowledge and then using the market process to exploit it for profitable gain.

> **Entrepreneurship** is about being alert to a set of opportunities, having a subjective expectation as to the value of such opportunities in the market *and* having the resources (or ability to generate them) to realize this value.

This may be no more than exploiting a price difference in two markets by buying cheap in one market to sell at a higher price in another market. Such an entrepreneurial discovery will eventually result in the disappearance of the price difference (consider the role of the speculator as described in Chapter 7) thereby bringing continual change to the market. The notion of equilibrium in the Austrian view of competition can only be temporary since new opportunities continually arise that cause future change. Entrepreneurship can also involve combining resources in a unique way that represents value to the consumer – something for which consumers are willing to pay.

Entrepreneurship, by definition, cannot be predicted. It brings chaos to markets in the sense that it generates price movements and resource allocation and reallocation decisions and all this is done in the search for economic profit. In the process 'mistakes' can be made either by incorrectly interpreting knowledge or by incorrectly judging the value consumers would place on such knowledge. Hence, we have some unsuccessful product launches, unsold inventories and bankruptcies. But through the discovery process more knowledge is gained which feeds back into entrepreneurial decision-making and so the cycle continues.

Competition in the context of entrepreneurship means one thing – free entry into any market. This is also known as contestable markets.

> **Contestable markets:** markets where entry costs and exit costs from markets are low.

Without this free-entry condition, discoveries cannot be made and so entrepreneurship is restrained. Discoveries could take the form of new technology, resulting in lower production costs (lower average cost curves), or new product attributes, resulting in more value to consumers (reflected in new or higher demand functions). Such discoveries would lead to resources being redirected in the economy to where their productivity is highest, and the impact of changes in markets would be reflected in changes in prices.

Discoveries might include a perception on changing consumer tastes. If consumers demand more computers and fewer typewriters then, through the market mechanism, the price of computers rises while the price of typewriters falls. As the equilibrium quantity changes so too can profits, and increasing profit levels would provide incentives for more producers to engage in the production of computers and fewer producers to engage in the production of typewriters. Changing profit opportunities result in increased computer production. As more computers are produced the price of computers will eventually start to decrease, whereas falling demand for typewriters will result in less production and falling prices in that market.

This outcome reflects society's change in preferences and it unfolded as individuals pursued their own self-interest without anyone or any government directing them to do so. Moreover, the market mechanism also operates as a check on individual self-interest. Any increases in price by one entrepreneur to take advantage of an additional profit opportunity may well be met with prices actually being bid down by more efficient entrepreneurs entering the market or through a switch to substitute goods.

> Markets are organized by a self-regulating process and what may seem at the first instance to be chaotic and disorderly is, in fact, not.

The marketplace by its very nature is constantly changing with knowledge being discovered, and any equilibrium state is only transitory. A major factor in causing such change is innovation.

Adam Smith explained that as markets increase in size, this leads to more specialization as producers seek better ways to produce goods and more ways to improve existing products. So both product and process innovation can be as a result of increased specialization. This is consistent with Schumpeter's views, introduced above, that market forces push down profits on existing goods, incentives are created to introduce new products and processes and avail of greater profit opportunities.

Accordingly innovation is a critical feature in the marketplace and again the entrepreneur is central to this process. This has led to debate on how best to increase the level of innovation and its by-product – economic prosperity. Patents are one way to increase innovation activity by providing the entrepreneur with added security through a system guaranteeing protection from imitation, thus encouraging them to undertake costly research and development expenditures searching for knowledge to be exploited in the market. Consumers gain immediately from patent-protected innovations in terms of the availability of previously unavailable products or processes. Consumers may also gain over time as the discovery embodied in patents eventually becomes dispersed more widely in the economic system once the patent runs out.

A limit to competition in the theory of entrepreneurship is the monopoly control of unique resources. This control can occur naturally, through ownership rights (that is, property rights) or through government regulations and the issuing of patents, for example, both of which have the effect of restricting entry to markets. The presence of patents in some markets indicates the precedence given to benefits from innovation over potential costs from greater market competition. There is a trade-off and decisions must be made on how the greatest benefit is provided to society.

Other types of barriers to entry that can limit competition are government regulations including licensing agreements. This is again related to what role governments should play in the marketplace. Depending on political ideology, some argue for an extensive role for government involvement in the market. Others, such as the Austrian school, believe that government involvement should be kept to an absolute minimum on the basis that any government intervention to prevent a free-market solution attempts to devise alternative allocation mechanisms that are rarely, if ever, better than the free-market solution. The role of government in this latter case would then be limited to supplementing the market process, to facilitate its smooth functioning.

6.3 ALTERNATIVE MODELS OF COMPETITION AND MARKET STRUCTURE

Traditional models of competition evolve around four types of market structure, each of which is examined separately below in terms of its implications for a firm's ability to earn profits, which we see is related to a firm's market power.

> **Market structure** refers to certain characteristics of an industry, such as the level of concentration, the extent of entry barriers and the extent of product differentiation.
> **Market concentration** refers to the number of firms in a specific market and their relative market share.
> **Market power** exists when firms in a market hold a sufficiently large market share that their actions can change the market price of a product – producing more results in a falling equilibrium price, producing less leads to a rise in equilibrium price, *ceteris paribus.*

At one extreme there can be just one firm in a market and we call this *monopoly*. At the other extreme a market can be characterized by many firms; each small, relative to the overall size of the market – this is called *perfect competition*. All examples of market structure apart from perfect competition come under the heading of *imperfect competition*.

Between the extremes of monopoly and perfect competition there are two additional forms of market structure: *monopolistic competition* and *oligopoly*. Monopolistic competition is characterized by many firms each with some power to set the price of their product, which they hold because they supply a particular brand of product – they differentiate their product. Oligopoly is characterized by a few firms of large size relative to the total market, so each firm has some degree of market power.

Market concentration is often used as the primary measure of market structure. To calculate the level of concentration in a market, a concentration ratio (CR) can be calculated.

A **concentration ratio** measures the market share of the biggest firms in the market. For example a **CR4** calculates the market share of the largest four firms.

Even though a concentration ratio only counts the top firms this can be quite accurate since if the purpose is to calculate the degree of market power in an industry, it is assumed the biggest firms have the most power. The Herfindahl Index is a more accurate measure of concentration.

The **Herfindahl Index** measures the market share of all firms in the industry by summing the squares of each individual firm's market share:

$$H = \sum_{1}^{N} S_i^2$$

where S_i denotes each firm's market share and summation is from firm 1 to N, the total number of firms in the market. The squared term indicates that firms with large market shares will have higher weight.

Market share can be measured in terms of, for example, total sales, net output, numbers employed or capital asset values. However, depending on the measure used, the calculation of market share will differ.

In the airplane manufacturing industry, different measures resulted in different results. Boeing and Airbus have both claimed to be the largest in the industry. With just two firms in this industry it should have been obvious that both could not be correct in their analysis. But as it happens both were right! This happened because each firm used a different measure of market share. Boeing, the older firm and once also the dominant firm in the industry, used the number of airplanes *delivered* as their measure of market share. Airbus, the younger but rapidly growing firm, used the number of airplanes *ordered*. Using these different measures both firms could claim to be the largest firm.

Concentration and market structure are the key ingredients in market analysis.

6.3.1   PERFECT COMPETITION

Assumptions underlying this model are:

- Products are *homogeneous* – all products are alike and so no perceived differences exist.
- All participants in the market have perfect knowledge – full information on prices, costs and product availability exist.
- There are a large number of buyers and sellers in the market. Each firm provides a fraction of the output of the industry.
- Firms have no control over price and are, therefore, *price takers*. Each firm's demand curve is perfectly elastic. At the market price, firms can sell as much output as they like.
- No barriers to entry or exit exist in the market.

Further characteristics of this market structure include:

- Prices are set by *market* supply and demand. Market demand is a downward sloping relationship, while market supply is upward sloping.
- At the market price, firms earn normal profits in the long run, no opportunities exist to earn supernormal profits in the long run.
- Factors of production are fully mobile and can be easily transferred from one industry or market to another.
- There is efficient use of resources.

How equilibrium emerges in the short run and long run are considered separately below.

Short-run equilibrium

Figure 6.1 presents the short-run equilibrium for the industry in panel A and the firm in panel B. Industry price is determined by the intersection of the demand and supply curves in panel A. At the short-run equilibrium price P^* one firm in the industry (panel B) can sell as much output as it likes, but will selling nothing either above or below this price. The firm faces a horizontal demand curve at this price. Industry output is Q^I, while the firm's profit-maximizing output Q^F is determined by the intersection of its MR and MC curves.

Since there are many firms in this industry, the quantity each firm produces, Q^F, is very small relative to the total output of the industry, Q^I. In Figure 6.1, the firm is making supernormal profits since the lower section of its AC curves is below the price. With each individual firm in a perfectly competitive industry able to earn only P^* for its output, P^* represents a firm's additional revenue (MR) if it sells extra output. Since the price the firm receives on any unit of its output is P^*, this price also represents the firm's average revenue (AR) on each unit of output. With perfectly elastic demand at the price P^*, marginal revenue and average revenue are all given by P^*.

At Q^F the firm's supernormal profit per unit is equal to the distance between price and the AC curve. The firm's total supernormal profits is represented by the dashed area in Figure 6.1 panel B. If the distance between the price and the AC curve at Q^F is £2 and the firm produces 1200 units ($Q^F = 1200$), then the total supernormal profits earned by the firm in the short run is £2400. Conversely, if the firm's AC curve is above price then the firm is losing money and it will only survive in the short run if it can cover its average variable costs. As explained in Chapter 4,

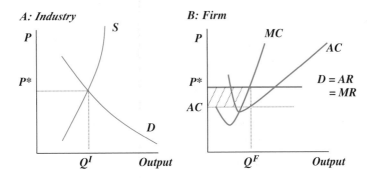

FIGURE 6.1 SHORT-RUN EQUILIBRIUM IN PERFECT COMPETITION

the critical short-run survival decision for the firm is whether or not it can cover its average variable costs.

Long-run equilibrium

Logically, the supernormal profits earned in Figure 6.1 will encourage new firms into the industry and result in the supernormal profits declining as firms compete by charging lower prices. Firms will not compete by offering different quality goods, as goods are presumed to be homogeneous. Existing or incumbent firms may wish to take advantage of such profitable opportunities and may also increase their output. The net result is a shift of the industry supply curve to the right as in panel A in Figure 6.2.

A new lower industry price results at P^1. Panel B outlines the effect of this price reduction for the same firm considered in Figure 6.1. The firm's price and AR fall in response to the corresponding fall in the industry price. This reduction in both industry price and firm's AR continues until such time as the AR is tangential to the firm's long-run average cost curve ($LRAC$). Additional industry supply continues until equilibrium emerges where it is just economically profitable for the firm to stay in business, since it can cover long-run average costs. Were the industry price to fall any further, the firm would be better off exiting the industry in the long run. No further incentive for new firms to enter the industry exists.

No supernormal profits are earned by a firm in a perfectly competitive market in the long run.

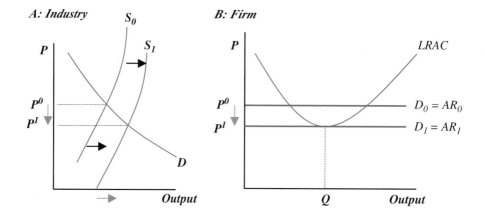

FIGURE 6.2 LONG-RUN EQUILIBRIUM FOR THE INDUSTRY AND THE FIRM UNDER PERFECT COMPETITION

Output is produced efficiently in a perfectly competitive industry:

- Production occurs at the minimum point of each firm's average cost curve.
- The price charged to consumers is the minimum price that could be charged while encouraging firms to stay in the industry.
- Economic resources are used to their maximum efficiency by all firms since prices cover marginal costs (this is **allocative efficiency**).
- Firms earn normal profits but not supernormal profits, so consumer surplus is maximized.

All outcomes indicate the model of perfect competition to be efficient *in theory*. Of course, very few examples, if any, of perfectly competitive industries exist in today's business world. Instead economists tend to use the outcomes of the model as *benchmarks* for comparison across all types of market structure.

6.3.2 MONOPOLY

In a monopoly, one firm supplies the entire market. Such cases are quite rare but do exist. In focusing on the model, we can compare and contrast its implications with the perfect competition case.

The assumptions underlying monopoly market structure are:

- There is only one firm in the industry.
- Entry barriers exist to prevent entry by other firms.
- The monopoly firm maximizes its profits.
- The monopoly product has no close substitutes, therefore each monopoly firm has control over price.

In a monopoly, the firm's demand function and the industry/market demand function are one and the same – a downward sloping demand curve. The monopoly firm sets its price depending on what it considers the market will bear, evident in the demand function for its product, given its costs.

The monopolist has a large degree of market power or control over price.

The firm sets price so as to maximize profits, i.e. sets $MC = MR$ at point X in Figure 6.3, leading to the monopoly price P^m and quantity Q^m shown. At this price the firm earns supernormal profits because the price is above average cost. The dashed area in Figure 6.3 represents the total amount of supernormal profits

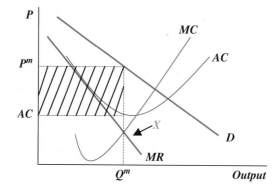

FIGURE 6.3   EQUILIBRIUM UNDER MONOPOLY

earned by the monopolist. New firms cannot bid these profits down due to barriers to entry in the industry.

> If scale economies imply that only one firm could supply efficiently, i.e. at low cost to the market, a **natural monopoly** exists.

Monopolies sometimes have a different shaped *AC* curve to that shown in Figure 6.3. This can arise from the existence of substantial economies of scale in the industry (see Figure 4.7 to refresh your memory). Scale economies result in average costs continually falling over large levels of output. This would be the case in, for example, capital-intensive industries such as the rail industry or electricity provision.

Figure 6.4 illustrates the characteristics of the *AC* curve and equilibrium in such an industry. Here the monopolist's *AC* curve is falling over a large range of output

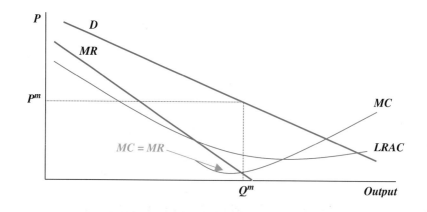

FIGURE 6.4   NATURAL MONOPOLY

and starts to rise only at very large output levels. Again, the profit-maximizing monopolist sets $MC = MR$ to maximize profits and earns supernormal profits at price P^m and output Q^m.

This ability to earn supernormal profits under monopoly market structure can be a major cause of concern for governments and competition watchdogs since such profits imply lower consumer surplus than if profits were lower.

6.3.3 PERFECT COMPETITION VS. MONOPOLY

The extent of the impact on welfare and consumer surplus is evident from Figure 6.5 where perfect competition and monopoly market structures can be compared and contrasted.

One striking difference between monopoly and perfect competition is the equilibrium price and output levels when facing an identical market demand curve.

> Under monopoly price is higher and output is lower than under perfect competition.

This implies that consumer surplus is lower and producer surplus higher under monopoly, due to this redistribution of income away from consumers and towards the monopoly producer. There is also an area that is lost completely in welfare terms, which neither consumers nor producers gain: defined by the triangle *abc*. This is called a deadweight loss.

> A **deadweight loss** represents the welfare lost to society from relatively inefficient production.

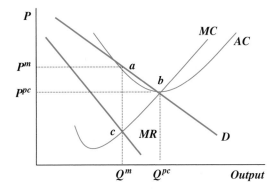

FIGURE 6.5 PERFECT COMPETITION AND MONOPOLY COMPARED

Unlike under perfect competition, a monopoly firm does not produce at maximum efficiency since it does not produce at the minimum point of the AC curve (Q^{pc}). Hence, resources are not used at maximum efficiency since under monopoly output is restricted.

Given these seemingly negative consequences of monopolies, why do they exist at all? Because the underlying assumptions of product homogeneity and free entry and exit in the perfect competition model rarely if ever hold true in the business world!

> The challenge for the economic system is to acknowledge that perfect competition is not achievable and to ensure that the beneficial effects of competition are maximized.

Barriers to entry exist in many industries and these impede the ability of new firms to come into the market and bid down price.

Barriers to entry may be based on:

- *Type of product*: standardized versus differentiated products. The ability of firms to differentiate their products and thereby create **brand loyalty** can make it difficult for new entrants to gain a foothold in a market, especially if consumers are unwilling to switch from a brand they know and trust.
- *Economies of scale*: Some industries require the firm to produce a relatively large output in order to operate at or near the minimum point of their average cost curve. In this case the ability of the firm to secure a large output will determine whether they can profitably enter the market. In the extreme case of the average cost curve continuing to fall over large output ranges, only very large firms could compete or, in the natural monopoly case above, just one firm would be profitable.
- *Experience curve effects*: Sometimes experience by the incumbent firm in the industry can result in lower average costs for that firm. New entrants who therefore do not have this experience are faced with higher average costs. This puts them at a competitive disadvantage.
- *Capital requirements*: Some industries require a large amount of initial capital in order to set up production. A firm's ability to access such capital may determine their ability to enter the market.
- *Cost disadvantages independent of size*: Incumbent firms may have long-established relationships with suppliers or distributors that give the firm valuable access to important resources. Dealing with a long-established

supplier over a period of time can provide the firm with access to a reliable source of high-quality raw materials at competitive prices at a time that suits the firm's production schedule. A new entrant, not having such access, may be at a competitive disadvantage.

- *Legal protection*: The firm's ability to secure patents can prevent a new entrant from competing in the market. Licences granted by, for example, national governments, or trade agreements between countries would have similar effects.

Benefits from monopoly?

Despite the potentially negative aspects of monopolies, there are instances where monopolies generate economic benefits. Central to the positive aspects of monopolies is their potential for innovation, emphasized by Schumpeter. The supernormal profits that monopolies earn can be used for investment into R&D facilities. However, this is only a positive result for society if firms carry out such investment rather than squandering their profits. There are some incentives that may encourage monopoly firms to invest, at least, a proportion of their profits back into the firm and these incentives centre around the ability to earn higher profits in the future as a result of successful innovation and thereby securing their dominance in the market.

Other arguments in favour of monopolies centre on their ability to exploit economies of scale in production such that society reduces wasteful inefficiencies. If a monopolist can gain efficiencies over and above those that could be gained in a perfectly competitive market (if small output shares are produced only at relatively high average cost) then monopolies have advantages. Coupled with such advantages is the potential, which always exists in monopolies, to exploit a market position and in doing so harm consumer interests. Critics of monopolies point to this potential damage as outweighing any potential advantages and will therefore be sceptical of them, especially as there are many cases where innovation and R&D take place in non-monopolistic industries.

6.3.4 MONOPOLISTIC COMPETITION

Markets characterized by monopolistic competition, first described by Edward Chamberlin, involve many sellers producing products that are close, but not perfect substitutes – there is product differentiation. Each firm has a monopoly in its own variety of the product. Examples of monopolistic competition include restaurants, petrol stations, corner shops and builders. This market structure is illustrated in Figure 6.6.

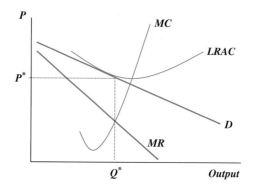

FIGURE 6.6 LONG-RUN EQUILIBRIUM UNDER MONOPOLISTIC COMPETITION

The assumptions of market structure characterized by monopolistic competition are:

- Large number of sellers each with a relatively small market share. Firms do not have to be overly concerned with what rivals are doing and how they are likely to react.
- Firms produce differentiated products – gives them some power over price but close substitutes are available – demand is elastic.
- Freedom of entry to the industry exists. Supernormal profits in the short run attract new entrants and new varieties so that long-run supernormal profits are not made.
- There is full and symmetric information – a new entrant takes market share from all competitors equally.

In the short run, any supernormal profits earned by a firm will disappear as new entrants enter the market, offering substitute products and attracting some customers, resulting in the demand curve facing each other firm declining – shifting to the left. In the long run, the demand curve is tangential to the long-run AC curve and normal profits are earned at price P^* and quantity Q^*. The industry is competitive containing several competing firms where none makes supernormal profits. Each firm produces along the negatively sloped portion of their $LRAC$, implying scale economies are not fully exploited, implying there is excess capacity in their plant.

With respect to efficiency, each firm does not produce at the lowest point on the $LRAC$ curve; therefore, production is not efficient. Also since price exceeds marginal cost, each firm has some degree of monopoly power, created through the existence of brand loyalty.

MAINTAINING AND ENHANCING BRAND LOYALTY IN MONOPOLISTIC COMPETITION

Incumbent firms purchase advertising and other promotional activities, while new entrants may have to spend substantially more in order to gain a foothold in the market. **Advertising** is one example of **non-price competition** and it is a major feature of this type of market structure. By spending on advertising, firms not only want to gain new customers but also keep existing customers; that is they want to make their customer's demand curves more inelastic. Yet advertising is expensive so firms must balance the perceived benefits of advertising against the actual costs of advertising.

How do firms do this? They continue to spend on advertising so long as the additional (marginal) revenue the advertising brings in exceeds the additional (marginal) cost of the advertising. Firms' profits increase as long as $MR_{advertising} >$ $MC_{advertising}$. **Advertising exhibits diminishing marginal returns**, such that more and more advertising will yield less and less revenue so eventually $MR_{advertising} = MC_{advertising}$ and the firm's advertising adds nothing to profits.

6.3.5   OLIGOPOLY

The final type of market structure considered is oligopoly.

The underlying assumptions of oligopoly are:

- Few sellers exist in the market – each taking account of the decisions of their competitors.
- Products of each firm are similar but not identical.
- Each firm produces a substantial amount of output and so has market power.
- Barriers to entry exist.

Oligopolies occur where a market has 'room' for a few large firms. This could be because of cost advantages through scale economies or through economies of scope.

Economies of scope exist when a firm produces many products and can share resources across them such that the unit costs of each product is lower than if they were produced by separate firms. Shared marketing or distribution costs may be sources of economies of scope.

In industries where mergers and acquisitions are commonplace (such as the car industry discussed in Chapter 4) the number of competitors decline as firms' business strategies guide them to 'grow' not by expanding the market, which is becoming saturated, but by buying up rivals, which may reduce competitive behaviour and allow for increasing profit margins once barriers to entry exist.

The essence of oligopoly markets is that firms' decisions are interdependent. When making decisions on output, for example, each firm takes account of how their rivals are *likely* to respond, as this will affect the profitability of such decisions. This complicates firms' decision-making processes because it can be very difficult to predict how each rival will respond and precisely how such responses will impact on the firm. Very often firms will seek out a 'simpler' solution. For example, instead of trying to guess how a rival will respond, firms may wish to seek agreements with their rivals on output (or other decisions) so as to maximize the profitability with the minimum of risk. With few firms in an industry this is not as difficult as it may first seem. Yet at the same time there are incentives for each firm to 'go it alone' so that it can get one step ahead of its rivals. This inherent conflict in oligopoly markets make for fascinating study.

Formal collusion by firms can take the form of a cartel where firms make explicit output agreements, for example, with the intention of maintaining a high price for the product.

> A **cartel** is an agreement between firms to cooperate in restricting the amount of output they produce, thereby influencing the price.

OPEC (the Organization of Petroleum Exporting Countries) is possibly the most well-known cartel and its agreements on levels of oil production (or extraction) for each country effectively controls the price of oil on world markets (this example is discussed in terms of its effects on international inflation in Chapter 8). However, there are two problems with cartels that inhibit their usefulness. First, cartels tend to be unstable because of each member's incentive to cheat on the agreement and make extra profits in the short term. When other firms see the agreement breached they would follow suit and, in the case of OPEC, increase oil production, thereby causing the world price to fall. Second, in a lot of countries, including Europe and the USA, cartels are *illegal* and any such agreements are prohibited under competition law.

As a result firms may engage in less obvious forms of collusion.

Implicit collusion may take the form of **price leadership**, where either

- a dominant firm in the industry sets price and all others follow and set their price with this information at hand; or
- a well-established firm becomes the 'leader' in the industry and is trusted with setting the price that all firms will charge.

Such a leader has usually gained the respect of the other firms and has a lot of experience in the industry. All types of implicit collusion are also illegal and therefore firms may not readily engage in such activities, despite the potential business benefits.

Oligopoly and game theory

Without collusion in oligopoly markets, firms make assumptions on how rivals react. Such interdependence can be analysed using game theory.

Game theory is a microeconomic approach or tool of analysis applied to understand the behaviour of individuals and firms. Pay-offs generated by following different strategies can be compared.

In game theory, a firm makes assumptions on how the other firm(s) will react and then chooses its best option. In such games the firm seeks a dominant strategy.

A **dominant strategy** is one that provides one firm with the best outcome, irrespective of the strategy another firm (or firms) chooses.

Firm interdependence and dominant strategies can be illustrated using the example shown in Table 6.1. Here we have two firms; *A* has two strategic options, *X* or *Y*, and

TABLE 6.1 GAME THEORY: STRATEGIC OPTIONS AND DOMINANT STRATEGY

		Firm B's strategic options	
		I (high)	*II (low)*
Firm A's	*X (high)*	(3, 4)	(2, 5)
strategic	*Y (low)*	(4, 3)	(4, 5)
options			

firm *B* has two strategic options, *I* and *II*. For firm *A*, Strategy *X* could be to set a high price and strategy *Y* to set a low price while for Firm *B*, Strategy *I* is high price and *II* is low price. By examining the pay-offs from each strategy we can analyse if a dominant strategy exists.

Here, if firm *A* chooses strategy *X* (high price) and firm *B* chooses strategy *I* (high price), then *A* earns £3 in profits and *B* earns £4. If *A* chooses strategy *Y* (low price) while firm *B* still chooses strategy *I* (high price), then *A* earns £4 and *B* earns £3 since lower prices entice consumers to buy more from firm *A*. When firm *B* chooses *I* (high), strategy *Y* (low) earns firm *A* higher profit.

When firm *B* chooses strategy *II* (low), firm *A* earns £2 with strategy *X* (high) and £4 with strategy *Y* (low). Again strategy *Y* earns Firm *A* higher profits. Therefore strategy *Y* is a dominant strategy for firm *A*; no matter what strategy firm *B* chooses, firm *A* will always do best by choosing strategy *Y*.

Similarly for firm *B*, no matter what strategy firm *A* chooses, firm *B* always does best by choosing strategy *II*, so *II* is *B*'s dominant strategy.

The equilibrium outcome in this game has firm *A* choosing strategy *Y* and firm *B* choosing strategy *II*. This outcome earns £4 for firm *A* and £5 for firm *B*.

Dominant strategies for either one or both firms result in a relatively easy determination of the outcome. However, dominant strategies do not exist for all cases.

Consider the Game in Table 6.2. Firms *A* and *B* again have two strategic options but with different pay-offs. In this game no firm has a dominant strategy. The firms are faced with two possible options:

- *Option 1*: Firm *A* chooses *X* and firm *B* chooses *I* – each firm earns £10 profit.
- *Option 2*: Firm *A* chooses *Y* and firm *B* chooses *II* – each firm earns £5 profit.

TABLE 6.2 GAME THEORY: STRATEGIC OPTIONS WITH NO DOMINANT STRATEGY

| | | Firm B's strategic options | |
		I	*II*
Firm A's	*X*	(10, 10)	(0, 0)
strategic	*Y*	(0, 0)	(5, 5)
options			

This is an example of a game with two Nash equilibria (after John Nash, the Nobel Prize winner in economics, 1994), where each firm is doing the best it can, given the strategy being pursued by the other firm.

A **Nash equilibrium** exists when each player in a game chooses their best strategy given the strategies followed by other players.

The two remaining options are less likely since both firms earning zero profits. Therefore, it is crucial that each firm chooses either option 1 or 2 and option 1 is preferable to option 2 for the firms concerned. But how can the firms ensure that either of these options will prevail? Collusion would ensure they do not end up with the worst outcome of £0 profits each.

In the absence of collusion there is still a way for the firms to achieve the better outcome. If one firm invests in a commitment of resources that will make it clear to all other firms that it intends to pursue one particular strategy, then this can guide the second firm in its strategy decision. For example, if firm A invests in a system of production that makes it clear it must pursue strategy X, then firm B, will do best by choosing strategy I and the resulting profit outcome for both firms is £10. Such an investment must be both *visible* and *irreversible* in order to convince firm B that strategy Y *will be* the strategy pursued by firm A. Pay-offs as before.

To make this example more tangible, consider that strategy X (and I) involve abiding by an agreement to restrict output and strategy Y (or II) represent cheating on such an agreement. If both firms abide by the agreement, they both earn £10; if they both cheat, they earn £5. Any deviations from these two strategies will result in zero profits for both, due to, for example, resulting price wars. To achieve the best possible outcome one firm could invest in machinery, or a production line, which is capacity-constrained – only a certain capacity can be produced. Such a firm could credibly commit a certain level of production. An agreement could then be made to set this level of production to maximize their profits.

Prisoner's Dilemma

An interesting outcome unfolds if the pay-offs to this game were as shown in Table 6.3. Such a game is an example of the Prisoner's Dilemma.

A **Prisoner's Dilemma** exists when the equilibrium from a game generates a sub-optimal outcome for **all** parties involved. With commitment (or a binding contract) between the firms, higher pay-offs could be achieved to the benefit of both players.

TABLE 6.3 GAME THEORY: STRATEGIC OPTIONS WITH SUB-OPTIMAL STRATEGY

		Firm B's strategic options	
		I	II
Firm A's	X	(10, 10)	(3, 15)
strategic	Y	(15, 3)	(5, 5)
options			

High price (or low output) strategies are X and I in Table 6.3, while low price (high output) strategies are Y and II. If both firms have low price strategies (Y and II), industry output is high and profits are relatively low at £5 per firm. With both firms following high price strategies resulting in low industry output, profits rise to £10 per firm. Firms' profits are maximized at £15 if one firm follows a low price (high

TABLE 6.4 SUMMARY OF MARKET STRUCTURE CHARACTERISTICS

	Type of product	No. of firms	Examples	Power of firm: price	Barriers to entry	Non-price competition
Perfect competition	Homogeneous	Many	None	None	None	None
Monopolistic competition	Differentiated	Many	Retailing, building and restaurant trades	Some	Low	Advertising and product differentiation
Oligopoly	Standardized or differentiated	Few	Steel, car and computer industries	Some	High	Advertising and product differentiation
Monopoly	Unique	One	Microsoft	A lot	Very high	Advertising

output) strategy when the other firm adopts the alternative strategy (earning £3); combined profits of £18 would be generated.

If firm A thinks B will select strategy I (high price), A's best option is to choose Y (low price) since its profits of £15 > £10. If B selects II, A's best option remains Y since £5 > £3. Similarly, B's best option is to select strategy II. Hence, when no co-operation is possible between firms a non-cooperative equilibrium emerges with pay-offs of £5 to each firm. This is sub-optimal when both could earn £10.

Some co-operation such as a binding commitment or a contract between the firms could generate an incentive for them both to simultaneously choose X and I (where profits of £20 shared equally are possible). This would be an example of a co-operative equilibrium.

Summary of market characteristics

To sum up this section, the main differentiating characteristics of each market structure are presented in Table 6.4.

6.4 AUSTRIAN AND TRADITIONAL PERSPECTIVES: A COMPARISON

The previous two sections present very different perspectives on competition, i.e. the Austrian 'competition as a process' view and the perspective of competition as a timeless state of events. Competition is a dynamic process in the former and a static process in the latter.

Knowledge and its use are key issues distinguishing the traditional view of competition from the Austrian view. In perfect competition, knowledge is 'perfect' or available to all. Decision-making becomes a problem not so much of making choices, but one of maximizing a series of price possibilities from a given set of resources. Individuals are in a sense 'programmed' to select a transaction that is a 'maximum' outcome attainable. Since knowledge is given, in effect, there is nothing to compete over. All producers and consumers know what is to be known about products and prices and there is no need to compete for anything.

In reality, characteristics of goods and what makes them scare and valuable are not known in advance and these are some of the issues that the events we call competition attempt to discover. In perfect competition, the decision-maker does not exercise genuine choice; everything is known in advance so there are no choices to be made. Consequently, it is assumed that no errors are made in this decision-making/maximization process.

To many consumers and producers the 'perfect competition' dramatization of the marketplace is not realistic. In making decisions, individuals rank objectives and available resources and in this process new knowledge is gained. This new knowledge becomes, in turn, part of future ranking processes. In addition, outcomes are not known in advance; instead individuals are confronted with choices to be made.

The Austrian perspective acknowledges the experience and learning of individuals where knowledge is not only limited, it is also constantly developing over time. Knowledge is crucial and central to the process of competition itself. It not only emerges from competition but also creates competitive forces. Every player in the market possesses different degrees of knowledge and can use it in exchanges to maximize their utility, the more specific in nature is the knowledge (as discussed in Chapter 2). This approach is intuitive from our own experiences as consumers. When we purchase goods we do not, and cannot, know everything there is to know about the good we are buying, the number of sellers of that good and the prices charged in different markets. Yet we do not need to know all this information in order to trade. We simply assess the amount of value or utility that we can derive from the product and decide whether the price subjectively represents good value to us.

Another feature of the perfect competition model is that no one firm can gain market power. Firms do not interact, they are price takers and accept given 'world' prices. Yet in business we see many firms with market power and they achieve this through, for example, superior use of knowledge or resources.

> Microsoft has become a very large and successful firm by developing a useful operating system for personal computers. In the process it displaced IBM, the previous leader in the industry. The amount of knowledge and, in particular, the use of knowledge that each firm had discovered allowed this situation to emerge.

Equilibrium, central to the traditional model of competition is considered in the Austrian approach as contradictory to the whole notion of competition. Equilibrium, by its very nature, assumes a steady state where the market has absorbed all relevant information and is in a position of stability from where there is no tendency to move – there is no more competition. As we can see from our discussion of the Austrian perspective, though, this can never be the case as knowledge constantly changes. Therefore equilibrium not only does not exist, moreover it *cannot* exist.

A further point that sets the Austrian perspective apart from the traditional model is that markets are unpredictable. Competition is more like a game of chance rather than a set of predictable moves and counter moves. This unpredictability comes from the central economic problem facing society, that is, the problem of the utilization of *knowledge* which no one individual possesses. Furthermore, this economic problem always arises due to changes occurring in the economy. Hayek (1978) sums up his position as follows:

> the point to keep constantly in mind is that all economic adjustment is made necessary by unforeseen changes; and the whole reason for employing the price mechanism is to tell individuals that what they are doing, or can do, has for some reason for which they are not responsible become less or more demanded. (p. 261)

Such change brings with it certain opposition. Competition is generally seen to benefit the consumer and indeed some producers, but it also introduces new ways of doing things that are better than current methods, the 'old' being replaced by the 'new'. With such displacement comes changing fortunes of those involved. Competition brings with it increased rewards for some and diminished reward for others. As explained in relation to trade in Chapter 5, such diminished rewards form the basis on which competition is usually opposed.

6.5 WHEN MARKETS FAIL

The portrayal and outcomes of competition describe how the self-motivated actions of consumers and producers leads to production and consumption of goods and services in an efficient, effective manner, given the incentives generated by the prices of goods and services. However, there are some events that occur that can interfere or even prevent this outcome – markets can sometimes *fail*.

> **Market failure** occurs when economic resources are not allocated efficiently caused by the price system working imperfectly.

6.5.1 WHY MARKETS MAY FAIL

The principal types of market failures are public goods, externalities, natural monopolies and monopoly power and information asymmetries. These are important in the context of policy as they provide the rationale underlying much of the government intervention in markets that we observe.

Public goods

Public goods (introduced in Chapter 1) are generally available to all, such that it is difficult if not impossible to exclude any person, even if they have not paid for the good, from consuming it. Markets often fail to encourage private firms from supplying such goods.

Externalities

As outlined in Chapter 4, an externality may result from a production or consumption process that affects some individual(s) not directly involved in the process.

> Positive externalities are private timber forests providing scenic benefits to all or immunization against contagious diseases in a community. Negative externalities are pollution from a factory harming local farmers or cigarette smoke reducing the enjoyment of a meal by another person.

Often, the prices of products do not fully reflect the true costs *including the external effects* of their production. It is the negative externalities that economists are mostly concerned with as they reduce the economic welfare of producers and/or consumers.

Natural monopoly and monopoly power

Monopoly power, or substantial power over price, is closely associated with the natural monopoly case such that a lower level of output may be produced and a higher price charged than in a more competitive market. These negative aspects can be sustained due to barriers to entry in the market, which facilitates the redistribution of income away from consumers and towards producers, thus harming consumer interests. Monopoly power also provides firms with the opportunity of engaging in anti-competitive practices, either on their own against other producers or potential producers or against consumers, which effectively means raising prices above competitive levels.

Information asymmetries

> **Information asymmetries** exist when one party has more information than another party in an exchange agreement.

Information asymmetries usually arise where a producer has more information on a product or service than consumers who are open to potential exploitation, usually in the form of high prices and/or poor quality. The functioning of competitive markets depends on the ability of consumers to adequately judge competing products. A lack of information naturally impedes this. If firms have market power they may have few incentives to produce relevant information for consumers or the information may be of such a technical nature that few consumers would be properly able to interpret and use it. The information asymmetry problem is most pronounced for experience goods as against search goods.

> **Experience goods** are goods where their quality attributes can only be assessed through trial (or experience) whereas the quality of **search goods** can be gained before purchase.

The resulting problems are of inefficiency and welfare loss.

6.5.2   IMPLICATIONS OF MARKET FAILURE

One implication of market failure is the redistribution effects from producers to consumers. Society may also suffer a deadweight loss, as considered earlier in Figure 6.5. This is particularly damaging since potential benefits are lost to the economy. By preventing such a loss someone in the market place would gain. In Figure 6.7 panel *A* we have a market performing efficiently where price and quantity emerge from the interaction of demand and supply as P^E and Q^E. If the quantity of output is limited below its free-market level (for example, because producers can set high prices as fewer goods than the equilibrium quantity may be sold due to distribution agreements) to Q^L, consumers pay higher prices at P^H. At a higher price, consumer surplus falls and producer surplus rises but we see that some of the original surplus is no longer part of consumer or producer surplus – this is a deadweight loss shown as a triangle in Figure 6.7 panel *B*.

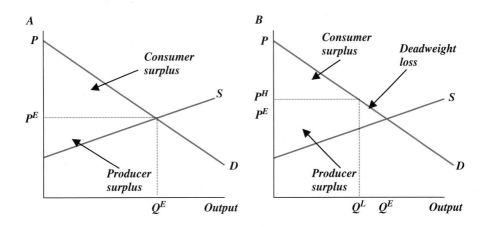

FIGURE 6.7   DEADWEIGHT LOSS

Preventing or correcting market failures can create positive economic benefits and can provide a justification for government involvement in the market. In an extreme case market failures can prevent a market from existing at all – hence the provision of public goods.

A government can control the behaviour of producers and consumers through 'indirect command' where they provide incentives by making certain activities more or less rewarding. Government involvement can take the form of intervention in the market, either as a direct supplier of a good or service, or as a policy instrument to force a positive outcome arising from a market failure. For example, governments will usually provide public goods such as national defence and security and also *may* provide the goods associated with natural monopoly characteristics, such as in the utilities industry where governments have in the past supplied electricity, gas, telecommunications, water, etc.

Less direct government involvement arises in attempts to reduce the impact of other types of market failure.

- To reduce information asymmetries governments can introduce regulations compelling producers to release accurate and affordable information in the form of standardized product labelling, setting minimum safety and health standards or banning false or misleading advertising.
- Governments can also step into the market, in the form of regulation, to reduce welfare losses arising from negative externalities.
- To reduce monopoly power and reduce the effects of anti-competitive practices, the government can introduce a specific legal instrument in the form of competition law, to enforce standards and a policy of competition in the economy.

6.6 GOVERNMENT REGULATION OF COMPETITION

Across Europe, governments' role in reducing monopoly power and in anti-competitive practices has evolved substantially over recent decades, particularly from the 1980s on. One traditional response – for governments to step in and take ownership of natural monopolies and to impose strict regulations on business activities – was considered to be an efficient method until the realization emerged that it may also generate significant costs. This conclusion arose from:

- weighing up of the costs versus the benefits of regulations;
- comparing whether the restrictions imposed under regulation were proportionate to the potential harm done in their absence;
- examining whether there was a more efficient way of achieving the goals of regulation.

Furthermore, it was possible in some circumstances that governments' regulations might harm consumers. This occurs if business interests are put ahead of consumer interests *and* if there is a weak consumer voice. Both of these can result in regulatory capture.

> **Regulatory capture** occurs where regulations set up to protect consumers – to lead to greater competition and lower prices – become captured by the industry for the benefit of producers in that industry. This happens where producers can convince the government or a regulator to introduce rules favouring producers.

Furthermore, the notion of a natural monopoly and the role of governments in running such enterprises began to change. Advances in technology and the development of financial markets, for example, both helped to change the perception of natural monopolies. No longer were such industries considered to be optimal if operated by one firm and instead many were broken up into small sub-industries. For example, in the electricity market, four sub-industries were developed comprising:

- *generation*: the production of electricity by either hydro, nuclear or fossil fuels, for example;
- *transmission*: the transfer of electricity from the generation site through the national grid to different parts of the country;
- *distribution*: the transfer of electricity from the national grid to local grids and sub-stations;
- *supply*: the transfer of electricity to homes and industries.

The idea then was to introduce competition into as many of these sub-industries as possible. Generation and supply were sub-industries where competition was seen to be possible whereas transmission and distribution were considered to have natural monopoly-type characteristics. Hence, it did not make economic sense to have duplicate transmission and distribution networks when the product could be transferred more efficiently through just one.

When introducing different competitors in rail transport, it would not make economic sense to have separate tracks and stations for each train operator. If this were to happen, hundreds of train stations would be scattered around the country, along with thousands of miles of train track. Exactly the same scenario applies to gas, water and other utility industries.

In addition, governments also reconsidered their ownership of certain industries, driven in some cases by EU policy. Moves towards privatization were not only an attempt to bring the benefits of competition to industries, including improving efficiency, but also to reduce bureaucracy and political interference.

Privatization: the sale of government-owned businesses (and associated assets) in whole or in part to the private sector. Examples include electricity, gas and telecommunications industries.

Governments' entire industry philosophy changed, becoming broadly less interventionist in industry with a redirection of their efforts to other policy issues. The idea was to introduce competition where competition was possible and to have regulation where it was not. Such regulation could take the form of access/price regulation so that competitive supply industries could gain access to a product at a 'fair' price and then sell it on to the end user for a 'reasonable' profit where the relevant regulator would decide on the interpretation of fair and reasonable.

Many regulations no longer serving their purpose – either because they were outdated, or had been captured by industry – encouraged a process of deregulation or re-regulation of private industry – where old rules were abandoned or amended to reflect current market conditions. At the same time the EU pushed for greater liberalization of markets as part of its drive for a single European market. The result was a changing competitive landscape in many industries including airlines, utilities and some professional services.

Market liberalization: reducing barriers to the free movement of goods and services to encourage entry by new competitors.

With liberalized markets came government competition policy to ensure a fair and level playing field for all competitors. Broad-based competition policy is seen as less burdensome than industry regulations in attempting to create a well-functioning marketplace.

Competition policy at the national level mirrors EU competition policy established under the Treaty of Rome. Two sections of the treaty form the foundations of national competition policy in individual EU countries.

> Section 81 of the Treaty of Rome prohibits any collaborative agreement between firms whose aim is to prevent, distort or restrict competition within the EU.
> Section 82 prohibits firms with market power from distorting competition within the EU.

Competition law is the legal instrument used to enforce competition policy. The final stage in this process was the establishment of competition agencies to monitor and police government competition policy at the national level.

6.6.1 COMPETITION SPECTRUM

If we consider competition as a spectrum with perfect competition at one end and monopoly at the other, then the role of government in the competition arena is to try to maximize the positive effects associated with perfect competition and avoid or minimize the negative aspects associated with monopoly. Even though these two positions are extremes, and thus rarely exist in practice, they are still very useful concepts if we consider them as representing two opposite ends of the competition spectrum.

> As *theoretical abstractions*, models of market structure are useful in so far as we know that the greater the level of competition, the greater are the incentives to:
>
> - drive price down towards costs;
> - provide incentives to reduce costs; and
> - develop new products that consumers are willing to buy.

So the closer an economy moves towards the perfect competition end of the spectrum, the greater the possibility of achieving efficient allocation of resources, efficient production and dynamic efficiency.

6.6.2 STRUCTURE, CONDUCT AND PERFORMANCE

Much of the basis for thinking on competition originates from the structure, conduct, performance (SCP) paradigm. When this first emerged in the 1950s (e.g. Bain, 1956), a one-way causal relationship was considered to exist between the structure of a market, the conduct of firms within that market and the performance of the firms.

Structure: e.g. the number of firms and the market share of each, the extent of entry barriers and the extent of product differentiation.

Conduct: e.g. the ability to practise **price discrimination** (charging different market segments different prices for the *same* product – as with airline seats in the same class) the pursuit of efficiency improvements, the setting of prices (high or low) and the pursuit of strategies aimed at preserving monopoly power or discouraging competition.

Performance: e.g. profitability, efficiency levels or the quality of the product.

Empirical studies of different industries indicate that the proposed one-way causal relationship was in fact multidirectional, with all three issues affecting each other. So, for example, the competitive conduct of firms pursuing efficiency improvements can result in other firms finding themselves unable to compete and thus leaving the industry, thereby affecting the structure of this industry. The result was a reformulation of the paradigm as

$$S \Leftrightarrow C \Leftrightarrow P$$

This paradigm provided insights for thinking about how to change the performance of firms. Governments realized that if they wanted market performance to change then market conduct and/or market structure had to change first. Explicit rules were introduced as part of achieving such change. The result was government competition policy.

6.6.3 COMPETITION POLICY

Competition policy has both economic and social objectives. The economic objective is based on the view that markets are an efficient mechanism for the allocation of scarce resources. Building on the ideas of Hayek, the knowledge contained within the market therefore exceeds the knowledge that even the 'best' regulators or government legislators could possess. The aim of a policy of competition is to break down barriers to new entry or dismantle business practices that discourage competition among existing firms. Once this can be achieved, the market makes decisions of resource allocation. The anticipated result is one of increased resource efficiency, increased innovation and a reduction in prices at the microeconomic level. These microeconomic effects then can lead to macroeconomic effects such as increased employment and productivity, through the efficient production of more goods and services, leading to increased prosperity for society.

The social objective of competition policy can be achieved only if the above economic objectives are first achieved, since the social objective is based on the aggregate (positive) outcome of the economic effects in the wider economy. These include the diffusion of economic power and the maximization of opportunities for all.

> There is an inherent conflict within competition policy. It may allow firms to become:
>
> - large enough to gain efficiency through economies of scale;
> - profitable enough to enable firms to invest in R&D and develop new products/processes.
>
> *But* large scale may:
>
> - generate market power;
> - lead to harmful anti-competitive practices for other (smaller) firms and consumers.

A delicate balance needs to be struck between these two potential conflicts, and competition policy attempts to achieve such a balance.

Principles of competition policy

The USA and the EU are at the forefront in advancing competition policy. Over the years both US and EU competition policy have converged and common standards of evaluation have been developed.

In the USA competition policy (or *Antitrust* as it is referred to) began with the Sherman Act of 1890, which was enacted largely in response to growing consolidation of big companies. The Act made illegal any restraints on competition. Interestingly, the one exception to this was any monopoly that was based on applying a superior technology or offering new products. This was an attempt to encourage innovation by providing firms with the opportunity to gain substantial profits from successful innovations. The Clayton Act of 1914 further strengthened competition policy by restricting specific practices if they could substantially lessen competition or if such practices could lead to a monopoly. This Act was introduced to restrain instances of economic power that were beginning to emerge.

The goal of EU competition policy is to establish a system which safeguards against the distortion of competition, either by restraints placed by private firms or by government involvement. It explicitly acknowledges the potential for national governments to distort competition and this has significant effects on the provision of state aid (as in the airline industry, for example). EU competition policy was established under the EU Treaty of 1957 and the two pillars of this policy are Articles 81 and 82, cited above, which prohibit contractual restraints on competition and prohibit an abuse of a dominant position. Rules governing mergers came into effect in 1990.

Table 6.5 summarizes the benefits of competition broken down into the benefits to consumers, businesses and the economy as a whole.

Implementation of competition policy

If the objectives of competition policy are to be met then proper and full implementation of the policy is essential. This involves an analysis of some key issues, such as the identification of competitors, the identification of a firm's product market and identification of the firm's geographical market, which may be more complicated than they first appear.

Identification of competitors is typically based on the degree of substitution between two products, where substitution is measured by the cross-price elasticity of demand.

TABLE 6.5 SUMMARY OF BENEFITS OF COMPETITION

Consumers:

Price, quality, choice, innovation and bargaining power

Example: airline industry prices reduced by: 25% (UK), 33% (USA), 50% (Spain), 65% (Ireland) accompanied by large increases in demand

Business:

Freedom to enter new markets and win market share

Benefits as buyers of production inputs – as for consumers above

Economy:

One-off effect of increased competition

Lower prices and higher output over time

Increased productivity, innovation and competitiveness

It is important to make a distinction here between direct and indirect competitors.

Indirect competition arises when the strategic choice of one firm affects the performance of the other due to strategic reaction by a third firm.

For example, innovation in the tyre market can bring about new competitive pressures in the car market if one car manufacturer uses the tyre innovation to attract customers. This recognizes the dynamics taking place in the market where action by one firm provokes a reaction by a series of other firms.

With **direct competitors**, two products tend to be close substitutes when they have similar uses and are sold in same geographic area.

In the world aviation market, Boeing's 737–800 jet and the Airbus A321 jet were considered by both Ryanair and easyJet to be close substitutes when they entered negotiations with both producers to add to their fleets. Both aircraft have similar passenger and range capabilities. In a local housing market two houses of similar size, in the same neighbourhood, may be considered close substitutes.

Identification of a firm's market is important, but difficult.

Two firms are in the same product **market** if they constrain each other's ability to raise price.

There are two markets that need to be considered: the product market and the geographical market. A market is well defined if customers could not switch between available substitutes in response to a hypothetical small but permanent relative price increase by all firms in the market. In other words, would a firm's customers switch to available substitutes or to a different supplier located elsewhere in response to a proposed permanent price increase of say 5%? If substitution were possible and this made the proposed price increase unprofitable, due to the resulting loss in sales, then these substitutes would form part of the same 'market'.

For a geographical market definition the flow of goods and services across geographic regions must be analysed. The idea here is to first find out where customers come from and then find out where the customers shop. A crucial issue in this analysis is transportation costs. Where such costs exist this would imply that identical products in two different geographic markets might not be substitutes.

As we saw in Chapter 5, advances in technology can reduce the importance of transportation cost, and the same is true with Internet shopping, for example. Once the market is defined, the most appropriate measure of market share must be identified and the relevant data accessed in order to compute accurate market shares.

Examples to illustrate the main issues in competition policy are provided below. The first example deals with mergers and the problem of defining the market in order to measure market share and therefore potential power/dominance. For those interested in case materials, a good starting point for EU material is http://europa.eu.int/comm/competition/index_en.html and for US material is http://www.ftc.gov/ftc/antitrust.htm.

COMPETITION POLICY EXAMPLE 1: ACQUISITION

In 1986 Coca-Cola wanted to acquire Dr Pepper and the US authorities investigated whether such an acquisition should be allowed. In that year Coca-Cola was the largest seller of carbonated soft drinks in the USA, while Dr Pepper was the fourth largest. Coca-Cola wished to expand Dr Pepper's market by applying its own skills in marketing and at the same time keeping up with its main rival – Pepsi-Cola – also expanding at the time. How to define the market became the central issue in the case to determine whether the acquisition could proceed. Coca-Cola's market could potentially be defined as the market for carbonated soft drinks, the market for cola drinks or the market for all drinks (including tap water). Depending on the definition used, the proposed merger would have left Coca-Cola with either significant or no significant market share, and this would naturally have very different effects on competition. Coca-Cola considered the relevant market definition to be the wider 'all drinks' market. However, in this case the market was defined as carbonated soft drinks and data was produced to show that the proposed merger could increase Coca-Cola's market share by over 4.5% at the national level and by as much as 10% to 20% in many geographical markets. On this basis the proposed merger was blocked.

COMPETITION POLICY EXAMPLE 2: SUBSIDIES

At the EU level, the issue of state aid where national governments provided subsidies to companies of national interest arose in several cases. One of the most common industries affected was airlines. In the early 1990s the European Commission announced that airlines would no longer qualify for state aid and put forward a proposal that aid could be given to assist with restructuring on a 'one last time' basis under which Iberia Airlines received almost $1bn in 1992. In 1994 the Spanish government provided Iberia with a further $1bn in aid to avert bankruptcy. The credibility of the 'one last time' policy was further diminished when, also in 1994, the Belgian government gave financial aid to Sabena. The EU then adopted the 'market economy investor principle' in deciding whether state aid is anti-competitive. This principle stated that if state aid takes place in circumstances that would not be acceptable to a private investor under normal market economy conditions, then such aid would be banned. In 2001 Belgian airline Sabena requested state aid to fight off bankruptcy arising from industry shocks. It was refused and the airline subsequently went out of business. The Irish airline, Aer Lingus, also requested state aid in 2001 and was also refused. It faced the stark choice of restructuring or going out of business. Following restructuring the company subsequently turned significant losses into substantial profits, indicating that state aid is not the only option for a company facing bankruptcy.

COMPETITION POLICY EXAMPLE 3: MARKET ABUSE

This case involved British Airways (BA) and Virgin Airlines and concerned the issue of market abuse. Here BA had 40% of the market for ticket sales in the UK and the next largest competitor had sales of 6%. BA was subsequently deemed to have dominance when other factors such as number of routes and its control over a large number of landing slots were factored in. Virgin took issue with BA over its commission scheme to travel agents. The scheme paid agents 7% for ticket sales on top of a 'performance reward', which paid up to an additional 3% on international flights and 1% on domestic flights, by matching current year sales to levels of performance in the previous year. This incentive scheme was seen as persuading agents to sell more BA tickets, thus giving BA an unfair advantage against other airlines. BA claimed that these rewards were linked to cost savings and efficiencies and had no damaging effects on other airlines. The European Commission did not accept these arguments and ruled that such a scheme was abusive.

6.7   SUMMARY

- Efficient functioning of a market economy depends on a robust state of competition.
- Through competition knowledge is discovered and exploited in the marketplace through the use of the price system.
- If markets are not contestable, entry barriers result in different market structures, ranging from monopolistic competition to oligopoly to monopoly, each with different effects on consumers, in terms of their ability to maximize their welfare and on producers in terms of their ability to earn supernormal profits.
- Market failure is used to justify government intervention in markets in the form of direct controls (becoming increasingly uncommon), or it can take the form of regulations or rules governing the behaviour of firms. Since all such rules impose costs on businesses it is important to assess the perceived benefits of these rules against their costs.
- Competition policy is an instrument to impose strict rules of competitive behaviour on firms. One aim is to reduce the role of government involvement in the economy and yet curb any negative effects from market failures. Competition law is the legal enforcement for competition policy and creates incentives for firms to obey such a policy.

REVIEW PROBLEMS AND QUESTIONS

1. How does Schumpeter's view of competition as 'creative destruction' link with the idea of competition as a process?

2. Patents prevent firms from copying inventions or innovations by other firms. Discuss what you think might happen if patents were eliminated so that firms could imitate successful innovations by other firms.

3. What are the key features of the following market structures: perfect competition, monopolistic competition, oligopoly and monopoly? If perfect competition does not exist in practice, what is the purpose of the model?

4. Use a diagram to show equilibrium price and quantity for a monopoly firm. Explain why supernormal profits result under monopoly. What are possible negative effects resulting from monopoly? Why do monopolies persist, given their possible negative effects?

5. With reference to the pay-off matrix below explain what you understand by the terms
   - dominant strategy;
   - Nash equilibrium;
   - co-operative equilibrium.

		Firm B's Strategic Options	
		I	*II*
Firm A's	X	(10, 10)	(15, 5)
Strategic Options	Y	(5, 15)	(18, 18)

6. In comparing the Austrian and traditional approaches to competition, what are the main conclusions? Would you see the Austrian and traditional views as being substitutes for or complementary to each other?
7. What is meant by 'market failure' and what might cause markets to fail? What, if anything can be done in response to market failure?
8. What is the structure, conduct, performance paradigm? What is the relationship between this paradigm and competition policy?

FURTHER READING AND RESEARCH

- For analysis of the US, UK and German manufacturing sector considering the efficiency of large scale production see Chandler, 1990.
- For the SCP approach to industry analysis see Bain, 1956, esp. pp. 1–19.
- For a modern applied perspective on markets, market structure and efficiency (among other issues) see Kay, 2003, particularly Parts 3 and 4.
- For consideration of a range of 'mythical' examples of market failure see Spulber, D. (ed.), 2002.

REFERENCES

Bain, J. (1956) *Barriers to New Competition*. Harvard University Press, Cambridge, Mass.

Chandler, A. (1990) *Scale and Scope: The dynamics of industrial capitalism*. Harvard University Press, Cambridge, Mass.

Hayek, F. (1978) *New Studies in Philosophy, Politics, and History Ideas.* University of Chicago Press, Chicago.

Kay, J. (2003) *The Truth about Markets: Their genius, their limits, their follies.* Allen Lane.

Spulber, D. (ed.) (2002) *Famous Fables of Economics: Myths of market failures.* Blackwell, Mass.

CHAPTER 7

MONEY AND FINANCIAL MARKETS IN THE ECONOMIC SYSTEM

LEARNING OUTCOMES

By the end of the chapter you should be able to:

✪ Explain the three functions of money and describe how money underpins exchange.

✪ Define what is meant by money and clarify alternative definitions (broad or narrow).

✪ Describe how banking systems work to create money.

✪ Outline the main motives underlying demand for money.

✪ Use the demand and supply model to describe how demand for and supply of money interact to determine the equilibrium interest rate and quantity of money.

✪ Describe the relationship between real and nominal interest rates.

✪ Explain the relationship between money supply and inflation.

✪ Apply the demand and supply model to the foreign exchange market to study:
  ● how demand for and supply of currency interact to determine equilibrium exchange rates and quantity of currency exchanged;
  ● the causes and consequences of changes in equilibrium exchange rates.

✪ Illustrate how the activity of speculators has potential to generate both costs and benefits in the economic system.

✪ Describe how monetary policy works and outline difficulties experienced in implementing such policies.

✪ Explain the logic underlying adoption or non-adoption of single currencies.

7.1 INTRODUCTION

So far we have implicitly used the concept of money in our discussion of the economic system. We mentioned the circular flow of income and output which we measure in money terms. Quite often the role of money is taken for granted but given its central role in the operations of an economy, it requires specific analysis. In fact the role played by money in the economic system is complex. Focusing on money and its place in the economy we realize even more the organized and interdependent nature of the various features and units within the economic system. For instance, what we consider as money today has no value other than that which we are happy, by convention, to afford it.

To be used as money, coins, notes, plastic cards (or whatever) must meet a number of criteria, set out in section 7.2. The supply of money in an economy is organized via central banks and commercial banks as explained in section 7.3. To allow us to analyse the money market we next consider demand for money in section 7.4 focusing on motives that explain demand. Bringing supply and demand together in section 7.5, we can consider how equilibrium is determined. The difference between real and nominal data is addressed once again, although here it is with reference to the 'price' of money – the interest rate.

The potential relationship between money supply and inflation is addressed in section 7.6, which also focuses on how monetary policy might be used to try to control inflation and affect interest rates. The focus then moves to broader international money markets with consideration of how exchange rates are determined, again using a demand and supply approach. This has relevance for central banks since one of their functions is to maintain the stability of their national currency.

The activities of speculators in foreign exchange markets has received much attention in recent times and this activity is examined in section 7.8 with interesting outcomes regarding the potential benefits speculators may bring to markets.

Section 7.9 focuses on monetary policy and how it can be used to affect economic activity. The final section assesses the arguments underlying monetary integration focusing on the specific case of the euro.

7.2   MONEY AND EXCHANGE

Life would be considerably more complicated were it not for money to the extent that we almost take it for granted and certainly do not consider the various functions it serves.

The various **functions of money** are:

- medium of exchange;

- unit of account;
- store of value.

Starting with the medium of exchange function, we know when we hand over the agreed amount of money in any transaction, we receive something we want and value in return. Whether we hand over cash, cheque or plastic (credit card) we know that there is agreement that our 'money' will be accepted in transactions. The fact that money is light and easily portable certainly facilitates exchange and just thinking about how barter systems work (where goods rather than money are exchanged for other goods) reveals how much more straightforward it is living in a monetary rather than a barter economy.

That we treat money as a unit of account means that it is the general language we use to quote prices and compare them. It would be possible to use any good as a unit of account if we were all happy to measure prices in mobile phones, for the sake of argument. This would mean that the price of tables, chairs, books and groceries would all be quoted in terms of the number of mobile phones required to buy them. In theory its sounds possible, but in practice who would want to carry around mobile phones to pay for everything they buy? And what about the different phones that are available – this would require an exchange rate relationship to be developed where the purchasing power of one phone would be quoted relative to another. Even if all prices were quoted in a more basic unit of account, like gold, this still would not get around the problem of having to carry around the gold to pay for purchases. History also reveals that when gold coins were used as an acceptable unit of account, some dishonest people engaged in shaving off some of the gold from the coins, thus devaluing them, but without the knowledge of the person accepting the gold. Since we are generally unwilling to treat commodities such as gold or phones as a unit of account, we require an alternative. This alternative is fiat money.

Fiat money exists where paper with no intrinsic value itself fulfils the functions of money, and government legislation ensures that it must be accepted for transactions.

By convention and tradition we are willing to accept paper and certain coins as payment because we have monetary systems that we trust sufficiently.

Since not all of consumers' purchases are made out of current income – people save and borrow – money must also be durable enough to allow for purchases to be made in the future or loans to be paid back. Money fulfils this function since it can be kept from one period to another although its purchasing power may not be exactly the same. In that way it can be said to be a store of value.

7.3 LIQUIDITY, CENTRAL BANKS AND MONEY SUPPLY

Different examples of financial assets exist that fulfil the functions required to define them as 'money'; for example, notes, coins, bank deposits, credit cards, travellers' cheques. Other financial assets such as stocks, shares, or government bonds could not be described as money since they cannot be exchanged for goods and services until they are first converted into money. The easier it is to use a financial asset to buy goods or services, the more liquid it is said to be.

In general a country's currency and 'money' are managed by its central bank, which deals with the formulation and implementation of monetary policy and tries to promote a sound and efficient financial system in which its citizens have confidence in the sense that they trust that their currency fulfils all the functions money should. Later in this chapter examples of monetary policies and their effects are considered.

> **Monetary policy** is the broad term used to describe how the supply of money is regulated in an economy, including how inflation is controlled and how the stability of the currency is maintained.

The amount of money held by banks in their reserves plus the currency in circulation is known as the monetary base.

Different central banks have their own definition of what constitutes money in the sense of which more and less liquid assets are included. For example according to the Federal Reserve, the central bank in the United States (the Fed), there are three definitions of what is included as money, from very narrow M1 including essentially the notes and cash and bank deposits available immediately for purchases (including travellers' cheques) to broader definitions called M2 and M3 that include less liquid financial assets. (The definitions used by the European Central Bank (ECB) are similar but not exactly the same.) The monetary base is smaller than M1 or M2 and only changes with specific activities of the central bank (explained later in this section). Recent figures for the different definitions of money are provided in Table 7.1 for the USA and Europe.

We can draw the supply curve for money (defined as M1, for example) as shown for the USA for April 2003, shown in Figure 7.1. The money supply is drawn as a vertical line because the decision about the quantity of money to supply to an economy is independent of the rate of interest. When discussing the price of money,

TABLE 7.1   MONEY IN CIRCULATION, USA AND EUROPE, APRIL 2003

	US ($bn)				EU (€bn)			
Currency	M1	M2	M3		Currency	M1	M2	M3
642	1236	5921	8600		337	2423	5027	5949

Sources: http://www.federalreserve.gov and http://www.ecb.int

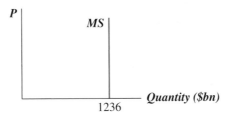

FIGURE 7.1   MONEY SUPPLY: USA, APRIL 2003

again like any other price we refer to its opportunity cost. The price of money is the rate of interest since the cost of holding onto money in its most liquid forms is the interest that could be earned if it were on deposit or used to buy a financial asset.

The main channel open to the central bank for affecting money supply is through open-market operations.

> When the central bank buys or sells government bonds it conducts an **open-market operation**.

Government bonds are issued to generate funds for the government and usually mature after ten years or more. Buyers of bonds pay money in return for an agreed rate of return on their investment in the future. If the central bank wants to increase money supply it buys government bonds from the public thereby releasing additional money into supply. To reduce the money supply the central bank could sell some of its own reserves of government bonds thus taking money out of circulation and transferring it into its reserves.

A further mechanism central to the determination of the money supply in an economy is the required reserve ratio held by banks.

The required reserve ratio is the percentage of all deposits received by banks that must be held in the bank and not used for loans or other purposes.

Through the required reserve ratio, banks manage to create money, thereby increasing the supply of money, in an economy. Central banks indicate what the desired reserve ratio is and commercial banks must retain that specified amount of reserves. Reserves are held so that any depositors requiring to withdraw their deposits are sure to be able to do so and will have confidence in their banking system. If on average, the central bank observes that banks need to hold 8% of their deposits for customers wishing to withdraw their deposits, this will be the preferred reserve ratio. For a ratio of 8%, a bank that has deposits of £50m must retain £4m in reserves but it is free to loan out the remaining £46m as it sees fit, within the guidelines set out by its central bank.

Since banks must hold a fraction of their deposits in the form of reserves, **the banking system** is known as **a fractional reserve system**.

The incentive for banks to loan out funds is generated once the interest they pay on deposits is less than the interest they can charge on loans so they can make profits. Since the banking market contains several competitors, each bank needs to ensure that its interest rates compare well to those offered by other competitors.

7.3.1 THE MONEY MULTIPLIER

If loans are created, they produce money in the economy in a multiplicative manner based on the money multiplier. This is easily explained using an example. Taking the case of the hypothetical BankOne, which has reserves of £4m and deposits of £50m. We can consider what happens to the money supply if the bank receives an additional deposit of £1000 from a customer, Moneybags Inc.

BankOne's deposits rise to £50 001 000 so it needs to increase its reserves at the central bank by £80 (8% of £1000). When the reserves have increased by £80, the remaining £920 can be loaned out by the bank. If a loan of £920 is issued to Grandon's, Ltd, their account at the bank is credited with this amount, thus increasing deposits by £920 to £50 001 920. As deposits rise, reserves must increase

TABLE 7.2   MONEY CREATION VIA THE MONEY MULTIPLIER

	Assuming a required reserve ratio of 8%		
	Deposit £	Required reserves £	Loan £
Moneybags	1000	80	920
Grandon's	920	73.6	846.4
Next customer	846.4	67.7	778.7
Next customer	778.7	62.3	716.4
. . .	. . .	. . .	. . .
Total	12 500	1000	11 500

in line and 8% of £920 is £73.60. When £73.60 is held in the bank's reserves, again the remainder of £846.40 (£920 − £73.60) can be used for loans by the bank. Then the bank can issue a further loan to Safelock Ltd, which is credited to their account in the bank, increasing bank deposits, requiring an addition to the bank's reserves ... and so on as shown in Table 7.2.

This process ensures that the initial addition to the bank's deposits generates an increase in the money supply considerably greater than the initial change.

The **money multiplier** describes how a change in money supply leads to an ultimate change in money supply by a multiple of the initial change.

The size of the money multiplier depends on the required reserve ratio according to the formula:

$$\text{Money multiplier} = \frac{1}{\text{required reserve ratio}}$$

Since the ratio is 8% in the example, the money multiplier is $1/0.08 = 12.5$. This means that any change in deposits will lead to an increase in the money supply 12.5 times the initial increase. If the initial change is £1000 it generates £12 500 in additional money supply as shown by the process in Table 7.2. Hence, banks create money.

7.4 MONEY DEMAND

Taken together, money supply and money demand determine the equilibrium price and quantity of money in the money market.

> We hold money or demand money (in more liquid forms) for different purposes – for **transactions**, as a **precautionary** measure and for **speculative** purposes. These are known as the **motives for holding money**.

The transactions demand for money relates to the medium of exchange function of money in that it is the demand for day-to-day spending on things like groceries, bus fares, and so on. The amount of money people demand for their transactions will vary depending on their income – generally those earning more spend more – and on the general price level – if prices are high, then relatively more money is needed to pay for purchases.

The precautions demand for money relates to the money demanded for unexpected emergencies and is again associated with the money's medium of exchange function. The amount of money demanded for precautionary purposes again depends on individuals' incomes, and their age.

> The transactions and precautionary demands for money are known as **the demand for active balances** because the money is actively used to buy goods and services.

The price of money – the interest rate – is not of interest in explaining the demand for active balances.

The third motive for money demand is for speculative purposes. This motive is related to money's store of value function because individuals concerned about the value of financial investments in the future who are afraid the value of their investments will fall prefer to hold money rather than financial assets.

> The speculative demand for money is also called the demand for idle balances since it relates to the desire to demand money to avoid potential losses from holding interest-bearing financial assets.

The demand for speculative purposes depends on the interest rate, which is the opportunity cost of holding money. With a relatively high rate, people will prefer the more attractive option of holding interest-bearing assets rather than more liquid forms of money.

Figure 7.2 shows the demands for active, idle and total money balances. Note that the price of money P is the interest rate. This demand for money or the liquidity

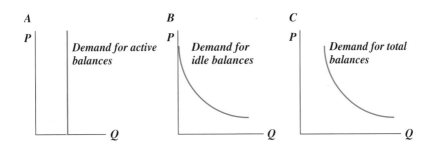

FIGURE 7.2 MONEY DEMAND: LIQUIDITY PREFERENCE CURVE

preference curve is shown in Figure 7.2 panel C, which is the sum of the demand for active and idle balances. This indicates the desire for holding assets in liquid form, i.e. cash rather than in other financial asset forms.

7.5 THE MONEY MARKET: DEMAND AND SUPPLY

Equilibrium in the money market requires an assessment of both demand and supply together, as presented in Figure 7.3. The opportunity cost of money is determined by the intersection of demand and supply, and this is shown as r^* in Figure 7.3 panel A.

If there is a fixed quantity of money supply then, depending on the demand for total balances, the interest rate may vary as shown in the comparison between Figure 7.3 panels A and B. In both panels the money supply is the same and money demand is different. The intersection between demand and supply gives rise to an interest rate r^* in panel A, while it is higher at $r^\wedge$ in panel B. The demand for money in panel B is greater than in A (the demand curve in panel B is above and to the right of that in panel A) but because supply is fixed the price must rise to bring the market to equilibrium. If the interest rate did not rise the demand for total balances at r^* would exceed the available supply – there would be a shortage of money – and the market would not clear.

In Figure 7.3 panels C and D we can examine what happens when the central bank conducts open-market operations and expands the money supply (when it buys government bonds). Initially the interest rate is r^* but once the open market operation increases the supply of money the interest rate declines to $r+$.

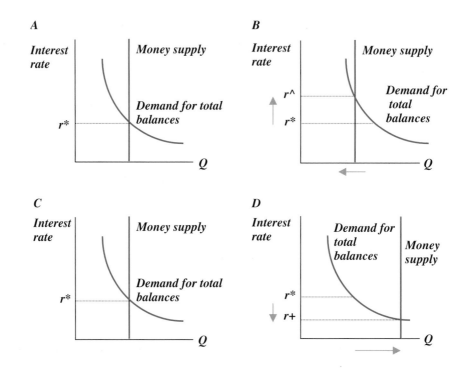

FIGURE 7.3   MONEY MARKET: DEMAND AND SUPPLY

The interest rate must decline when the supply expands because, as shown in Figure 7.3 panel D, at the original interest rate of r^* the expanded money supply is greater than demand at that price. The market only clears if the interest rate drops to bring demand and supply together.

7.5.1   WHICH INTEREST RATE?

Figure 7.3 simplifies the process by which the interest rate is determined because there is more than one interest rate determined in an economy at any time. For example, one interest rate is charged for mortgages. Mortgages are a feature of the capital rather than the money market since they are long-term debts – debts shorter than one year are features of the money market. Another interest rate is earned on deposits held by savers, while another is earned on deposits held for one month, or three months, and so on. Two main elements help to explain differences in interest rates:

- *Loan term*: loan repayment periods vary in time; some are short like the overnight borrowing that some banks engage in with their central bank, others like mortgages are for up to 30 or 35 years. Generally speaking long-term rates are higher than short-term rates, although mortgages do enjoy lower rates than other types of loan

● *Risk associated with borrower*: not all loans are repaid as individuals go bank-rupt and businesses shut down. Lenders are free to take into account the probability of default when providing loans and higher interest rates are associated with riskier loans.

All of the above interest rates tend to change together following a similar trend, however, which means the simplifying assumption that there is only one rate can be used.

7.5.2 NOMINAL AND REAL INTEREST RATES

Economists are interested in real variables because this allows for comparisons to be made in terms of purchasing power over time. Interest rates, like any prices, can be quoted in real or nominal terms. The nominal interest rate on deposit accounts, for example, is the rate quoted by banks – say 0.75% – meaning that you could earn 0.75% interest on any deposits held for one year.

When nominal interest rates change, individuals' incentives to save or borrow are affected. An increase in the nominal rate raises returns for savers but makes borrowing more expensive while a cut in the nominal rate has the opposite effects. Since savings create the deposits that banks use for creating money via providing loans, the amount of savings in an economy is of crucial importance for the real interest rate, which takes purchasing power into account.

> **The real interest rate (r)** is computed as the difference between the nominal interest rate and the rate of inflation.
>
> $$r = i - \pi$$
>
> where i denotes the nominal rate and π is the rate of inflation.

If the annual rate of inflation is 4% while the nominal interest rate is 0.75%, then the real interest rate is −3.25%. This means that any deposits held in a bank will buy 3.25% fewer goods at the end of a year as the purchasing power of money has declined – prices rose faster than the rate of return on money. The real interest rate is a positive number once the inflation rate is less than the nominal rate of interest. If real interest rates are expected to be negative, it may be logical for consumers to make purchases today rather than hold onto money that will buy fewer goods in the future so savings might be relatively low. Hence, via individuals' consumption behaviour, nominal and real interest rate effects have implications for aggregate demand.

With negative real interest rates, borrowers' debts would decline in real terms so people might be happy to borrow knowing that without making any repayments the real value of their borrowings will decline! In this case, consumption and aggregate demand are also affected. There is evidence that, when real interest rates are negative *and large*, consumers prefer to spend and can even cause asset prices and/or property prices to rise rapidly if supply cannot expand sufficiently quickly to meet demand. Furthermore, if share prices rise rapidly as well due to increased demand for such financial assets this can cause further increases in consumer spending and may even lead to inflation (if aggregate demand shifts rightwards intersecting aggregate supply at a new equilibrium point with higher output and a higher price level).

Financial or property bubbles are often associated with negative real interest rates as people are willing to invest or speculate on assets with an amount of certainty that because real returns on assets are falling, their losses will be partially 'protected'. In markets where bubbles exist, there tends to be an over-enthusiasm on the part of investors who believe that increases in asset values will continue into the future and so they are increasingly willing to invest, pushing up the price of the asset and as long as people expect that asset values will continue to rise, the bubble gets bigger and bigger and may eventually burst, as in the case of the technology stock market in 2000. Alan Greenspan the Chairman of the Federal Reserve famously asked in a speech in late 1996: 'How do we know when irrational exuberance has unduly escalated asset values, which then become subject to unexpected and prolonged contractions as they have in Japan over the past decade?'

His concern was in relation to monetary policy and his fears were that there could be effects that would impact 'the real economy, its production, jobs, and price stability'. Clearly expectations about the future play a key part in bubbles but as Mr Greenspan pointed out can affect the 'real' economy in adverse ways if the bubbles burst.

For firms thinking about making investments and who need to finance those investments via bank loans, the nominal and real interest rates also play a central role in their decisions. Their strategies regarding buying and selling shares in both their own and other companies will also be affected by the interest rates. *Ceteris paribus*, firms will be most likely to borrow when nominal interest rates are low and this is why you often hear business analysts arguing that cuts in interest rates by the Federal Reserve or the European Central Bank are needed to 'stimulate business activity'. If interest rate cuts lead to consumers buying more, then both the investment and consumption effects in the economy would boost economic activity via a shift in the aggregate demand function.

In May 2003, commentators correctly predicted a cut in the ECB's interest rate from 2.5% to 2% given the poor economic growth in the French and German markets and the fact that inflation of 1.9% was below the target rate of 2% for the euro zone. In fact some analysts were predicting falling prices (deflation) in the German market and argued one way to attempt to avoid this was to cut interest rates significantly by half a percentage point to 2.0% stimulating consumption (and thereby aggregate demand) and reducing any downward pressure on the price level. Such a drop in the interest rate to 2.0% when inflation was at 1.9% would imply a real interest rate of 0.01%.

Finally, in relation to Figure 7.3, the real interest rate is determined if real money supply and real money demand are considered, while if nominal supply and demand are of interest, the nominal interest rate is determined.

7.6 QUANTITY THEORY OF MONEY AND EXPLAINING INFLATION

From the motives for holding money considered earlier, we know that people demand money in order to make transactions and logically the more money needed for expected transactions, the more money people will want to hold.

Another way of stating this is via the **quantity equation**:

$$M \times V = P \times Y$$

where M denotes the nominal money supply in an economy, V denotes velocity of money, P denotes the average price level, Y denotes the level of real economic activity and hence $P \times Y$ is the nominal value of economic activity (i.e. income or output).

The velocity term is a measure of how often an average unit of money is used in a period of time. If £100bn-worth of nominal output is produced in an economy in a year and the stock of money in that economy is £10bn, then the velocity term is equal to 10, implying that each unit of money (£1) is used ten times per year appearing as ten separate transactions in the circular flow.

If any of the terms in this equation change, there is an impact on one or more of the other variables so if the quantity of money falls and the velocity is unchanged, either the price level or the level of activity must fall.

Another way of expressing the quantity equation is in terms of velocity where:

$$V = \frac{P \times Y}{M}$$

which defines the velocity of money as the ratio of nominal income to the quantity of money in the economy. In practice the velocity of money does not change hugely over time and it can be assumed that V is constant. If this assumption is made the quantity equation becomes a relationship between the quantity of money and the nominal level of income in an economy whereby any change in the amount of money in an economy would lead to a similar change in nominal income: when V is constant, if the quantity of money increases by 10%, so too will the nominal value of income.

To see what this implies (assuming still that V is constant) take the case where an economy produces £100bn of real output in a given year and has an average price level, P, so nominal output is given by $P \times$ £100bn. The same economy has £10bn of money. Any change in the quantity of money must lead to a change in the price level in the economy because the real output is the actual quantity of output produced (if this causes you problems think of real output as 100 'bags' or 'bales' of output!). If the money supply rises by 20% to £12bn, the effects are felt through P, which rises also by 20% as the 'bags' of output produced are 100, whatever happens.

A change in P, the aggregate price level, is caused by a change in money supply. An increase in the price level is called **inflation**. Hence, **inflation** is caused by increasing the money supply.

By implication, central banks – through their setting of money supply – can affect the rate of inflation. Analyses of the correlation between inflation rates and money supply growth (according to the *M1* definition) reveal a strong positive relationship over the long run.

In order for the money supply to be the *sole* determinant of inflation, we assumed no change in real output. This would be true for an economy operating in the long run at its potential output level with all resources fully employed. From our previous analysis of economic activity, however, we know that real output tends to be cyclical in the short run. We know too that there is a marked upward trend in real output in developed countries over time.

> Hence, a change in the money supply results in the same proportional change in P, the aggregate price level, if we treat real output as constant.

We can go one step further and consider what that would imply for the demand for money. If real output (income) rises by 5%, the demand for money should do so too to buy the extra output/to spend the extra income. If money supply grows by 8% then prices need rise only by 3% because 5% of the extra money supply is needed due to the growth in economic activity. By implication, long-run inflation should equal the rate of growth of the money supply minus the real rate of growth in economic activity.

> **Inflation** = rate of money supply growth − rate of real output growth
> e.g. inflation = 8% − 5% = 3%

7.6.1 INFLATION EXPECTATIONS, INTEREST RATES AND DECISION-MAKING

If I lodge money into a deposit account preferring to save rather than buy consumption goods, I expect to earn some interest, depending on the deposit account I select. I know that if there is a change in the interest rate announced by the central bank, that change, or at least a portion of it, will be passed on to me by my bank. This means that I cannot be sure of the nominal return I will earn on my account. Since I also do not know what inflation will be in the future, I cannot compute the real interest rate with certainty. I can, however, make my best guess at the inflation rate and hence the real interest rate.

Similarly for borrowers taking out loans where the nominal interest rate varies depending on what the central bank dictates and the real repayments can be guessed with varying amounts of accuracy depending on how close the economic outcome is compared to the decision-maker's forecast. In decision-making when we base our choices on our best guesses of what we expect the inflation rate to be, we use an *ex-ante* real interest rate. This is our best guess given available information about a future occurrence. The actual real interest rate that we can measure once we know what the inflation and nominal interest rates are is called the *ex-post* real interest rate.

The *ex-ante* **real interest rate** is $r = i - \pi^e$ where π^e is expected inflation.

Rearranging this expression, the nominal interest rate $i = r + \pi^e$. (This is known as the Fisher equation and is explained below.)

The *ex-post* **real interest rate** is $r = i - \pi$ where π is actual inflation.

Expectations regarding future inflation are central to economic decision-making when current and future flows of income must be considered. This has implications for our analysis of the role of a central bank in setting the interest rate via its money supply. Consider the case where a central bank conducts an open-market operation by increasing the money supply, i.e. it buys bonds and pays money in return, which it takes from its reserves. Increased money supply implies excess supply for money at the original interest rate and the money market can clear only if the nominal interest rate *falls*. This may not always happen.

If money market analysts interpret the increase in money supply as a policy direction of the central bank to indicate that there will be rise in the rate of growth of the money supply (not just an increase in its level), they may predict further increases in money supply in the future. This would mean that the expected rate of inflation would rise, from the relationship described as:

% inflation = % money supply growth − % real output growth.

From the Fisher equation, a rise in the expected rate of inflation would put *upward pressure* on the nominal interest rate since it depends on the real interest rate and expected inflation. Fisher showed that if expected inflation increases by 1% then the nominal interest rate also rises by the same amount.

If the money market analysts got it wrong in predicting faster growth of the money supply, over time people would see that the expectations of higher inflation were mistaken and the expectation would disappear. In that case the nominal interest rate would certainly fall.

A central bank has only limited control of the interest rate in the short run. Changes in inflation expectations can change the outcome predicted by the money demand and supply model.

If a central bank really wants to lower interest rates, it should lower inflation or, more specifically, inflationary expectations. It can attempt to do this by reducing the rate of growth in money supply and by being a credible institution. Credibility in its policies basically implies that the central bank means what it says and if it sets a policy target of 2% inflation (for example) it will stick to this target. This credibility of policy generates certainty for consumers and firms facilitating their economic decisions.

The credibility of central banks' policies is tied to their independence. By independence we mean the extent to which the central bank is free to set its own targets for inflation and interest rates without political interference from a government, Minister for Finance, or Chancellor of the Exchequer. Studies have shown that economies with the most independent central banks have lower inflation performance and less variable inflation (DeLong and Summers, 1993). The countries did not appear to have any higher unemployment, lower real income growth or larger short-run fluctuations in real output. In order to establish credibility, it appears central banks have to prove themselves as sticking to their word – if they set an inflation target then the policy is credible if they have managed to successfully stick to previously declared targets for inflation. Central banks are often judged on their ability not only in terms of inflation but in terms of maintaining a stable value for their currency, which is addressed next.

7.7 THE FOREIGN EXCHANGE MARKET

The price of a currency (in terms of other currencies) depends on demand for the currency and supply of that currency. The demand for euros on the foreign exchange market is called a derived demand, derived from the demand for goods or financial assets. Holders of other currencies – US dollars, for example – purchase euros in order to pay for European goods and services or European financial assets, e.g. shares, government bonds and property.

> The price of one currency in terms of another is called an **exchange rate**.

When exchange rates change currencies either appreciate or depreciate.

> An **appreciation** of the euro occurs when £1 buys more foreign currency today than it did yesterday (when it costs more in terms of foreign currency to buy £1). A **depreciation** of the euro occurs when £1 buys less foreign currency today compared to yesterday (when it costs less in terms of foreign currency to buy £1).

Exchange rates are considerably more volatile than most prices, as you will know if you've ever had to buy foreign exchange when the price varies day-to-day if you buy from a bank or in real time as currencies are traded on international money markets. On 9 June 2003, €100 would have bought almost $118 whereas five months earlier on 9 January 2003, it would have bought less than $105. As a given quantity of euros bought more dollars, the euro can be said to have appreciated in value. The corollary is that the dollar depreciated. To consider how exchange rates are determined we consider both demand for and the supply of foreign exchange.

7.7.1   DEMAND IN THE FOREIGN EXCHANGE MARKET

In Figure 7.4 the demand curve for euros is shown in terms of dollars. Three different prices or exchange rates are shown. At the highest price of the euro, when it costs $2 to buy €1, the quantity demanded of euros is *Q1*. If the price were lower at €1 for $1, a higher quantity of euros is demanded at Q2 while if the price is only $0.50 for €1, the quantity demanded is higher again at Q3. Hence, as you would expect, when the price of the euro is high, the quantity demanded of euros is relatively low. At a high exchange rate (€1/$2) holders of dollars would prefer to buy domestic goods and services, where possible, rather than those from Europe and so their demand for euros is relatively low. At cheaper exchange rates, the incentive to buy European goods and assets increases.

7.7.2   SUPPLY IN THE FOREIGN EXCHANGE MARKET

Supply of foreign exchange is also derived and is shown in Figure 7.5. Holders of euros want dollars to buy US goods and services and US financial assets. When people buy goods/assets they supply euros in exchange (if they are going on holidays and exchange their currency, for example). Or European importers make purchases from US producers and pay in dollars.

The supply of US goods, services or financial assets is greater the cheaper the price of dollars in terms of euros, as shown in Figure 7.5. When €1 buys $2, Europeans have an increased incentive to buy US goods, services or financial assets compared to when the price is higher, e.g. when €1 buys only $0.50.

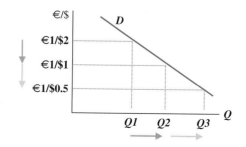

FIGURE 7.4   FOREIGN EXCHANGE: DEMAND

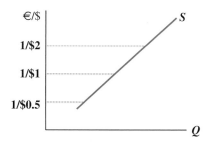

FIGURE 7.5 FOREIGN EXCHANGE: SUPPLY

7.7.3 EXCHANGE RATE DETERMINATION

The exchange rate between any two currencies is based on their relative demands and supplies. Equilibrium in the foreign exchange market is found in the usual way, where demand and supply intersect, shown in Figure 7.6. From the demand and supply curves the equilibrium exchange rate is €1 = $1. We know that exchange rates change quickly, meaning information that changes either demand or supply of foreign exchange occurs frequently and the exchange rate required to clear the foreign exchange market changes quickly.

Consider what might happen to the exchange rate if holders of euros want to buy extra US goods and need to buy dollars to pay for them. This might happen if, for example, US computer producers use some new technology that allows them to produce better machines at a lower price than European competitors. If the supply of euros (for dollars) rises as shown in Figure 7.7, then at the original exchange rate, the market does not clear and supply is greater than demand and at the original exchange rate a surplus exists. This means that at the original exchange rate there are more euros on the market than people holding dollars wish to buy. This surplus of euros can only be eliminated if the exchange rate falls. As the

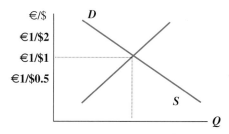

FIGURE 7.6 DETERMINATION OF AN EXCHANGE RATE: THE EURO IN TERMS OF DOLLARS

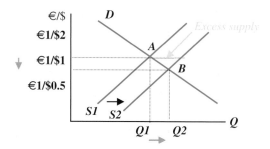

FIGURE 7.7   CHANGE IN THE EQUILIBRIUM EXCHANGE RATE

exchange rate falls, the quantity of euros demanded by holders of dollars increases. The new equilibrium emerges at Figure 7.7 point *B*.

7.7.4   CAUSES OF CHANGES IN EXCHANGE RATES

Many different factors affect exchange rates, due to interdependencies of foreign exchange markets internationally. These can be examined using the demand and supply framework and considering equilibrium changes derived from changes in either currency demand, supply or in some cases changes in both currency demand *and* supply.

The main factors causing exchange rates to change include:

- interest rate differentials;
- inflation differentials;
- growth differentials;
- speculation.

An *interest rate differential* exists between the euro zone and the USA when their interest rates differ and would be expected to have an effect on the euro–dollar exchange rate. Take the case where the euro interest rate is set (by the European Central Bank) at a rate above that in the USA (set by the US Federal Reserve). Holders of dollars might wish to earn a higher interest rate on their savings, demand more euros and supply more dollars to the foreign exchange market. An increase in demand for euros would mean a rightward shift of the demand curve drawn in Figure 7.7, bringing about an *appreciation* of the euro.

Furthermore, if holders of euros are also less willing to buy US assets, fewer euros may be supplied and the supply curve may shift to the left (at each exchange rate, the supply of euros falls). The result of a leftward shift in supply is, again, to increase in the value of the euro against the dollar. The net effect of the interest rate differential depends on the extent of the changes on both demand and supply but in this example brings about an appreciation of the euro. The appreciation of the euro results in reducing the benefit of the initial interest rate differential!

An *inflation differential* exists between the USA and Europe if prices are rising faster in one economy relative to the other. European goods become relatively more expensive if a positive inflation differential exists between the euro zone and the USA. As euro goods are more expensive, demand for them may fall, reducing demand for euros by holders of dollars – a leftward shift of the demand curve. If US goods also become more attractive for European buyers, the supply of euros increases also – a rightward shift in the supply curve. The net result is a depreciation in the value of the euro versus the dollar.

In the case where one economy is growing faster than another (e.g. faster growth of GDP in the EU) a *growth differential* exists. We know from earlier analysis that additional income results in extra consumption, some of which is met by imports. As import demand increases, so does the supply of euros to pay for them, resulting in a depreciation in the value of the euro for the dollar.

The vast majority of demand for and supply of foreign exchange takes place not in order to pay for goods or services but for the purpose of *speculation*, which amounts to gambling on the future movements of an exchange rate. We know this because the amount of foreign exchange traded greatly exceeds the value of international purchases of goods and services (including tourism). In 1998, for example, the average *daily* turnover in foreign exchange markets was equivalent to the *annual* GDP of Germany! Estimates of the amount of foreign exchange transacted worldwide on a daily basis over the period 1998 to 2001 are $1.2tr. (This figure is down 14% from 1998, as quoted by the Bank for International Settlements in their *Central Bank Survey of Foreign Exchange and Derivatives Market Activity* available from http://www.bis.org.) The most traded currencies are the dollar, euro, Japanese yen and sterling. In percentage terms each currency's respective share of foreign-exchange trade is 90%, 38%, 23% and 13% (note that the sum of all foreign currency shares adds to 200% not 100% since two currencies are involved in each transaction).

People trade in foreign exchange because of arbitrage opportunities.

Arbitrage is the possibility of buying an asset (e.g. foreign exchange) in one market and selling it at a higher price in another market.

Speculators speculate on the price they expect to earn on an asset in another market or in the future. Given the ease and speed with which traders in foreign exchange gather and receive information on exchange rates, currency exchange rates tend to converge quickly between the various foreign exchange markets (London being the largest) so that arbitrage opportunities in money markets are less common.

7.8   SPECULATION IN MARKETS

Speculators can only make a profit if they have information not available to the rest of the market. We argued earlier that holders of specific information should use it for their economic decision-making to make best use of economic resources. We also considered that the market system allowed individuals to use their specific information and generated incentives for them to use such information. Hence, speculators must guess (and bet on) changes in exchange rates from which they can benefit. Since speculators cannot know future currency rates with certainty, speculation is a risky activity.

In many cases speculators can act in such a way as to bring about their expectations. If speculators believe that a currency will fall in value, the rational action is to sell any holdings of that currency and buy others. If a large number of speculators follow the same strategy and sell a particular currency, its supply on the market increases and so the price of the currency will fall as supply exceeds demand. The role played by speculators in exchange rate determination is quite substantial and estimates for the level of speculation on the London ForEx (foreign exchange) market are up to 80% of all trades.

Despite the actions of speculators, economists argue that if a country's economic fundamentals are right, its currency should not be too volatile and the exchange rate should remain steady. Quite often we hear economic commentary that a currency is over- or under-valued based on an economy's fundamentals.

> **Economic fundamentals** is a very broad term and includes such economic measures as interest rates, the government's budget deficit, the country's balance of trade account (relating to exports and imports), the level of domestic business confidence, the inflation rate, the state of (and confidence in) the banking and wider financial sector, and consumer confidence.

The fundamentals are elements of the economic system that need to 'fit' well together or else speculators might try to sell the currency. If speculators see any of the fundamentals as a potential problem, they may sell the currency, changing its exchange rate(s). Speculators operate across all kinds of markets such as art, rare coins, property (real estate), and agriculture. Some speculative activities relate to futures markets.

In **futures markets** agreements are made relating to a payment that will be made for delivery of goods in the future.

In **spot or cash markets** money changes hands today for goods or services received today.

The usual goods exchanged on futures markets are primary (unprocessed) commodities like agricultural output, wheat, barley, corn, coffee as well as stocks and bonds. Futures markets provide information to growers/producers today about how prices are expected to change in the future. If the futures price of a kilo of wheat in 12 months' time is £3.50, and is £2.50 today, this indicates that given predictions about future plantings, expected weather conditions (and whatever other factors affect corn output) the expert opinion based on the best specific information available is that wheat prices will rise.

Speculators often receive bad press as individuals or businesses that exploit the market system to make a profit. Interestingly, however, speculators who accurately predict the future price of corn, as an example, can help to stabilize the price and output in a market. Take the case for the corn market shown in Figure 7.8. The market for this year and next year are considered respectively in panels *A* and *B*. Demand is considered to be the same for both years. Initially we examine the situation if no speculation occurs but there is an expectation that next year's crop will be smaller than this year's. If no speculation occurs, the contraction in production of corn from *S1* to *S2* results in different equilibrium prices and output over both periods.

However, if speculators are correct in predicting that prices will rise in period 2 their rational behaviour would be to buy at the cheaper price this year and hold onto some of the output until the following year, selling it at the higher price. This activity would change supply for periods 1 and 2 as shown in Figure 7.8 panels *C* and *D*. For year 1, supply drops back (to S_S1) as shown in panel *C*, if speculators store some of the wheat. For year 2 supply expands in panel *D* (to S_S2) and the outcome is an equilibrium price that is equalized over the two periods – the price is £3 in both periods and consumption is 50 million kilos. If speculators were completely correct in predicting year 2's supply then prices and output (and hence, consumption) could remain stable over time. Both price and consumption would be smoother over both periods compared to the situation that would prevail without speculative activity.

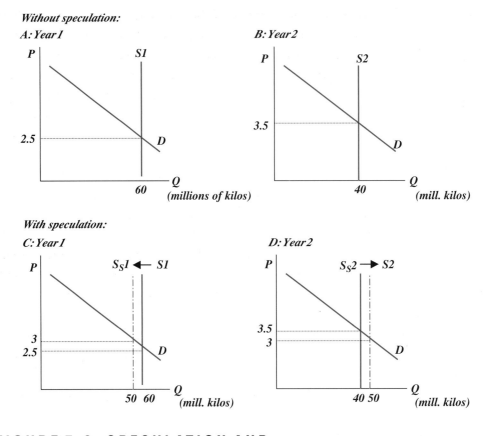

FIGURE 7.8 SPECULATION AND CONSUMPTION SMOOTHING

When speculators' expectations are incorrect, however, they can exacerbate problems further. This occurs if a speculator buys at one price, expecting it to rise. If the price is already high and speculators are wrong about future price rises, their purchase today of goods will drive today's price higher still (because of the leftward shift of the supply curve, *ceteris paribus*). If prices in the future fall, the speculator sells their purchases and drives the price further down (as the supply curves moves rightwards) by releasing their goods onto the market. In such circumstances the speculators only serve to magnify the trend in prices and consumption over both periods.

A similar analysis can be conducted for the money market although we know currencies to be considerably more volatile than other prices. A key difference with speculation in currencies is the possibility that comprehensive financial crises can result with devastating consequences for the affected economies. It is little solace to the victims of the Asian currency crises that the speculative attacks of the 1990s led to the identification of problems in the economic fundamentals and the crises forced the economies to try to address these economic weaknesses and problems (for more on this topic, see Further Reading and Research). It is also unfortunate that speculative attacks on a currency can cause effects over very short periods and can be passed quickly onto neighbours and trading partners yet the time required to rebuild a shattered economy in which investors have little confidence takes years.

A possible solution to the potential cost of currency speculation, facilitated by the ease with which capital can flow internationally, would be to set limits on such flows (such as existed until the 1980s in many countries) or impose taxes on such flows. However, not all speculation is bad and some speculation, as we see above, leads to stability in currency prices, hence using taxes or limits on speculation could create the very price differences that speculators try to exploit and therefore it is difficult to know how to deal with the issue. What we can say with certainty is that:

- Speculators dealing with uncertainties are experts in their fields and they have the incentive to be as well informed as possible before investing in uncertain future events.
- Society benefits when specific information is used by economic decision-makers and when speculators 'get it right'.
- Speculators who are consistently incorrect are pushed out of business by their losses.
- There are both costs and benefits associated with speculative activity.

7.8.1   INVESTMENT IN BOND MARKETS

Speculation takes place in markets where uncertainty prevails regarding the returns on speculative activity. An alternative, safer investment strategy exists by investing in bonds.

A **bond** represents an agreement between two parties in a transaction where one party lends money to the other for an agreed rate of interest (usually) over a specified period and where the lender receives back the total value of their investment when the bond matures.

Both governments and companies issue bonds when they wish to raise funds for investments they could not otherwise afford. When attempting to raise funds, businesses have the option of debt or equity financing.

> **Debt financing** results in borrowing money that must usually be repaid with interest.

Debt financing is described as short-term if repayments are made within one year or else is denoted as long-term debt.

> **Equity financing** involves selling a share of the business ('shares') in exchange for finance where no specific future payment is defined.

With equity financing there is often a fear that ownership interests will be reduced and that a certain amount of control reverts to the additional shareholders. Clearly, governments do not have the option of equity financing; however, they use bonds to finance some of their activities. Clearly, while companies can become bankrupt, countries cannot (notwithstanding financial problems experienced by some developed and developing countries). This implies that riskier corporate bonds must offer higher returns than government bonds. The extent of the difference in bond returns depends on the belief that market participants have in the ability of a corporation to repay the purchaser of the bond.

In the same way as shares are traded on the stock exchange, a market for bonds also exists, which is known as the securities market. As with any other market, demand and supply analysis allows us a framework for considering how the prices of bonds are determined.

Bonds are less risky investments than shares but as a consequence generate lower returns for this lower risk. Some bonds must be retained until maturity while others may be sold before that date, depending on the initial agreement. Different bonds have different regulations attached to them.

- Convertible bonds can be exchanged for a predetermined number of common stocks in a company although once converted, stocks cannot be reconverted back into bonds.
- Zero-coupon bonds do not pay interest. They are purchased at a deep discount from their face value. On maturity investors receive a sum equal to the initial investment plus interest that has accrued.
- Foreign (or international) bonds generate returns in foreign currency, which means the value of the bond issuer's currency must also be considered when thinking of making such investments.
- In some countries municipal bonds are sold to finance public works (i.e. street lights, fountains, etc.).

In attempting to decide between investing in various bonds it is possible to consider their relative rankings.

Companies such as Moody's and Standard & Poor's provide rankings of bonds that are determined by their expected ability to generate interest payments and repay the principal. The best ratings is triple A (AAA), next is double A, next A followed by BAA, BA, B, CAA, CA and C.

Any changes in rankings by these companies clearly have repercussions for investors' willingness to buy them.

In terms of its size the bond market has a similar market value to the stock market (around $31 000 bn in 1999). Government bonds represent 45% of US and euro zone bonds but in 1999 were over 70% of the Japanese bond market. Together the USA, euro zone and Japan represent over 88% of the world bond market with shares of 47%, 23% and 18% respectively.

A substantial amount of businesses' corporate investment is made through selling bonds and, hence, businesses' desire to sell bonds (the supply of bonds) is related to the amount of investment they plan. The flip side of the price of bonds, both government and corporate, is the return that investors are willing to earn on their investments, i.e. the interest rate.

Hence, the **demand for bonds** is dependent on their rate of return or interest.

Remembering that people have the choice between saving and consumption, the demand for bonds is a mirror image of individuals' planned savings. Therefore, firms' investment decisions, the supply of bonds, households' savings decisions and the return on bonds versus other financial assets feed into the determination of equilibrium bond quantities and prices. Firms' investment decisions include their analysis of the marginal revenue product of investment which is the revenue-producing potential of additional investment (and this is analytically similar to the marginal revenue product of labour examined in Chapter 2).

In terms of the main options for saving, bank deposits are one possibility while bond purchases are another. The return on either investment in a stable economic environment will have to be approximately similar, otherwise destabilizing movements of investment funds to the more profitable savings option (increasing its supply and pushing down its price/return) would occur. We can say, therefore, that interest rates on deposit accounts and returns on bonds, which are similar in risk level and for which the maturity period is similar (e.g. the purchase of a five-year bond and a savings deposit to be withdrawn in five years' time) will be similar. If interest rates are high, so too are returns on bonds, also known as bond yields.

Bond yields are closely related to expectations of future interest rates. The reasons for this have to do with how central banks deal with inflation and use interest rates in conducting their monetary policy. If the Bank of England, which sets the interest rate for the UK, announces that it does not expect inflation to be a problem financial analysts expect no changes in the interest rate. (If the bank considers inflation to be too high it tries to reduce the amount of money in circulation, which leads to upward pressure on the interest rate.) If expectations are that interest rates are not going to change in the short run then bond yields will be assumed similarly not to change. Expectations about what future interest rates will be are important in the determination of bond yields.

7.8.2 BONDS, INFLATION AND INTEREST RATES

Holders of 'standard' bonds receive an agreed fixed return over time on their investment. This agreed return is based on the market's best guess of future economic conditions, which is uncertain. If the agreed return on the bond is 5% per annum and inflation unexpectedly jumps to 6% over one year of the life of the bond, the real rate of return – the nominal return less inflation – is negative and holders lose 1% of their return.

> The real value of the fixed-income investment is reduced when inflation is greater than the rate of return.

Thus, anyone earning a fixed income dislikes inflation because the value of a fixed income is eroded. Index-linked earnings are preferable to fixed income payments because they are linked to the inflation rate and rise if inflation rises. An index-linked pension, for example, has a built-in facility that ensures it increases by 4% if the general price level rises by 4%.

If an economy experiences inflation, higher interest rates usually follow as the monetary authority or central bank tries to deal with it by reducing money supply. We know that increased inflation reduces real earnings from fixed-income investments.

Interest rate reductions are often welcomed by bond-market analysis as they affect the *present value* of the investment. A £1000 bond to be repaid in 10 years is worth less than £1000 received today due to expected inflation and the cost of having to wait rather than use the money for consumption today.

To compare the future receipt of the bond with a current receipt of the same value requires a method for comparing benefits in different time periods known as the **present value determination**.

The present value of £1000 to be received in ten years' time is the amount of money that would need to be set aside today to receive that specified amount at the specified future date. What must be determined is the amount of money that should be set aside to earn sufficient interest (or rate of return) to yield £1000 in ten years.

The standard formula used to determine **present value** is

$$PV = \frac{£X}{(1 + r)^T}$$

where PV denotes present value;
$£X$ is the amount to be received in the future;
r is the market interest rate;
T is the number of years before the investment is repaid.

If a bond of £1000 will be repaid in 10 years' time, its present value can be calculated once the current interest rate is known. If r is 3% the present value is computed as $£1000/(1 + 0.03)^{10}$. This is computed as $£1000/1.34 = £744.09$. Thus, the present value of a £1000 10-year bond is just over £744.

The present value of an investment varies with T and with r. If the bond is repaid in nine rather than ten years, this changes the present value, which is recalculated as £766.42. If the period is eight years the present value rises to £789.41 and if the period is two years the value is £952.50.

The present value increases as the period of the investment declines because of people's preference for £1 today rather than one year, two years, etc. from now.

To undertake an investment a rational person must be paid for the inconvenience and risk of foregoing their money now for its use only in the future. The further away the return on the investment, the more we expect the purchasing power of money to decline, and hence the lower its present value (I would prefer £1000 next year to the same amount the following year and so on).

As r varies so too does present value. If r is 2% rather than the 3% used in the above example the present value for $T = 10$ changes to £820.35. When interest rates fall, the present value of bonds rises representing a capital gain for holders of bonds, which is why bond market analysts often consider it positive news when interest rates fall.

A lower interest rate increases the present value of a bond.

7.9   MONETARY POLICY

In recent times, monetary policy has largely become synonymous with central banks' attempts to control inflation. Alternative targets for monetary policy include output growth and employment but since central banks deal with interest rates and reserve requirements, effects on real economic variables such as output and employment are indirect. A central bank's influence on inflation is also indirect via changes to the money supply and through the monetary instrument of the setting of short-term interest rates. Central banks usually make the public explicitly aware of what their inflation target is and depending on whether it can be achieved and maintained they are judged to be credible or not. Credibility is a key characteristic required of a sound central bank. We know that expectations play a central role in the determination of interest rates and in the bond market and the extent to which a central bank can follow through on its stated objectives is considered as an important factor that allows markets to deal with some of the uncertainty with which they must deal.

Independence from government is another factor that is important for central bank credibility.

Central bank independence usually implies that a government has no direct input into the economic decisions taken by the central bank regarding money supply, interest rates and inflation.

However, some central banks are independent only in the choice of how they meet targets set by their government. Independence matters because traders in financial markets trade based on their best analyses of how supply and demand are determined. Any attempts by a government to manipulate supply or demand for their own purposes would create additional uncertainty in the market. There may be grounds to argue that governments should produce additional money in an economy to pay for deficits it runs but unfortunately any additional money just serves to initially lower interest rates (by increasing money supply) but after a time the extra money in the economy would lead to higher inflation and invariably to higher interest rates. Governments might be liable to follow unsuitable monetary policies prior to elections to increase the likelihood of re-election but central bank independence mitigates this potential problem.

7.9.1 DIFFICULTIES IN TARGETING MONEY SUPPLY

In designing its monetary policy, an economy could choose particular targets for its money supply, its inflation rate and its exchange rate. From the quantity equation, the relationship between money supply and inflation is described and this can be used as the basis to target the money supply and bring about the desired rate of inflation.

Unfortunately, this is not as simple as it sounds because the quantity theory relates to long-run changes in the price level and central banks are interested in stabilizing short-run inflation (among other things). Controlling inflation in the short run is difficult because:

- Not only are there different definitions of the money supply (M1, M2, etc.), but they do not always move together. This means that targeting a specific rate of growth of money supply is difficult and in practice central banks have often switched from targeting one measure to another
- Central banks have no way of ensuring that the commercial banking sector fully passes on changes in interest rates to their customers. If the central bank changes (i.e. drops) the interest rate expecting the money supply to increase, commercial banks may not fully pass this on and limit the extent of any increase in the money supply.
- Assumptions are made about aggregate supply. Given the quantity theory, the rate of change of money supply and its relationship to inflation involves taking account of the rate of growth of long-run output growth. Whether output growth is 1% or 4% makes a difference when planning on achieving a specific inflation target via targeting money supply growth. Furthermore, if an economy is operating at capacity or potential output, an expansion of the money supply should lead to an increase in aggregate demand (caused by a drop in interest rates) and the result would be a rise in the price level. However, in dealing with an economy in the short run, it may well not be operating at its potential output. Hence the results of a rise in aggregate demand would be both an increase in the price level and in national output.

- Unexpected events – economic shocks – occur. Unexpected changes to aggregate supply, for example, imply that the best targeted policies may not have the desired outcome. The standard examples used are the oil-price shocks which resulted in aggregate supply contracting (moving leftwards) increasing the average price level and reducing equilibrium output. If such effects are short-term they are of less importance than if the effects endure over time.

7.9.2   ALTERNATIVE TARGETS

Some economies use exchange rate targets as part of their arsenal of monetary policies. Many countries fix their exchange rate to the dollar (e.g. Argentina, Hong Kong), or a basket of currencies (the most important trading partners, for example), in the hope that they can control inflation. This could be achieved by officially depreciating or appreciating the currency by altering interest rates, as required.

If exchange rates are set by demand and supply they are known as **floating exchange rates**. If one country's exchange rate is tied to another country's rate, it follows a **fixed exchange rate** regime.

Fixed or floating exchange rates?

More precisely, countries usually fix their currency over a range rather than to one particular value, otherwise the central bank would be forced to intervene every time the currency was not at its fixed value. Only if the currency moves outside its range, its target zone, would the central bank intervene, buying up excess supplies of the 'fixed currency' if required or supplying additional currency in times of excess demand. If the central bank did not follow such policies then excess supply could lead to depreciation of the exchange rate or excess demand could lead to appreciation. Altering interest rates to create interest rate differentials could similarly be used to entice capital to flows into or out of the country, as desired by the central bank.

Countries with fixed exchange rates should have similar inflation rates as the country to which the currency is fixed because of how currency demand and supply function. For example, if two countries have different levels of inflation and are economically linked via trade, holders of currency in the high-inflation country can buy fewer goods and services domestically than in the lower-inflation country. People will have an incentive to sell some of their high-inflation currency for the other currency, causing supply of the high-inflation currency to increase – resulting in its depreciation. For an exchange rate to remain fixed and for markets to find this a credible monetary policy, holders of the fixed currency must have no preference for one currency over the other and, therefore, inflation would have to be similar. A lack of credibility in a fixed currency could generate speculation on the currency, as discussed earlier.

The business sector is generally in favour of fixed exchange rates because of the increased certainty generated. Speculators have no incentive to buy or sell the currency against the currency to which it is fixed. Governments with fixed exchange rates cannot follow irresponsible expansionary policies, fiscal or monetary. Since such polices lead to rising aggregate demand and a higher aggregate price level (inflation) they make exports more expensive and imports less expensive, creating a tendency towards a trade deficit. While this could be cleared by a devaluation of the currency (caused when the central bank allows it or forces it to depreciate) it is not a policy option when the exchange rate is fixed. Inflation cannot be out of line with competitors' rates.

In floating exchange rate systems no such central bank intervention is required as market demand and supply alone determine equilibrium. This means no reserves of international currencies are required to purchase any excess supply. Governments have more discretion in selecting the level of aggregate demand it deems suitable while the central bank selects the interest rate it deems suitable given its targets.

A major difference between fixed or floating exchange rates is on how they can be used to bring about changes in the domestic economy. A country that has decided to fix its exchange rate but which might be at a different position in its business cycle to the country to which its currency is fixed is limited in how to deal with its domestic economy. One reason often voiced to explain the fact that the UK has not adopted the euro is that its business cycle is different to that of mainland Europe. Different interest rates being set by the ECB and the UK's Monetary Policy Committee are indicative of the different needs of both economies.

There is consensus that exchange rate and money supply targeting are difficult tools to use to achieve the goal of stable prices and that strict rules on money supply targets or fixing (or quasi-fixing) of rates do not leave economies with much room for manoeuvre. Many central banks instead have explicit publicly stated goals for their inflation targets. Their expectation is that via public announcements and communication, markets can be reasonably sure what monetary policies will be used *and why*. This recent behaviour is in marked contrast to previous secretive and closed-door deliberations on monetary policy but points to and reflects an understanding of the important role played by expectations within the economic system.

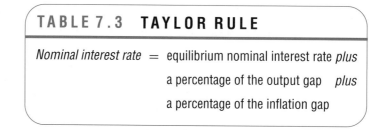

TABLE 7.3   TAYLOR RULE

Nominal interest rate = equilibrium nominal interest rate *plus*

a percentage of the output gap   *plus*

a percentage of the inflation gap

7.9.3   TAYLOR RULES AND ECONOMIC JUDGEMENT

Because of the nature of the economic system, with so many separate features related to others, it is a difficult feat to control inflation. Rather than targeting any one measure, an alternative exists in the form of Taylor rules (Taylor, 1993). These rules describe how interest rates are set by a central bank. A general form of such a rule is shown in Table 7.3.

The rule indicates that three pieces of information feed into the determination of the nominal interest rate set by a central bank, each of which requires some clarification.

- The equilibrium nominal interest rate is the real interest rate plus the inflation target of the central bank.
- As identified in Chapter 5, the output gap is the difference between potential output (also known as full employment output) and actual output.
- The inflation gap is the difference between the actual rate of inflation (or some banks use the future expected rate of inflation) and the central bank's target for inflation.

The decision on what percentages to use in the rule vary from bank to bank based on their assessment of how sensitive inflation and output are to changes in the interest rate. In the USA, 0.5 is the percentage of the output gap used and 1.5 is the percentage of the inflation gap used by the Federal Reserve. Essentially economic judgement is brought to bear on the expected relationships between output, the price level and nominal interest rates.

7.10   INTERNATIONAL MONETARY INTEGRATION

As we have already discussed in relation to trade (in Chapter 5) there are many signs to indicate that economies are becoming more interdependent. So too with money and currency markets which are intrinsically related internationally as goods, assets and services are bought and sold across borders. On the one hand if only one currency existed all international exchanges would be simpler. However, it is quite likely that different regions would have different requirements of monetary policy and interest rates. Forces leading to different business cycles might mean, for example, that Ireland requires policies appropriate to dealing with a boom at the same time as the USA requires policies to focus on recession, while the UK requires policies to deal with an expansionary phase of their business cycle.

Whether any single currency will be economically successful depends on whether the members constitute an optimal currency area (OCA).

> **Optimal currency area (OCA) theory** identifies the factors that determine whether a single currency maximizes single-currency benefits for members given the costs generated.

Four factors have been identified as playing a central role in the determination of the success or failure of any common currency:

1. Extent of trade with currency partners.
2. Effect of economic shocks vis-à-vis currency partners.
3. Extent of labour mobility between currency partners.
4. The extent of fiscal transfers between currency partners.

Countries that trade substantially with each other enjoy economic linkages that are enhanced by stability in their exchange rates. Exchange rate volatility has been found, in some cases, to increase the perceived costs of trading and so reduce the amount of trade that could take place if that volatility were removed.

If countries with the same currency do not experience similar effects of economic shocks, they have limited scope in how best they can react to deal with the shock. With one currency, monetary policy is guided by what is required by the majority or the largest countries – an example of a 'one size fits all' policy. Should another country require an alternative policy, they must bear the cost of not having an independent monetary policy.

With easy labour mobility between countries, the labour market becomes the short-run adjustment mechanism in the absence of monetary policy. If two countries experience differences in their business cycles at the same time with one booming and another in recession, both will have the same interest rate. The booming country cannot increase its interest rate and attempt to slow its economy down. Neither can the other cut the interest rate to create incentives for investment. With flexibility in the labour market, however, unemployed workers can move to the other country experiencing the boom.

In the absence of high labour mobility, sufficient transfers of income enable redistribution from higher-income areas that can help ease the plight of countries experiencing recession.

7.10.1 CONSIDERING THE EURO

The euro was launched by 11 European countries (Austria, Belgium, Finland, France, Germany, Ireland, Italy, Luxembourg, the Netherlands, Portugal and Spain) at the beginning of January 1999. When euro notes were introduced in 2002, Greece also 'joined' the euro zone. For some this was the culmination of the post-World War Two attempts by European countries to ensure a repetition of the causes and consequences of war was not possible through the strengthening of economic and political ties between them.

Some of the main European events that preceded the euro were:

- *1951*: The European Coal and Steel Community (ECSC) was set up, with six members: Belgium, West Germany, Luxembourg, France, Italy and the Netherlands. This organization was proposed by the French Foreign Minister Robert Schuman to integrate the coal and steel industries of Western Europe.
- *1957*: The same six countries signed the Treaties of Rome and European Economic Community creating the European Atomic Energy Community (EURATOM) and European Economic Community (EEC) respectively. The aim of the EEC was to remove trade barriers to form a 'common market'.
- *1967*: The institutions of the three European communities (ESCS, EURATOM and EEC) were merged to create one European Commission, one council of ministers as well as the European parliament.
- *1973*: Expansion of Community to Denmark, Ireland and the United Kingdom.
- *1981*: Expansion of Community to Spain and Portugal.
- *1987*: Single European Act (SEA) came into operation in July. The goal was to create a single market in goods, capital, labour and services by 1992.
- *1992*: The Treaty of Maastricht (1992) introduced new forms of inter-governmental co-operation, for example on defence, and in the area of 'justice and home affairs' thus creating the European Union (EU).
- *1995*: Expansion of Union to Austria, Finland and Sweden.
- *2003*: Given past and future expansions of the Union, the Treaty of Nice came into force laying new rules governing the size of EU institutions and how they work.

- *2004*: Expansion of Union to Cyprus, the Czech Republic, Estonia, Hungary, Latvia, Lithuania, Malta, Poland, Slovakia and Slovenia.

By adoption of the SEA, members of the EC confirmed their aim to realize an economic and monetary union (EMU). The Delors Report on EMU of 1989 proposed how this might be achieved in a series of stages in a process to coordinate economic and monetary policy. A European system of central banks would take charge of monetary arrangements via a committee of central bank governors. The final stage would be the irrevocable fixing of exchange rates and introduction of a single currency.

Phase 1 began in earnest in 1990 when increased economic cooperation was required by the submission of currencies to the European Monetary System's exchange rate mechanism (ERM). The EMS had been created in 1979, before the road to EMU was begun. Its aims were to assist the maintenance of stable currencies by keeping currencies within exchange rate bands. The bands were altered from time to time and realignments occurred.

Realignments are simultaneous and coordinated devaluation or revaluation of currencies of several countries.

Stability was not always achieved. The UK joined in 1991 but withdrew along with Italy in 1992. In September 1992, there was widespread uncertainty on the outcome of the French referendum on the Treaty of Maastricht. This contributed to speculation on the weakest ERM currencies, sterling and the lira. Despite substantial increases in domestic interest rates, the markets were subject to intense speculation and sterling left the EMS in 1992. Over the four months that followed, the interest rate in the UK was cut by four percentage points to meet the requirements of a country dealing with a recession. The currency had depreciated by over 15% but subsequently appreciated as the economy recovered. The French franc, thanks to substantial intervention by the German central bank, the Bundesbank, survived speculative pressure in September 1992. The Irish pound succumbed to pressure from speculators and was devalued by 10% in January 1993.

ERM bands had to be widened to 15% in August 1993. In hindsight it appears currencies had been over-valued in the sense that their exchange rates were out of line with a sustainable balance of payments and devaluations were required.

The **balance of payments** is one account in a country's national accounts. It includes transactions between domestic residents and the rest of the world over a specified period. It consists of a **current account** and a **capital** account.

> The current account includes all trade transactions where the balance of trade might be in surplus or deficit. It also includes all income and current transfers.
>
> The capital and financial account tracks transactions relating to ownership of financial assets, including inward and outward direct investment.

Devaluations lead to increased competitiveness for export goods, boosting the balance of payments through the balance of trade. Import goods become less attractive as they are more expensive following devaluation.

The German economy had been a source of uncertainty in the EMS also because of its need to finance unification on the one hand and a desire not to increase taxes to fund it on the other. The increased demand for money to fund reunification meant the German interest rate was driven up. Through the EMS links, interest rates in other countries were also high.

Over time, the credibility of the EMS was re-established and by the end of 1996 all but Ireland were within 2.25% bands.

The EMS survived largely because many governments wished to fulfil requirements to qualify for EMU under the Maastricht criteria. These included:

- *Inflation*: a country's inflation rate (CPI) could be no higher than 1.5 percentage points above the three best performers for one year.
- *Interest rate*: a country's average nominal long-term interest rate (e.g. on government bonds) could be no more than two percentage points higher than the same three best performers above.
- *Budget deficit*: a country's current budget deficit could not be 'excessive' taken to mean it should not be higher than 3% of GDP.
- *Currency stability*: a country's exchange rate should have operated normally within the ERM for two years with no pressure to devalue against other members.
- *Public debt*: although not specifically mentioned it was considered that it should be no higher than 60% of GDP.

These specific convergence criteria are not supported by objective rationale or theory, e.g. why not choose 65% of GDP? No mention of unemployment is made, although what is happening in the labour market helps to determine success or failure of OCAs. (Indeed, as we will see in Chapter 8, the relationship between inflation and unemployment should not be overlooked in focusing solely on inflation.) Rather the 60% and 3% deficit figures were the trends or averages at the time. The need for movement toward convergence, in the light of the OCA discussion above, is however unquestionable if the currency is to be successful.

The advantages of one European currency include:

- Elimination of currency conversion costs associated with buying foreign exchange.
- Competition and efficiency improvements as prices of the same goods in the euro zone would be more comparable and create incentives for arbitrage and be pro-competitive and pro-consumer especially for high-cost markets.
- Removal of exchange rate volatility within the euro zone that results in enhancing trade and reducing possibility for speculation on individual currencies (as occurred in 1992 and 1993). Investment by foreign-owned companies is also sensitive to exchange rate volatility effects on their potential costs and revenues. The experience of the UK post-euro has been a decline in its share of EU-destined inward investment from 39% in 1999 to 24% three years later.
- Lower inflation and interest rates are possible once the European Central Bank is perceived as independent and achieves credibility. This boosts the market's impression of the euro as a strong currency, which can maintain low long-term interest rates, stimulating domestic and foreign investment in the EU.

Despite these potential advantages, the difficulties in meeting some of the OCA criteria remain too significant for some countries to concede that joining is optimal for them, or that on economic grounds the adoption of the euro made sense.

Clearly, adoption of the euro is not the result of economic decisions but political decisions also.

HOW DOES THE EURO SCORE IN TERMS OF THE FOUR OCA FACTORS?

- In terms of the euro, member countries conduct between 55% and 75% of their trade with other euro-zone members.
- Belgium, France, Germany, Italy and the Netherlands display highly correlated GDP growth patterns. The business cycles of other countries including Finland, Greece, Ireland and Portugal indicate lower correlations which implies they may find the transition to the single currency more difficult. Relatively speaking, the correlation appears higher among all euro-zone members than among all states of the USA, which has its single currency.

- European labour markets tend to be less flexible and labour less mobile than in the USA. (More on this in Chapter 8.) The language barrier explains much of this as well as historical relatively low labour mobility rates.
- Fiscal transfers between euro-zone member states are quite small and do not compare to the federal tax and expenditure system of the USA.

Not all four factors are fully satisfied. It does not follow, however, that the costs of the euro outweigh its benefits.

Some explanation is provided for the alternative stances taken by countries on the euro. The UK appears to follow a different business cycle to its European partners. France, Germany and the Benelux countries trade highly and follow similar business cycles. Greece and Italy may benefit from lower inflation under the euro than if they followed independent national monetary policies (such as with Ireland following its membership of the previous European monetary system).

The more problematic factors may become less important over time if/as the single market becomes more developed.

7.11   SUMMARY

- **To qualify as money, three specific functions must be served: medium of exchange, unit of account and store of value.**
- **The supply of money is regulated by each country's monetary authority (central bank or Federal Reserve), which operates monetary policy focused on maintaining a sound financial system in which people have confidence. Open-market operations are the main way that money supply is increased or reduced. Another mechanism is via the required reserve ratio.**
- **The banking system creates money according to the money multiplier relationship between deposits, the required reserve ratio and loans offered by banks.**
- **The demand for liquid money can be specified as precautions, transactions and speculative demands.**
- **Interest rates are determined in the money market (by money supply and money demand).**

- The real interest rate is the difference between the nominal rate and inflation. Both nominal and real interest rates are taken into account for consumption, saving and investment decisions, hence they affect aggregate demand.
- The quantity theory of money describes the relationship between money supply and inflation. Inflation expectations also have a role in the determination of *ex-ante* real interest rates used for decision-making.
- Credibility of central bank policies matter for the stability of a country's financial system.
- Exchange rates are determined in the foreign exchange market (by currency supply and demand).
- Speculation in money and other asset markets is widespread in the economic system. There are costs and benefits associated with speculation.
- Monetary policy can focus on a variety of targets.

REVIEW PROBLEMS AND QUESTIONS

1. Show, by using your own examples, that you understand the three functions of money.
2. Fill in the following table to consider the impact on money creation of deposit of £1000 according to the method explained in Table 7.2 taking into account here a required reserve ratio of 10%.

	Deposit £	*Required reserves* £	*Loan* £
Moneybags	1000		
Grandon's			
Next customer			
Next customer			
. . .	. . .	. . .	. . .
Total			

3. Use supply and demand curves to explain how equilibrium emerges in the money market to determine the interest rate – the price of money. Explain the impact of open market operations (if the government sells bonds) on equilibrium.

4. What are the nominal and real interest rates? How do changes in i) nominal and ii) real interest rates affect:
   - borrowers;
   - savers;
   - consumers?
5. What is the quantity equation and what relationship does it describe?
6. Use the demand and supply model to show:
   a. how exchange rates are determined;
   b. causes of fluctuations in exchange rates.
7. What is a bond and what is the bond market? What is the relationship between the price of a bond and the rate of interest?
8. Explain using some examples what you understand by the term 'monetary policy'. Using the example of controlling inflation, what difficulties may arise in implementing monetary policy?

FURTHER READING AND RESEARCH

- For an insight into how cigarettes fulfilled the main functions of money in a prisoner-of-war camp, see Radford, 1945.
- In relation to the Asian currency crisis see Nouriel Roubini's Global Macroeconomic and Financial Policy Website at http://www.stern.nyu.edu/globalmacro/ See also Krugman, 1998.
- For more on the European exchange rate mechanism see El-Agraa, 2001, pp. 124–48; and Mayes, 2001.

REFERENCES

DeLong, J. and L. Summers (1993) 'Macroeconomic policy and long-run growth' in Federal Reserve Bank of Kansas City. *Policies for Long-run Economic Growth.*

El-Agraa, A. (ed.) (2001) *The European Union, Economics and Policies.* 6th edn, Pearson.

Krugman, P. (1998) *Whatever happened to Asia?* Mimeo; online at http://web.mit.edu/krugman/www/

Mayes, D. (2001) 'The European monetary system', in El-Agraa, A. (ed) *The European Union, Economics and Policies,* 365–87.

Radford, R. (1945) 'The price system in a microcosm: a POW camp', *Economica*, **12**, 189–201.

Roubini, N. Global Macroeconomic and Financial Policy website at http://www.stern.nyu.edu/globalmacro/

Taylor, J. (1993) 'Discretion versus policy rules in practice', *Carnegie-Rochester Conference Series on Public Policy*, **39**(0), 195–214.

CHAPTER 8

CHALLENGES FOR THE ECONOMIC SYSTEM: UNEMPLOYMENT AND INFLATION

LEARNING OUTCOMES

By the end of this chapter you should be able to:

✪ Explain why unemployment and inflation periodically emerge as short-run economic problems.

✪ Describe alternative definitions and categories of unemployment.

✪ Use the labour demand and supply model to examine the effects of minimum wages on employment and wage rates.

✪ Apply the aggregate demand and supply model to compare/contrast alternative approaches to unemployment and how an economy deals with it.

✪ Explain the recessionary gap approach to unemployment.

✪ Outline the main costs associated with unemployment.

✪ Apply the aggregate demand and supply model to compare and contrast alternative approaches to inflation and how an economy deals with it.

✪ Explain the inflationary gap approach to inflation.

✪ Describe recent trends in international rates of inflation, and their causes.

✪ Outline the main costs associated with inflation if it is anticipated or not.

✪ Describe what the Phillips curve predicts for unemployment and inflation.

✪ Explain the alternative perspective to the Phillips curve offered by the natural rate of employment model.

8.1 INTRODUCTION

We have seen that in the context of economies experiencing business cycles over the short to medium terms, there is the possibility that an economy can find itself in an equilibrium situation where aggregate demand intersects with aggregate supply at a point where the economy is at less than full employment. Another potential macroeconomic equilibrium is possible where the average level of prices is unstable which, as we will see below, is possible with increasing aggregate demand or decreasing aggregate supply in the short run. In the case where the price level rises over time inflation can be a feature of the short- to medium-term experience for an economy. The two issues of unemployment and inflation have focused the minds of many economists over the years as they attempt to argue how economies should best deal with the challenges created by either unemployment or inflation, or sometimes both together.

In this chapter we consider the issues separately initially (in sections 8.2 and 8.3) and examine the causes of unemployment and inflation using standard economic theory based on both the microeconomic demand and supply and the aggregate demand and aggregate supply concepts and tools introduced in earlier chapters. We examine some alternative explanations for unemployment and inflation and in section 8.4 discuss the logic behind theories that hold that the one is a trade-off for the other and consider what implications that view has for government policy. We also examine the causes of different equilibrium rates of unemployment and find in sections 8.5 and 8.6 that it is possible under certain circumstances to observe both inflation and unemployment in the short run.

8.2   UNEMPLOYMENT

In any economy a number of individuals are willing and able to work. The number of people aged 16 (or in some countries 15) and over who are employed plus the number of people unemployed – those who do not have jobs but who are actively looking for work – makes up an economy's labour force. Not every individual in an economy falls into either the employed or unemployed category. For example, retired people, people who choose to take on home or childcare duties, and discouraged workers are not included in the calculation of the labour force.

> **Discouraged workers** have tried to find work in the past and are willing to take on a job but have given up on looking for work because they feel, or know, that nothing suitable is available.

The unemployment rate measures the percentage of the labour force that cannot find work.

If 9 million people are employed in an economy and 1 million are unemployed, the unemployment rate is:

$$\frac{1}{9+1} \times 100 = 10\%$$

Across the countries of the OECD a standardized unemployment rate is reported as the measure of unemployment. This measure is also used by the International Labour Organization (ILO).

The **standardized unemployment rate** measures those unemployed as people of working age without work who are available to start work within two weeks and who are actively seeking employment.

Some recent statistics for unemployment (using the standardized rate) are shown in Table 8.1. France and Germany's performances have been poor relative to the other countries shown.

Countries report standardized unemployment statistics based on labour force surveys conducted on a regular basis (often each quarter). An alternative measure of unemployment is found by counting all those who receive unemployment payments; however, those unemployed but ineligible for benefits are excluded in

TABLE 8.1 UNEMPLOYMENT RATES, %, SELECTED COUNTRIES 1998–2003

Year	Germany	France	Japan	Sweden	Ireland	UK	USA
1998	9.1	11.4	4.1	8.2	7.5	6.2	4.5
1999	8.4	10.7	4.7	6.7	5.6	5.9	4.2
2000	7.8	9.3	4.7	5.6	4.3	5.4	4.0
2001	7.8	8.5	5.0	4.9	3.9	5.0	4.7
2002	8.6	8.8	5.4	4.9	4.4	5.1	5.8
2003	9.3	9.4	5.3	5.6	4.6	5.0	6.0

Source: Excerpted from Table A, OECD, 2004.

this measure. Neither measure is perfect since the standardized measure excludes those in receipt of payments but not actively looking for work.

8.2.1   LABOUR MARKET ANALYSIS: TYPES OF UNEMPLOYMENT

Within the broad heading 'unemployment' it is useful to distinguish between frictional, structural, cyclical and seasonal unemployment.

> **Frictional unemployment** is unemployment that arises because of changes or friction in particular markets.

Frictional employment reflects changes in people's preferences or tastes, or the introduction of new technologies that alter demand for products over time, with knock-on effects on the demand for labour to produce them. The most appropriate ways to supply also change with technological developments, which can also impact on the demand for labour. Thus, within the normal activities of the economic system some firms go out of business while others open up. This means there are always people losing their jobs, switching from one job to another, and entering or leaving the labour force. Frictional unemployment is regarded as natural, and it is associated with the 'natural rate of unemployment'.

> The **natural rate of unemployment** is the rate of unemployment that would prevail when the labour market is in long-run equilibrium – some people choose to change jobs and even in boom periods it can take a worker time to find a job best suited to their skills.

The natural rate of unemployment is also called the non-accelerating inflation rate of unemployment – NAIRU – to emphasize that since it is a long-run phenomenon, it puts no pressure on prices to increase. Hence, frictional unemployment is also regarded as voluntary.

> **Structural unemployment** refers to unemployment arising from a permanent decline in employment in industries located in a particular region or area.

Structural unemployment differs significantly from frictional. It may be due to mismatch between job vacancies and the skill/occupations of the unemployed, e.g. there may be job vacancies for carpenters, but this will do little to alleviate unemployment among plumbers. It is a more serious types of unemployment than frictional unemployment because it takes time for mismatches to be addressed via reskilling, for example, or for new industries to be attracted to an unemployment black spot. Such unemployment is particularly harsh if a recession is prolonged. The natural rate of unemployment could be reduced if some of the structural unemployment were eradicated.

Cyclical unemployment is associated with the recessionary phase of the business cycle.

When the growth rate of economic activity slows down in a recession, there is a fall in aggregate demand and some firms will react to this fall in planned expenditure of consumers by reducing their output and may make some of their employees redundant. When the economy picks up again and the growth rate of economic activity rises, planned expenditures will rise and in response firms who wish to expand their output accordingly may hire additional workers. Cyclical unemployment refers to short-run employment.

Seasonal unemployment occurs in seasonal industries such as tourism and fishing. People in these industries may become temporarily unemployed over the winter months when the industries slow down.

In the long run, the labour market is in equilibrium at the natural rate of unemployment. In the short run, unemployment can be higher than the natural rate, in which case economic policies are often used to try to address the problem. In the short run it is also possible to have unemployment below the natural rate – the implications are discussed in a later section of the chapter.

Like other markets, labour supply and labour demand determine the equilibrium price – wage rate – and the quantity of workers employed. Many countries impose wages not determined by 'market forces' as in the case of the minimum wage.

Minimum wage: wage rate set by the government below which employers are not legally permitted to pay workers. Employers are free to pay workers above this wage rate if they choose.

Minimum wages are implemented to address arguments that workers would otherwise earn wages that are too low to allow them a reasonable standard of living. The determination of what constitutes 'reasonable' depends on the views of those involved in negotiations that lead to the decision to implement a minimum wage. In situations where a minimum wage applies the effects on employment can be analysed (similar to the situation of price floors considered in Chapter 2). The possible effects of a minimum wage are shown in Figure 8.1 where in panel A the wage is set above the 'free-market' level and where resulting effects on consumer

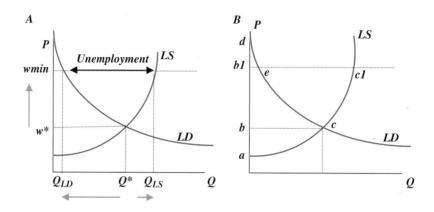

FIGURE 8.1   MINIMUM WAGES (PRICE FLOOR) AND THE
LABOUR MARKET: CASE 1

and producer surplus are considered in panel *B*. *LS* refers to labour supply and *LD* to labour demand.

In Figure 8.1 panel *A*, with no intervention in the labour market, the equilibrium quantity would be Q^* and the equilibrium wage would be at w^*. However, a minimum wage is set at *wmin* which is higher than w^*. At the wage *wmin*, labour supply is greater than labour demand implying an excess supply of labour. More workers wish to work at this wage rate than firms demand. The results of the minimum wage when it is set above the market wage is that the number of workers employed is lower – Q_{LD} is lower than Q^* – although those who can find employment at the higher wage (*wmin* compared to w^*) do earn a higher wage. Since a lower quantity of workers earn the higher wage it is difficult to determine which situation is best for workers in general. A worker who can find work at the higher wage will probably think it is a fairer situation than a worker who is unemployed when wages are high but can find work at the lower wage w^*.

Welfare analysis can be conducted to consider the changes resulting from a minimum wage. In Figure 8.1 panel *B* there is a direct transfer of consumer surplus to producer surplus arising from the implementation of the minimum wage. In the labour market, firms that employ workers are consumers of labour while workers offering their labour for payment are the producers. Producer surplus increases, as suggested by the increase in the area between the prevailing wage and the supply curve. Producer surplus is the area above the supply curve and below the price. Before the minimum wage, producer surplus is the area *abc* which rises to *ab1c1* if the minimum wage is used.

With the minimum wage consumer surplus falls. Without a minimum wage, consumer surplus (the area between demand function and price) is the area *bcd*. With the minimum wage consumer surplus falls to *b1de*. Some of the loss in consumer surplus, *bb1ec* is transferred to producer surplus. The area *cc1e*, however, is a net gain to producer surplus (not a transfer). This area represents the 'cost' in welfare terms of the minimum wage. It indicates the extra wages received by some suppliers over and above what they require to supply their labour. It could be called excessive since it entices some labour to enter the labour market for a wage beyond what is required to provide them with an incentive to work. Unfortunately, since the demand for labour is lower than the supply at *wmin*, all labour above Q_{LD} cannot find work.

Therefore, the minimum wage increases producer surplus, decreases consumer surplus and creates a cost for the economy. In terms of the outcome regarding employment, fewer people are employed, although those who can find work earn the higher minimum wage.

Such unemployment is explained by examples where trades unions negotiate wages above market-clearing levels. If wages reach such levels it is quite easy to offer a solution to the problem – wage rates need to fall. In practice, however, workers in employment and their union representatives will be unwilling to let this happen. A further potential problem with a drop in the average wage occurs if the decline is too large and workers overall respond by reducing their consumer expenditure which could lead to a decline in aggregate demand with no positive net impact on unemployment.

A similar situation is presented in Figure 8.2 with one significant difference, however, since the minimum wage is set below the 'free-market' level. Such a minimum wage could arise if the government is incorrect in its assessment of labour

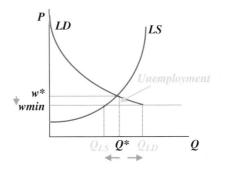

FIGURE 8.2 MINIMUM WAGES (PRICE CEILING) AND THE LABOUR MARKET: CASE 2

demand and labour supply and there are instances where such mistakes have been made. Here the effects of a minimum wage would be that some workers wishing to supply their labour at the higher wage w^* no longer have the incentive to work at the lower $wmin$ and so labour supply is lower at Q_{LS} than if the free equilibrium position prevailed at Q^*. At the lower wage of $wmin$, firms' demand for workers is higher than at the wage of w^* hence, Q_{LD} is higher than Q^*. Demand for workers outstrips supply and there is a shortage of workers at $wmin$. This shortage can be cleared only if wages are allowed to rise to w^*. The impact on unemployment in this situation is that fewer workers wish to supply their labour at the lower wage, hence unemployment is higher than under the 'free-market' situation.

Since policy-makers do not know with certainty what the labour demand and labour supply curves look like, any attempt to impose a minimum wage represents their 'best guess' or 'guesstimate' which may have either the consequences shown in Figures 8.1 or 8.2. The better the economic analysis provided to policy-makers, the more focused and successful the policy may be, but setting wage rates is never a policy without costs.

In practice, fears about reductions in employment as a result of minimum wages have appeared largely unfounded, i.e. the outcome has been different to that suggested in Figures 8.1 and 8.2. Employers have *not* reacted to the minimum wage by reducing their numbers of employees. Why? One plausible reason is that firms choose to absorb any additional costs generated by minimum wages, which essentially means they lowered their preferred profit margins. Firms may be happy to do this in the short run if workers become more productive when paid a higher wage so that an initial jump in firms' average costs caused by paying the minimum wage is balanced by a decline in average costs over time as productivity improves. It is also plausible that higher wages act as a signal to attract higher-skilled workers. The concept of efficiency wages may also provide an explanation.

An **efficiency wage** rate lies above the market clearing wage rate to provide motivation for workers, to keep worker turnover low (avoiding costs of hiring) and to act as a signal to attract appropriately skilled workers.

The implication of efficiency wages is that firms may have an incentive to pay higher wages than the market clearing rate or a minimum wage. Firm profitability may ultimately be higher due to the motivation, turnover and signalling effects provided by efficiency wages.

In many countries the actual process through which wages are determined is through collective wage-bargaining where government representatives, trades union representatives, employer representatives and sometimes others, negotiate wages for periods of one year, two years and sometimes longer. Some negotiations take place at a national level, others take place locally. There appears to be support for the view that the more coordinated are wage-bargaining negotiations – i.e. the more trades unions are involved collectively – the better the outcome for the unemployment rate. If unions negotiated unilaterally for wage rates for only their workers, each union would try to negotiate the highest wage possible.

> If all unions have to negotiate together with all employers and the government then it is clear to all that excessively high wages for all unions' workers would just lead to higher unemployment.

More modest wage negotiations are more likely, as is lower unemployment.

8.2.2 ANALYSING UNEMPLOYMENT: MACRO AND MICRO

The macroeconomic aggregate demand and supply framework can also be used when analysing unemployment. Beginning with the long-run case, where an economy faces a downward sloping aggregate demand function and a vertical aggregate supply function, unemployment occurs if the level of equilibrium national income is below potential output. In such circumstances the challenge for business and government is to get the economy to its long-run equilibrium position at or at least closer to potential output, so that a minimum of economic resources are unemployed. Such analyses follow in later sections.

Classical approach

One school of thought in economics, known as the classical school, maintains that labour markets would operate to ensure that unemployment did *not* exist and that in the long run economies would tend towards their full employment level of output. In a labour market with flexible wages and no intervention by governments, wages would adjust to clear the market and, therefore, any unemployment would necessarily be voluntary, i.e. only frictional or equilibrium unemployment would exist. Wages would fall in times of low demand for labour (relative to its supply) so that unemployed resources could be put to work. If demand for labour was high (relative to its supply) wages would rise to bring the labour market and eventually the economy back to equilibrium.

Supporters of the classical view see unemployment as a possibility in the short run where distortions exist that do not allow wages to change (perhaps due to a minimum wage policy, or to negotiations with trades unions or due to generous unemployment benefits). Solving such unemployment problems would be possible by allowing wages to be more flexible. With wages free to move up or down, unemployment would not be a feature of the long-run performance of an economy.

Classical vs. Keynesian approach

An alternative view was put forward by John Maynard Keynes (in 1936), who believed that unemployment and slow growth in economic activity could persist over the short run and maybe even for long periods and become ingrained in an economy. Such unemployment is also called demand-deficient unemployment since firms do not demand labour because consumers demand too few goods. Keynes argued that reducing wages to deal with such an unemployment problem would be inappropriate because wage cuts would lead to lower incomes which in turn lead to lower planned expenditure, lowering aggregate demand and further lowering employment and raising unemployment.

In the Keynesian approach to the economy, unemployment could be involuntary due to problems faced by economic agents who, for whatever reasons, do not have the capacity to boost aggregate demand to the degree required to cause firms to hire more workers. Accordingly, a possible solution for an unemployment problem would be for governments to increase their expenditure, increasing aggregate demand, recirculating more income so that demand for unemployed labour will increase. Keynes acknowledged, however, the potential for problems of persistent budget deficits that might be generated by such a strategy.

A comparison of the classical and Keynesian views on unemployment is presented in Figure 8.3 using microeconomic analysis of the labour market. In panel A the classical position is sketched where the prevailing real wage is $w1$ and is higher than the level required to clear the labour market. There is involuntary unemployment, which could be reduced in the short run and ultimately eliminated by a fall in real wages towards w^*. In the classical approach, such involuntary unemployment would not prevail very long because real wages are assumed to adjust down to clear the labour market.

In Figure 8.3 panel B the differences between classical and Keynesian views can be highlighted. In panel B, involuntary unemployment exists at the wage rate $w1$. In the Keynesian explanation of unemployment real wages do not simply fall to eliminate unemployment as real wages are essentially fixed or 'sticky' – workers are unwilling to accept cuts in wages required to bring the labour market into equilibrium. This could be a feature of an economy where nominal wages were set through a centralized bargaining approach regarding what level of wages and wage

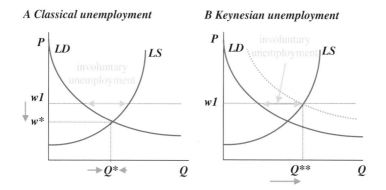

FIGURE 8.3   UNEMPLOYMENT: CLASSICAL AND
KEYNESIAN APPROACHES

inflation is acceptable. With such agreements there is no scope for cutting wages, or indeed for increasing them beyond agreed levels.

In Figure 8.3 panel *B* the unemployment problem could be remedied if labour demand increased to the dotted demand line indicated in panel *B*. Hence, unemployment here is caused by demand deficiency. A reduction in wages to below *w1* would lead the market to clear *but* the labour demand curve drawn represents demand for labour in an economy where demand for firms' output is below the full employment level. This means that an equilibrium position could prevail in the short run and persist as long as demand is less than the full employment level of output. Also, if wages are below *w1*, workers may reduce their planned expenditures, making the demand deficiency even worse.

So which model is correct – the classical or Keynesian? There is disagreement among economists on that issue in the sense that many believe that there is a self-correcting mechanism operating in the economy that brings the economy back towards equilibrium over time. However, the speed of this correction is what gives rise to the disagreement. Those who believe that the speed is rather quick consider that no action is required to induce the economy to move more quickly to equilibrium. Those following the Keynesian view support a more activist approach since the speed of economic adjustment is considered to be slow.

8.2.3   UNEMPLOYMENT AND THE RECESSIONARY GAP

The macroeconomic aggregate demand and supply model illustrates the problem of unemployment from both classical and Keynesian perspectives. In Figure 8.4 we have an economy in short-run equilibrium at a level of output below its long-run

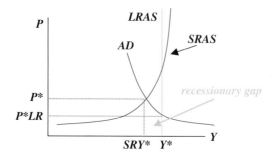

FIGURE 8.4 RECESSIONARY GAP

potential level. Since the economy is not operating at its potential level, this implies the economy has some unemployed resources and the level of unemployment is above the natural rate. The economy is in recession.

Note in Figure 8.4 that both long-run and short-run aggregate supply curves are included. We do not treat the *SRAS* as a 'combination' aggregate supply curve. Over the (almost) vertical portion of the *SRAS* lying to the right of the *LRAS*, the economy is producing at its maximum but unsustainable level of output. Many workers are working overtime, capital is being utilized over several shifts, for example, but the level of output could not be retained at such high levels without pressure on prices and wages. At any point on the *LRAS*, the prices of all outputs and inputs have fully adjusted to clear all markets in the long run.

> In a recession, the difference between the level of potential output and the lower actual output is described as the **recessionary gap**.

This recessionary gap is shown as the difference between short run output *SRY** and potential output *Y**, indicating that actual output falls short of its potential level. In comparing short-run to long-run equilibrium we also see that the price level differs in both cases. The short-run price level *P** lies above the long run level of *P**LR.

Following a classical theory of adjustment, wages, as one of the prices prevailing in the economy, are too high and must fall to bring the economy to long-run equilibrium. Hence the economy's price level would fall as the economy adjusts over time from its short-run to its long-run equilibrium, from *SRY** and *P** to *Y** and *P**LR. Firms would hire more workers at lower wage rates and output could expand. At a lower price level of *P**LR, aggregate demand would increase.

According to a Keynesian theory of adjustment, wages are fixed or sticky in the short run and what is required is government intervention to increase injections into the economy (increase government expenditure) or reduce withdrawals (taxes) to

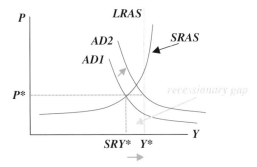

FIGURE 8.5 CLOSING THE RECESSIONARY GAP: KEYNESIAN APPROACH

close the recessionary gap. This implies a shift of the aggregate demand function. For example, if the government increases its expenditure it can, through the multiplier, close the gap as shown in Figure 8.5.

Aggregate demand rises from $AD1$ to $AD2$ as the government increases its expenditure or cuts taxes via its discretionary fiscal policy. Moving from the short-run equilibrium of P^* and SRY^* (from the intersection of $SRAS$ and $AD1$) to the long-run equilibrium of P^* and Y^* we see that the boost in aggregate demand gives rise to a higher output level at the same aggregate level of prices.

8.2.4 THE COSTS OF UNEMPLOYMENT

At the level of the macroeconomy, unemployed resources mean unproductive resources. Output is less than what it could be and income is below its potential level (at SRY^* relative to Y^*). Economic activity is lower than if the economy operated at its full employment level. Some unemployment – a natural rate – is normal for any economy but non-voluntary unemployment generates costs. As well as reduced output and income, unemployment reduces governments' revenue from tax income. With high employment, there is likely to be high demand for goods and services from firms. Firms may even make higher profits as consumers are able to buy more goods and services, but this depends on market structure, which we saw in Chapter 6. With high unemployment, profits surely suffer as demand is weakened.

Within modern welfare states, governments provide transfer payments as benefits to the unemployed (under certain conditions) and therefore, this represents an additional cost. Managing to create jobs for the unemployed would therefore increase national output, allow workers to earn a wage/salary, allow firms to make profits, allow the government to collect more in taxes and, if demand for labour were substantial, allow those already employed to increase their supply of labour.

All of the costs described above are at the level of the macroeconomy. Arguably, there are even more serious costs of unemployment if we consider the microeconomic, individual and social costs of unemployment. Even short-term unemployment can be disheartening and stressful for individuals and their families. This may result in higher personal costs for physical and mental health care, which can result from stress. Some authors have associated crime and delinquency with unemployment. In addition, individuals' human capital can decline. A broad assessment of the costs of unemployment would take these issues into account also.

8.3 INFLATION

In Chapter 5 an example was used to illustrate how inflation is measured using information on people's general expenditure patterns and the prices of goods and services. It is possible to consider the causes of inflation using the aggregate demand and supply model to examine what happens to the equilibrium price level if there are changes to either the demand or supply sides of the aggregate economy.

In Figure 8.6, beginning with panel A, we see a rise in aggregate demand, i.e. the AD curve shifting to the right from AD to AD1. The initial equilibrium occurs at P* and Y* while the new equilibrium arises at P1 and Q1. An increase in aggregate demand leads to both higher output for the economy and a higher aggregate price level as the economy was not initially operating at potential output.

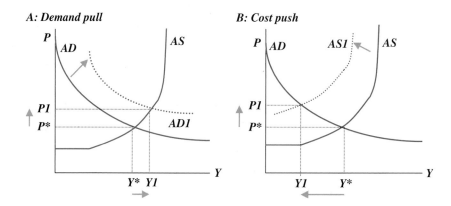

FIGURE 8.6   DEMAND-PULL AND COST-PUSH INFLATION

An increase in the price level of an economy caused by rising aggregate demand is called **demand-pull inflation**.

Demand-pull inflation is associated with boom periods in an economy where planned expenditures rise with the increasing income generated in a boom. This means the aggregate demand curve moves up or rightwards on a continual basis over a period of time. Firms react to the increases in planned expenditures by producing more, if they can, and by raising prices.

If an economy is operating at capacity where all firms are producing to capacity, or beyond its long-run level, which can occur for short periods if workers are willing to work overtime, any rise in aggregate demand leads to increases in prices only and no increase in output.

An alternative source of inflation is presented in Figure 8.6 panel *B* where aggregate supply falls in response to firms' reducing their output (in reaction to a rise in costs). For example, if firms' wages increase then at any level of prices, firms would cut back on their production and this is observed in a leftward shift of aggregate supply.

Cost-push inflation occurs when firms react to increased costs by reducing their output.

This occurs because when firms face increased costs, they react by raising their prices, and pass on the cost increase, to some extent (depending on price elasticity of demand for different products) to their consumers. The resulting equilibrium is seen at *P1* and *Y1*. The new equilibrium reflects a higher level of prices but a lower level of national output than the initial equilibrium. If the economy was not operating at full employment in the initial equilibrium of *P** and *Q**, this implies that more resources are unemployed if output drops to *Y1* from *Y**. Rises in firms' costs might come from other sources than wages. For example, import-price push inflation occurs with an increase in the price of raw materials (such as oil or inputs) that are imported. Cost-push inflation could also be due to firms raising prices to increase their profit margins.

It is possible that both demand-pull and cost-push inflation occur simultaneously, with some forces pushing aggregate demand rightwards and the aggregate supply curve leftwards.

8.3.1 THE INFLATIONARY GAP

Just as with unemployment, inflation is considered essentially as a short-run problem for an economy but one that can persist depending on the speed and process of

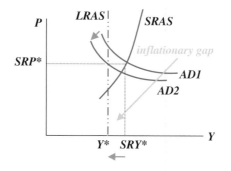

FIGURE 8.7 INFLATIONARY GAP: KEYNESIAN ANALYSIS

adjustment of an economy from the short to the long run. When an economy operates above its short-run capacity, an inflationary gap is said to exist.

> An **inflationary gap** is defined as the difference between equilibrium output and actual output when an economy is producing above its potential long-run level.

In Figure 8.7 there is an example of an economy in short-run equilibrium at a level of output above its long-run potential level. The economy is experiencing a boom in its real growth rate and is operating above potential output. Here the short-run equilibrium output SRY^* is greater than the long-run level Y^*.

In comparing the short-run to long-run equilibrium we see that the price level is the same in both cases, which corresponds to a Keynesian analysis of inflation. Although Keynes focused more on the issue of recessionary gaps, he also acknowledged that economies can be in short-run equilibrium as shown here. The unemployment rate is less than its natural rate, due to high demand for labour for which firms are willing to pay attractive overtime wages or higher wages than are sustainable in the long run with the given aggregate demand, *AD1*. Producing beyond potential output puts pressure on the price level and is not sustainable over time without a change in aggregate demand or aggregate supply.

The inflationary gap could be eliminated through an active or interventionist Keynesian policy by the government that implements policies to reduce aggregate demand to *AD2*. This would be achieved through fiscal policies such as a fall in government expenditure or an increase in the tax rate. According to a Keynesian theory of adjustment, wages are fixed or sticky in the short run and, in order to close the inflationary gap, injections into the economy must decline and/or withdrawals increase to slow the economy down.

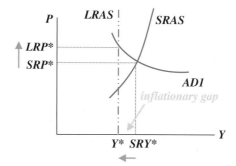

FIGURE 8.8   INFLATIONARY GAP: CLASSICAL APPROACH

According to a classical approach (as shown in Figure 8.8) no intervention by the government would be required, prices and wages would not be sticky in the short run and the economy would adjust from its initial short-run position by the price level rising from SRP^* to LRP^* and output would decline back from SRY^* to Y^*.

8.3.2   TRENDS IN INTERNATIONAL PRICE LEVELS

From Figure 8.6 we see that changes in either short-run aggregate demand (a rise) or short-run aggregate supply (a fall) give rise to inflation with different consequences for national output. A one-off jump in prices caused by rising aggregate demand or falling aggregate supply is not considered particularly damaging to an economy but policy-makers and analysts consider that attempts should be made to curtail persistent inflation, whatever its cause, if at all possible. A relevant question, though, is why we observe inflation in economies at all. In looking at the trend in price levels in a historical context we find that between 1661 and 1930, average UK prices did not show any continual upward trend and in fact it was not until the twentieth century that prices increased sharply (based on price data that were compiled by B.R. Mitchell, 1988; figures for the US display a similar pattern).

More recent inflation data are presented in Figure 8.9, which shows trends in the consumer price index (CPI) of some selected countries over the last three decades. We see that inflation has been observed for most countries shown for the vast majority of the last 30 years, being highest over the initial decade, and highest on average for the United Kingdom and Ireland. Deflation was observed in Germany for 1986, Sweden in 1998 but more persistently for the final four years of the sample period in Japan.

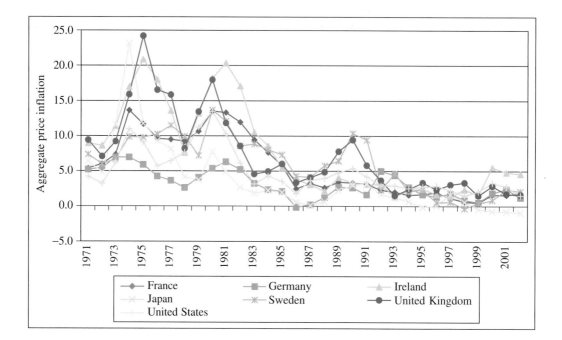

FIGURE 8.9 INTERNATIONAL INFLATION RATES: 1971–2002

Source: International Financial Statistics of the International Monetary Fund

The CPI is one measure of prices; alternatives exist in the form of indices of producer input and output prices, and the GDP deflator. An index of producer input prices provides information on the trend in prices of inputs experienced by suppliers, while producer output prices provide information on the sales prices in wholesale terms, i.e. to distributors or retailers, excluding any consumer taxes. Anyone with an interest in the trend in consumer prices should also examine producer output prices as it would be reasonable to expect any changes in the latter to be reflected to some extent in the former.

The GDP deflator is another quite commonly used measure of prices. Earlier, nominal and real GDP were defined and discussed. Since nominal GDP includes both changes in quantity and prices and real GDP measures only the quantity of output produced when price changes have been removed, the ratio of nominal GDP to real GDP provides a measure of inflation. Because GDP measures domestically produced output, however, using the GDP deflator as a measure of inflation focuses only on the prices of *domestically* produced output, excluding imports which are included in the CPI measure of inflation. No measure of inflation is particularly better or worse than the others and since they each include different items and goods they do not follow exactly the same trends over time; however, over the long run they tend to move together.

WHY INFLATION?

Why do the prices of goods and services generally tend to rise over time? Several possible reasons have been put forward. It could be because:

- Firms increase their prices trying to make higher profits and consumers cannot react by buying cheaper substitutes.
- Firms facing increased costs pass them on to consumers.
- Improvements in the quality of products mean goods cost more due to either better inputs or technology *and* consumers are happy to pay the increased price.
- Consumers' nominal incomes are rising and, following the quantity theory (and assuming money supply and velocity are constant), if income rises then so too will prices to keep real income unchanged.

Each potential explanation sounds plausible and provides a contribution to our understanding of why the average level of prices is upward over time. Unfortunately, no single or indeed simple explanation for inflation exists but as Figure 8.9 indicates it is a very pronounced international phenomenon. The role of oil prices in international inflation is considered in the text box.

OIL PRICES AND INFLATION

Across most developed countries inflation increased in the period following the first oil price shock of 1973 (see www.wtrg.com/prices.htm for trends in oil prices). The Organization of Petroleum Exporting Countries (OPEC) was formed in 1960 with five founding members: Iran, Iraq, Kuwait, Saudi Arabia and Venezuela, and by the end of 1971 six new members – Qatar, Indonesia, Libya, United Arab Emirates, Algeria and Nigeria – had joined too. These countries operated a cartel (as explained in Chapter 6). The aim of such collusion is to increase profit by reducing competition. These nations had experienced a decline in the real value of their product since foundation of the OPEC. Throughout the Post-World War Two period, exporting countries found increasing demand for their crude oil and a 40% decline in the purchasing power of a barrel of crude.

In 1972 the price of crude oil was about $3.00 per barrel. By the end of 1974 it had quadrupled to $12.00. The Yom Kippur War started with an attack on Israel by Syria and Egypt on 5 October 1973. The USA, among other western countries, showed strong support for Israel. As a result Arab oil-exporting nations imposed an embargo on the nations supporting Israel. Arab nations reduced production by 5 million barrels per day (MBPD). About 1 MBPD was made up by increased production in other countries. The net loss of 4 MBPD extended through to March 1974 and represented 7% of the free-world production. The extreme sensitivity of prices to supply shortages became all too apparent and is known as the oil-price shock. Since oil is a significant input into so much of the production process – machinery, equipment, transportation etc. – the oil-price shock had substantial inflationary implications as seen from Figure 8.9. From 1974 to 1978 nominal crude oil prices increased at a moderate pace from $12 per barrel to $14 per barrel, but in real terms, i.e. when adjusted for inflation, the prices were constant over this period of time.

A further sharp increase in oil prices in 1979 occurred on the back of the Iranian Revolution and became known as the second oil-price shock. The decline in production that occurred in 1985/86 was triggered by Saudi Arabia's rebellion against its role as the world's swing producer. It implemented a new and ultimately successful pricing strategy to regain its market share, which became the third oil-price shock. Although prices jumped up again in 1990, in response to Iraq's invasion of Kuwait, this was not sustained and, therefore, is not generally classified as a fourth shock.

It is worth remembering that as long as people are compensated in their earnings for rises in the average price level, people are no worse off *in real terms* as a result of inflation. This is an important point because when it comes to wages, in particular, we have seen already that under the Keynesian view of economic activity, wages tend to be 'sticky' or fixed in the short run, and that the short run can persist for some time.

Not only do wages not tend to fall in times of unemployment, but neither do wages tend to adjust upwards unless workers can put credible pressure on their employers to increase wages. Since wage-bargaining does not take place continually but occurs periodically there tend to be discrete jumps in wages rather than a steady increase. Where trades unions are involved in wage-bargaining, they argue for the best outcome possible for their members and attempt to secure the highest possible wage increases from employers rather than focusing on addressing the needs of the unemployed, who are not part of their membership – an example of an insider–outsider model where 'insiders' look after their own interests. For non-unionized workers, their effective credible threat in negotiating wage increases is that of finding work elsewhere, which is only really credible in boom times if there are shortages of workers with their specific skills set.

As well as 'standard' inflation in average prices of consumer goods and services, wage inflation is also of interest to economists. If at all possible, economies should avoid creating an environment conducive to escalating price inflation where price rises used to argue for increases in wages are in turn used by firms to argue for increasing their prices to cover costs, which is used to argue for increases in wages, in an unending spiral of rising prices and wages that leaves no one any better off and wastes time and energy, which are scarce resources best spent on other more productive activities.

Furthermore, the pattern emerging from trends across several countries is that their inflation rates tend to move together. This indicates that countries' economies are inextricably linked so that the tendencies for price rises often coincide across countries. Because countries trade with each other and given that capital flows across borders for investment and speculative purposes, many economic variables such as inflation tend to behave similarly across different countries.

8.3.3 GOVERNMENTS' CONTRIBUTION TO INFLATION

Reference was made earlier to government deficits where governments must borrow to make up for their overspending compared to their receipts. Governments that persist in running deficits can influence inflation in two ways: via aggregate demand and the money supply.

If a deficit is run because of a government increasing its expenditure (a rise in G) or because of a reduction in the tax rate (a fall in t), the result is an increase in aggregate demand, i.e. a rightward shift in the AD curve. This leads to an increase in the price level in the short run, presuming no change to aggregate supply. However, if consumers anticipate that a government running a deficit today may be likely to increase tax rates in the future to pay for the deficit, consumers may very well react to increased government expenditure or lowered tax rates by reducing their current spending. Savings would rise and, hence, some of the inflationary effects of a deficit can be reduced and maybe even eliminated, depending on consumers' behaviour and expectations.

Sometimes when a government issues debt its central bank purchases the debt, thereby increasing the money supply. The central bank, through its open-market operations, releases money into the economic system as it buys the debt in the form of government bonds, for example. While the central bank is under no obligation to purchase the debt, it may choose to do so if it prefers to maintain the interest rate constant. Depending on the scale of the debt, if the general public bought the bonds the impact could be to increase the demand for credit and put upward pressure on interest rates. As we know from the quantity theory, any increase in the money supply results in an increase in the price level, hence the link between the deficit, money supply and inflation.

8.3.4   ANTICIPATED AND UNANTICIPATED INFLATION – THE COSTS

Economic analysts regularly provide and publish forecasts on their inflation expectations. These can then be used by parties engaging in wage negotiations (for example) to use in supporting arguments for specific rises in wage rates: if inflation of 5% is predicted for each of the next two years, workers will want to earn increases of *at least* 5% each year to keep their real income levels constant. If workers expect profits to rise also then individually and through their trades unions they try to negotiate increases higher than expected inflation. Inflation forecasts can also be used by those with responsibility for setting interest rates in the knowledge that savers and investors are more likely to save and invest when positive real returns are possible, *ceteris paribus*. Any anticipated inflation can be taken into account to some degree, at least, but no matter how people attempt to plan for inflation, because its extent is uncertain, any adjustments will probably not be perfect (either over- or under-predicting the rate) and any adjustments will take time to implement.

> **Anticipated inflation:** expected inflation that is taken into account in economic decision-making.
> **Unanticipated inflation** is inflation that takes people by surprise.

Governments and individuals dislike unanticipated inflation, because they have not allowed for it in interest rate changes, bond issues, wage-bargaining, etc. Anticipated inflation is built into people's/governments' terms of borrowing and lending, but unanticipated inflation is not. Both types of inflation are associated with certain costs, but the costs are more severe in the case of unanticipated inflation. Specifically, the costs of inflation are outlined in the text box. Points 1 to 3 occur with both anticipated and unanticipated inflation, being more severe when inflation is unanticipated. Points 4 to 8 are particularly relevant to unanticipated inflation.

COSTS OF INFLATION

1. *Loss of purchasing power*: inflation lowers purchasing power, and people living on fixed incomes suffer a decline in living standards as a result.

2. *Shoe-leather costs*: during periods of inflation, people hold less currency. Therefore, they must make more trips to the bank to withdraw cash. These extra trips are known as 'shoe-leather costs of inflation', i.e. the extra time and effort that people put into transactions, when they try to get by with lower real money balances.

3. *Menu costs*: during periods of inflation, prices may change frequently. This imposes costs on firms and shops, which have to reprint price lists. Also, customers have to go to some trouble to keep up-to-date with price changes.

4. *Effects on income distribution*: inflation can result in a redistribution of income. Savers are penalized, borrowers gain by going into debt and repaying the loan in money which value has declined. This amounts to a transfer in wealth away from savers to borrowers.

5. *Fiscal drag*: when tax rates are not fully inflation-adjusted, fiscal drag occurs. This means that people are pushed into higher tax brackets in a progressive income tax system. A progressive income tax system is one in which individuals pay a higher percentage of their income in tax, the more they earn (alternative tax systems are either regressive or neutral).

6. *Effects on international competitiveness*: inflation can have serious effects on the ability of domestic firms to compete with international rivals if domestic prices are rising faster than for competitor firms in other countries. Exports may fall, causing growth and employment to fall also.

7. *Balance of payments effects*: countries with high inflation relative to others find their quantity of exports decline as the prices of their goods become less competitive and imports rise. In the national accounts, the value of exports falls while imports rise and a deficit on the trade account is possible. This might lead to a drop in demand for the country's currency and have an effect on the exchange rate or interest rate.

8. *Business uncertainty and lack of stability effects*: inflation increases the complexity of making long-term plans, e.g. investment. Also, most people are generally risk-averse, and prefer to make plans and contracts in real terms, rather than in nominal terms. With unanticipated inflation, this may not be possible.

8.4 LINKING UNEMPLOYMENT AND INFLATION

It may appear from the foregoing analysis that unemployment is a problem associated with recessionary periods in an economy while inflation is often associated with boom periods. Both unemployment and inflation appear to be linked, under a Keynesian approach to the economy, to aggregate demand and differences between short-run and long-run macroeconomic equilibrium. This implies that unemployment and inflation are problems that occur in the short run. Inadequate aggregate demand is associated with recessions and unemployment while excessive aggregate demand is associated with booms and inflation. From policy-makers' point of view, they would either have to attempt to deal with unemployment or inflation. This pattern appeared to hold true for over 100 years until the mid-1960s but thereafter, it oversimplifies the inflation–unemployment relationship. Based on analysis of wage inflation and unemployment data from 1861 to 1957 (hence, not based on theory but observation) the economist William Phillips (in 1958) considered that inflation and unemployment tended to move in opposite directions. High wage inflation was associated with low unemployment and low inflation was associated with high unemployment. This relationship became known as the Phillips curve. A similar curve describes the relationship between price inflation and unemployment.

> The relationship between unemployment and inflation, called **the Phillips curve**, is negative, meaning that high unemployment is associated with low inflation and vice versa.

Central to our understanding of the Phillips curve today is the role of the expected inflation rate predicted by the general public, based on their best guesses given all available information, including advice from inflation forecasters. The original Phillips curve made no mention of inflation expectations, however, following the work of other economists (Edmund Phelps and Milton Friedman) both inflation expectations and the natural rate of unemployment have been incorporated into the Phillips curve. The Phillips curve presented here is correctly called the expectations-augmented Phillips curve.

> The **expectations-augmented Phillips curve** explains inflation in terms of a negative relationship between inflation and unemployment *and* a positive relationship between actual inflation and expected inflation.

Think of the situation where people predict an inflation rate of, say, 2%, for both wages and general prices. If there is an increase in aggregate demand above the level producers expected so that demand for firms' output is higher than firms envisaged, firms' prices may be driven up by more than 2%, say by 4%. This would occur via a rightward movement of the aggregate demand curve, caused by rising consumption expenditure, leading to a new macroeconomic equilibrium.

However, wages are usually negotiated for relatively long periods so wages are fixed in nominal terms for some period of time. When nominal wages are fixed and are associated with rising price levels, the implication is that *real wages* decline. Since economic decisions are made on the basis of what happens to relative prices, a fall in real wages creates an incentive for firms to hire extra workers since labour costs have become cheaper, and with increased demand for firms' output it makes economic sense for firms to hire additional workers. The result is a fall in unemployment associated with the increase in inflation.

> The formula for **the expectations-augmented Phillips curve** is
> Actual Inflation rate = expected rate of inflation + X (natural unemployment rate − actual unemployment rate)
> where X denotes a positive number, which is different for different economies.

The actual rate of inflation in an economy will be the same as the expected rate if output and unemployment remain at their equilibrium levels so that unemployment is at its natural level. Where this is not the case, actual and expected inflation will differ.

> If the natural rate of unemployment is 8%, if X is 0.75 and inflation is expected to be 4% then actual inflation is 4% if unemployment is 8%. If instead unemployment is 10%, inflation must be 1.5 points less than expected (since 0.75 (8−10) = −1.5) which would be 2.5%.

The negative unemployment/inflation relationship is logical in this case since with higher-than-equilibrium unemployment due to insufficient aggregate demand, producers have an incentive to moderate any increase in prices. Hence price inflation is less than expected although since nominal wages are fixed, wage inflation remains at the expected level. The effect is an increase in real wages (relative to what was expected) so that labour is more expensive and some workers lose their jobs. When inflation is lower than expected, unemployment goes up.

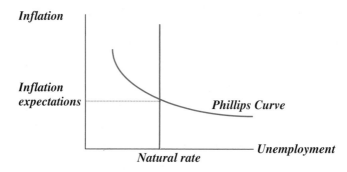

FIGURE 8.10 THE PHILLIPS CURVE

The alternative would also hold that when inflation is higher than expected, unemployment would fall.

Graphically the Phillips curve as described above is shown in Figure 8.10. This figure shows a negative relationship between unemployment on inflation and vice versa. When inflation is in line with expectations, unemployment is at its natural rate. Since wages are sticky only in the short run but will be renegotiated in the light of actual inflation and expectations in the future, the inflation – unemployment relationship underlying the Phillips curve is something we expect to observe in the short term only and, hence, government intervention would require action to affect aggregate demand in the short run only.

The policy choice for government implied by the relationship described in the Phillips curve was in terms of trading off inflation for unemployment. The 'cost' of low unemployment would be higher inflation while low inflation would be associated with higher unemployment.

From the mid-1960s onwards, outcomes implausible under the Phillips curve relationship were observed across developed economies – both rising unemployment and rising inflation. Some economists argue that over time the Phillips curves of individual countries move around, the position being determined by factors unrelated to aggregate demand explanations of inflation and unemployment. Such explanations include frictional and structural unemployment and cost-push inflation and expectations-generated inflation. The Phillips curve moves to the left if any of these factors changes leading to falling inflation or unemployment (or to the right if the result is rising inflation or unemployment).

The next section on determinants of the natural rate of unemployment explains how it is possible to observe inflation and unemployment in certain circumstances.

8.4.1 A MODEL EXPLAINING THE NATURAL RATE OF UNEMPLOYMENT

Given the earlier definition of the natural rate of unemployment, several economic features help us to understand why some countries tend to have higher natural rates of unemployment (e.g. Spain, Italy, Greece) than others (USA, Austria, the Netherlands). Remember the natural rate is a long-run equilibrium rate. By appealing to analysis we have already conducted in the labour market and in terms of firms' pricing behaviour we can develop a model to understand how the natural rate of unemployment comes about. (This section draws on the model presented in Miles and Scott, 2002, ch. 8).

We saw in Chapter 2 that real wages and the number of workers employed is determined as shown in the labour market model of labour demand and labour supply. We saw how firms' demand for labour reflected the marginal revenue product of labour. We also saw in Chapters 4 and 6 that firms attempting to maximize profits, when facing downward sloping demand curves, can earn profits above the normal level once their cost curves lie below the demand curve. Wages represent a large portion of firms' costs and we see that when supernormal profits are earned, firms earn more than required to pay for all their costs.

In thinking about how the natural rate of unemployment is determined, we assume here that firms over the long run set themselves rates of profit that they wish to earn expressed as mark-ups over their costs. The mark-up would depend on the line of business a firm is in, the mark-up targeted by competitors, the firm's strategy (i.e. how it tries to compete in its chosen market, e.g. by offering lower prices or higher quality).

> The **profit margin**, also called the **price-cost margin**, describes the mark-up over costs that a firm makes or wishes to make. Some firms will be happy to earn low mark-ups, other firms wish to earn high mark-ups.

In attempting to set prices for their output and generate a desired mark-up, when costs rise over time firms put pressure on the real wage rate to fall. Higher prices on average feed into lower real wages. Workers too can affect real wage rates. This happens most directly if we think about the role of labour unions in wage-setting negotiations if they try to use their bargaining power to increase wages for their members. Non-unionized workers can also exert an influence on real wage rates because employers generally wish to minimize the turnover rate of good staff because it is costly:

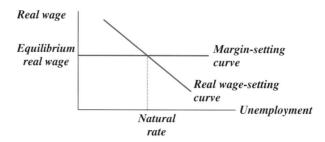

FIGURE 8.11 DETERMINATION OF THE NATURAL RATE OF UNEMPLOYMENT

- to have a post vacant since the post generates no revenue product of labour;
- to advertise, interview and train new staff.

The extent to which individual workers or unions try to negotiate higher nominal wages with their employers will vary with the unemployment level, as high rates of unemployment mean there is greater competition for available jobs and neither workers nor unions wish to price themselves out of a labour market which is characterized by high unemployment. This information is presented graphically in Figure 8.11.

The margin-setting curve (MSC) indicates the long-run real wage corresponding to firms' average desired profit margins. This profit margin in the figure is assumed to be constant, hence the MSC is a horizontal line.

The real wage-setting (RWS) curve is downward sloping reflecting the tendency for workers and unions to link demands for real wage increases to the level of unemployment. The intersection of the MS and RWS curves determines the natural rate of unemployment.

The equilibrium position generated by this model indicates that there is one real wage rate that unions (and workers) are willing to accept that corresponds to what firms are willing to accept.

> There is only one real wage rate and one level of unemployment where firms' desired profit margins match the wages desired by unions and workers.

As we have seen earlier, the macroeconomy can be away from its long-run equilibrium position for certain periods. The model shown in Figure 8.11 can be used to consider what we can expect if the economy is out of its equilibrium position. We begin with an example where the natural rate of unemployment lies above the equilibrium level, as shown in Figure 8.12.

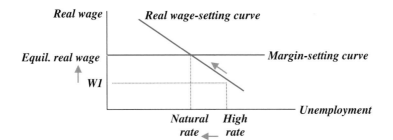

FIGURE 8.12 DISEQUILIBRIUM: HIGHER THAN NATURAL UNEMPLOYMENT

With a rate of unemployment above the natural rate, demands for real wage levels by unions and workers are moderate at *W1*. With such moderate wage rates, firms can hire more workers so unemployment tends to move to its long-run natural rate. As the economy adjusts towards the natural rate, unions and workers wage demands will rise. Up until the natural rate, firms still have incentives to hire more workers to produce additional output (for which they perceive a demand). Although real wage rates rise from *W1*, as long as wage demands are below the equilibrium level, there is no pressure on the average price level so not only does unemployment fall in this case, but so too does inflation as the economy moves back to its equilibrium position.

Next we look to the opposite situation in Figure 8.13 where the economy begins in a disequilibrium situation initially with lower than natural unemployment and a higher than equilibrium real wage rate of *W2*. Workers and unions have high wage demands in this case as they are aware that firms have little choice in a limited

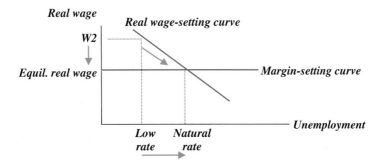

FIGURE 8.13 DISEQUILIBRIUM: LOWER THAN NATURAL UNEMPLOYMENT

labour market. With too high real wage demands, firms will start letting workers go because the costs are out of line with firms' desired profit margins.

Firms might respond to the cost pressure by increasing their own output prices (in an attempt to cover high wage costs) to maintain their margins. Increasing unemployment will lead to lower wage demands and the wage rate declines from *W2* towards equilibrium. Hence, in this case rising inflation *and* unemployment would be observed as the economy moved towards the long-run equilibrium position.

8.4.2 CAUSES OF DIFFERENCES IN NATURAL RATES OF UNEMPLOYMENT

From the model shown in Figure 8.11, we can conclude that there are three determinants of the natural rate of unemployment. Each is considered below.

1. Firms' desired margin – reflected in the height of the MS curve.
    If firms set relatively high profit margins, this is associated with relatively high prices of goods implying *lower* real wages. The MS curve for firms setting high margins would, therefore, lie below those shown in Figures 8.12, 8.13 and 8.14 and would have the effects as shown in Figure 8.14.
    We see from Figure 8.14 that higher desired margins by firms are associated with a lower real wage and a higher natural rate of unemployment. Higher margins imply higher prices of goods and we know from the law of demand that higher-priced output is demanded in relatively lower quantities by consumers. Lower quantities of output demanded by consumers require fewer workers to produce the output, so the end result is higher equilibrium unemployment.
2. The responsiveness of unions and workers wage demands to the level of unemployment – reflected in the position and slope of the RWS curve.

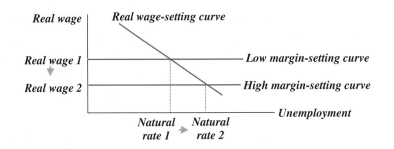

FIGURE 8.14 NATURAL UNEMPLOYMENT AND FIRMS' MARGIN-SETTING

3. The strength/negotiating power of labour unions – reflected in the share of unionized workers.

The strength and responsiveness of unions and workers wage demands to unemployment can be seen from the comparison presented in Figure 8.15.

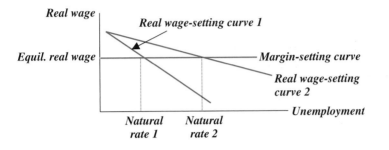

FIGURE 8.15 NATURAL UNEMPLOYMENT AND UNIONS' BEHAVIOUR

When unions and workers have a lot of bargaining power the real wage-setting curve lies above the curve for lower bargaining power. A relatively flatter real wage-setting curve (such as curve 2 in Figure 8.15) indicates a greater responsiveness of wage-setting behaviour to unemployment. The bargaining power of workers and unions is usually high when:

● The share of workers affected by unions' negotiations is high. Many non-union members are still affected by the wage negotiations agreed by unions with other decision-makers.
● Unemployment benefits are high and long-term. This affects some individuals' incentives to find new jobs. This explains a general tendency by countries to offer sliding scales of unemployment benefits that decline over time. Reasonable levels of benefits also increases the likelihood that workers will search out jobs best suited to their skills – maximizing their potential productivity. If the cost of becoming unemployed is low in the sense that the benefits are high, this can lead to high demands for wages by those in employment.
● The share of long-term unemployed is high. A high proportion of long-term unemployed signals that those individuals are not competitive in the job market – their skills may be out of date and this problem is exacerbated the longer an individual remains long-term unemployed and is outside the active labour force.

- There is substantial mismatch between labour demand in various locations within a region or between skills available and skills in demand.
- The tax wedge is high. When the tax wedge is high, unions and workers demand relatively higher real wage rates to compensate for higher taxes that must be paid.

Tax wedge: the difference between the real wage paid by an employee and the real wage received by an employee. Differences are accounted for by payroll taxes (usually related to social insurance/security contributions), income taxes, consumer price taxes.

8.5 CROSS-COUNTRY DIFFERENCES – INFLATION AND UNEMPLOYMENT

The general pattern evident in international prices (Figure 8.9) is that consumer prices tend to move similarly internationally. This is largely explained by the substantial economic linkages between industrialized countries due to the size and nature of flows of traded goods and services, financial capital and people. Firms competing internationally are under pressure to keep abreast of 'best practice'. Manufacturing firms attempt to source inputs from their most cost-effective location (as with out-sourcing – see Chapter 5) and so similar pressures are extended on firms operating out of different locations. Consumers become aware of international availability of products through their own travel patterns and through the information increasingly available via the national and international media facilitated by information technology developments.

Greater disparity exists in terms of international unemployment rates, which is evident from publications such as the OECD *Employment Outlook*, the source of the data in Table 8.1. From the discussion of the determinants of the natural rate of unemployment, it is possible to identify ways of addressing a rate of natural unemployment, which is higher than desired by identifying its cause and by focusing policies, where possible, on

- reducing firms' desired profit margins;
- reducing the strength/power of labour unions and workers in negotiating wage increases.

Governments do not generally enact laws governing the profit margins that firms are permitted to set because this goes against all economic arguments regarding the ability of the market system to bring about the most appropriate resource allocation by allowing most prices to be set freely within the functioning of markets. However, governments do keep a watchful eye on the conduct of firms in terms of whether firms follow pro-competitive or anti-competitive practices. If firms are setting high desired profit margins, this could only occur in practice on a sustained basis if there are some barriers to competition, as considered in Chapter 6.

A low-cost competitor producing a similar good to an incumbent can take over a market if they set a lower price for consumers. The extent to which goods are differentiated from each other in terms of the attributes of the goods or the levels of quality may create 'switching costs' for consumers to buy from one supplier than another. As long as entry to a market is easy, however, we would expect firms who identify profitable opportunities, as reflected in high profit levels, to have incentives to enter and compete in such markets. Competition would generally mean that more low-cost competitors would exist in markets and pass on benefits to consumers in the form of lower prices. Hence, governments focusing on addressing high profit margins in some sectors of the economy could focus on supporting increased competition in those markets by removing any obstacles to new entrants, where they exist. This might involve increasing licences where they are required to compete, as in the taxi market cited in Chapter 3.

To address the power of labour and workers in wage negotiations the process by which wages are negotiated appears important since collective wage-bargaining, as mentioned earlier, increases the likelihood that adverse unemployment effects of strong unions will be low. A set of policies known as active labour market policies (ALPS) is the term given to the various measures governments use to focus on increasing employment and reducing unemployment. Examples of ALPS include:

- increasing information on available vacancies via employment agencies, providing retraining and reskilling programmes;
- providing courses on filling application forms, presenting CVs and interview techniques;
- providing subsidies to firms that hire unemployed workers;
- providing financial and other supports to people wishing to start their own business.

Furthermore, given the reference to the tax wedge earlier, government policies that try to reduce the taxes that create large differences between wages paid and received would change incentives regarding the demand for and supply of labour.

8.5.1 EMPLOYMENT LEGISLATION

Labour market flexibility is a term often used in the explanation for differences between unemployment rates across countries.

> **Labour market flexibility:** the ability of the labour market to adjust to economic shocks.

Countries differ significantly in their legal requirements in terms of hiring and firing workers. These differences can be found, for example, in redundancy payment requirements, notice requirements prior to redundancy, and in government policy on corporate restructuring. Research shows that the labour market of the United States is the most flexible in the OECD since there are few administrative requirements firms must observe before they can make workers redundant and neither notice nor severance pay are general legal requirements. By contrast, employment protection policies across Europe are much stronger. There is, however, a debate on the effects of more flexible labour markets on income inequality (which we address in Chapter 9) that indicates that labour market flexibility is not without costs.

Theoretically at least, better worker protection can have positive labour market effects through increasing workers' motivation following on from job security. Negative effects are also possible since firms' hiring decisions are in the knowledge of the difficulties of letting people go, if required, and so with higher redundancy costs, lower employment levels are likely.

There is some general consensus on the effects of labour protection legislation from research on OECD countries' experiences (published in their *Employment Outlook*). First, low employment rates are associated with countries that have strong labour protection policies because it is more costly to hire workers. Second, there is no statistical correlation between unemployment and labour protection legislation. This is due to effects of the legislation regarding part-time workers, who have similar rights to full-time workers. There is a lower incentive to firms to offer part-time jobs when employment legislation is strong. A significant portion of workers who work part-time are women, hence, there are implications for female participation in the workforce. Lower participation is a corollary of strong employment legislation. Third, job security is higher and people hold jobs for longer when employment legislation is strong. Fourth, unemployment tends to last longer, on average, when employment legislation is strong. Somewhat paradoxically the conclusion is that unemployed workers appear to carry the costs of strong labour legislation while the employed carry the benefits. This is logical in terms of political economy explanations where strong unions can lobby government to enact legislation protecting their member-ship.

As with most economic issues finding a solution to unemployment is complex and can require a range of coordinated policies to achieve a satisfactory outcome. Since countries (and regions within them) are characterized by specific economic circumstances, what addresses one problem would not be appropriate in dissimilar situations. Economic analysis helps to understand what precisely characterizes the unemployment situation so that appropriate remedies can be found and enacted.

8.6 SUMMARY

- When the economy is out of long-run macroeconomic equilibrium, inflation and/or unemployment can result in the short run.
- Minimum wages and their effects can be considered via the labour market model although efficiency wages should be considered before drawing conclusions based on the model alone.
- Classical and Keynesian analyses of unemployment incorporate different assumptions about how the economy adjusts.
- Unemployment may be analysed by considering the recessionary gap approach using the aggregate demand and aggregate supply model.
- The sources of inflation – demand-pull and cost-push – can be analysed using the aggregate demand and aggregate supply model. The same model allows for consideration of an economy operating above its short-run capacity when an inflationary gap is said to exist. Both classical and Keynesian approaches can be used to analyse how the economy can eliminate an inflationary gap.
- Several hypotheses have been put forward to explain why aggregate prices tend to increase over time. International trends in oil prices have played a role in international inflation patterns.
- Governments may contribute to creating inflation.
- Several costs arise from inflation, both anticipated and unanticipated.
- The relationship between unemployment and inflation, called the Phillips curve, states that high unemployment is associated with low inflation and vice versa.

- **A model of the determination of the natural rate of unemployment implies that inflation and unemployment can occur simultaneously in an economy. Conclusions can be drawn on how to try to address the unemployment problem.**

REVIEW PROBLEMS AND QUESTIONS

1. Use the labour market supply and demand model to show and explain the effects of the imposition of a minimum wage on unemployment and the wage rate. What factors outside your model might also have an impact on your conclusions regarding the level of unemployment?
2. Use the labour market supply and demand model to explain the different approaches of Keynesian and classical economists to how an economy reacts to unemployment.
3. Explain what is meant by a recessionary gap.
    a) From a Keynesian perspective how can a recessionary gap be eliminated?
    b) From a classical perspective how can a recessionary gap be eliminated?
4. Explain, using a figure of aggregate demand and aggregate supply, the difference between demand-pull and cost-push inflation and their respective impacts on macroeconomic equilibrium.
5. Explain what is meant by an inflationary gap.
    a) from a Keynesian perspective how can a inflationary gap be eliminated?
    b) from a classical perspective how can a inflationary gap be eliminated?
6. What are the main trends evident in the CPI of industrialized countries? Can you identify reasons behind the trends?
7. What is the Phillips curve (include a graph in your answer) and what are its implications for government policy on employment or inflation?
8. Describe the main elements of the model of the natural rate of unemployment. How according to the model is the natural rate determined?

FURTHER READING AND RESEARCH

- For an examination of labour mobility within the EU see sections 21.4 onwards in Mayes, 2001, ch. 21, 472–497.
- For literature on the effects of minimum wages see Brown, 1988; and *Economic Journal*, 2004.

- For recent consideration of the Phillips curve see Lansing, 2002; and Mankiw, 2000.

REFERENCES

Brown, C. (1988) 'Minimum wage laws: are they overrated?' *Journal of Economic Perspectives*, **2**(2), 133–145.

Economic Journal (2004), **114**(494), 86–116, March.

Friedman, M. (1968) 'The role of monetary policy', *American Economic Review*, **58**(1), 1–17.

Lansing, K. (2002) 'Can the Phillips curve help forecast inflation?' *Federal Reserve Bank of San Francisco Economic Letter*, No. 2002–29.

Mankiw, N. (2000) 'The inexorable and mysterious tradeoff between inflation and unemployment', *Economic Journal*, **111**, c45–61.

Mayes, D. (2001) 'Factor mobility', in El-Agraa, A. (ed.) *The European Union, Economics and Policies*. 6th edn, Pearson, 472–497.

Miles, D. and A. Scott (2002) *Macroeconomics: Understanding the wealth of nations*. John Wiley & Sons, Ltd.

Mitchell, B. (1988) *British Historical Statistics*. Cambridge University Press, London.

OECD (2004) 'Standardised unemployment rates in 27 OECD countries', *OECD Employment Outlook*.

Phelps, E. (1967) 'Phillips curves, expectations of inflation and optimal employment over time', *Economica*, **34**(3), 254–281.

Phillips, A. (1958) 'The relation between unemployment and the rate of change of money wage rates in the United Kingdom, 1861–1957', *Economica*, **25**(2), 283–299.

CHAPTER 9

DEVELOPING THE ECONOMIC SYSTEM: GROWTH AND INCOME DISTRIBUTION

LEARNING OUTCOMES

By the end of this chapter you should be able to:

✪ Describe the relationship between the level of people's living standards and their economy's level of labour productivity.

✪ Reason as to why economic growth matters for people's living standards.

✪ Illustrate why rising productivity may not always translate into rising living standards.

✪ Explain the main elements of the Solow model of growth and its main conclusions.

  ● Use the model to illustrate the effect of changes in savings for an economy.

  ● Use the model to illustrate the effect of changes in the labour input on an economy.

  ● Use the model to illustrate the effect of changes in technology on an economy.

✪ Assess productivity growth patterns across countries to identify their main sources of growth.

✪ Clarify the extension to the Solow model as outlined in newer (endogenous growth) models.

✪ Comment on the main trends in international income distribution and their implications for welfare and equity.

9.1   INTRODUCTION

One of the most fundamental and important economic issues, especially from a macroeconomic perspective, is that of economic growth. This issue focuses on how an economy can achieve a sustainable level of growth in economic activity that generates improvements in people's living standards – real output per capita. Although this is of macroeconomic interest, given our earlier examination of how firms operate and attempt to maximize their profits, it is clear that what happens at the firm and microeconomic level impacts on living standards also – firms and their employees produce the real output. Understanding the determinants of economic growth is vital for identifying the links that exist within the economic system that impact on the level of aggregate economic activity and on its rate of growth. This is the focus of the first four sections of this chapter. In section 9.2 trends in living standards are presented and the relationship between living standards and labour productivity is explained. While rising labour productivity is one necessary condition for economic growth we will see that it is not sufficient *on its own* to ensure rising living standards, which is of key interest to economists.

The rate at which an economy grows or expands is usually quoted in terms of the annual percentage increase (or decrease) in GDP or GNP. The long-run implications of high or low economic growth are considered in section 9.3. The central model used to consider growth – the Solow growth model – is presented in section 9.4, where the effects of changes in savings behaviour, in employment, in capital investment and in technology for economic growth are all considered. Recent extensions to the model are also considered in terms of examining potential causes of changes in technology.

In section 9.5 the focus turns to the manner in which the 'spoils' generated by economic activity are distributed. The distribution of income across and within countries is examined and the extent to which these have changed over time is considered.

9.2   LIVING STANDARDS AND LABOUR PRODUCTIVITY RELATIONSHIPS

Examining the trend in living standards over time reveals the pattern of living standards across economies. Table 9.1 provides some data on living standards over time.

TABLE 9.1 GDP PER CAPITA GROWTH, IN %, SELECTED COUNTRIES, 1960–2000

		1960–80	1980–2000	Change
High HDI[a]	Austria	104	42	⇓
	Belgium	102	67	⇓
	Cyprus	160	122	⇓
	Czech Republic[b]	133	0.5	⇓
	Denmark	68	49	⇓
	Finland	105	56	⇓
	France	102	40	⇓
	Greece	182	34	⇓
	Hungary	170	4	⇓
	Ireland	106	144	⇑
	Italy	126	43	⇓
	Japan	241	54	⇓
	Latvia[b] (from 1965)	103	−22	⇓
	Luxembourg	50	122	⇑
	Netherlands	86	47	⇓
	Poland[b] (from 1970)	50	25	⇓
	Portugal	167	82	⇓
	Spain	137	68	⇓
	Sweden	64	34	⇓
	United Kingdom	49	55	⇑
	United States	55	56	⇑
Middle HDI	China[b]	71	180	⇑
	India[b]	15	102	⇑
	Malaysia[b]	168	85	⇓
	Romania[b]	229	10	⇓
	Turkey[b]	77	53	⇓
Low HDI	Burkina Faso[b]	0.22	26	⇑
	Mali[b]	−0.6	6	⇑
	Niger[b]	35	−37	⇓
	Sierra Leone[b]	30	−60	⇓

Source: Excerpted from Table 1 in Weisbrot, Naiman and Kim (2000).

[a]HDI denotes the human development index reported by the United Nations, and explained in the text.

[b]Data taken from Penn World Table 5.6 (Heston *et al.*, 2002). Czech Republic and Latvian data finish in 1997.

Note: As mentioned in Chapter 1, updated Penn World Tables (version 6.1) are available at the Center for International Comparisons at the University of Pennsylvania. See http://pwt.econ.upenn.edu/

A broad cross-section of countries is included in Table 9.1 ranked in groups according to their human development index (HDI) score in 2004. The HDI is based not on income solely but also includes criteria including health, education, life expectancy, income, poverty levels and environmental quality.

The broad trend that emerges is there has been a slowdown in economic growth, measured as GDP per capital internationally over the periods 1960 to 1980 and 1980 to 2000. The first period includes the 'Golden Age' period between 1950 and 1973 following World War Two and prior to the first oil-price shock when economies internationally, particularly the industrialized countries, expanded substantially. A minority of countries (highlighted in italics in Table 9.1) experienced higher growth in GDP per capita in the second period.

While real output per capita provides an indicator of living standards, another measure – real output per person employed – provides information on the productivity of an economy's workforce. This measure is called labour productivity.

Labour productivity: the amount of real output, on average, produced by each worker in the economy. It is computed as

$$\frac{\text{Real output}}{\text{Workers employed}}.$$

Measurement of labour productivity differs from living standards in terms of the denominator used because **living standards** is computed as

$$\frac{\text{Real output}}{\text{Population}}.$$

In 2003 Finland's real output was approximately €137bn (quoted in 2000 prices) and the number of workers employed was 2 365 000 (see http://www.stat.fi for statistical information; figures for real GDP are taken from http://www.stat.fi/tk/tp/tasku/taskue_kansantalous.html while numbers employed is available at http://www.stat.fi/tk/tp/tasku/taskue_tyoelama.html). Computing Finnish labour productivity yields a figure of €57 928. Comparing this to 2002 when real output was €134.5bn (in 2000 prices) and 2 372 000 workers were employed indicates that labour productivity was €56 703.

Repeating this exercise for 2001 gives rise to a figure of €55 555 (€131.5bn/2 367 000). Hence we can say that real labour productivity increased in this economy between 2001 and 2003. This means that each worker *on average* increased the quantity of goods/services they produced.

The corresponding figures for living standards can be computed using figures for population. The population figure for 2001 was 5 201 000 and for 2002 (latest available data) was slightly higher at 5 213 000. Hence, living standards for each Finnish resident in 2002 were €25 801 and in 2001 were €25 284 indicating a rise in living standards of 2.04%. Over the same period the rise in labour productivity was quite similar at 2.06%.

When labour productivity rises over time this means that output is growing at a faster rate than the number of workers employed (the labour input). The importance of labour productivity for economic growth is evident if we consider that increased labour productivity reflects an increase in the productive efficiency of an economy. An economy that is able to increase the real output of the average worker may be making more efficient use of available resources, using them in more productive ways. In terms of our discussion of the production possibility frontier (refer back to Chapter 1), an economy that increases its average labour productivity with *no* change in the amount of available resources or technology over time experiences efficiency that allows it to increase its output and move its production point closer to its PPF. This would represent an improvement in the *technical efficiency* of the economy as better ways of using the resources are put in place. If more and more firms in an economy adopt the 'best practice' methods for producing their goods and services, technical efficiency would improve.

Logically, any barriers to the dissemination of best practice methods have repercussions for efficiency and it would be in the economy's interest to eliminate such barriers where possible. Firms that are in industry or trade associations whereby they visit each others' premises or are in regular contact and are aware of how best to produce their output are usually quick to implement and imitate improvements introduced by their peers, which has a positive impact on the firms and on the economy as labour productivity could also be expected to rise in an economy that applies improved technology.

In the 1970s and 1980s many international manufacturing companies tried to imitate the best practice production methods originating in Japan that allowed Japanese producers to become efficient and competitive in many consumer electronics products and in the car/automobile markets. Many firms in the USA, and elsewhere, found it difficult to produce products that could compete on price and quality relative to the available Japanese alternatives. Some firms went out of business, others attempted to adopt best practices, although this proved difficult since the Japanese model of production had many cultural aspects not easily imitated in non-Japanese firms.

Alternatively, an economy that experiences rising labour productivity might be enjoying the results of an increase in its resources (of capital, for example) available to each worker, allowing each worker to produce more. If the capital input expands because firms invest more in new machinery and equipment, for example, the country's production possibility frontier moves outwards reflecting increases productive capacity of the economy. Again a higher amount of output can be produced caused by the rise in capital resources. If capital increases with no change in the labour input and output produced rises, once again labour productivity increases.

A complex mix of economic factors affect labour productivity and are, therefore, important in the context of economic growth. For example,

1. The income taxation structure within an economy can have significant implications for individuals' incentives to work as individuals will not necessarily be willing to give up welfare payments if faced with poverty traps.

   A **poverty trap (also sometimes known as an unemployment trap)** exists when the opportunity cost of moving from unemployment benefits to paid employment does not exist. Unemployed workers are often entitled to various benefits in addition to unemployment payments. These may include housing or rent allowances, reduced medical costs, food vouchers, etc. On taking up paid employment, especially of a low-paid nature, the benefits foregone may be greater than the wages earned. A vicious circle of poverty can be created which is difficult to break.

2. Women (and men) who opt to take care of children and not work outside the home may not be enticed into the workforce unless sufficient incentives exist to compensate them for childcare costs so that even if more employees are in demand by firms, they cannot attract additional workers without increasing wages.

3. High taxes on firms' profits affect the location decisions of multinational firms and high employers' taxes reduce their incentives to increase their workforce.

4. If a government attempts to attract firms via capital grants and/or the provision of buildings they essentially change the relative prices of capital and labour making capital relatively cheaper which again impacts firms' incentives to increase employment.

5. The ease and availability of finance for investment matters for investment purposes. Overall business confidence in an economy in terms of favourable expectations of future demand and economic developments feeds into firms' decisions regarding how much to invest in capital and research and development which ultimately contributes to economic growth.

The myriad of factors that affect economic growth (not exhausted above) implies that it can be extremely difficult to attempt to address the problem of slow economic growth. Given the relationship between living standards and labour productivity, however, adopting a perspective of economic growth based on improving labour productivity through a more efficient use of resources is central.

9.2.1 THE DEPENDENCY RATIO

Unfortunately labour productivity improvements do not *necessarily* or immediately lead to higher living standards because the dependency ratio must be taken into an account.

A country's **dependency ratio** is the portion of the population not in employment (including the unemployed, those who have retired and children) relative to the total population in employment. The percentage of employed people in the population is known as the **participation rate**. Dependents are also often classified as 'non-economically active' as they are considered to consume but not produce economic outputs.

Table 9.2 provides information relating to 2001 on dependency ratios for a selection of countries.

For Austria 16.5% of its population is between 0 and 14 years of age, 11.8% is in the segment between 15 and 24, etc. The dependency ratio is the sum of the shares of the non-economically active segments (defined as children up to 14 years and those of 65 years and older) stated as a percentage of the rest of the population (those between 15 and 64 years).

TABLE 9.2   INTERNATIONAL DEPENDENCY RATIOS AND POPULATION SHARES, 2001

	Dependency ratio	0–14 years	15–24 years	25–64 years	65+
Austria	47.2	16.5	11.8	56.1	15.5
Belgium	52.5	17.6	12.1	53.5	16.9
China[a]	46.4	36.4	–	–	10.0
Cyprus	51.8	22.7	15.4	50.5	11.4
Czech Republic	43.7	16.1	14.8	53.5	13.8
Denmark	50.3	18.7	11.2	55.3	14.8
Estonia	49.0	17.6	14.7	52.4	15.3
Finland	49.4	18.0	12.7	54.3	15.1
France	53.8	18.8	13.0	52.0	16.2
Germany	47.7	15.4	11.3	56.4	16.9
Greece	47.9	15.3	14.1	53.5	17.1
Hungary	46.4	16.5	14.3	54.0	15.2
India[a]	62.5	54.4	–	–	8.1
Ireland	53.7	21.4	17.2	43.4	11.2
Italy	48.4	14.4	11.4	56.0	18.2
Japan	46.8	21.6	–	–	25.2
Latvia	47.9	17.0	14.6	53.0	15.4
Lithuania	50.2	19.3	14.5	52.1	14.1
Luxembourg	48.8	18.8	11.5	55.7	14.0
Netherlands	47.2	18.0	11.9	56.1	14.1
Poland	44.8	18.5	17.0	52.1	12.4
Portugal	48.1	16.0	14.2	53.4	16.5
Slovakia	44.0	19.0	16.9	52.2	11.4
Slovenia	42.6	15.6	14.3	55.8	14.3
Spain	46.2	14.6	13.8	54.6	17.0
Sweden	55.0	18.3	11.6	52.9	17.2
United Kingdom	52.8	18.9	12.1	53.3	15.6
United States	50.6	21.2	14.0	52.4	12.4

Sources: Data compiled from United Nations, 2003; except for countries marked [a] where data taken from United Nations, 2002.

The percentage of each country's population that falls into different age groups is shown in Table 9.2.

> The dependency ratio for Austria is 47.2 which is found by
>
> 1. summing up the share of the population between 0 and 14 (16.5%) and the share over 65 (15.5%) = 32%;
> 2. summing up the economically active population between 15 and 64, i.e. 11.8% + 56.1% = 67.9%;
> 3. expressing 32 as a percentage of 67.9 = 47.2%.
>
> This dependency ratio implies that for every 100 people in the population, 47 are dependents. Note these measures do not account for unemployment.

It is also possible to compute separate 'young dependency' and 'elderly' dependency ratios. Concern has been raised recently in industrialized countries about increased life expectancy (rising elderly dependency) and the pressure thus created on pension-systems. The proportion of the world's population over 65 is predicted to double by 2030, from about 8% to more than 16%. For members of the Organization for Economic Cooperation and Development the percentage is expected to rise from 18% to 32% over the same period. Coupled with falling fertility rates this means smaller populations will have to support greater shares of non-economically active people.

Fertility rate: the number of children born in a year, usually expressed per 1000 women in the reproductive age group.

> In 1970 average international fertility rates were 3.33; currently they are 2.96 and are expected to drop to 2.5 by 2020. In fact Ireland had the distinction in the 1990s of being the sole European country where the fertility rate was sufficiently high to lead to a rise in the overall population – in all other European countries populations were declining as the fertility rate was less than the replacement rate, i.e. that required to replace deaths.

These international trends create challenges that will have to be faced by governments, pensions-administrators and by workers in the not too distant future. (For more on the pensions debate see *Cato*, 1998.)

The importance of the dependency ratio for understanding trends in labour productivity and living standards can be considered using an example.

Before the 1990s in Ireland, labour productivity growth did not translate into proportional growth in living standards because of high levels of unemployment and dependency. However, during the 1990s growth in labour productivity eventually coincided with improved living standards because it reflected a more efficient use of resources and allowed Irish goods and services to become more competitive relative to those produced elsewhere. Up to the late 1980s high Irish unemployment reflected general international recessions and the inability of many inefficient Irish producers to compete either domestically or internationally. By the mid 1990s the 'Celtic Tiger' had emerged (a reference to the name often used to denote the four Asian Tiger economies of Hong Kong, Singapore, Taiwan, and South Korea that achieved relatively high rates of growth over the 1960s to the mid-1990s) and rising employment meant that growth in productivity translated into living standards figures also, as shown in Table 9.3.

Table 9.3 shows that real output of the Irish economy accelerated from 1993 onwards at 8.3% on average each year to 2000. To explain this jump we see that from 1993 annual growth in employment also increased substantially to

TABLE 9.3   ECONOMIC GROWTH, PRODUCTIVITY AND EMPLOYMENT

Period	GDP	Population	Employment	Living standards, i.e. GDP/capita	Productivity, i.e. GDP/worker
Annual average growth rates %					
1960–1980	4.1	0.9	0.5	3.1	3.5
1980–1993	3.3	0.4	0.0	2.9	3.3
1993–2000	8.3	0.8	4.7	7.4	3.5

Source: Kennedy, 2001. Data taken from Irish *National Income and Expenditure*, various issues; ESRI *Quarterly Economic Commentary*, December 2000; and Kennedy, K. (1971) *Productivity and Industrial Growth: The Irish experience*. Clarendon Press, Oxford.

4.7%. Living standards too jumped dramatically from 1993 onwards. Although the growth in labour productivity was almost stable since 1960, because increasing numbers of people could find work since 1993, the overall output of the economy increased substantially. The dependency ratio fell as the unemployment rate dropped from 15.5% in 1993 to 4.2% in 2000. The gap between the population and the employed population explains why growth in living standards was below that for productivity until the period beginning 1993. As employment increased this gap closed, allowing living standards to grow faster than productivity and allowing a greater proportion of the population to share in the economic growth through their new-found jobs.

9.3   ECONOMIC GROWTH OVER TIME

Economies are not static entities. The *ceteris paribus* assumption helps economists theorize about the economy and facilitates their analyses of the economy but factors do not remain constant for very long. Economic decisions are made, goods and services are bought and sold, demand conditions change, supply conditions change, population and unemployment rise and fall, real output is produced and real income is earned and spent. Ideally economies should expand or grow over time meaning more real output is produced. The more output produced, the more income generated for the citizens of a country. We all probably hope that our children and grandchildren will be materially (and non-materially) better off than ourselves, which implies that there will be more real output/income generated by their economies to be shared among the population. Table 9.1 indicates quite different outcomes across various countries in terms of their growth experiences as revealed by average living standards internationally over the last 40 years.

The rate at which an economy grows matters if we consider what happens to real income if long-run growth is 3% each year. Real national output for Ireland in 1978 was IR£15 815m (expressed in 1995 prices). We can compute how long it would take for real income to double (to £31 630m) assuming a growth rate of 3%. The following formula applies:

Future value = initial value $(1 + $ growth rate$)^n$; where n denotes time period

    (i)   **To compute n** rearrange the above:

$$\frac{\text{Future value } (FV)}{\text{Initial value } (IV)} = (1 + \text{ growth rate } (GR))^n$$

(ii)   It is true that log $(FV/IV) = n \log (1 + GR)$

(iii)   Dividing both sides by log $(1 + GR)$ gives log $(FV/IV)/\log (1 + GR) = n$

(iv)   **To compute GR** rearrange the above:

$$\frac{\text{Future value } (FV)}{\text{Initial value } (IV)} = (1 + \text{growth rate } (GR))^n$$

(v)   This can be rearranged as $(FV/IV)^{1/n} = (1 + GR)$

(vi)   Finally GR can be found as $[(FV/IV)^{1/n}] - 1 = GR$

Applying the formula to this example:

(i) $£31\,630\text{m}/£15\,815\text{m} = (1 + 0.03)^n : 2 = (1.03)^n$

(ii) $\log (2) = n \log (1.03)$

(iii) $\log (2)/\log (1.03) = 0.301/0.013 = \mathbf{23.15}$

This means that it would take 23.15 years for real output to double assuming the above information holds. What we would find for a lower growth rate of say 1.5% (half of 3%) is that it would take *twice* as long – over 46 years – for output to double. This indicates that the rate of economic growth really matters for economies, for their real output and hence for living standards.

In actual fact 23 years after 1978, in 2001, Irish real output was £67 615, more than trebling over the period. This implies a substantially higher rate of growth than 3%. We can compute what the growth rate was again using the above formula. This time the future value is £67 615m and the variable we wish to compute is the growth rate (GR). (For simplicity the time period used is 23 years rather than 23.15.)

(v) $(£67\,615\text{m}/£15\,815\text{m})^{1/23} = (1 + GR) = 4.28^{1/23} = (1 + GR)$

(vi) $1.0653 = (1 + GR) = 1.0653 - 1 = \mathbf{0.0653}$

A growth rate of over 6.5% corresponds to the observed real growth in Irish output between 1978 and 2001. This figure of 6.5% is an average computed over the entire period but in fact, as Table 9.3 showed earlier, real Irish output grew mostly after 1993.

To understand the processes underlying economic growth Solow's growth model is considered further in the sections that follow.

9.4 MODELLING ECONOMIC GROWTH: THE SOLOW GROWTH MODEL

In 1956, Robert Solow, who received the Nobel Prize in Economics in 1987, developed a model of economic growth that focuses on long-run economic growth and its determinants, as opposed to the short-run fluctuations we considered earlier in the discussion of the business cycle. (This approach to modelling economic growth is also called the neoclassical growth model.) Long-run growth is related to the production possibilities or productive capacity of an economy, which usually change very little over short periods of time but which can change over longer periods. In terms of the tools we have already met, economic growth corresponds to an outward expansion of the production possibilities frontier or a rightward shift of the aggregate supply curve.

Solow's growth model uses the production function approach discussed in Chapter 5 (see section 5.8). The production function summarizes the relationship between the factors of production (K and L), the level of technology (T), and output (Y), as:

$$Y = F(K, L, T)$$

From this relationship, any change in the quantity or quality of the productive factors or technology has an impact on the level of output the economy can produce.

Just how changes in K or L actually affect Y (e.g. Y increasing by 5% if L rises by 10%) is not covered in this text but would be described in a more specific production function than the general function presented here as $Y = F(K, L, T)$.

One example of a more specific functional relationship between Y, K, L and T would be $Y = T \times (K^\alpha) \times (L^\beta)$ with values provided for T, α and β (these values could be estimated from analysis of available economic data).

Where the value of α plus β is less than 1, e.g. 0.3 and 0.5 (summing to 0.8), it would imply that decreasing returns to scale describe the relationship between the factors of production and output – if inputs both doubled, output would rise but by less than double. If α plus β sum to greater than 1, increasing returns to scale are described (output rising faster than a joint input rise) and if they sum exactly to 1, constant returns to scale apply to the economy.

Relating the production function to our discussion of labour productivity (and assuming that resources are used efficiently) any change in labour productivity is due to either a change in the quality or quantity of capital available to each worker or to a change in available technology.

In the Solow model, technology is assumed not to be influenced by K and L implying that changes in the capital stock, K, or labour input L do not affect technological progress. In other words, technology is assumed to be *exogenous* to the Solow model as it is determined outside the model itself and not influenced by other variables in the model: technological change just happens without explanation. (A number of economists have examined this exogeneity assumption with interesting results but before discussing these it is necessary to initially consider the Solow model and its implications).

Figure 9.1 presents an illustration of a production function. To draw the production function in two dimensions – here we use output and capital – we assume that the production function is drawn for one given level of technology and for a given level of labour supply. This allows us to focus on how output is related to the capital input, given T and L.

The production function indicates the amount of output produced for different levels of capital input (given T and L). We see that long-run output depends on the level of the capital stock in the economy. If the level of capital stock is $K1$, output is $Y1$; when it is $K2$, output is $Y2$. Furthermore, for any two economies with similar production functions if the level of capital in one country is $K1$ while it is $K2$ in the other country, the output levels in both countries will differ substantially.

We also see that output rises as the stock of capital employed increases but the relationship is nonlinear. This implies that output does not rise by a constant

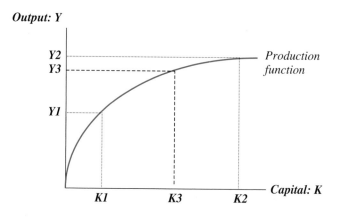

FIGURE 9.1 PRODUCTION FUNCTION IN THE SOLOW GROWTH MODEL

amount if the capital stock changes. For example as the capital stock rises from zero to *K1*, output rises relatively sharply from zero to *Y1*. As the capital stock rises further from *K1* to *K3* (an increase of roughly 200% here), output also rises but by a smaller proportion – approximately 50%. This nonlinearity illustrates diminishing returns to capital. For a given number of workers, adding more and more capital contributes ever declining amounts to total output. The initial benefit of doubling capital when the capital stock is low allows workers to increase their output substantially. Doubling capital when the capital stock is high and each worker already has a lot of capital with which to work generates lower additional increases in total output.

Since the level of output in the long run depends on the level of capital stock, any change in the capital stock causes a change in output. If an economy has a level of output at *Y1* and wishes to expand output to *Y2*, investment in more capital stock is required. Such investment is undertaken by both firms and governments; firms make private investments that change the stock of private capital and governments engage in public investment that change the amount of public capital.

To increase the capital stock investment in new capital must be sufficient to more than cover any depreciation that normally occurs as capital is used for productive purposes. Once capital investment is greater than depreciation the capital stock rises and so too does output (assuming that the output is in demand!). If investment is less than depreciation, an economy experiences a decline in its capital stock and in output. If investment just covers or offsets the capital lost due to depreciation, the levels of capital stock and output remain constant or unchanging. Solow called this case the steady state.

At any level of investment, either above or below the level required to cover depreciation in the economy, the economy is not at its steady-state level of output and the capital stock will either rise or fall with knock-on effects on the level of output.

The **steady state** is the term used by Solow to describe the equilibrium state of output and capital stock in the long run. (The term is also used in physics.) An economy that reaches a steady-state level of capital stock and level of output has no tendency to change from these levels, *ceteris paribus*.

Figure 9.1 can be extended to consider investment and depreciation further. Having discussed investment in Chapter 5, we know that expectations play a key role in firms' determination of their investment levels. Predicted future demand is central to the investment decision.

Many factors enter into governments' decisions regarding public investment but it is closely related to the level of development of the economy – classified as low, medium or high – and to the government's policy goals. It may take the form of *hard investments* in physical infrastructure or *soft investments* including services, education or technology.

If we consider that national savings is the main source of actual investment funds we can describe actual investment as equal to national savings, which itself is a fraction of national income (equating investment with national savings is strictly true only if there is no government expenditure or trade). Including government and foreign sectors implies:

Investment = savings − government deficit (or + government surplus)

+ foreign financing.

If Y denotes national income then savings or the funds for investment is a fraction of Y. If the fraction of Y saved were 25% we can add this as the savings = actual investment function shown in Figure 9.2.

To include depreciation in the diagram, it is assumed that a constant fraction of the capital stock requires replacement annually as it becomes obsolete. If this fraction is 20% then 20% of K depreciates each year and will be written off in the national accounts; if no investment takes place the capital stock declines. It is reflected in Figure 9.2 by a straight line with a slope of 0.20. The linear relationship between depreciation and capital stock implies that for any change in capital stock, depreciation will always be 20% of this change (so if the level of K is 10, depreciation is 2).

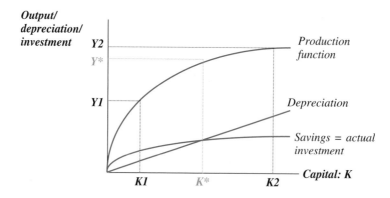

FIGURE 9.2   SOLOW GROWTH MODEL WITH INVESTMENT AND DEPRECIATION

In Figure 9.2, K^* denotes the level of the capital stock required for investment to just cover depreciation. This is the steady-state level of capital stock, the only level from which the economy has no tendency to change, *ceteris paribus*. At other levels of capital stock, this is not the case. If $K1$ is the level of capital stock and $Y1$ the output of the economy, investment is greater than depreciation and the tendency is for the capital stock to rise with an impact on output also. For levels of capital stock above K^* such as $K2$, depreciation is above investment, and investment is insufficient to replace depreciating capital stock, hence the tendency is for the capital stock level to decline and, therefore, for output to fall. Whenever the level of the capital stock is not at K^*, it tends to move towards K^*.

The steady-state level of capital stock K^* corresponds to a level of output of Y^* on the production function.

Another implication of the production function drawn here is that of convergence.

Convergence is the tendency for poorer countries to grow faster than richer countries for a given increase in capital stock. Hence, poorer countries would be expected to catch up with richer countries if the countries share similar steady states.

Richer countries (i.e. those with higher per capita income levels) have higher levels of capital stock than poorer countries. Given the assumption of diminishing returns to capital, this implies that for any increase in the capital stock the additional output produced from the capital will be lower in the richer country than the poorer country starting from a lower level of capital stock and lower level of income. The productivity of capital will be higher in the poorer country. Historically, following World War Two, Japan and Germany invested heavily in renewing and improving their capital stock relative to the USA and UK and this is one of the factors that is considered to explain their relatively better productivity. Similar arguments are used to explain the Asian Tiger phenomenon.

9.4.1 MORE ON SAVINGS

Savings rates for many countries are published on a regular basis. A recent report by the Organization for Economic Cooperation and Development (OECD) provided the information presented in Table 9.4 on household saving rates across a range of industrialized countries. Countries' ranking are presented in the final column while an indication of the general trend is shown in the second-last column of the table. The predominant trend in household saving has been a decline. In some countries,

TABLE 9.4 INTERNATIONAL HOUSEHOLD SAVINGS RATES

Country	1985	1990	1995	2000	2002[a]	Change	Rank '02
Australia	10.8	9.3	4.8	3.4	0.3	↓	19
Austria	10.5	14.0	11.7	8.3	7.5	↓	12
Belgium	15.9	18.0	18.8	13.4	13.7	≈	2
Canada	15.8	13.0	9.2	4.8	4.4	↓	17
Czech Republic	− [b]	−	20.6	13	11.3	↓	5
Denmark	−	11.2	6.9	4.8	6.2	↓	14
Finland	3.4	2.2	5.2	−0.9	−0.3	↓	20
France	8.9	7.8	11.2	10.8	12.2	≈	3
Germany	12.1	13.9	11.2	9.8	10.4	↓	7
Ireland	10.6	6.5	8.5	6.0	7.5	↓	12
Italy	30.7	27.8	22.5	14.5	16.0	↓	1
Japan	16.5	14.0	11.9	9.8	5.8	↓	15
Korea	14.8	22.0	16.8	11.5	9.6	↓	9
Netherlands	5.6	11.6	14.9	6.7	10.7	↑	6
New Zealand	−	0.5	−3.6	−3.8	−0.3	≈	20
Norway	−3.3	0.8	4.6	4.5	7.0	↑	13
Portugal	−	−	13.6	9.5	11.9	↓	4
Spain	11.1	12.3	14.4	10.6	10.1	↓	8
Sweden	3.2	0.0	8.3	2.4	8.2	↑	11
Switzerland	−	8.7	9.4	8.3	9.0	≈	10
United Kingdom	9.8	8.0	10.0	4.3	5.2	↓	16
United States	9.2	7.8	5.6	2.8	3.7	↓	18

Source: OECD, 2002
Notes: [a] 2002 figures are projections.
[b] Data unavailable.

the decline has been dramatic – Australia, Canada, Italy (from a very high share), Japan, the USA, and the UK.

There are many possible reasons why the savings rate varies a lot across countries. Different demographic patterns between countries lead to different savings rates as countries with a high proportion of the population in older age groups tend to have higher savings rates. National tax policies affect people's saving/consumption incentives and decisions. Cultural differences also play a role, as does the level of development, and political and economic stability. Savings rates tend to be highest in countries with high income-levels, which could mean also that high income promotes high rates of saving. Economists have not identified which of the many possible explanations is most important to explain international differences in savings rates.

The Solow model can be used to consider what happens if a country's savings rate changes. A decision to increase the proportion of income saved, for example, moves the savings = actual investment function up, as shown in Figure 9.3.

With the higher savings rate, at any level of capital stock the amount of investment is higher, so the new savings function *2* lies above the initial function. We can consider the implications of this change beginning at the initial steady state. Using savings function 2, we see that at K^*, savings = actual investment lies above the depreciation line. This means there is a tendency for the economy to move from its steady state and the capital stock rises due to increased net investment. In fact, the capital stock increases until $K2$ is reached (where the new savings function intersects the depreciation line and where savings = actual investment just covers capital depreciation). The higher capital stock of $K2$ denotes a *new steady state* involving both higher capital stock and higher output.

Governments sometimes intervene to affect savings. Remember consumers have the options to either save or spend on consumption goods. High levels

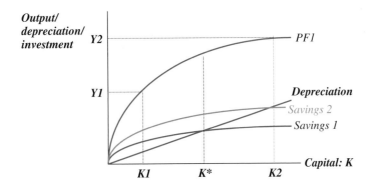

FIGURE 9.3   INCREASE IN THE SAVINGS RATE

of consumption correspond to low levels of saving. High levels of aggregate demand correspond to booms and to encourage consumers to change their savings behaviour government might be anxious to try to reduce aggregate demand (if inflation or inflation expectations were rising, for example). Or to encourage greater savings for pensions, governments often offer tax concessions as an incentive to change savings behaviour. But is there an ideal or optimal savings rate for an economy?

Imagine that consumers wish to maximize their consumption out of the income generated in their economy and income is either consumed or saved (i.e. used for investment). There are, in fact, unique levels of capital stock (K^*) and output (Y^*) that correspond to maximizing consumption, which are shown graphically in Figure 9.4.

The production function indicates the maximum levels of consumption possible if no income/output is diverted for savings/investment (and if no taxes were diverted to government and if no external trade occurred!). Even if no income is saved a certain amount of capital depreciates each year, reducing the amount of income available for consumption. For Figure 9.4 panel A we can consider just by looking at the graph where the biggest difference exists between output and depreciation; this indicates the unique values of output (Y^*) and capital stock (K^*) at which consumption would be maximized. The intuition behind this result is that only at these points is the marginal return to capital (the slope of the production function) the same as the rate of depreciation. At any higher (lower) capital stock

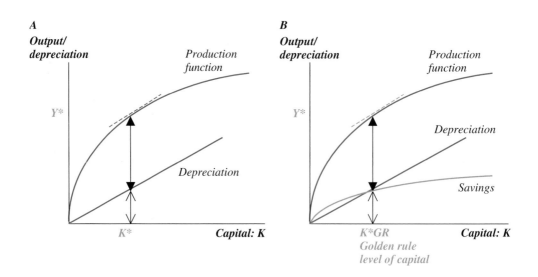

FIGURE 9.4   SOLOW GROWTH MODEL: SAVINGS AND CONSUMPTION

the rate of deprecation would be greater (less) than the return of the capital in the economy. Only at these points is there no incentive to change the capital stock.

In Figure 9.4 panel B a savings function is added. The golden rule level of capital (K^*GR) corresponds to the point where depreciation = savings *and* consumption is maximized. This outcome is far from certain for an economy. One unique savings function must apply, as shown in Figure 9.4 panel B. For any other savings function, the optimum level of consumption does not occur and the level of capital stock differs from K^*GR.

9.4.2   THE SOLOW MODEL AND CHANGES IN LABOUR INPUT

Using the Solow model to examine the impact of changes in labour on output and economic growth is complicated. Why? Because using the production function approach we assumed T and L are fixed. Relaxing this assumption for a while, take the case where the labour input increases and we assume the economy is initially operating efficiently. With a rise in quantity of the labour input (L) only and no change in capital, each worker (on average) has less capital with which to work. The net effect on output depends on the relative effects of

1. lower *average* productivity due to the drop in capital per worker;
2. rising *total* output produced by the extra workers.

See the box for examples.

An economy produces output efficiently. It has 100 workers and average productivity is 10 baskets of output. Therefore, national output is $100 \times 10 = 1\,000$.

Example 1

Labour rises by 5% to 105 workers. Capital does not change. Each worker has less capital and so their productivity declines by 10% to 9 baskets. New national output is $105 \times 9 = 945$. This represents a drop of 5.5%.

Example 2

Labour rises by 10% to 110 workers. Capital does not change. Each worker has less capital and so their productivity declines by 5% to 9.5 baskets. New national output is $110 \times 9.5 = 1045$. This represents a rise of 4.5%.

Thus, the impact on output depends on the precise relationship between output, capital, labour and technology for the economy at that point in time, i.e. its production function!

There is a further possibility. It could be envisaged that an increase in the labour input could occur *either* if more workers become available or if the quality of the workforce improves (due to better education or skills, for example). In such a case, greater numbers of more efficient or productive workers might reduce or even cancel out the effect of having less capital with which to work. All of this implies that it is difficult to predict exactly what the effect of changes in the labour force will have on real output.

If the *quantity* of workers and capital are *both* increasing, however, the Solow model is useful for considering the effects of increasing labour inputs for output and economic growth. A rising labour input reduces capital per worker (as with depreciation). In order to maintain a constant amount of capital for each worker in the economy if the labour input is rising, investment must cover not only depreciation but also the capital required to supply all new workers with capital: capital widening is required.

> In an economy where the capital stock increases at the same rate as the labour force *and* covers depreciation, **capital widening** occurs.
>
> **Capital deepening** occurs when the capital stock increases faster than the labour force so that the amount of capital per worker rises.

At the level of the macroeconomy, if capital widening occurs, a given level of capital per worker (*K1* for example) can be maintained, which is associated with a specific level of output (*Y1*). To maintain *Y1* if the labour input is rising requires greater investment than if labour is unchanging.

Capital deepening would be funded through savings leading to higher investment. In an economy with a workforce growing by 5% each year, for example, investment would have to grow by 5% just to keep a constant amount of capital available to each worker. This is apart from the investment required to replace depreciating capital. If our economy above experiences 20% depreciation and 5% labour force growth then investment to the value of *25%* of the capital stock is required to maintain a constant level of capital stock per worker.

A rise in labour coupled with capital deepening would lead to a further expansion of the production function. In an economy where constant returns to scale prevail, output grows at the same rate as input growth. In other words if *both* capital and labour increase by 5% then output grows by 5% also, reflected in an upward shift of the production function.

In measuring the changes in labour input, economists usually use average annual hours worked in an economy, which is estimated based on broad surveys of companies usually carried out by national statistical agencies. This measure of labour input is preferred to a measure of the number of workers because of the changing patterns of work for many individuals. Focusing solely on the numbers of workers employed reveals that numbers employed internationally have risen (this is true using historical data going back to 1870) but since part-time work is quite commonplace and given labour policies and regulations, hours worked per person have actually fallen internationally.

9.4.3   THE SOLOW MODEL AND CHANGES IN TECHNOLOGY

The Solow model assumes a given level of technology. Allowing technology to improve, *ceteris paribus*, allows more output to be produced from a given amount of inputs. This means the production function moves up as shown in Figure 9.5.

An economy with an amount *K1* of capital can increase its output from *Y2* to *Y1* given better technology. If the economy begins with *K2* capital its output increases from *Y3* to *Y4*. The country with the higher initial capital stock experiences a greater absolute rise in output. We can extend this figure to illustrate that technology improvement is a more important source of growth than increased capital for more industrialized countries, *ceteris paribus*.

This case is shown in Figure 9.6. Imagine two countries with production functions like *PF1* that both experience technology improvements allowing their production functions to move to *PF2*. One country is relatively poor with a low capital stock of *K1*; the second country has a higher capital stock of *K2*. Both countries experience the same absolute increase in capital stock.

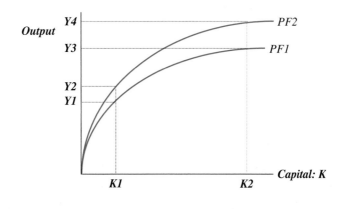

FIGURE 9.5   IMPROVED TECHNOLOGY

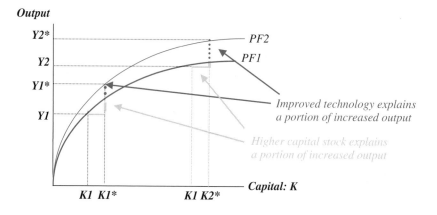

FIGURE 9.6 IMPROVED TECHNOLOGY: RICH VS. POOR COUNTRIES

K1 rises to *K1** as shown in Figure 9.6 while *K2* rises to *K2**. Since the marginal product of capital is higher for the poorer country with the lower stock of capital, the expansion of its capital stock is responsible for approximately half of its increase in output from *Y1* to *Y1**. Compare this to the rise in output for the richer country. Because the production function is relatively flatter for the richer country since its capital stock is higher, most of the expansion in its output from *Y2* to *Y2** is caused by the shift in the production function.

This implies that developing or non-industrialized countries benefit *more* from increasing their capital stock than do more advanced economies. Advanced economies can expand their output but technology improvements are a relatively more important source of their growth.

9.4.4 EXPLAINING GROWTH: LABOUR, CAPITAL AND TECHNOLOGY

Any change in national output can be explained by changes in capital or labour or technology. More specifically a technique known as growth accounting categorizes the separate sources of output changes.

Growth accounting is a method of identifying the proximate causes of changes in output and its rate of growth. The main causes are:

1. *The marginal product of capital* – linked to where on the production function an economy produces, ultimately explained by past investment decisions influencing the capital stock.

2. *The amount of capital in use.*
3. *The marginal product of labour.*
4. *The amount of labour in use*
5. *Total factor productivity* – a measure of the efficiency with which inputs are employed to produce output. **TFP** is a catch-all term that measures the effect on output not only of any changes in technology, but also in the social and political systems that affect the quantity and quality of output that an economy can produce from its labour and capital resources. TFP is effectively that portion of output change that cannot be accounted for by changes in the quantity and quality of labour and capital.

Any change in output *not* accounted for by changes in capital accumulation or changes in labour input is called total factor productivity (TFP). It is also known as the Solow residual – growth left unexplained after inputs have been accounted for.

The extent to which differences in the quality and quantity of inputs explain differences in productivity across countries is shown in Table 9.5. The first column indicates each country's labour productivity expressed as a percentage of that of the United States. The other columns present counterfactual analysis, best interpreted by taking an example. Australia's output was measured as 83% of that of the USA. If Australia's labour and TFP were the same as in the USA, with capital being the only different factor, its labour productivity *would have been* 109% of that in the USA. This implies greater relative capital productivity in Australia but since its output is less than the USA, differences in its other input (labour) and/or TFP reduce its overall relative productivity performance.

9.4.5   CONCLUSIONS FROM THE SOLOW MODEL

- The level of output is determined by the amount of capital in an economy, given labour and technology. This supports the general observation that countries with substantial capital investments (per worker) have relatively high levels of output and productivity.
- The long-run equilibrium level of output and capital depends on the savings rate of an economy. In equilibrium the level of capital (and output) is constant. Investment is sufficient to cover depreciation and any growth in the labour force. International evidence indicates high correlations between savings rates and living standards (e.g. Summers and Heston, 1991).
- An increased savings rate leads to a new equilibrium with higher capital investment and higher output level. A higher savings rate leads to economic growth *temporarily* until the new equilibrium is reached.

TABLE 9.5   SOURCES OF INTERNATIONAL PRODUCTIVITY DIFFERENCES

Country	Output per worker as % of US output	Capital	Labour	TFP
Australia	83	109	90	86
Austria	71	108	67	98
Belgium	84	102	84	98
Canada	94	100	91	103
China	6	89	63	11
Czechoslovakia	21	115	76	24
Denmark	69	108	91	71
Finland	73	120	86	73
France	82	109	67	113
Germany (west)	82	112	80	91
Greece	47	102	68	67
Hungary	31	112	93	29
India	9	71	45	27
Ireland	58	105	77	71
Italy	83	106	65	121
Japan	59	112	80	66
Korea	38	86	76	58
Netherlands	81	106	80	95
New Zealand	72	112	102	63
Norway	76	120	91	70
Portugal	37	96	50	76
Spain	68	102	61	111
Sweden	79	103	85	90
Switzerland	87	119	83	88
United Kingdom	73	89	81	101

Source: Excerpted from 'Data Appendix' for Hall and Jones (1999).

Hence, high savings rates *do not* generate *persistent* economic growth.

- Growth in the population or labour force matters for living standards. With a growing labour force, *ceteris paribus*, labour productivity falls. Correlations indicate that countries with fast rates of population growth experience relatively lower levels of living standards.
- In the steady state, growth can only occur via TFP changes.

The Solow model does not deal with causes of technology improvement since technology is exogenous or not explained within the growth model itself. We can allow technology to become an endogenous factor and such endogenous growth models are considered in section 9.4.6, which follows.

The conclusions do not help us understand why some countries do not experience convergence of income levels. We need to look elsewhere to understand this phenomenon. Nor do we have an indication of welfare implications of economic growth, which is also examined in section 9.5.

9.4.6 ENDOGENOUS GROWTH

Endogenous or new growth models essentially try to explain how and why changes in technology occur. Technology is not assumed to be unchanging and the result of things occurring outside the models. Some endogenous growth models discard the assumption of diminishing marginal product of capital so that a change in capital leads to a constant proportional increase in output irrespective of the initial level of capital stock. This implies a rising but linear production function, as shown in Figure 9.7. This means that every one-unit increase in the capital stock increases output by the same amount, irrespective of an economy's initial level of capital stock.

Adding our assumption about savings being a constant proportion of output, we draw a corresponding savings function, which is also linear. By further including the depreciation line, we complete the essential elements of the model. By definition the steady state occurs where there is no tendency to change from one level of the capital stock. But in Figure 9.7 no such point exists. Investment lies above depreciation indicating that the level of capital stock can rise indefinitely *without* any technological change, allowing output to rise also.

Another interesting result from the model occurs with an increase in the savings function. If people's savings behaviour changes so that savings increase and the savings function moves up, the result is an increase in the economy's stock of capital and in its rate of output growth – the production function also moves up indicating

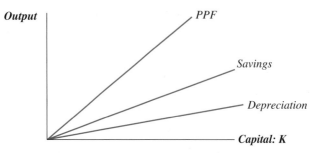

FIGURE 9.7 PRODUCTION FUNCTION WITH CONSTANT MARGINAL PRODUCT

a positive link between savings and a *permanent* rise in output growth (a new steeper slope of the new PPF indicates a change in the rate of growth).

A key issue arises as to the credibility of assuming a constant marginal product of capital. This may be possible if we allow investment to have an impact on the quality of labour, and vice versa. The greater the amount of physical capital (buildings, equipment, machines, etc.) in an economy, the greater the output that human capital (skills, education, etc.) can produce and the higher the return on further investment to improving education and skills to maximize the productivity of physical capital. Each separate component of capital may exhibit diminishing marginal product but in combination, they could give rise to a constant marginal product of combined, or total, capital. Poorer countries with not only low levels of physical capital, but also of human capital, face a double disadvantage in trying to catch up. Not only is investment in physical capital required but spending on training and education is also required and by its nature the return on such investments takes years to yield rewards. Many poorer countries with very limited budgets do not have the luxury of spending in the hope of generating future growth as the opportunity cost of such spending is considered too high. What is important for long-term growth is subordinated to urgent expenditures required today.

Growth benefits from investment may go beyond individual firms who undertake the investment indicating that diminishing returns to capital may be relevant for a firm but not for society overall. Consider the effect on economic growth of a utility company investing in providing broadband technology. The provider will decide to invest in the broadband technology taking account of its own costs and potential revenues. The provision of broadband technology, however, can increase output and productivity of those firms that adopt it allowing them to increase their output for a set amount of inputs. The social benefit may outweigh the private benefit and create constant or even increasing returns to capital investment for the economy.

The potential for such a scenario creates challenges for government and whether or not it should try to encourage capital investments by private firms that generate economy-wide benefits. Private firms usually do not take social benefits into account in their investment decisions (and consider only their private costs and benefits) so maybe government should subsidize investments that give rise to broader economy-wide benefits? This sounds somewhat logical. Yet investment by firms is often in new products and innovations that can be quite costly and often very risky. Innovation that underlies many technological improvements is based on research and development, which does not have a certain outcome. Governments will not be able to correctly gauge which investments will yield positive economic results no more than firms themselves can so it will be a guessing game to decide on how much support to provide for investment purposes. Many examples exist of such supports via favourable treatment of savings, investment, or the provision of R&D tax incentives or tax credits.

A generally sound economic system organized around markets and firms where people enjoy property rights that are supported by law, where money fulfils its main functions, where modern infrastructure is provided (publicly and/or privately), and where people are free to buy, sell and invest as they choose usually provides an environment that facilitates growth. The extent to which governments facilitate such an environment may be even more important in the context of growth than the funding they might provide in support of research and development.

9.5 INCOME DISTRIBUTION

Information on economic growth provides a partial perspective on living standards across countries because it is an average measure. The living standards of some people in an economy lie above the average while that of others lie below it so that real income is not divided up equally across the population.

How real income is divided up both internationally and within countries is an issue of interest from a welfare perspective. Are citizens actually better off if their average national living standards rise? Arguably, you need to examine income distribution *as well as* living standards in order to get a more comprehensive and accurate indication of if and how economies develop and to identify the trend in living standards for the majority of the population. For example, in a country of 5 million people, consider what happens if the income of the richest quarter of the population increased by £5m while the income of the least-well-off quarter fell by £2.5m (all in real terms). Although total real income and average income per capita have undoubtedly risen it does not automatically follow that the society overall is 'better off' because in this example the gap between rich and poor widens. It's a matter of being clear on how economic growth is measured and on what it actually means. Rising average living standards do not necessarily mean that the welfare of all, a majority or even the worst-off citizens in an economy improves.

The extent to which income is shared depends on where – and by whom – the factors of production (land, labour, capital, entrepreneurship, etc.) are held in an economy. If the factors are concentrated in the hands of a small number of individuals (or in a particular region), these individuals (or their region) will be disproportionately wealthier than the vast majority of their fellow citizens (or other regions). Within countries, policies (e.g. tax) are often used by governments to redistribute income to increase some people's consumption possibilities beyond those provided by their income, in an attempt to close the income distribution gap. The extent to which countries consider this as an issue to be addressed is revealed by their actions and related policies. Addressing income inequality between rather than within countries is somewhat more complicated since it requires international cooperation and formal agreement.

Information in Table 9.6 indicates the extent to which income was distributed internationally over the last 40 years relative to world population. It indicates that the developing world (all countries except industrialized countries and Eastern Europe) increased its share of the world population from 71% to 81% since 1960 and also its share of world income from 29% in 1960 to 42% in 2000.

While on the basis of Table 9.6 it appears that income is better shared internationally in 2000, income remains concentrated in the countries that make up less than 20% of the world's population. Since the table does not deal with within-country income distribution, we cannot say whether inequality has changed within any country.

Many people and NGOs (non-governmental organizations) disagree with the international income distribution and attempt to change it through supporting programmes for economic development and cancelling debt repayments for the poorest countries. Clearly, much still remains to be done to bring about a more equitable or fairer international income distribution.

TABLE 9.6   INTERNATIONAL INCOME AND POPULATION SHARES

Region	1960 Income[a]	1960 Pop.	1980 Income	1980 Pop.	2000 Income	2000 Pop.
Developing world	29	71	33	79	42	81
of which China and India	*8*	*36*	*7*	*39*	*17*	*38*
Developed world	71	29	67	21	58	19
Total	100	100	100	100	100	100

Source: Adapted from Tables 2.2 and 2.3 in Bhalla (2002).
[a]Income is estimated as GDP in PPP terms based to 1993, provided by the World Bank.

Equity in terms of income distribution is an example of **vertical equity** whereby people with intrinsically different characteristics (education, experience, abilities) would be treated differently in order to reduce the disparate income resulting from their differences.

Horizontal equity is a related concept but refers to treating identical people in an identical manner (i.e. not discriminating based on gender or race between individuals who are economically identical and can perform similar tasks).

In developed countries, laws and practice appear generally to *attempt* to achieve horizontal equity. The extent to which countries attempt to achieve vertical equity is more varied, depending on political ideology, preferences and culture.

9.5.1   INTRA-COUNTRY INCOME DISTRIBUTION

Measurements of income of the richest and poorest proportions of a population are used to estimate inequality and allow us to consider the extent to which income has been distributed more or less equitably within countries over time. From Table 9.7 it appears that over the last 40 years income inequality within countries has not substantially changed or improved.

Contrary to the data in Table 9.7, Sala-i-Martin (2002) found that global income inequalities fell over the 1980s and 1990s. But in further research published in 2002, Milanovic estimated that the richest 1% of the world population received as much as the world's poorest 57% . He also found that the ratio between the average

TABLE 9.7 INTERNATIONAL INCOME DISTRIBUTION WITHIN COUNTRIES

Country	Income[a] of poorest 20%			Income[a] of richest 20%		
	1960	1980	2000	1960	1980	2000
Austria	6.8	6.6	10.4	36.6	38.3	33.4
Belgium	7.9	7.9	9.5	36.1	36.1	34.5
China	7.9	7.9	5.9	36.7	36.7	46.6
Czech Republic	8.2	11.4	10.2	35.1	32.1	36.4
Denmark	5.0	7.0	6.4	41.2	38.0	39.5
Estonia	10.0	10.0	7.0	32.7	32.7	45.1
Finland	2.4	6.6	10.6	49.3	40.0	33.6
France	1.9	8.3	7.2	53.7	38.5	40.2
Germany	10.5	6.6	8.2	37.7	39.0	38.4
Greece	6.4	6.4	6.2	41.7	41.7	41.2
Hungary	9.2	10.8	9.9	34.8	32.4	34.5
India	8.4	8.5	8.7	41.4	40.9	41.8
Ireland	4.8	4.9	6.7	42.2	43.6	42.9
Italy	7.0	7.9	8.7	42.0	39.1	36.3
Japan	5.3	6.3	10.6	45.1	39.6	35.6
Latvia	10.4	10.4	7.5	32.8	32.8	40.4
Lithuania	10.6	10.6	6.7	32.9	32.9	41.7
Luxembourg	10.2	10.2	9.4	34.0	34.0	36.5
Netherlands	4.0	8.4	7.3	48.4	36.7	40.0
Poland	9.5	9.8	7.8	35.2	34.5	40.1
Portugal	5.8	5.5	7.3	46.3	42.5	43.4
Slovakia	10.4	10.4	9.3	34.2	34.2	38.6
Slovenia	10.1	10.1	9.1	36.1	36.1	37.7
Spain	8.2	8.2	10.2	35.1	35.1	33.1
Sweden	4.4	7.0	9.6	44.0	39.5	34.6

(*continued overleaf*)

TABLE 9.7 *(continued)*

Country	Income[a] of poorest 20%			Income[a] of richest 20%		
	1960	1980	2000	1960	1980	2000
United Kingdom	9.4	10.2	6.6	36.9	37.6	42.9
United States	4.8	4.3	3.6	41.3	43.6	49.4
Average: Table Total	7	8	8	39	37	39
Average East Europe	10	10	8	34	33	39
Average China/India	8	8	7	39	39	44
Average Others	6	7	8	42	39	39

Source: Excerpted from Appendix Table C.1 in Bhalla (2002).
[a] Income is income per capita based on survey data measured as GDP in PPP terms based to 1993.

income of the top 5% in the world to the bottom 5% increased from 78 to 1 in 1988 to 114 to 1 in 1993 indicating greater inequality. So what is the correct welfare interpretation of these disparate data? It is a hotly debated issue, as shown by the discussion at www.foreignaffairs.org and an interesting article in *The Economist* of 11 March 2004 entitled 'More or less equal?'.

The Milanovic results are based on household survey data (rather than national income data) which are considered to provide more reliable estimates of income that people actually earn and, hence, more reliable estimates of poverty and inequality. The data period is quite short, however, and probably does not allow for a fair comparison with Sala-i-Martin's research. Milanovic's finding that inequality increased between 1988 and 1993 due to slower income growth in highly populated Asian countries relative to richer OECD countries also changes if a longer period is examined. Because almost 40% of the world's population live in China or India, the impact of strong economic growth in both has a considerable impact on measures of inequality that focus on average incomes in these countries (see how these countries fared in Table 9.1). However, again from a welfare perspective, some economists argue that if inequality within China is considered then there are widening urban–rural income disparities emerging there. Further difficulties arise in assessing the equality question depending on whether exchange rates or purchasing power parity data are used.

Disagreement among economists in the equality debate is more than just an academic exercise. Many critics of capitalism argue that widening inequality is simply a reflection of the problems inherent in the capitalist system of order and organization. The above data are not especially helpful in this debate since world income distribution has improved while individual country inequality remains.

Irrespective of the debate around rising or falling inequality a renowned Indian economist and Nobel laureate for Economics, 1998, Amartya Sen, considers that the sheer scale of world poverty is still too high, with the concentration of over 80% of world income in the hands of the wealthiest 20% of the world's population. He argues for greater focus on addressing this central issue. Fortunately, there appears to be agreement among several different researchers that the proportion of the world's population living on less than a dollar a day (a standard poverty measure) has fallen sufficiently over the 1980s and 1990s to offset rising population in developing countries (see Table 9.5). The United Nations goal (announced in its millennium development goals) to reduce the number of people living on less than a dollar a day in 1990 by half by the year 2015 has, they have claimed, been achieved already. Not everyone, however, agrees with these findings and the debate goes on.

Evidence on convergence?

And what of the convergence debate? Have poor countries (those with low living standards) enjoyed higher growth than rich countries? This is another substantial research area in economics yielding disparate results depending on definition and measurement. In considering this question Fischer (2003) illustrated that if you graph countries' levels of living standards in 1980 and their growth until 2000, there is no evidence of convergence. The upward sloping trendline in panel 1 of Figure 9.8 indicates that countries with lower income (in 1980) grew more slowly than countries with higher income (in 1980). He also showed that if you plot each country taking into accounts its share of the world's population – thereby allowing consideration of *the number of people* in the poorest countries rather than simply the poorest countries – you observe convergence since the poorest are catching up in terms of living standards.

Many countries, however, still lack the political, social and economic structures required to allow them to reorganize as required to benefit from the convergence potential.

Trade and development

In the context of the discussion of developing countries, it is also worth noting that both the United States and European Union maintain trade restrictions that harm developing countries by limiting their ability to export goods. Through the WTO (and its predecessor the General Agreement on Tariffs and Trade)

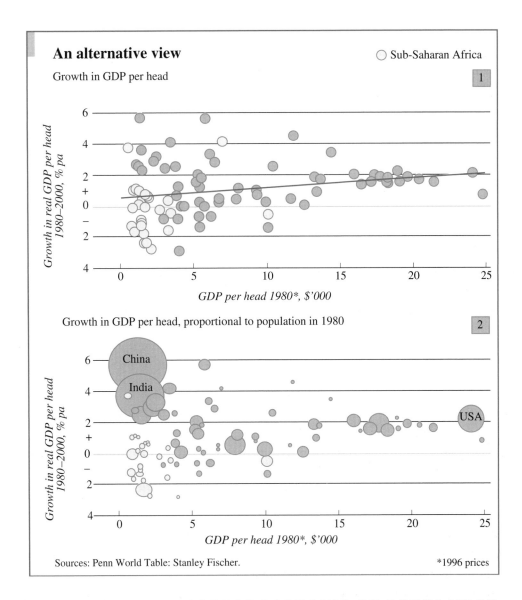

FIGURE 9.8 CONVERGENCE FOCUSING ON POPULATION
Source: © *The Economist* Newspaper Limited, London (11 March 2004).

improvements have been attempted but reform has been promised for many years without substantial results. It is still the case that average tariff levels in agriculture (predominantly exported by developing countries) are about nine times those in manufacturing. Industrial countries subsidize agriculture, effectively cutting world prices because of the supply incentive subsidies create for farmers in industrialized countries.

> Not only does the EU spend around £2.7 bn *per year* to make sugar profitable for European farmers but it also shuts out low-cost imports of tropical sugar through trade barriers.

Minimizing or overlooking the negative microeconomic effects of trade is a problem with many free-trade advocates. It may well make the free-trade argument more palatable and popular if these issues are dealt with explicitly. In this context the link between the arguments for free trade and for greater focus on national income distribution appear quite close. Both relate to normative judgements on the fairness and equity of the economic repercussions on the least well off of economic measures that may well favour an economy overall and maybe even the majority of its citizens. Economic models showing the welfare improvements to an average or representative citizen hold little weight for those interested in costs borne by minority groups who are not adequately compensated for their losses.

9.6   SUMMARY

- **Economies undergo transformations as they change and develop. The pace and extent to which real output expands is one measure used to assess economic growth. A broader measure is the human development index of the United Nations.**
- **Living standards indicate the average output of an economy per person. Trends in living standards are directly related to and affected by trends in labour productivity *but* the two do not necessarily move together.**
- **The Solow growth model provides a useful framework for considering the main causes of economic growth using a production function approach.**
- **Persistent growth cannot be explained by investment/savings behaviour. Improvements in technology can explain persistent growth.**
- **Technology improvement is a more important source of growth than increased capital for more industrialized countries, *ceteris paribus*.**
- **In the steady state, growth can only occur via total factor productivity changes.**
- **Endogenous growth models provide explanations as to why and how changes in technology occur.**

- How real income is distributed both internationally and within countries is an issue of interest from welfare and equity perspectives.
- Some improvement in international income distribution has occurred in the last 40 years with little change in national income distribution
- Depending on definition, there is some evidence of international convergence in living standards.
- Internationally trade has been growing faster than production, creating opportunities and generating threats in terms of economic growth, development and restructuring.
- Focusing on the effects on those worst affected by economic developments (be it trade, growth, etc.) and how they might best be addressed would enhance understanding and functioning of the economic system.

REVIEW PROBLEMS AND QUESTIONS

1. For each of four countries, draw a graph showing both its living standards and productivity. Compare the trends across the two measures in terms of their similarities and dissimilarities. Can you explain their similarities or dissimilarities over time?

2. Draw a production function. What assumptions are made when drawing the production function? Explain why at low levels of capital stock a rise of £100m in the capital stock has a larger effect on output than at relatively higher levels of capital stock.

3. Draw a production function.
   (a) Add a savings = investment function. Explain why the savings = investment function has a similar shape to the production function you have drawn.
   (b) Add a depreciation function. Explain why the depreciation function has a dissimilar shape to the production function you have drawn.
   (c) Use your diagram to explain how the equilibrium output and capital stock are determined.

4. You are given the following information about an economy:

   number of workers = 8 million

   average productivity = £124 000 per annum.

   (a) Compute the value of output of the economy for the year in question.
   (b) Explain what might happen to:
      - total output;
      - productivity;

if 50 000 migrant workers found work in the economy with no change to the capital stock.

(c) If you were told that average productivity in the following year changed to £135 000, how would you explain this outcome?

5. What is total factor productivity and how might it be measured? For four countries in Table 9.5 explain whether labour, capital or TFP explains the country's productivity differential with the USA.

6. Explain the central difference between the Solow growth model and endogenous growth models. Draw a production function that assumes endogenous growth and explain how and why it differs from the standard production function you have drawn for earlier answers.

7. What questions and issues can be analysed by considering
   (a) the international distribution of income?
   (b) national distributions of income?

8. What factors, in your opinion, explain recent trends in
   • the international distribution of income?
   • the national distribution of income?
   (Refer to any three countries in Table 9.7 to answer this question).

FURTHER READING AND RESEARCH

• For more on the Japanese model of economic growth and development take a look at Porter *et al.*, 2000.

• For the original articles providing apparently opposing evidence on inequality see Sala-i-Martin, 2002; Milanovic, 2002.

• For comprehensive and topical analysis of growth and inequality see Bhalla, 2002.

• For Sen's perspective on economic development see Sen, 1999.

REFERENCES

Bhalla, S. (2002) *Imagine There's No Country*. Institute for International Economics, Washington.

Cato Online Policy Report (1998), **20**(2) March/April, at http://www.cato.org/pubs/policy_report/cpr-20n2-6.html

Fischer, S. (2003) 'Globalisation and its challenges', American Economic Association Papers and Proceedings, *American Economic Review*, 93(2), 1–30, May.

Hall, E. and C. Jones (1999) Why do some countries produce so much more output per worker than others? *Quarterly Journal of Economics*, **114**(1), 83–116. Data Appendix as it appears on the link from Hall's website at www.stanford.edu/~rehall/CV.htm

Heston, A., R. Summers and B. Aten (2002) *Penn World Table Version 6.1.* Centre for International Comparisons at the University of Pennsylvania (CICUP), October.

Kennedy, K. (2001), 'Reflections on the process of Irish economic growth', *Journal of the Statistical and Social Inquiry Society of Ireland*, **30**, read before the Society on 26 April 2001.

Milanovic, B. (2002) 'True world income distribution 1988 and 1993: first calculation based on household surveys alone', *Economic Journal*, **112**, 51–92, January.

OECD (2002) *Economic Outlook*, Annex Table 24, December (www.oecd.org).

Porter, M., M. Sakakibara and H. Takeuchi (2000) *Can Japan Compete?* Macmillan.

Sala-i-Martin, X. (2002) 'The disturbing ''rise'' of global inequality', *National Bureau for Economic Research Working Paper 8904*, April.

Sen, A. (1999) *Development as Freedom.* Oxford University Press, Oxford.

Summers, R and A. Heston (1991) 'An expanded set of international comparisons 1950–1988', *Quarterly Journal of Economics*, 327–368, May, Supplement (Mark 5.6) to the Penn World Table (Mark 5).

United Nations (2002) *World Population Ageing, 1950–2050.* Population Division of the United Nations, Dept of Economic and Social Affairs.

United Nations (2003) *Trends in Europe and North America, The Statistical Yearbook of the Economic Commission for Europe.* United Nations Economic Commission for Europe (available online in the Demographic Database of the Population Activities Unit (PAU-DB) at http://w3.unece.org/stat/pau.asp).

Weisbrot, M., R. Naiman and J. Kim (2000), 'The emperor has no growth: declining economic growth rates in the era of globalization', Centre for Economic and Policy Research, Briefing Paper.

GLOSSARY

Absolute advantage
When a product is produced more efficiently (using less resources) in one country, that country has an absolute advantage in that product. It is measured by comparing relative output across countries. See also **comparative advantage**.

Aggregate demand (AD)
The demand for output (of all goods and services) at different price levels.

Aggregate economic activity
See **national economic activity**.

Aggregate expenditure function
Indicates total planned expenditure in an economy for different levels of income or output (denoted Y).

Aggregate supply (AS)
The amount of output firms are willing to supply at different price levels.

Anticipated inflation
Expected inflation that is taken into account in economic decision-making. See also **unanticipated inflation**.

Appreciation
The increase in value of an asset over time. An appreciation of sterling occurs when £1 buys more foreign currency today than it did yesterday (when it costs more in terms of foreign currency to buy £1). See also **depreciation**.

Arbitrage
The possibility of buying an asset in one market and selling it at a higher price in another market.

Arc price elasticity of demand (arc PED)
A method for estimating elasticity of demand, based upon average price and average quantity demanded. It is calculated as follows:

$$\frac{\Delta Qd}{\Delta P} \times \frac{1/2[P1 + P2]}{1/2[Qd1 + Qd2]}$$

It is most appropriately used for large price changes.

Arc price elasticity of supply (arc PES)	A method for estimating elasticity of supply, based upon average price and average quantity supplied. It is calculated as follows:

$$\frac{\Delta QS}{\Delta P} \times \frac{1/2[P1 + P2]}{1/2[QS1 + QS2]}$$

Asymmetric shocks	Economic shocks that affect one economy or a part of one economy more than other economies or other parts of an economy.
Automatic stabilizers	Measures that automatically counter the business cycle without government action. They result in reducing the response of GDP to changes in autonomous spending.
Autonomous consumption	Consumption expenditure that is independent of the level of income. It occurs if people borrow to buy consumption goods or if they spend their savings (or borrow) when they have no income to pay for consumption goods.
Average cost (AC)	Total costs per unit of output. AC is computed as total costs divided by output (TC/Q).
Average product of labour	Total output divided by the number of workers: Q/L.
Average total cost (ATC)	Average variable cost (AVC) plus average fixed cost (AFC): $ATC = AVC + AFC$.
Balance of payments	A country's national account which includes transactions between domestic residents and the rest of the world over a specified period. It consists of a **current account** and a **capital account**.
Barriers to entry	Exist when new firms cannot freely enter and compete in a market. With no barriers, all firms competing in the same market would have access to similar technology allowing them to have similar cost structures.

Bond	Represents an agreement between two parties in a transaction where one party lends money to the other for an agreed rate of interest (usually) over a specified period and where the lender receives back the total value of their investment when the bond matures.
Business cycles	The tendency for real output to rise and fall over time in a reasonably regular pattern.
Capital	A factor of production that has been produced (e.g. machines, factories, tools) and is used with labour to produce and/or market more goods and services.
Capital account	A country's national account which tracks transactions relating to ownership of financial assets, including inward and outward direct investment. See also **current account**, **balance of payments**.
Capital deepening	Where the capital stock increases faster than the labour force so that the amount of capital per worker rises. See also **capital widening**.
Capital intensity	The amount of capital each worker in the economy (on average) has at their disposal.
Capital widening	Where the capital stock increases at the same rate as the labour force and covers depreciation. See also **capital deepening**.
Cartel	An agreement between firms to co-operate in restricting the amount of output they produce, for example, thereby influencing the price.
Cash markets	See **spot or cash markets**.
Central bank independence	Usually implies that a government has no direct input into the economic decisions taken by the central bank regarding money supply, interest rates and inflation.
Ceteris paribus **assumption**	From the Latin, meaning all things being equal or unchanged. An assumption that allows economists to construct models that highlight the fundamental nature

of a relationship they are trying to describe and understand. Subsequently they use their models to incorporate other factors of most relevance to that relationship.

Circular flow	The way in which products, services, resources and money flow around the economic system.
Commodity	An undifferentiated product such as wheat or oil or computer memory chips. Commodities are usually of uniform quality, often produced by many different producers where each producer's output is considered equivalent or interchangeable. **Futures markets** exist for many commodity products.
Comparative advantage	When output is produced at a lower **opportunity cost** in one country, that country has a comparative advantage in production. It is measured by comparing relative opportunity costs between countries. See also **absolute advantage**.
Competitiveness	A range of factors from measures of income and prosperity to economic creativity and innovative ability that describe the performance of one economy relative to others.
Concentration ratio	Measures the market share of the biggest firms in the market. For example a CR4 calculates the market share of the leading four firms.
Concepts, theories and models	Simplified representations of phenomena, which are intended to serve as tools to aid thinking about complex entities or processes.
Consumer confidence	The degree of optimism that consumers express (in surveys, for example) about the state of their economy through their saving and spending patterns and plans.
Consumer surplus	The benefit to consumers due to the difference between what consumers actually pay to consume a good and what they would have been willing to pay.

Contestable markets Markets where entry costs and exit costs from markets are low.

Contractionary fiscal policy A fiscal policy that results in lower activity and a reduction in the circular flow of income. See also **expansionary fiscal policy**.

Convergence The tendency for poorer countries to grow faster than richer countries for a given increase in capital stock. Hence, poorer countries would be expected to catch up with richer countries if the countries share similar steady states.

Cost-push inflation Caused by firms reacting to increased costs by reducing their output.

Costs of inflation These are: loss of purchasing power, **shoe-leather costs, menu costs**, effects on income distribution, **fiscal drag**, effects on international competitiveness, effects on **balance of payments** and business uncertainty and lack of stability.

Countercyclical fiscal policy Policies which have the opposite effect on economic activity to that caused by the business cycle, reducing income flows during booms, increasing income flows in recessions.

Cross price elasticity Indicates the responsiveness of the quantity demanded of one good (good A) when the price of another good (good B) changes. It is computed as $\% \, \Delta \, \boldsymbol{Q}d_A/\%\Delta \, \boldsymbol{P}_B$.

Current account A country's national account which includes all trade transactions where the balance of trade might be in surplus or deficit. It also includes all income and current transfers. See also **capital account, balance of payments**.

Cyclical unemployment Unemployment associated with the recessionary phase of the business cycle.

Cyclically adjusted budget Provides information about the discretionary fiscal polices a government has followed to deliberately achieve specific macroeconomic goals. These might include trying to achieve a particular level of inflation, or employment or government deficit, for example.

Deadweight loss	The welfare lost to society from relatively inefficient production.
Debt financing	Debt financing results in borrowing money that must usually be repaid with interest.
Deflation	A fall in the average price level. See also **inflation**.
Demand	The quantity of output buyers are willing to buy over a range of possible prices
Demand for active balances	The transactions and precautionary demands for money are known as the demand for active balances because the money is actively used to buy goods and services.
Demand for idle balances	The speculative demand for money is also called the demand for idle balances since it relates to the desire to demand money to avoid potential losses from holding interest-bearing financial assets.
Demand-pull inflation	An increase in the price level of an economy caused by rising aggregate demand.
Dependency ratio	The portion of a country's population not in employment (including the unemployed, those who have retired and children) relative to the total population in employment. Dependents are also often classified as 'non-economically active' as they are considered to consume but not produce economic outputs.
Depreciation	The decline in value of an asset over time attributable to deterioration due to use and obsolescence. See also **appreciation**.
Differentiated products	Products for which several different varieties are provided (e.g. cars). Differentiation between varieties depends on producers' choices of the product attributes for which consumers are willing to pay. See also **standardized products**.

Direct taxes	Taxes paid on income. See **indirect taxes**.
Discouraged workers	Those who have tried to find work in the past and are willing to take on a job but have given up on looking for work because they feel, or know, that nothing suitable is available. They are excluded from calculations of the labour force, together with groups such as retired people or people who choose to take on home or childcare duties.
Diseconomies of scale	Inefficiencies that are associated with a firm's scale of output which varies over the long run; diseconomies of scale are experienced when average costs of output rise as output increases. See also **economies of scale**.
Dominant strategy	A strategy that provides one firm with the best outcome, irrespective of the strategy another firm (or firms) chooses.
Dynamic efficiency (economic growth)	The outward expansion of the **PPF**.
Economic efficiency	Optimum production given the quantity and quality of available factors of production and their cost.
Economic fundamentals	A very broad term which includes such economic measures as interest rates, the government's budget deficit, the country's balance of trade account (relating to exports and imports), the level of domestic business confidence, the inflation rate, the state of (and confidence in) the banking and wider financial sector and consumer confidence.
Economic growth	An expansion in the quantity of goods/services produced and sold.
Economic profit	An economic profit is made if a producer earns enough from supplying their product (or service) to the market to cover all their costs and pay themselves for the cost of the time and effort put into the business.
Economic shock	An unexpected event that affects the economy.

Economies of scale	Efficiencies that are associated with a firm's scale of output which varies over the long run; economies of scale are enjoyed when average costs of output decline as output increases. See also **diseconomies of scale**.
Economies of scope	These exist when a firm produces many products and can share resources across them such that the unit costs of each product is lower than if they were produced by separate firms. Shared marketing or distribution costs may be sources of economies of scope.
Efficiency wage	An efficiency wage rate lies above the market clearing wage rate to provide motivation for workers, to keep worker turnover low (avoiding costs of hiring) and to act as a signal to attract appropriately skilled workers.
Efficient production	All available resources are used to produce a maximum combination of goods/services with no resources unemployed.
Elastic PED	See **price elasticity of demand**
Entrepreneurship	Entrepreneurs exploit knowledge by converting knowledge discovered into profitable gain. Entrepreneurship is about being alert to a set of opportunities, having a subjective expectation as to the value of such opportunities in the market and having the resources (or ability to generate them) to realize this value.
Equity financing	Selling a share of the business ('shares') in exchange for finance where no specific future payment is defined.
Ex-ante real interest rate	$r = i - \pi^e$ where π^e is expected inflation. Rearranging this equation gives the **Fisher equation**. See also **ex-post real interest rate**.
Exchange rate	The price of one currency in terms of another.
Expansionary fiscal policy	A policy whereby the government manages to increase activity by injecting extra income into the circular flow by changing government expenditure or the tax rate. See also **contractionary fiscal policy**.

Expectations-augmented Phillips curve	The expectations-augmented Phillips curve explains inflation in terms of a negative relationship between inflation and unemployment and a positive relationship between actual inflation and expected inflation. The formula for the expectations-augmented Phillips curve is

$$\text{actual inflation rate} = \text{expected rate of inflation}$$
$$+ X \text{ (natural unemployment}$$
$$\text{rate} - \text{ actual unemployment rate)}$$

	where X denotes a positive number, which is different for different economies. See also **Phillips curve**.
Experience goods	Goods where their quality attributes can only be assessed through trial (or experience). See also **search goods**.
Ex-post real interest rate	$r = i - \pi$ where π is actual inflation. See also **ex-ante real interest rate**.
Externalities	Either positive or negative effects of a transaction by one set of parties on others who did not have a choice and whose interests were not taken into account.
Factors of production	These are the resources necessary for production. They include **land**, **labour**, **capital**, **entrepreneurship** in business organization and willingness to take business risks.
Fertility rate	The number of children born in a year, usually expressed per 1000 women in the reproductive age group.
Fiat money	Paper with no intrinsic value itself which fulfils the functions of money; government legislation ensures that it is accepted for transactions.
Final goods	Goods that are not purchased for further processing or resale but for final use.
Fiscal drag	A cost of inflation whereby people are pushed into higher tax brackets in a progressive income tax system because tax rates are not fully inflation adjusted.

Fiscal policy	Governments use fiscal policy whenever they affect government spending or tax rates (which affect **aggregate demand**). See also **contractionary fiscal policy**, **expansionary fiscal policy**, **countercyclical fiscal policy**.
Fisher equation	The nominal interest rate $i = r + \pi^e$. Rearranging this equation gives the **ex-ante real interest rate**.
Fixed costs	Costs, such as rent and rates, that must be paid even if the firm produces no output. See also **variable costs**.
Fixed exchange rate	An exchange rate that is tied to another country's rate.
Floating exchange rate	An exchange rate that is set by currency demand and supply.
Fractional reserve system	Describes the requirement of the banking system that banks must hold a fraction of their deposits in the form of reserves. See also **required reserve ratio**.
Free-rider problem	Exists due to the non-rival and non-excludable nature of public goods. There is no incentive to supply or pay privately for goods with public-good characteristics. Such goods, if desired, are provided by governments and paid for collectively through taxes. The free-rider problem is one example of market failure, a reason why the market requires government intervention to change what would otherwise be produced.
Frictional unemployment	Unemployment that arises because of changes or friction in particular markets.
Functions of money	These are: <ul><li>medium of exchange;</li><li>unit of account;</li><li>store of value.</li></ul>
Futures markets	Markets in which agreements are made relating to a payment that will be made for delivery of goods in the future.

Game theory	A microeconomic approach or tool of analysis applied to understand the behaviour of individuals and firms. Pay-offs generated by following different strategies can be compared.
Gross domestic product (GDP)	A location-based measure of economic activity which measures the value of real output produced in an economy.
Gross investment	The value of new capital created by investment plus depreciation. See **net investment**.
Gross national income (GNI)	**GNP** is also called gross national income (GNI), since national economic activity is the same whether measured in terms of output (the product in GNP) or income that is generated by citizens providing their factor resources to markets for payment.
Gross national product (GNP)	The value of real output that is retained by the citizens in a country after all inflows and outflows are allowed for.
Growth accounting	A method of identifying the proximate causes of changes in output and its rate of growth.
Herfindahl Index	Measures the market share of all firms in an industry by summing the squares of each individual firm's market share: $$H = \sum_{1}^{N} S_i^2$$ where S_i denotes each firm's market share and summation is from firm 1 to N, the total number of firms in the market. The squared term indicates that industries consisting of firms with large market shares will have high indices. See **market concentration.**
Horizontal equity	Treating identical people in an identical manner (i.e. not discriminating based on gender or race between individuals who are economically identical and can perform similar tasks). See also **vertical equity**.

Human capital	Includes all the skills, knowledge and expertise that people accumulate over time that allow them to increase their productive capacity as individuals, members of firms and within society more broadly.
Import tariffs	Rates imposed by governments on imported goods, which raise the price paid by consumers, thereby making the goods less attractive to buy.
Income effect	The adjustment in quantity demanded due to the change in real income alone caused by a price change.
Income elasticity of demand	Measures the responsiveness of the quantity demanded of a good to changes in consumers' income (Y). It is computed as $\% \Delta Qd/\%\Delta Y$.
Indirect competition	Arises when the strategic choice of one firm affects the performance of another due to strategic reaction by a third firm.
Indirect taxes	Indirect taxes are paid on expenditure whereas **direct taxes** are paid on income.
Inelastic PED	See **price elasticity of demand**.
Inferior good	A good for which demand rises if real income falls or for which demand falls if real income rises.
Inflation	A rise in the average price level. Inflation = rate of money supply growth – rate of real output growth See also **deflation**.
Inflationary gap	The difference between equilibrium output and actual output when an economy is producing above its potential long-run level.
Information asymmetries	Exist when one party has more information than another party in an exchange agreement.
Injections	Injections into the circular flow of income include: • investment expenditure by firms; • government expenditure; • income earned as payment for exports. See also **leakages**.

Intermediate goods	Goods sold by firms to other firms and used in making final goods.
Investment function	This describes the macroeconomic or aggregate investment behaviour in an economy.
Labour	All human resources used in production.
Labour market flexibility	The ability of the labour market to adjust to economic shocks.
Labour productivity	The average output of each worker in the economy. It is generally measured as the value of a country's production per worker, e.g. UK national output divided by the employed workforce of the UK for a particular period of time.
Land	All natural resources including minerals and other raw materials.
Law of diminishing marginal returns	When a firm adds workers to a given amount of capital – machinery, equipment, etc. – it eventually leads to a less efficient match between labour and capital to the extent that, if all capital is used by workers, hiring an additional worker will only lead to workers getting in each other's way and the marginal product of labour declining.
Leakages	Leakages of income out of the circular flow include: • savings; • taxes; • income paid for imported goods. See also **injections**.
Living standards	The level of material well-being of a citizen. It is generally measured as the value of a country's production per person, e.g. UK national output divided by the population of the UK for a particular period of time.
Long-run aggregate supply (LRAS) curve	A vertical line drawn at potential output.

Macroeconomics	The study of: • The relationships between aggregate or combined elements in the economic system such as national production and employment. • Causes of changes in aggregate economic performance including economic structure and economic institutions.
Marginal analysis	The process of considering the effect of small changes in one factor relevant to an economic decision (e.g. on output levels or pricing) and identifying whether an economic objective will be met. The objective may relate to profit maximization, benefit maximization, cost minimization or revenue maximization as examples. The logic of marginal analysis is that a small incremental change should be made once an economic objective is met – there is economic rationale to increasing price only if profits rise, if that is the economic objective. If no change enhances the economic objective (if it is already maximized/minimized) the decision variable should be changed no further. It is a method for optimizing decision-making within a reasonably well-defined setting.
Marginal cost (MC)	The change in total costs as output changes ($\Delta TC/\Delta Q$).
Marginal physical product of labour (MPPL)	The change in the quantity of output produced by each additional worker: $\Delta Q/\Delta L$.
Marginal propensity to consume (MPC)	The relationship between a change in income and the resulting change in aggregate consumption expenditure.
Marginal rate of substitution	At different points on the indifference curve, the consumer is willing to trade different amounts of one good for another good. This is also reflected in the slope of the indifference curve at any point.
Marginal revenue	The change in total revenue associated with a change in quantity demanded.

Marginal revenue function	Shows the amount of additional revenue generated for a firm at different levels of quantity demanded. It is computed as the change in **total revenue** divided by the change in output: $\Delta TR/\Delta Q$.
Marginal revenue product of labour (MRPL)	The change in **total revenue** (price of output × number of units sold) generated by each additional worker. It is computed by multiplying the product price by the **marginal physical product of labour**.
Marginal utility	The change in **total utility** for each additional good/service consumed. It is estimated as $\Delta TU/\Delta Q$.
Market concentration	The number of firms in a specific market and their relative market share. See also **Herfindahl Index**.
Market failure	Occurs when economic resources are not allocated efficiently caused by the price system working imperfectly.
Market liberalization	The reduction of barriers to the free movement of goods and services to encourage entry by new competitors.
Market power	Exists when firms in a market hold a sufficiently large market share that their actions can change the price of their product – producing more results in a falling equilibrium price, producing less leads to a rise in equilibrium price, *ceteris paribus*.
Market structure	This describes the main characteristics of an industry, such as the level of concentration, the extent of entry barriers and the extent of product differentiation. Examples of market structures are **monopoly, perfect competition, monopolistic competition** and **oligopoly**.
Markets	Situations where exchange occurs between buyers and sellers or where a potential for exchange exists. Markets cover the full spectrum from physical locations where buyers and sellers meet to electronic markets (such as auction websites) facilitated by the Internet.
Menu costs	A cost of inflation to firms and shops, which have to reprint price lists during periods of inflation because of frequent price changes.

Microeconomics	The study of the causes and effects of the behaviour of individual economic units within the economic system (or groups with broadly similar interests and goals) such as consumers, producers, trades unions, firms and their impact on the markets in which they interact.
Minimum efficient scale (MES)	The size/scale of plant required if a firm wishes to produce sufficient output to allow it to produce at its minimum long-run average cost.
Minimum wage	Wage rate set by the government below which employers are not legally permitted to pay workers. Employers are free to pay workers above this wage rate if they choose.
Monetary policy	The means by which the supply of money is regulated in an economy, including how inflation is controlled and how the stability of the currency is maintained.
Money multiplier	How a change in money supply leads to an ultimate change in money supply by a multiple of the initial change. The size of the money multiplier depends on the required reserve ratio according to the formula: $$Money\ Multiplier = \frac{1}{required\ reserve\ ratio}$$
Monopolistic competition	A market structure where there are many firms, each with some power to set the price of their product because they supply a particular brand of product – they differentiate their product – but where many imperfect substitutes are available.
Monopoly	A market structure where there is just one profit-maximizing firm in a market.
Motives for holding money	We hold money or demand money (in more liquid forms) for different purposes – for transactions, as a precautionary measure and for speculative purposes. These are known as the motives for holding money.
Multiplier	Indicates how much income/output changes after a change in autonomous expenditure. It is calculated

according to the following formula:

$$\frac{1}{(1 - MPC^*)}$$

Nash equilibrium

Exists when each player in a game chooses their best strategy given the strategies followed by other players.

National economic activity

National economic activity is the sum of activity by all of the economic decision-makers including households, producers and government. For this reason it is also called **aggregate economic activity**.

National output or income

National output or income, denoted **Y**, is calculated as the value of
- all the goods bought for consumption purposes; **C** plus
- all the investment expenditures by firms; **I** plus
- all government expenditures; **G** plus
- the net value of all goods traded by the economy, exports minus imports: **X** − **M**.

Natural monopoly

Where scale economies imply that only one firm could supply efficiently, i.e. at low cost to the market.

Natural rate of unemployment

The rate of unemployment that would prevail when the labour market is in long-run equilibrium – some people choose to change jobs and even in boom periods it can take a worker time to find a job best suited to their skills.

Net investment

Investment which creates new capital assets, whereas **gross investment** includes the value of capital depreciation plus new capital investment.

Net property income from abroad

The difference between **GDP** and **GNP**.

Normal (economic) profit

The minimum profit a firm is willing to make rather than go out of business. Any level of profit beyond this is called **supernormal profit**.

Normal good

A good for which demand falls if real income falls or for which demand rises if income rises.

Offshore outsourcing	Offshore outsourcing (known as **offshoring** in the United States) involves relocation of elements of the supply chain to a foreign location for more efficient production. Both production and services may be outsourced.
Offshoring	See **offshore outsourcing**.
Oligopoly	A market structure where there are a few firms of large size relative to the total market, so each firm has some degree of market power.
Open-market operation	When the central bank buys or sells government bonds.
Opportunity cost	The cost of what is given up in following one course of action such that other choices are no longer possible. It is subjective and can be estimated in terms of the cost of the next-best preferred alternative but only when the choice made cannot be reversed.
Optimal currency area (OCA) theory	This identifies the factors that determine whether a single currency maximizes single-currency benefits for members given the costs generated.
Output gap	The difference between **potential output** (also known as full employment output) and actual output.
Perfect competition	A **market structure** where there are many firms, each small relative to the overall size of the market.
Phillips curve	The relationship between unemployment and inflation, which is negative, meaning that high unemployment is associated with low inflation and vice versa. See also **expectations-augmented Phillips curve**.
Political economy	The term given to the study of how the rules, regulations, laws, institutions and practices of a country (or a state, region, province) have an influence on the economic system and its features.
Potential output	A country's output level if all resources were fully employed.

Poverty trap	A poverty trap (also sometimes known as an **unemployment trap**) exists when the **opportunity cost** of moving from unemployment benefits to paid employment is too high. Unemployed workers are often entitled to various benefits in addition to unemployment payments. These may include housing or rent allowances, reduced medical costs, food vouchers, etc. On taking up paid employment, especially of a low-paid nature, the benefits foregone may be less than the wages earned. A vicious circle of poverty can be created which is difficult to break.
Present value (PV) determination	A method for comparing benefits in different time periods in order to compare the future receipt with a current receipt of the same value. The standard formula used to determine present value is

$$PV = \frac{£X}{(1 + r)^T}$$

where PV denotes present value;
$£X$ is the amount to be received in the future;
r is the market interest rate;
T is the number of years before the investment is repaid.

Price cap	See **price ceiling.**
Price ceiling	A price that puts an upper limit on the price that suppliers can charge.
Price elasticity of demand (PED)	The responsiveness of quantity demanded to a change in price. It is calculated as:

$$PED = \%\Delta Qd/\%\Delta P$$

PED differs at different points on the demand curve. In absolute terms (ignoring the minus sign) PED is greater than one when the percentage change in quantity demanded is greater than the percentage change in price. This is elastic PED. PED is less than one when the percentage change in quantity demanded is less than the percentage change in price. This is inelastic PED.

Price elasticity of supply (PES)	The responsiveness of quantity supplied to changes in price. It may be elastic, inelastic or unit elastic. It is computed as the proportional change in quantity supplied divided by the proportional change in price:

$$\%\Delta QS / \%\Delta P$$

Price floor	A price that suppliers can be sure to receive for their output.
Price leadership	Where either a dominant firm in the industry sets price and all others follow or a well-established firm becomes the 'leader' and is trusted with setting the price that all firms will charge.
Price-cost margin	See **profit margin**.
Prisoner's Dilemma	Exists when the equilibrium from a game generates a sub-optimal outcome for all parties involved. With commitment (or a binding contract) between the firms, higher pay-offs could be achieved to the benefit of all players.
Privatization	The sale of government-owned businesses (and associated assets) in whole or in part to the private sector. Examples include electricity, gas and telecommunications industries.
Producer surplus	The benefit to producers due to the difference between the price suppliers are willing to receive for their output and what they actually receive.
Product differentiation	The features or attributes that explain consumers' decisions to buy one variety or brand instead of another are the basis for product differentiation.
Production function	A relationship describing how economic activity, specifically output, depends on the factors of production

and technology. It describes a technically efficient use of the factors of production and technology necessary to produce output, i.e. no resources are unemployed.

Profit margin

The mark-up over costs that a firm makes or wishes to make. Some firms will be happy to earn low mark-ups, other firms wish to earn high mark-ups. Also called the **price-cost margin**.

Progressive income tax system

A tax system in which individuals pay a higher percentage of their income in tax, the more they earn.

Public goods

Goods that would not be provided in a free-market system. They are goods that

- if consumed by one person can still be consumed by others; non-rival in consumption. Private goods once consumed are not available to others.
- if provided, cannot be excluded from the consumption of anyone who desires the good, even if they do not wish to pay for it. Public goods are non-excludable in consumption.

Purchasing power parity (PPP)

A measure of the relative purchasing power of different currencies. PPP is the exchange rate that equates the price of a basket of identical traded goods and services in two countries. It is often very different from the market exchange rate.

Quantity equation

$$M \times V = P \times Y$$

where M denotes the nominal money supply in an economy, V denotes velocity of money, P denotes the average price level, Y denotes the level of real economic activity and hence $P \times Y$ is the nominal value of economic activity (i.e. income or output).

Quotas

Quantitative restrictions set by governments on the amount of imports permitted from another customs area. Because quotas limit the supply of a good, they drive the price of the good up.

Real business cycle (RBC) theory	This theory is based on the view that changes in technology explain **business cycles**.
Real interest rate (r)	This is computed as the difference between the nominal interest rate and the rate of inflation. $$r = i - \pi$$ where i denotes the nominal rate and π is the rate of inflation.
Realignments	Simultaneous and coordinated devaluation or revaluation of currencies.
Recessionary gap	In a recession, the difference between the level of potential output and the lower actual output.
Regulatory capture	Where regulations set up to protect consumers – to lead to greater competition and lower prices – become captured by the industry for the benefit of producers in that industry. This happens where producers can convince the regulator to introduce rules favouring producers.
Required reserve ratio	The percentage of all deposits received by banks that must be held in the bank and not used for loans or other purposes.
Reservation wage	The lowest wage a worker will accept to take a job.
Search goods	Goods where their quality attributes can be assessed before purchase. See also **experience goods**.
Services	Non-material or intangible items of consumption that are consumed as they are created.
Shoe-leather costs	The effect of people holding less currency during periods of inflation, thereby needing to make more trips to the bank to withdraw cash.
Short run	The period of time it takes for a firm to change its scale of production and this depends on its fixed factor of production – usually capital.

Speculative demand for money	See demand for idle balances.
Spot or cash markets	Markets where money changes hands today for goods or services received today.
Standardized products	Products for which many substitutes are available and which use readily available technology in their production. See also **differentiated products**.
Standardized unemployment rate	The standardized unemployment rate measures those unemployed as people of working age without work who are available to start work within two weeks and who are actively seeking employment.
Steady state	The term used by Solow to describe the equilibrium state of output and capital stock in the long run. (The term is also used in physics.) An economy that reaches a steady-state level of capital stock and level of output has no tendency to change from these levels, *ceteris paribus*.
Structural unemployment	Unemployment arising from a permanent decline in employment in industries located in a particular region or area.
Subsidy	A payment or a tax concession from the government that reduces producers' average production costs.
Substitution effect	The adjustment in quantity demanded due to the change in relative prices alone, i.e as the price of one good increases, people buy less of it preferring its relatively cheaper substitutes.
Supernormal profit	See **normal profit**.
Supply	The activities of firms that organize the factors of production to produce output and make it available to buyers.
Supply chain	The resources and processes that are involved in acquiring components and raw materials and includes delivery of end products to final consumers. It includes

the activities of sellers, distributors, manufacturers, wholesalers and any other service providers and contributors to the buyer's decision to buy.

Tacit knowledge   Knowledge that is highly personal, not easily visible or expressible and cannot easily be copied. It usually requires joint, shared activities in order to transmit it. Examples of tacit knowledge include subjective insights, intuitions and hunches.

Tariffs   See **import tariffs**.

Tax wedge   The difference between the real wage paid by an employee and the real wage received by an employee. Differences are accounted for by payroll taxes (usually related to social insurance/security contributions), income taxes, consumer price taxes.

Total costs (TC)   The sum of **variable costs** and **fixed costs** incurred by a firm.

Total factor productivity (TFP)   A measure of the efficiency with which inputs are employed to produce output. TFP is a catch-all term that measures the effect on output not only of any changes in technology, but also in the social and political systems that affect the quantity and quality of output that an economy can produce from its labour and capital resources. TFP is effectively that portion of output change that cannot be accounted for by changes in the quantity and quality of labour and capital.

Total revenue (TR)   Price times the quantity of goods sold: $TR = P \times Q$.

Total utility (TU)   The total benefit perceived by the consumer from consumption of a good/service.

Trade barriers   Policies or practices that reduce the amount of imports into a country. Examples include **import tariffs** and **quotas**.

Transactions costs   The complete price plus non-price costs of a transaction, including search, information, bargaining and policing costs.

Unanticipated inflation	Inflation that takes people by surprise and therefore has not been taken into account in economic decision-making. See also **anticipated inflation**.
Unemployment trap	See **poverty trap**.
Variable costs (VC)	Costs that depend directly on the amount of output a firm produces, such as the costs for production inputs and workers. The higher the quantity produced the higher the variable costs. See also **fixed costs**.
Vertical equity	Treating people with intrinsically different characteristics (education, experience, abilities) differently in order to reduce the income disparity resulting from their differences. See also **horizontal equity**.

INDEX